STRATEGIC PLANNING AND POLICY

Strategic

WILLIAM R. KING
University of Pittsburgh

DAVID I. CLELAND
University of Pittsburgh

Planning and Policy

 VAN NOSTRAND REINHOLD COMPANY
NEW YORK   CINCINNATI   ATLANTA   DALLAS   SAN FRANCISCO
LONDON   TORONTO   MELBOURNE

Van Nostrand Reinhold Company Regional Offices:
New York   Cincinnati   Atlanta   Dallas   San Francisco

Van Nostrand Reinhold Company International Offices:
London   Toronto   Melbourne

Library of Congress Catalog Card Number: 78-3398
ISBN: 0-442-80440-7

Manufactured in the United States of America

Published by Van Nostrand Reinhold Company
135 West 50th Street, New York, N.Y. 10020

Published simultaneously in Canada by Van Nostrand Reinhold Ltd.

15 14 13 12 11 10 9 8 7 6 5 4 3 2 1

Library of Congress Cataloging in Publication Data

King, William Richard, 1938–
    Strategic planning and policy.

    Includes index.
    1. Planning.   I. Cleland, David I., joint author.
II. Title.
HD30.28.K56   309.2'12   78-3398
ISBN 0-442-80440-7

PREFACE

This book deals with the field of strategic or long-range planning and the policy-making functions of managers in a variety of organizations. It is intended to serve as an exposition of modern strategic planning thought and practice for the manager as well as a supplement to the "cases" usually emphasized in courses in "Business Policy."

The book emphasizes the methodological "how to do it," aspects of strategic decision making and planning rather than the "what to do" aspects usually emphasized in policy courses. It should therefore prove useful both to the experienced manager who is concerned with achieving more effective organizational strategic planning and to the student of planning for whom the methodological focus can serve to complement the important "what to do" decision-making skills that can be developed through case analysis and other simulations of real-world decision situations.

The methodological emphasis of the book is not an exclusive one, however. We believe that this book's broad view of the organizational strategic planning function—one that emphasizes long-run, truly strategic thinking about opportunities as well as problems—is an extremely effective device in stimulating strategic thought processes in managers and students.

Based on our consulting experience, which forms a primary empirical basis for the book, we have concluded that the ability to "think strategically" in comprehensive policy terms is perhaps the least homogeneously distributed personal managerial trait. Those few managers who have the ability to think strategically are generally extremely successful and move readily to the top of their organization, whereas those who do not, move less quickly.

In working with many firms and agencies in developing the ideas and methodologies of this book, we have found that the process of designing and developing a strategic planning methodology in an organization may well be the single best device for stimulating strategic thinking. This is so because, in thinking about the vast range of considerations that must be explicitly, yet economically, taken into account in an organizational strategic planning process, the individual expands his own horizons and level of awareness of the overall system of which he and his organization are a part.

Thus, the methodological emphasis of the book has payoff in *both* the methodological and substantive areas. We have tried to amplify these substantive learning benefits by incorporating many real-world examples and by discussing methodology using substantive contexts.

In treating the methodological aspect of strategic planning, this book deals with systematic approaches that can serve to amplify the value of the ever-necessary managerial judgment. It focuses on strategic decision-making within the supportive framework of a strategic planning system. Such a system provides procedures, processes, informational support, and a facilitative organizational structure to permit managers to "break out" of an emphasis on day-to-day operating problems and give appropriate attention to the development of *contrived organizational change*.

The strategic-planning system is treated at both the conceptual and operational levels. This dual approach reflects our belief that the field of strategic planning has developed few integrating concepts, even though, at the same time, its literature is filled with "motherhood and sin" prescriptions of how strategic planning *should* be accomplished. Here, we attempt to provide some integrating concepts, as well as to show how these concepts have been applied in real-world situations.

Much of the material in the book is based on our personal consulting experience with a variety of business and public organizations; however, we have supplemented our personal experience with ideas and approaches adapted from some of the world's best strategic-planning organizations. In all instances, we have adapted language and approaches to a single conceptual framework and set of terminology that is used throughout the book. This attempt to do more than catalog various strategic-planning approaches addresses a major problem in the field: a "semantics jungle" in which words are used by different authors to mean different things and old ideas are given new names to make them more appealing and "saleable."

The premises on which this book is based, although they are not eternally established truths, have been developed and tested in real-world situations to a degree that makes them worthy of serious consideration by any organization with a need and desire to do better strategic planning. These basic premises are as follows.

1. Professional planners can facilitate a planning process, but they cannot themselves do the organization's planning.
2. Planning activities should be performed by the managers who will ultimately be responsible for the implementation of the plans.
3. Creative strategic planning is inherently a group activity, since it must involve many different subunits of the organization and many different varieties of expertise.

4. A "planning organization" must be created to deal with the conception and development of strategic plans. This organization provides the climate and mechanisms through which individuals at various levels are provided a greater opportunity to participate in determining the organization's future.

5. Strategic planning involves much more than numerical extrapolations of trends; it involves as well the selection of missions, objectives, and strategic alternatives.

6. Managers must be motivated to spend time on strategic planning through a formalized system and organization approach, which also permits their contribution to the planning process to be assessed.

7. The planning process must provide for the development of relevant data bases—qualitative as well as quantitative—that facilitate the development of environmental forecasts and the evaluation of strategic alternatives.

8. An evaluation of future environmental trends, competitive threats, and internal organizational strengths and weaknesses are essential to the strategic-planning process.

9. Evolving ideas within the organization provide the point of departure to develop future products and markets.

10. The chief executive's responsibility for developing future organizational strategy centers around the development of a "strategic planning culture" in the organization, the final evaluation and selection of strategic alternatives, and the design of a master plan of implementation for those alternatives.

These premises form the broad bases for the strategic-planning approach developed in this book.

The book begins with an Introductory Section that develops basic ideas and outlines the overall scope of the strategic planning system. Subsequent major sections deal with the principal subsystems of the strategic-planning system: The Outputs of Strategic Planning (Section II), The Strategic-Planning Process (Section III), The Strategic-Decision Subsystem (Section IV), The Information Subsystem (Section V), The Organizational Subsystem (Section VI), and The Planning-Management Subsystem (Section VII). Each of these subsystems is treated in one or more chapters at both the conceptual and operational level, thus giving both the "how to do it" and the "why" treatments essential to effective use of the ideas.

The dual nature of the audience to which the book is focused—practicing managers and students—is addressed through the incorporation of two sets of exercises at the end of each chapter. One set, "Strategic Questions for the Manager," is intended to summarize the chapter in a concise fashion, which stimulates the reader to apply the ideas to his own situation. The questions serve to illustrate a personal bias about strategic planning that authors hold that questions about planning may be more important than answers, or, to paraphrase Albert Einstein: "I wish I knew what questions I should be asking myself!". The strategic questions are addressed to the manager in his organizational setting. When the manager finds the question unanswerable or only partially answered, then he knows that someone in the organization has some work to do!

The other set of questions at the end of each chapter, labeled "Questions and Exercises," is intended to serve the more traditional purpose of chapter review and the elaboration and expansion of ideas from the chapter. They are directed primarily to the student. However, while the managerial-oriented strategic questions are primarily intended for managers, they should also be reviewed by student readers. This will serve to stimulate the student to think in managerial, rather than academic, terms.

We are indebted to a large number of students, colleagues, consulting clients, and professional planners for their inputs to this book. However, since we have adapted their ideas to our own mold, we take seriously the traditional claim of total responsibility for the results.

Our debt is especially great to Dean H. J. Zoffer of the Graduate School of Business and Dean M. L. Williams of the School of Engineering of the University of Pittsburgh, both of whom provided the "facilitative organization" conducive to the completion of the manuscript and to Claire Zubritzky, Carol Capone, Lois Aurila, Arlene Wycich and Olivia Harris, who typed the many drafts.

William R. King
David I. Cleland
Pittsburgh, Pa.

CONTENTS

PART I

Introduction

Chapter 1

PLANNING, STRATEGY, AND POLICY

Change and the organizational implications of change are very much on the minds of modern managers. Managers are becoming increasingly aware of the need for better information, techniques, and processes to cope with the risks and uncertainties that are the handmaidens of change. Management assessments of the likely impacts of the constantly occurring social, economic, and technological changes have become essential to organizational survival and growth. Among the most perplexing problems facing contemporary managers is how to anticipate future problems and opportunities and how to design strategies to cope with and take advantage of them.

Although there is much that continues to be said about the accelerating rate of change that faces contemporary organizations and managers, the notion of change as a way of life has become accepted, at least in principle by most modern managers.[1] Indeed, throughout society, change has become simultaneously more rapid and more familiar, whereas in the past change was relatively slow and was often surprising when finally perceived.

Organizational behavior to cope with change was, in the past, reactional in nature. Today, most institutions in our society recognize the need for the deliberate *contrivance of change* carried out through a rigorous process of anticipating change, plotting its course, and shaping the change for intended organizational purposes.

Terms such as "long-range planning" and "strategic planning" connote philosophies and approaches through which the *future impact* of change is assessed and integrated into *current decisions*. These terms deal with broad, important, far-reaching forces that beset the organization as opposed to the more parochial and shorter range issues involved in day-to-day operating decisions. Yet, despite the fact that the literature of management is replete with exhortations concerning the importance of such high-level, long-range approaches, they are among the least well-developed and least understood concepts of man-

---

[1] See Toeffler, A., *Future Shock,* Random House, New York, 1970, and Drucker, P., *The Age of Discontinuity: Guidelines to Our Changing Society,* Harper & Row, New York, 1968.

agement. Moreover, even in those organizations and situations where these ideas are understood, they are among the least practiced of the many elements of the manager's job.

Most large organizations attempt to perform activities labeled "long-range planning" or "strategic planning," but few actually have developed structured approaches and effective processes for exploring the broad range of opportunities and strategies available to enhance future prospects. For the most part, activities conducted under these labels are either highly formalized exercises that narrowly focus on financial extrapolations or, at the other extreme, creative efforts performed in an unstructured way and having little real impact on the organization.[2]

There is a good deal of empirical evidence suggesting that high-level managers recognize the great significance of strategic planning, but that, paradoxically, they devote only a small proportion of their time to it. As a consequence of this incongruity, planning is often entirely neglected by managers, or relegated to staff people with top management playing only a reviewing role. Sometimes managerial involvement in planning primarily occurs when one level of manager, say at the divisional level, approves the plans prepared by his staff and submits them to a higher-level manager who promptly sends them to his staff for review.

The reasons for the pervasive failure to implement the sound strategic planning practices that are almost universally regarded to be worthwhile are manifold. Among them is the natural tendency for the day-to-day short-run problems of the organization to occupy so much of the manager's time that the long run is neglected. The greater difficulty and uncertainty inherent in consideration of the long run unquestionably discourages managers from devoting their limited time and energy to "blue sky" thinking about the uncertain future when that time can be applied so effectively to solving the "real" and more easily understood issues of today.

However, perhaps most important in this regard is the *lack of effective management systems for the conducting of strategic planning.* Put simply, the field is much less well developed, in terms of the sort of processes, approaches, techniques, or even principles that managers are used to applying to their short-range tactical activities, than are most other areas of management. Strategic planning is time consuming, complicated, and has long-run payoffs at best. Many managers are therefore willing to forego these practical problems and the consequent promise of long-run benefits on the premise that if they don't solve today's problems, they may not be around to experience the long run.

This tendency is undoubtedly amplified in the many organizations in which

---

[2] For instance, see Zoglin, R., "The Futurists—Seers in a Shortsighted Industry," *New York Times,* July 23, 1975, pp. 1 and 27.

managers are evaluated primarily in terms of current performance. The corporate executive whose pay and promotions depend largely on this year's profits is unlikely to willingly trade off current profits for potentially larger future ones, especially if his personal advancement will ensure that he will not be in his current position when those future profits are realized. Thus, when managers are assessed in short-run terms, they are unlikely to devote much thinking to anything other than the short run.

Long-Range and Strategic Planning

The primary purpose of this book is the conceptualization and operational development of an approach to strategic planning and policy that can be applied to a wide variety of contemporary organizations. Although the approach taken to satisfy this objective has something of a business bias, one of the important points to be made is that the traditional business emphasis on "the market", the environment of the organization and the marketing function is as important to other types of organizations as it is to business.[3]

This book deals with *systematic processes for the assessment of the future impact of present strategic decisions, how those decisions can best be made and effectively implemented, and how the organization can be structured to facilitate, rather than hinder, this process.*

LONG-RANGE PLANNING

Just what is long-range planning? The term is often used to denote planning for actions that will impact on the organization only in the long run. In some organizations, such as a paper firm that must plant forests 30 or more years in advance, long-range planning may be done for very long planning horizons. Elsewhere, such as a firm that manufactures style goods, the planning horizon, at least in the product dimension, may be only about a year. In this new product context, other firms, such as pharmaceutical manufacturers, need to plan for much longer than a decade. This is so because the lead time required to develop new products, test and evaluate them, and obtain federal government approval for placing them on the market may well be of that duration.

Many other organizations, such as public agencies, try to plan for the very long run (i.e., decades), but find that they are limited in their ability to do so. Most organizations find that some dimensions of their planning *must* be done in

---

[3] Kotler, P., *Marketing in Nonprofit Organizations,* Prentice Hall, Englewood Cliffs, N.J., 1975.

the range of five years hence, e.g., planning for facilities, since the time required to complete facilities is often of that magnitude.

Thus, precisely what is meant by "long" in the term "long-range planning" depends very much on the context in which the planning is being done. What is long-range to one organization may be short-range to another, and the planning horizon feasible in one area of an organization's activities may be impractical in another.

STRATEGIC PLANNING

In this book, we prefer to use the term "strategic planning," rather than long-range planning, because it does not have the confusing time horizon connotation and because it has the connotation of importance. Thus, whereas some authors[4] have tried to avoid this linkage of strategic planning and important decisions, it is clearly true that *the decisions that are the province of strategic planning are those most important to the organization's future.*

A variety of definitions have been put forth for strategic planning. One appears in a book on another topic (management control):

> Strategic planning is the process of deciding on the objectives of the organization, on changes in those objectives, on the resources used to attain these objectives, and on the policies that are to govern the acquisition, use and disposition of these resources.[5]

Thus, strategic planning involves the development of objectives and the linking of these objectives with the resources which will be employed to attain them. Since these objectives and resource deployments will have impact in the future, strategic planning is inherently future oriented. Strategic planning, therefore, deals primarily with the contrivance of organizational effort directed to *the development of organizational purpose, direction, and future generations of products and services,* and the design of implementation policies by which the goals and objectives of the organization can be accomplished.

Identifying the Need for Strategic Planning

There is a glaring need in modern organizations for more effective strategic planning processes and systems. That need can be exemplified by a variety of symptoms that tend to inhibit an organization from achieving its potential:

[4] For example Ansoff, H. I., *Corporate Strategy,* McGraw-Hill, New York, 1965, p. 5.
[5] Antony, R. N., Dearden, J. and Vancil, R. F., *Management Control Systems,* Richard D. Irwin, Homewood, Ill., 1965, p. 4.

1. A tendency for each manager to view his current domain from the standpoint of the discipline in which he first acquires credentials, regardless of its broader scope and the requirements for more diverse considerations.
2. A "tunnel vision" phenomenon, in which managers fail to recognize the multiple objectives of the organization even though they have moved to a general management position and can no longer afford the luxury of the simplistic efficiency-oriented objectives that are the forté of managers at lower levels.
3. A bureaucratic organizational structure designed more for maintaining efficiency and control in current operations than in fostering long-range innovation.
4. The lack of an "organization" or process designed specifically for fostering the managerial participation and innovativeness for developing new products and services.
5. An assumption that the chief executive or, alternately, a professional planning staff should *do* the planning.
6. An incentive system wherein performance oriented toward the production of short-range results is rewarded more highly than that oriented toward long-range opportunities.
7. The introduction of radically new planning systems into organizations without proper concern for their effect on the motivations and behavior of those managers who must use them.

If these symptoms exist in an organization, it is likely that it is incapable of significantly affecting its future. Organizations possessing these traits are reactive rather than proactive, and whether or not they devote significant resources to planning, they are not likely to be effective planners.

It is a primary objective of this book to show why this is so and how these organizational characteristics can be rectified to permit effective planning.

The Nature and Scope of Strategic Planning

The strategic planning activity in an organization should provide managers with an opportunity to address some basic questions about the organization in a way that they cannot do in the course of their day-to-day operational activities. These critical questions are simply: (a) What has been our "business" or organizational purpose? (b) What is our present business? (c) What should our business be in the future? (d) How can we best act to assure that our business becomes what we want it to be? In addressing these questions the manager must identify and analyze historical fact and culture, present circumstances, and future "images."

WHAT IS STRATEGIC PLANNING?

Strategic planning involves important, high-level organizational choices. A question important to the understanding of the field, therefore is, "How can one identify those crucial choice situations with which strategic planning deals?"

The answer to this question is deceptively simple. *Strategic planning is applicable to any situation so long as:* (a) it is directly related to *overall organizational purposes,* (b) it is *future-oriented,* (c) it significantly involves *uncontrollable environmental forces* that affect organizational performance.

OVERALL ORGANIZATIONAL PURPOSE. A decision aimed at reducing costs in the production department would probably *not* be within the purview of strategic planning since cost reductions are not generally *directly* related to overall purposes. Such activities normally focus on *efficiency* (the way in which inputs are transformed into organization outputs) rather than *effectiveness* (the degree to which outputs achieve organizational purposes). *It is organizational effectiveness (the relationship between outputs and purposes) that is the primary concern of strategic planning.*

Thus, broad decisions regarding new products (e.g., which products to introduce and when) would normally be strategic in nature. But, more detailed elements of the new product situation (e.g., which advertising appeal to use) would not normally be considered strategic to the organization.

FUTURE ORIENTATION. Since virtually any decisions can be argued to be future oriented in the sense that the consequences of the choice will be felt only in the future, the second element of the above definition of strategic planning warrants further explanation. In fact, the idea of "future orientation" is not really explicit, so that it requires an operational definition [6] to make it useful.

Here we shall consider a decision regarding an element of an organization to be *future oriented if the element, at least in part, does not currently exist.* This view therefore takes decisions regarding products, personnel, organizational skills, etc., as being *future-oriented* if one is deciding about such things as products that are not in the current mix, people who are not currently employed, or skills that the organization does not currently possess.

Thus, if one is planning for new products, new skills, new facilities, etc., *and these entities are important to the achievement of the organization's objec-*

---

[6] An operational definition is one that relates a concept to the observable criteria which, if satisfied, indicates the existence of the thing being defined. Operational definitions are important in science, where everything must be defined in terms of what would be observed if certain operations were performed. The use of the term here is not precisely that familiar to scientists, but it is closely related to it. See Ackoff, R. L., *Scientific Method,* Wiley, New York, 1962, Chapt. 5.

tives, he is doing strategic planning. Decisions regarding current products, markets, and skills, are not normally strategic in nature, although important *changes* in existing ventures, such as consideration of discontinuing a product are often strategic.

Similarly, a decision about whether to hire a specific individual would not normally be a strategic one (although in the case of a new chief executive or someone with unique talents who can directly help the organization in achieving its overall goals, such a decision could be strategic),[7] and a decision to add some technological forecasting expertise to the planning department would generally not be strategic.

ENVIRONMENTAL FORCES. The third element used in describing the scope of strategic planning is that of environmental forces. *Strategic planning normally involves issues that are significantly affected by a variety of external environmental elements.* Thus, the social, economic, technological, legal, and political factors in the organization's future must be understood before the questions of future strategic purpose or direction can be addressed. To do otherwise would be to select a strategy that could fail if contingencies, such as an economic downturn or a change in political alignments, affected the organization.

Within this three-dimensional realm of future-oriented environmentally-related activities that directly affect overall organizational purpose, virtually *anything that significantly changes the character or direction of the organization* is within the province of strategic planning. Strategic planning is an innovative process, which may affect all of the inputs, outputs, and resources of the organization. Illustrative of such changes are:

Acquisition and disposition of facilities

New markets to be served

New distribution channels

Redesigned organizational structure

New product research and development

Revised dividend policy

New sources of financing

[7] However the growing body of federal and state legislation directly affecting the relationship between the corporation and its employees tends to make hiring of an employee somewhat "strategic" in nature. Over the past twenty years there has been more than one hundred pieces of such federal legislation. One large U.S. corporation views the hiring of an individual as "strategic" in nature somewhat on par with a capital expenditures decision considering the "ownership costs" commitment that is involved if the employee were to remain with the corporation for a lifetime of work. These lifetime "ownership costs" for an hourly employee have been estimated as $1.7 million, and for a salaried employee $2.2 million assuming a 40-year working lifetime. These costs include cost of wages and benefits for a typical employee.

Mergers and acquisitions

New organizational skills

Executive succession

Thus, strategic planning decisions ultimately will affect the overall "systems" framework (physical, organizational, financial, etc.) within which the organization operates.

THE STRATEGIC-OPERATING DICHOTOMY

This view of the nature of strategic planning establishes a natural dichotomy within the framework of the organization—the current generation of outputs and resources versus future organizational missions and generations of "products" and resources. Strategic planning deals primarily with the latter, whereas other managerial activities (sometimes called management control and/or operational planning) deal with the former.

This dichotomy is conceptually sound because it emphasizes *change and innovation* in organizations. The ability to deal with change and to foster organizational innovation has always been associated with good planning. Indeed, they are the essence of good management.

> For centuries, one of the defining characteristics of a good manager has been his ability to think and move faster than the economic, political, social, and technical norms of the environment in which he operates. It is precisely his ability to anticipate and lead among environmental hazards and opportunities and his skill in organizational modification that have been in demand.[8]

In addition to this conceptual viability, the "existing versus new" dichotomy is operationally practical. Much of the remaining chapters of this book are devoted to demonstrating this practicality. Suffice it to say here that the organization itself, its processes, information, and other salient elements can be structured to accommodate this view. Moreover, in doing so, one is designing an organization that is more likely to survive and to prosper and less likely to be diverted from its purpose than is an organization that is not so structured.

EFFICIENCY AND EFFECTIVENESS. The "existing versus new" viewpoint serves to rather clearly distinguish strategic considerations and activities from operating ones. This is important in part because of the nature of the management activities involved in the two areas.

When managers are concerned with operating decisions, such as the size of a production run, the number of workers to lay off, or the negotiation of the

---

[8] Baughman, J. P., Lodge, G. C., and Pifer, H. W., *Environmental Analysis for Management,* Irwin, Homewood, Ill., 1974, p. V (preface).

best possible terms for a loan, the objectives are well defined and limited in scope. *Efficiency* is the primary concern of the operational decision maker. Whether this is reflected in maximizing output, minimizing cost, or in "getting the best deal" that it is possible to obtain, the goal is clear and singular.

Strategic choices, on the other hand, involve decisions on the basic purpose of the organization, the objectives to be sought, as well as the general way in which they will be sought. Thus, strategic decisions are much less structured and much more ill-defined than are operational ones. Moreover, greater attention is paid to organizational *effectiveness* (the degree to which performance meshes with goals) than to simple efficiency.

MANAGERIAL IMPLICATIONS OF THE DICHOTOMY. The "existing versus new" dichotomy implies that different skills and processes may be required to cope with strategic choice than with operational choice. If this is so, it might suggest that different kinds of people, possessing different mixes of skills, should be assigned to strategic and operating responsibilities.

Even though such a division of labor may be theoretically reasonable, and though most organizations do follow this principle to some limited degree by creating planning staffs with no operating responsibilities and by charging high-level executives with more strategic responsibilities than lower-level managers have, modern organizations operate on the principle that its *managers should have both strategic and operating responsibilities*.

The justifications for this are manifold. Among these rationales are the importance of having those who make the strategic choices also have a "stake" in the outcome of their choices, the desirability of involving lower-level managers in the decisions regarding the future of the organization, and the possible loss of realism if plans are developed by people who are insulated from day-to-day operations.

How then can the basic strategic-operating dichotomy be a practical basis for operating an organization if the "simple" solution of assigning strategic decisions to strategic specialists and operating choices to operational specialists is not to be used? If both operating and strategic responsibilities are vested in individual managers, day-to-day "fire fighting" seems certain to dominate the less immediate, but nonetheless, more important, strategic considerations.

The solution to this apparent dilemma is easy to state and less easy to implement. The answer simply is that since strategic choices are important, they must be allocated appropriate time and resources. The tactical must not be permitted to drive out the strategic; the present cannot be allowed to dominate the future.

Just as the intelligent manager chooses to allocate more funds to the most important project than he does to one of lesser importance, the organization and its managers must consciously choose to appropriately allocate their time, attention, and other resources to the important process of strategic planning.

This somewhat pontifical statement recognizes that planning requires resources, the most significant of which is the time and attention of managers who have important and pressing operating responsibilities. Therefore, if this principle is to be put into practice, the strategic choice process must be made to be as demanding on the manager as are his operating responsibilities. In other words, *he must be formally charged with strategic responsibilities in a manner that makes it impractical to shirk them or to perform them in cursory fashion in the time "left over" from his operating responsibilities.*

This conclusion is in keeping with the best available evidence on the actual nature of the manager's job and the ways in which he can reasonably be expected to improve his effectiveness. Mintzberg has studied the nature of managerial work and concludes that:

> The manager is challenged to gain control of his own time by . . . turning those things that he wishes to do into obligations.[9]

To turn the recognized need for strategic planning into an obligation requires that strategic responsibilities be clearly stated, that resources be provided to support the carrying out of these responsibilities, that measurable outputs be defined, that appropriate information be available, and that a schedule be established for the accomplishment of planning tasks. In short, *the accomplishment of effective strategic planning, within the framework of the "operating versus strategic" dichotomy that characterizes most organizations, requires the development of a strategic planning system.*

The Need For a Strategic-Planning System

A strategic-planning system is only one of the management-support systems of the organization. However, because the substance with which such a system deals is so important and far reaching, the system itself must be broad and comprehensive.

Management systems may be simple systematic procedures for dealing with prescribed situations, or they may be complex formalized processes that encompass many dimensions of the organization. Glans et al.[10] define a management system as ". . . the methods by which an organization plans, operates and controls its activities to meet its goals and objectives by utilizing the resources of money, people, equipment, materials, and information."

---

[9] Mintzberg, H., "The Manager's Job: Folklore and Fact," *Harvard Business Review*, July–Aug., 1975, pp. 49–61.

[10] Glans, T. B., Grad. B., Holstein, D., Meyers, W. E., and Schmidt, R. N., *Management Systems*, Holt, Rinehart & Winston, New York, 1968, p. 3.

Thus, a management system is a structured way of performing the activities of the organization and *a strategic-planning system is the organizational system which focuses on its strategic "business."*

Perhaps the best way to illustrate the glaring need for a systematic approach to strategic planning is by considering two decision-making situations in an urban police department.[11] On a busy street, a police officer begins to pursue a speeding automobile while simultaneously inquiring into a police information system with the car's license number. The patrolman, in the seconds that elapse before he must confront the driver, is provided with information that tells him such things as if the automobile has been reported stolen, if the registered owner has a police record, and if the automobile has been involved in recent accidents. This information provides the patrolman with a *guide to action* in approaching and dealing with the speeder.

At the same time, the police chief is faced with the problem of establishing a policy for the utilization of police resources in maintaining order in the city's school system. He phones a number of people in his department, in the city administration, and in the school administration. Drawing on their experience with disorders that have occurred in the recent past, they counsel him on the various positions that the department might take. Finally, the police chief determines a course of action to be implemented.

In both of these situations, the individual in question is faced with the problem of making a decision on largely subjective grounds. Indeed, neither the patrolman's decision about how to deal with the speeder nor the police chief's policy determination decision could have been dealt with solely on objective grounds. The need for human judgment is paramount in both instances. The salient difference between the two situations, however, is that the patrolman's decision is based on the sound guide to action of objective information from a supporting information system. The police chief, on the other hand, has to deal with his strategic question in an unsystematic fashion without the support of a formal information system.

The two situations described here are typical of the state of the art in many organizational information systems for the support of decisions made at the operational level and the strategic planning level. Computer technology and information systems have been much more extensively developed and implemented for operational purposes than for the more complex higher level needs of strategic planning and decision making. In strategic planning, the benefits that may be derived from management systems, such as decision making processes and organizational roles, are largely relegated to the level of the informal and ad hoc, whereas at operational decision areas, these elements are clearly specified.

---

[11] Adapted with permission from King, W. R. and Cleland, D. I., "Decision and Information Systems for Strategic Planning," *Business Horizons*, April 1973.

This complex of elements—decision making, organization, motivation, information, etc., all integrated into a consistent structure—are called a *strategic planning system*. Systematization in this context means that a formal planning *process* is used in the organization, that *information support* is provided in a structured way, that there is an *organization* devoted to planning, that the *outputs* of the planning process are defined in a way that they can be effectively used by managers, and that *planning decisions* are made within some structural framework of missions, objectives, and strategies.

The concept of a strategic planning system is becoming widely accepted in modern organizations. Many large business firms such as General Electric, Westinghouse, Texas Instruments, and 3M have extensively developed such systems and rely on them to ensure that they will be able to do effective strategic planning, despite the pressures of everyday operations. Smaller organizations both public and private, have also developed strategic planning systems. In many cases, these systems have been credited with impressive results,[12] and in general, many studies have demonstrated the payoff in terms of organizational performance and profitability of formalized planning.[13]

Of course, the positive impact of formalized planning has not been conclusively demonstrated, and there are those who hold that strategic planning is an inherently ad hoc activity dealing with unique strategic problems. Since they see every strategic question as being unique, they see little place for planning systems or systematic approaches.[14]

Although it is true that strategic planning decisions are inherently less structured, less programmable, and less repetitive in nature than are operational decisions, they can be approached in a systematic fashion to a greater degree than is generally perceived. In making this point, we will draw on the experience of a variety of firms and other organizations that have successfully used various elements of strategic planning systems and thereby demonstrate that it is both feasible and desirable to systematize planning.

Of course, all of this emphasis on systematization and structure does not imply that strategic planning can be accomplished in the same highly structured way that may be applied to tactical decisions, such as production schedules. However, it does imply that *structural frameworks may be developed to guide the many management judgments that are the essence of organizational strategy formulation.*

---

[12] For instance, see "At Potlatch, Nothing Happens Without a Plan," *Business Week,* Nov. 10, 1975, pp. 129–134.

[13] For instance, Malin, Z. A., and Karger, D. W., "Does Long-Range Planning Improve Company Performance?" *Management Review,* Sept., 1975, pp. 27–31.

[14] See Wrapp, H. E., "Good Managers Don't Make Policy Decisions," *Harvard Business Review,* Sept.–Oct., 1967.

Summary

Strategic planning is that element of a manager's job and of the organization's function that deals with the contrivance of change, rather than the simple reaction to it. Strategic planning involves those choices related to overall organizational purposes, oriented toward the future, and importantly involving uncontrollable environmental forces. Strategic choices are those that emphasize future missions and future generations of "product" outputs and resource inputs. In contrast, the organization's day-to-day operating environment emphasizes current objectives and the existing generation of outputs and resources.

The organizational implications of this simple dichotomy are profound. *Efficiency,* the transforming of inputs to outputs, is the focus of the operating environment, whereas *effectiveness,* the degree to which future goals are achieved, is the focal point of the strategic planning function. The implications of the "existing versus new" dichotomy to managers is no less important. Managers have dual, and possibly conflicting, responsibilities: those related to present operations and those related to the strategic future. Managers must allocate their time and attention between these two tasks and not permit the more apparent and higher-pressure present to drive out consideration of the future.

Strategic-planning systems (formalized approaches to doing the job of strategic planning) can help the organization and individual managers to resolve this conflict. Such systems are both useful and feasible if they are designed and implemented in a sensible manner recognizing that planning choices are inherently less structured and more uncertain than are most of the other decisions that managers face. Thus, although they can be dealt with systematically, they are not subject to the same degree of routinization as are many operating decisions.

Managerial judgment reigns supreme at the strategic-planning level. Strategic-planning systems can support this judgment, focus it, and permit it to be applied at the points where it will have the highest impact on the organization's future. However, such a system cannot supplant the crucial role that must be played by judgment, experience, and intuition in guiding the organization into the future.

Chapter 1—Questions and Exercises

1. The authors state that the most perplexing problem facing contemporary managers today is how to anticipate future organizational challenges and needs. Do you believe this to be a credible statement? Why or why not?

2. Under what circumstances might the need for strategic planning not be of high priority to an organization? Give examples.

3. What are some of the reasons why executives might be unable to implement adequate strategic-planning practices within their organizations?

4. What is the value in trying to design an effective management system for the conduct of strategic planning within an organization? If you were to design such a management system, where might you start?

5. Strategic planning deals with the uncertainty of the future. It is time-consuming, risky, complicated and may have limited cost-effective payoffs for the organization. Since it is so uncertain and risky, why bother with it at all?

6. Under the concept of "profit centers" managers are evaluated primarily in terms of the effectiveness of the current performance of their organization. Does this reward for current operational effectiveness detract from the development of a strategic planning system within the organization? Why or why not?

7. What is meant by "long" in the term "long-range planning"? What is the difference between long-range planning and short-range planning?

8. Define a strategic decision. Demonstrate by example that you understand your definition of a strategic decision.

9. What is the meaning of the word "strategy." Select an organization of your choosing and state what you believe that organization's strategy to be.

10. The best strategy for an organization can often be stated in very simple terms. Why?

11. A poor strategy is better than no strategy at all. Do you agree with this statement? Why or why not?

12. What is a policy? What is the relationship of an organizational policy and the executive decision-making activity in an organization?

13. What is the difference between a "reactionary" decision and an "anticipatory" decision? Which kind of decisions do you typically make?

14. What proportion of an executive's time should be spent on developing a sense of direction for his organization in its future? How do you think your estimate compares with that which is actually spent?

15. Select an organization of your choosing (educational, industrial, ecclesiastic, military, etc.) and delineate some of the key environmental changes that you feel have influenced the organization in recent years. Does it appear that the organization anticipated these environmental changes?

Chapter 1—Strategic Questions for the Manager

1. What mechanisms, processes, techniques and such things have been developed in my organization for dealing with change?

2. What major changes have occurred in my organization's environment in the past several years for which the organization was not prepared? Could these changes have been foreseen?

3. What major changes are expected in my organization's environment in the future?

4. Do the principal executives in my organization have a "conceptual understanding" of long-range planning?
5. Has long-range planning been attempted in my organization? Has it been a success? Why? Has it failed? Why?
6. What proportion of my time is spent on long-range planning? What proportion of my time am I willing to spend on long-range planning?
7. What is the typical long-range planning horizon for my industry? What industry factors determine this planning horizon?
8. What is the "general direction" by which my organization's objectives are currently sought? Do the key executives in the organization subscribe to this "general direction"?
9. Have I developed any "contingency strategies" for my organization?
10. Have any policies been developed that deal with the long-term growth and/or survival of this organization?
11. What recent decisions have I made whose impact might be considered long-term? Were these decisions "reactionary" or "anticipatory"?
12. What professional reading have I done lately on the subjects of *change, long-range planning, futurity,* and such related material?

References

Ackoff, R. L., *A Concept of Corporate Planning,* John Wiley, New York, 1970.

Andrews, Kenneth R., *The Concept of Corporate Strategy,* Dow-Jones, Irwin, Homewood, Ill., 1971.

Ansoff, H. I., *Corporate Strategy,* McGraw-Hill, New York, 1965.

Branch. M. C., *Planning: Aspects and Applications,* Wiley, New York, 1966.

Carson, I., "The Big Leap in Corporate Planning," *International Management,* April 1972.

Christensen, C. Andrews, R., Bower, L., *Business Policy, Test and Cases,* Irwin, Homewood, Ill., 1973.

Denning, B. W., *Corporate Planning: Selected Concepts,* McGraw-Hill, New York, 1971.

Eppink, D. J., "Corporate Planning in the Netherlands," *Long Range Planning,* Oct. 1976.

Forsyth, W. E., "Strategic Planning in the Seventies," *Financial Executive,* Oct. 1973.

Gluck, F. W. et al., "Cure for Strategic Malnutrition," *Harvard Business Review,* Nov.–Dec. 1976.

Golightly, H. O., "What Makes a Company Successful?" *Business Horizons,* June 1971.

Gotcher, J. W., "Strategic Planning in European Multinationals" *Long-Range Planning,* Oct. 1977.

Greiner, Larry E., "Evolution and Revolution as Organizations Grow," *Harvard Business Review,* July–Aug. 1972.

Harvard Business Review, "Participation Management at Work: An Interview with John F. Donnelly," Jan.–Feb. 1977.

Henry, H. W., "Formal Planning in Major U.S. Corporations," *Long Range Planning,* Oct. 1977.

Higgins, J. C., and Finn, R., "The Organization and Practice of Corporate Planning in the U.K." *Long Range Planning,* Aug. 1977.

Hofer, C. W., "Research on Strategic Planning: A Survey of Post Studies and Suggestions for Future Efforts," *Journal of Economics and Business,* Spring-Summer, 1976.

Irwin, P. M., and Langham, F. W., Jr., "The Change Seekers," *Harvard Business Review,* Jan.-Feb. 1966.

Kahn, H., *The Future of the Corporation,* Mason and Lipscomb, New York, 1974.

Kono, T., "Long Range Planning—Japan-USA—A Comparative Study," *Long Range Planning,* Oct. 1976.

Kudla, R. J., "Elements of Effective Corporate Planning," *Long Range Planning,* Aug. 1976.

Lorange, P., and Vancil, R. F., "Strategic Planning in Diversified Companies," *Harvard Business Review,* Jan. 1975.

Malin, Z. A., and Karger, D. W., "Does Long-Range Planning Improve Company Performance?" *Management Review,* Sept. 1975.

Marley-Clarke, B. W. G., "Policy Planning for Environmental Management," *Long Range Planning,* Oct. 1976.

Miller, D., "Common Syndromes of Business Failure," *Business Horizons,* Dec. 1977.

Mintzberg, H. "Policy As a Field of Management Theory," *Academy of Management Review,* Jan. 1977.

Morgan, John S., *Managing Change,* McGraw-Hill, New York, 1972.

Pohlman, R. A., Ang, J. S., and Ali, S. I., "Policies of Multinational Firms: A Survey," *Business Horizons,* Dec. 1976.

Prout, G. R., "Corporate Social Strategy In a Post Industrial World," *Conference Board Record,* Sept. 1975.

Punt, T., "Social Trends and Corporate Plans," *Long Range Planning,* Oct. 1976.

Ringbakk, K. A., "Organized Planning in Major U. S. Companies," *Long Range Planning,* Dec. 1969.

Rothschild, W. E., *Putting it all Together: A Guide to Strategic Thinking,* American Management Association, New York, 1976.

Rue, L. W., "The How and Who of Long-Range Planning," *Business Horizons,* Dec. 1973.

Scott, B. W., *Long Range Planning in American Industry,* American Management Association, New York 1962.

Smith, R. A., *Corporations in Crisis,* Doubleday, Garden City, N.Y., 1963.

Springer, C. H. "Strategic Management in General Electric," *Operations Research,* Nov.–Dec. 1973.

Steiner, G. A., and Miner, J. B., *Management Policy and Strategy,* Macmillan, New York, 1977.

Van Dam, André, "Planning For a New International Economic Order," *Long Range Planning,* Oct. 1976.

Warren, E. K., *Long Range Planning: The Executive Viewpoint,* Prentice-Hall, Engle-wood Cliffs, N.J., 1966.

Wrapp, H. E., "Top Managers Don't Make Policy Decisions," *Harvard Business Review,* Sept.–Oct., 1967.

Wright, V. C., "Corporate Planning in the Mineral Industry," *Long-Range Planning,* Apr. 1976.

Chapter 2

STRATEGIC-PLANNING SYSTEMS

This chapter introduces the broad framework for a strategic planning system. Subsequent chapters elaborate on the various aspects of that framework and deal with the translation of the concepts into working processes and procedures.

The strategic-planning system so developed is a management system in which strategic decisions are made in a systematic manner, with information supplied by an information subsystem and within the framework of an explicitly designed supportive organizational and managerial environment.

Evolution of Strategic-Planning Systems

This modern systems-oriented concept of a strategic planning system may be viewed as the outgrowth of an evolutionary process.

TRADITIONAL VIEWS OF STRATEGIC PLANNING

The traditional view of strategic planning sees it as a function that is a part of the job of general managers. Concomitant with this view is the virtual absence of systematic support for planning. The only "systems" that exist are those the individual manager may develop for himself.

Because people do not naturally think in terms of the future rather than the present and because strategic decisions inherently depend on information about external forces not usually provided to managers by the organization's internally oriented information system, this approach often leads to poor planning, or to little real planning at all. Certainly, under this traditional viewpoint *it is difficult for an organization, composed of many different people supported by inward-looking systems, to do planning which is truly strategic in nature.*

The recognition of these deficiencies of the traditional view led to a view of strategic planning that saw it as an identifiable *organizational* function, rather than merely an individual managerial one. Unfortunately, this viewpoint

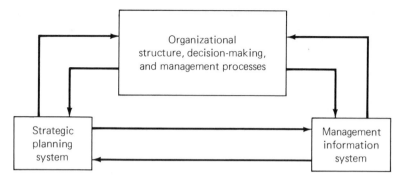

FIGURE 2.1   Relationship of Strategic Planning System to Other Organizational Subsystems.

has often been institutionalized by creating a planning staff and charging that staff with the primary responsibility for planning.

The "systems" used to support this staff approach to strategic planning are largely procedural. For instance, many organizations that use this concept of planning go through an annual cycle during which managers make financial and sales forecasts and budgets for their area of responsibility. These are then reviewed and aggregated by planners of the highest organizational level, and are thereby viewed as "plans" for the future. Unfortunately, such plans are seldom really strategic in nature. All too often the processes for preparing them degenerate quickly into "a ritual of numbers with no analysis of reality."[1]

MODERN VIEWS OF STRATEGIC PLANNING SYSTEMS

A more modern approach to strategic planning recognizes the interdependence of planning and other functions and activities in the organization and attempts to take cognizance of these interdependencies in designing the organization's planning systems, information systems, and other processes and systems.

The view thus given to strategic planning is one that relates it to other critical elements of the organization, as shown in Figure 2.1. The implementation of the conceptual viewpoint shown in Figure 2.1 may be accomplished through the design of organizational systems and procedures. For instance, the organization using this view would consider the information requirements of the strategic-planning activity during the design phase for a new computer system and it would also consider whether new organizational forms, such as a product

[1] Roger E. Williams, as quoted by *Business Week* in "Top Management Ferment at Koehring," January 19, 1976, p. 74.

management approach, might be effective ways to accomplish the goals established for planned new products.

The Concept of a Strategic-Planning System

Figure 2.2 shows a strategic-planning system that totally encompasses three subsystems: a system of plans, a planning process, and a planning-management subsystem and partially encompasses three others (an organizational subsystem, an informational subsystem, and a decision subsystem). The details of these subsystems will be explained in the next section. For the moment, it is sufficient to recognize that this means that, in addition to the organizational elements that are integral parts of a strategic planning system, other elements of the organization, involving information, decisions, and the "organization" itself, are, in part, also within the domain of the strategic-planning system.

In the informational context, this means that a strategic-planning system

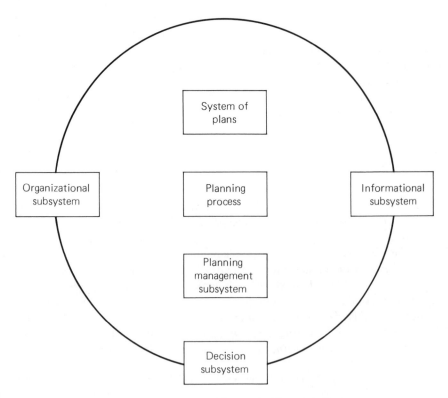

FIGURE 2.2   Elements of Strategic Planning System.

must be designed to address such questions as: What is the flow of information that will provide insight into future environmental forces? What is the nature of this information? What "information system" can be used to identify emerging ideas concerning future organizational pursuits? How is the information integrated into appropriate data bases, which then can be analyzed to predict future environmental and competitive forces?

The partial integration of the organizational subsystem into the strategic-planning system in Figure 2.2 represents much more than just a specialized organization developed to "do" planning. The design of the organization that is developed to accomplish the process of strategic planning involves the answers to questions such as: What are the specialized skills necessary to accomplish planning? How are these skills to be put together? Who performs what specialized function? Who has the ideas? Who does the analysis? Who makes the final selection of strategic alternatives?

The concept of a strategic planning system shown in Figure 2.2 emphasizes *the interdependence of these subsystems. This interdependence is so pronounced that one subsystem cannot be effectively implemented without at least making appropriate changes in the others.* In other words, the informational, decision, and organizational subsystems are not merely related to the planning system; *they are, at least in part, a part of the strategic-planning system itself.*

With this introduction to the concept of a strategic-planning system, we shall go on to outline the substance of the various interrelated subsystems. Before doing this, however, it will be useful to deal with the underlying premises on which these subsystems are based.

Strategic-Planning Premises

Every management system is explicitly or implicitly founded on underlying premises that reflect the roles that should be played by various managers in using the system, the nature of the information processed by the system, and how that information is to be used to improve managerial effectiveness.

The strategic planning system depicted in Figure 2.2 is based on a variety of premises that reflect the hard-won lessons of various companies and public agencies in instituting planning in their organizations. These premises, although they are not eternally established truths, have therefore been developed and tested in real-world situations to a degree that makes them worthy of serious consideration by any organization with a need and desire to do better strategic planning.

These basic premises are as follows:

1. Professional planners can facilitate a planning process, but they cannot themselves do the organization's planning.

2. Planning activities should be performed by the managers who will ultimately be responsible for the implementation of the plans.

3. Creative strategic planning is inherently a group activity, since it must involve many different subunits of the organization and many different varieties of expertise.

4. A "planning organization" must be created to deal with the conception and development of strategic plans. This organization provides the climate and mechanisms through which individuals at various levels are provided a greater opportunity to participate in determing the organization's future.

5. Strategic planning involves much more than numerical extrapolations of trends; it involves as well the selection of missions, objectives, and strategic alternatives.

6. Managers must be motivated to spend time on strategic planning through a formalized system and organization approach that also permits their contribution to the planning process to be assessed.

7. The planning process must provide for the development of relevant data bases—qualitative as well as quantitative—that facilitate the development of environmental forecasts and the evaluation of strategic alternatives.

8. An evaluation of future environmental trends, competitive threats, and internal organizational strengths and weaknesses are essential to the strategic-planning process.

9. Evolving ideas within the organization provide the points of departure to develop future products and markets.

10. The chief executive's responsibility for developing future organizational strategy centers around the development of a "strategic culture" in the organization, the final evaluation and selection of strategic alternatives, and the design of a master plan of implementation for those alternatives.

Strategic Planning Subsystems

Like any system, a strategic planning system may be thought of as being composed of a number of subsystems. The major subsystems incorporated into the strategic planning system of Figure 2.2 are:

1. A system of plans
2. A planning process
3. A decision subsystem
4. A management information subsystem

5. A facilitative organizational structure
6. A planning management subsystem

A SYSTEM OF PLANS

The output of the strategic planning process is planning documentation (a "system of plans") that portrays planning results for all organizational activities and all relevant periods.

The idea of a system of plans—a collection of interrelated and interdependent plans—is motivated by the recognition that the solutions to complex strategic questions are often themselves quite complex. Most organizations are sufficiently sophisticated to recognize that simple solutions will not suffice for complex problems. The day is gone when a "war on poverty" could be considered a solution to a complex problem which has plagued mankind from time immemorial. So too is the day past when a purely technological solution will suffice for complex technology-related problems. One need only consider the failures of new transport vehicles to solve the transportation problems of major cities to recognize that problems are made up of many complex parts and that problems are themselves related in complex ways. For instance, the transportation and air pollution problems of the cities are inextricably intertwined by the automobile's role in present-day transportation.

Complex solutions will also inevitably be required for most strategic organizational problems. The solutions will be complex in the sense that they will require many different elements (technological, financial, marketing, etc.) and they will require the participation and support of a wide variety of the organization's clientele groups (its employees, owners, suppliers, etc.).

Since plans are importantly composed of the proposed "solutions" to complex problems, the plans must be at least as complex as are the problems. This means that a simple plan or simple heirarchy of plans will not be adequate for a complex organization. Rather, there must be a system of interrelated and interdependent subplans that reflect the various dimensions of the problems being faced, the opportunities presented, the relevant clientele groups, and the interrelationships among these elements.

Taken in this context, four interrelated subplans may be distinguished:[2]

1. The *Mission Plan* outlines the broad purposes and strategies for the extended future.
2. The *Development Plan* deals with periods beyond one year and typically deals with "product" improvements and the next generation of products and services.

[2] This framework is based on one originally developed in *A Framework for Business Planning*, Stanford Research Institute, Report No. 162, Menlo Park, Calif., Feb. 1963.

3. The *Operational Plan* supports the current generation of products. This plan is the blueprint for current organizational actions and usually emphasizes a one- or two-year horizon.
4. The *Project Plan* deals with ad hoc activities such as the development of a new facility, developing a new product, an emerging market or technological area, or effecting an organizational merger.

Such interrelated plans serve to document the planning effort within the organization, and to provide the basis for communicating goals, objectives, and strategies throughout the organization. They also serve to relate planning outputs that are at different conceptual levels, that relate to different elements of the organization, and that affect different time periods.

For instance, the mission plan documents the choices made in the strategic planning process concerning what business the organization is to be in and what its general strategy will be in pursuing that mission. The development plan is more detailed and deals with long time periods and future generations of products and resources. The operations plan deals with much shorter ranges, but it is also broad in scope. Program and project plans may deal with various time horizons, but they are narrow and focus on limited objectives and limited resources commitments.

The two highest level elements of this set of plans constitute the primary product, or output, of the strategic-planning system. However, these plans must be based on present operational and project plans. Moreover, they must be translated into future operational and project plans. Hence, these levels of plans constitute a part of the overall strategic-planning system.

The nature of the content of the various subplans in the system of plans is as important as is their relationship to each other. For the moment, let us simply say that the plans should represent *adaptive mechanisms* that enable the organization to change: survive, grow, or be liquidated.

These adaptive mechanisms are such things as acquisition plans for other companies, plans for facilities that will enable the organization to perform its future missions, plans for acquiring new capital, and the myriad of other things that will enable the organization to prosper in a future environment that will be quite different than the present one.

The "adaptive" nature of these plans suggests that they should themselves be flexible and adaptable to the vagaries of an uncertain future. For instance, facilitates may be planned to be multipurpose rather than single purpose, and acquisitions may be planned to complement existing capabilities in order to broaden the range of organizational competencies. If plans are purposefully developed to be adaptive, they have a much better chance of being effective, despite the fact that current visions of the future may necessarily change, than do plans which are "cast into concrete" on the basis of a singular view of the future.

A PLANNING PROCESS

If a complex system of plans is to be effectively developed and utilized by an organization, it must be done in an organized fashion. A loose process for planning might well be feasible in a small organization, or even in one in which the various subplans can be simply stapled together to form the overall plan. However, one basic aspiration of planning is the achievement of synergy—that the whole can be more than the sum of the parts. This in turn means that some process must be developed for assessing the relationships, interactions, and interdependencies among the subelements of the organization and among the activities and programs of each. For planning to truly achieve synergy, some mechanism must be developed for using these assessments as a basis for *taking advantage of the interactions and interdependencies.*

Figure 2.3 shows a conceptual model of an adaptive planning process. The "adaptive" nature of this process simply means that the output (the system of plans) should be flexible enough to deal with changing circumstances.

This variety of adaptation may be thought of in terms of *contingency*

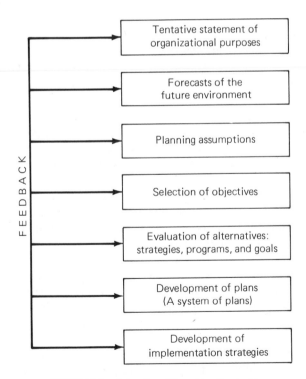

FIGURE 2.3   Adaptive Planning Process.

planning in which specific plans are developed for a variety of contingencies that may occur, usually with "trigger levels" to specifically identify when such contingencies will be considered to have occurred.

Although the strategic-planning process shown in Figure 2.3 is described in a step-by-step sequential pattern, this simple sequence applies only to the *beginning* of each step. Thus, step one begins before step two begins, but, through the feedback loops, each step may be reperformed a number of times and various steps may therefore be going on simultaneously.

TENTATIVE STATEMENT OF ORGANIZATION PURPOSE. The strategic-planning process begins with the delineation of *tentative organizational purposes,* essentially a mission statement describing the "business" that the organization might pursue in the future. This statement, preliminary in nature, is intended to put boundaries on future opportunities and to provide a point of departure from which the informational requirements for assessing future opportunities can be assembled and evaluated. The statement of future organizational purpose may be challenging, even shocking, in the hope of getting organizational participants to think about the future in other than traditional or existing business terms.

FORECASTS OF THE FUTURE ENVIRONMENT. Forecasts have as their key purpose the development of insights that enable planners to build a model of expected future environments. This model portrays the nature of the social, economic, political, legal, and technological forces with which the organization must deal in the future.

PLANNING ASSUMPTIONS. Assumptions represent basic background information required for strategic planning. They can be specific, such as one dealing with the rate of inflation, or more general, such as one dealing with shifts in people's basic values.

Planning assumptions provide complementary information bases to those provided by forecasts. These assumptions permit the planner to complete his model of the future that can be used as the basis for evaluating and selecting strategic objectives.

SELECTION OF OBJECTIVES. This step involves the specification, in greater detail and refinement, of the tentative statement of organizational purposes previously made. Objectives (broad aspirations for the organization) serve to focus and direct the subsequent stages of the planning process.

EVALUATION OF ALTERNATIVES. The next step in the process, the evaluation of alternatives, deals with the definition and evaluation of the alternative ways in which the resources of the organization are to be employed to achieve the organization's objectives. Thus, the process of evaluating alternatives is one of deciding on the best route for the organization given the conditions and limitations of the future.

The evaluation of alternatives, using some form of cost-benefit analysis, should be performed in terms of the previously selected objectives and should therefore lead to the selection of alternatives congruent with these objectives. These alternatives, together with a statement of risk and uncertainty, constitute the core of strategic planning. To be meaningful, they must be cast in the framework of *what can be done* and *what should be done,* given the existing organizational purposes and the risks in the future.

DEVELOPMENT OF PLANS. Once these evaluations and choices have been made, the process of developing plans focuses on ensuring that there is consistency among the choices made by different organizational units and across the various activities of the enterprise. It also involves ensuring that the plans are congruent with the overall objectives. This step produces the written and documented description of the choices made and the activities that will be performed to achieve the realization of the choices; thus, it must be again more detailed than the previous step.

Too often, this step is the only one that is really accomplished with any effectiveness by organizations purporting to do planning. The overall process here emphasizes that the plans are merely the output (the written record), which serve to document the choices made, ensure that the choices are consistent, and define the choices in specific action-oriented terms so that they can be implemented.

DEVELOPMENT OF IMPLEMENTATION STRATEGIES. Just as careful consideration should be given to a range of activities that the organization might undertake, once those choices have been made consideration must be given to alternative ways of accomplishing the desired ends through the strategies and activities selected. In part, this implementation strategy is treated within the scope of the plans themselves, since in developing the plans one considers alternative ways of effectively doing that which the evaluation process has determined should be done. For instance, if a new plant is to be built, the plan would certainly specify an orderly sequence of steps involving site selection, design, etc. which would lead to the implementation of the planning decision concerning a new plant.

However, there is another aspect of implementation strategy that may often be required. That element of the implementation strategy is more subtle than the former in that it deals with the intangibles of motivation and human behavior. The planner here asks questions like: What will be the response of our employees to this decision? How can this plan be conveyed to them in a manner that will motivate them to help make it a success? What portions of the plan should be publicly announced? When? Should any public officials be communicated with before public announcement?

Such a treatment of the human behavioral implications of the plan serves to make the plan more comprehensive by incorporating into it a strategy for implementation. This strategy serves to guide *all* of the activities that emanate from the plan rather than just those job and task assignments usually thought of as the major activity outputs of planning.

THE DECISION SUBSYSTEM

As the planning-process description shows, planning intrinsically involves *decisions* about such things as organizational purposes, goals, objectives, strategies, and implementation strategies. No systematic planning process would therefore be complete without a systematic approach to the crucial decision-making phase.

Of course, no planning decision process can be made totally objective and systematic. The decision subsystem should serve as a means of integrating executive judgment into a formal decision-analysis framework. This complementarity of executive judgment and formal analysis amplifies the manager's ability to deal with complex strategic-decision situations.

Formal decision analysis involves the use of some variety of *decision model,* an explicit statement of the relationship between organizational *performance* (say, in terms of profitability) and the controllable and uncontrollable forces that determine the level of performance. For instance, a decision model might relate organizational profitability to economic conditions (uncontrollable) and to *strategic choice variables* such as the size of the advertising budget (controllable).

Such models can serve as *guides* to the evaluation and selection of strategies, programs, and the other decision elements of planning. With the aid of models, the planners need not rely solely on intuitive judgments or a trial-and-error approach of limited scope. Rather, he can explore a wide range of alternative actions that can be taken in terms of their overall future impact on the organization.

Of course, the planning-decision subsystem need not be entirely formalized. Many decision models do not involve fancy symbolic expressions or sophisticated mathematics. Indeed, many strategic decisions *must* be made without the aid of models because they are unique or because appropriate models cannot be developed within the time and cost constraints under which the choice is being made. In such instances, the decision subsystem may simply be a well-structured process of discussion and negotiation.

However, if a planning process becomes focused on the process itself (the performance of certain required planning activities) to the exclusion of a focus on decision making (the heart of any planning process), it is likely to result in poor planning. In some organizations, planning has become an end in itself, rather than a means to an end. Usually, this is because the *process* is so emphasized that the real decision making must be accomplished in an ad hoc fashion or, in some instances, totally outside of the planning process. When this is so, planning becomes a charade carried on by actors in the belief that they must do planning. The crucial organizational decisions are then made separately from the formalized activity.

The incorporation of a decision subsystem into the planning system serves to emphasize the decision aspect of planning. It also importantly requires that certain information be obtained and processed in a fashion that will contribute to better decisions.

THE MANAGEMENT INFORMATION SUBSYSTEM

Many planning failures are caused by a lack of supportive information relevant to planning (the "data bases" on which decisions can be made). Most of the information currently processed by organizational information systems is largely descriptive of the past history of the internal organizational subsystem. Much of it is outdated and inwardly directed. To be useful for strategic planning, such information must be prospective and focused toward those environmental and competitive elements of the organization that will most critically affect its future.

Relevant and adequate information is essential to carry out effective strategic planning in any situation. Information concerning future political, economic, technological, social, and legal forces facing the organization must be assembled and analyzed to build assumptions about the future.

The extreme importance of objective information in making planning choices is made clear by the following excerpt from the planning guidebook of Westinghouse Electric:[3]

> The gathering and organizing of information in a logical step-by-step analysis so as to recognize and evaluate the important aspects of the business now and for the future, enabling the development of a set of strategic moves with acceptable costs, benefits and risks which will optimize performance for the Business Unit and the Corporation.

This sort of planning information serves to motivate the need for a formal intelligence gathering, processing, and monitoring system. A useful broad de-

[3] "The Business Unit Strategic Plan," 1977–1981, Westinghouse Electric Corporation, March, 1976, p. 1. Used by permission.

lineation of the various kinds of business intelligence is given in Figure 2.4, which summarizes the content of a strategic-planning data base and portrays their relationship to the elements of the planning process as well as to the diverse sources of planning information.

To even attempt to address such a broad diversity of planning information without systematization would be utter folly. No individual or group could reasonably be expected to be aware of, and much less to have evaluated, such a range of data. Therefore, any action taken without such a system is necessarily made without the full informational support that could be provided.

To systematize planning information does not mean that an expensive computer system must be developed; rather it means only that questions such as the following be answered and that the answers be made operational: What needs to be known? Where can the data be obtained? Who will gather the data? How will the data be gathered? Who will analyze and interpret the data? How will extracted information be stored most efficiently for equally efficient future retrieval? How can extracted information be disseminated to the proper parties at the right time for consideration?

Unless the needed information is focused toward a single program or objective and can therefore be approached on a somewhat ad hoc basis, reasonable answers to these questions sometimes do dictate that a computer system be utilized for effective storage and retrieval operations. Dissemination that goes beyond periodic briefings and responses to specific inquiries can be facilitated by assembling user interest profiles and feeding them into the computer. Then, as additions are made to the file, match-ups with those profiles can automatically trigger outputs that might have been missed by the human data interpreter.

A FACILITATIVE ORGANIZATIONAL STRUCTURE

There are many different roles that organizational elements play in strategic planning. These often represent some combination of the following:

1. A strong central planning staff that develops long-range strategies.
2. A central planning staff that facilitates long-range planning by providing supporting services to organizational elements engaged in planning.
3. The decentralization of long-range planning responsibilities to "profit center" executives responsible for carrying the long-range plans.

Most questions of "organizing for planning" generally involve issues of "line versus staff" and whether the long-range planning staff should be at the corporate level, division level, or both, on the organization chart. There is a need of creative organizational approaches to long-range planning. Some creative approaches are finally beginning to emerge in the planning practices of

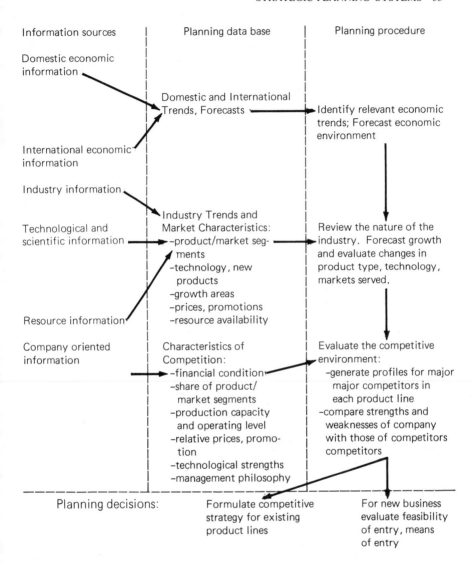

FIGURE 2.4   Strategic Planning Data Base.*

*Adapted from Francis E. de Carbonnel and Roy G. Dorrance, "Information Sources for Planning Decisions," Copyright 1973 by the Regents of the University of California. Reprinted from *California Management Review*, Vol. XV, No. 4, pp. 43 by permission of the Regents.

larger corporations, such as General Electric, Westinghouse, and Texas Instruments.

Of course, the concept of a "planning organization" is itself not well understood in any context other than that of a professional planning staff. As noted earlier, many organizations operate as though strategic planning were simply another aspect of the manager's job, or alternately, as though only top management and professional planners should have anything of substance to do with strategic planning for the overall organization. These two concepts, either alone or in combination, presume that strategic planning should be done within the framework of the existing traditional bureaucratic organization.

Modern organizations are much too complex for either of these simplistic approaches. If the organization is to be opportunistic, to adapt to change, and to influence the future, all of the things that planners constantly promise as the benefits of comprehensive organizational strategic planning, it must not be bound to either the practices or the organizational structures of the past. There is a wealth of evidence to support this pontifical statement. First, some of the main thrusts of change in our industrial society serve to remind us that strategic planning is inescapable if the organization is to survive: protracted product development cycles, accelerating product obsolescence, rapid state-of-the-art proliferation, changing social values, increasing demand of people for more participation in the decision process, and growing organizational complexity and interdependency. Second, coincident with these changes has come the recognition that good ideas for the future are not the special prerogative of top managers or professional planners. Yet, many organizations continue to operate with a multilayered chain of command where many people can say "no," but few can say "yes." Such an organization stifles the generation of ideas and complicates the process of bringing them to fruition.

Innovative ideas may be the harbingers of the organization's future, and, if those ideas are truly new, they may be lost in the bureaucratic milieu. If, for instance, new products and markets are to be developed that are not simply extensions of existing products and markets, effective ways of generating ideas, evaluating those ideas, and developing them to fruition must be found.

For strategic planning to accomplish this, the planning effort must be supported with the skills and knowledge that exist in the organization at all levels and in all subunits. In most organizations, organizational interfaces between subunits are "cracks" through which good ideas are lost. The goal of a strategic-planning system should be to convert them into organizational assets to be used in the creation of the organization's future.

The concept of a planning organization is one that views the organization as actually being made up of two (or more) parallel organizations. If one thinks of each of these parallel organizations as being described as an organizational chart or some other two-dimensional representation, the overall organiza-

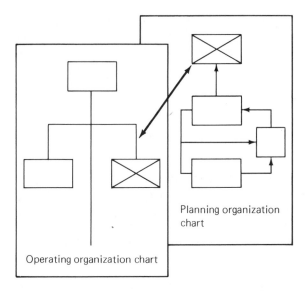

FIGURE 2.5 Parallel Organizations Within a Firm.

tion may be thought of in the manner of Figure 2.5. There, the two organizations are in parallel and the *same people play different roles in each.* Thus, the crosses in Figure 2.5 depict an individual filling one slot on the operating organizational chart at some times and filling another slot on the planning organizational chart at other times. He may, within the scope of one day, move back and forth several times between his two jobs in the two parallel suborganizations that make up his overall organization. In this way, through *parallel organizations,* the operating and planning goals and activities can be separated to some degree and each may be dealt with effectively and efficiently.

THE PLANNING MANAGEMENT SUBSYSTEM

Strategic planning does not just happen; it must be motivated. An important part of motivation is the attitude that managers create and the climate that exists in the organization. Since it is people who perform the planning functions, the strategic-planning process must itself be structured and managed. Just as the planning process described earlier dictates that a strategy for the implementation *of plans* be developed, so too is a strategy for the implementation *of planning* required if strategic planning is to be newly introduced or radically changed in an organization. Thus, planning must itself be planned for and managed.

This seeming play-on-words is, in fact, most crucial to successful planning. Planning is a major time-and-resource-consuming organizational activity. As such, it will degenerate if it is not perceived as being important, if people are not positively motivated toward it, and if it is not carefully managed in the same way that other organizational activities are managed.

Part of this "management of planning" involves giving attention to the organizational climate necessary for creative planning. An effective way of enhancing the climate for such planning is to encourage widespread participation at all levels. Individuals can be encouraged to submit their own planning ideas in terms of product modification, new products, new organizational arrangements, new strategy for the organization, and so forth. Such ideas should have enough justification and documentation to enable the planning staff to perform an initial appraisal and to see if each idea is worthy of further investigation.

In creating a suitable climate for strategic planning, it is important to stress the idea that change is normal and is to be expected as the organization faces a dynamic environment. Top executives must not only be adaptable to change, but must convince other people in the organization of the inevitability of change. Part of this convincing can be accomplished by drawing up organizational policies that reflect the official attitude toward change and planning, but there is more to it than just the paper work. In this respect, Irwin and Langham[4] have noted:

> Top managers must be change seekers. Their leadership role is to provide a climate for rapid improvement toward excellence. The success their business achieves in the future will be in geometric proportion to their understanding of, planning for, dedication to, personal involvement in, and self-motivation toward the implementation of purposeful change. For many companies this demands a reorientation in the thinking of senior executives. It means honest commitment to a new concept. Insincerity or lip service will soon destroy confidence.

Of course, the only truly effective way of creating a proper climate for strategic planning is to permeate the organization with planning, to demonstrate that it works, and to make use of it. When this pragmatic test of results has been passed, skeptics will be stilled and the organizational climate will be ripe for the institution of strategic planning.

Summary

Systems for strategic planning have evolved as planning has been recognized as a formal organizational activity that requires the involvement of top managers and middle managers as well as staff planners. For planning to be successful in

---

[4] Irwin, P. M., and Langham, F. W., Jr., "The Change Seekers," *Harvard Business Review,* Jan.–Feb., 1966, p. 83.

such a complex organizational context, it must be integrated into the organization, its information systems, and its general "way of doing things" in a systematic fashion. A strategic-planning system encompasses a system of plans, a planning process, a decision subsystem, and a planning-management subsystem. It also directly interfaces with the organizational subsystem and the information subsystem of the organization.

A system of plans is a planning product, or output, which is sufficiently complex to enable the organization to cope with and to influence the future environment. A planning process is a systematic procedure for producing adaptive plans in an effective and efficient manner in a situation that involves many individuals, parochial interests, and conflicting personal objectives.

A decision subsystem represents a way in which the organization can explicitly consider the choices that are often only implicit in planning. A planning-management subsystem permits the overall planning system to be managed in the same way as other organizational activities are managed.

The organization's information system, as well as the organization itself, must be designed to facilitate, and not deter, effective planning. Organizations and information systems primarily designed to support the effecient operations of the organization are generally not well equipped to support planning. Therefore, new organizational and informational concepts must be applied if planning is to be facilitated by these elements of the organization.

Chapter 2—Questions and Exercises

1. There are certain basic strategic questions a manager should ask about his organization that are considerations over and above the day-to-day operational matters. What are some of these critical strategic questions?
2. How can one identify those criticl choice situations in an organization with which strategic planning should deal?
3. What are some examples of a strategic decision in a business organization? How does a manager determine if a decision is strategic in nature?
4. Some U.S. corporations now view the hiring of an individual as a kind of strategic decision. What valid basis might there be for such a view?
5. What are some of the external environmental elements that can affect the strategic direction of an organization? Give some examples of these external forces in an organizational context with which you are familiar.
6. Give a specific example of how the management information system, the organizational structure, its decision-making processes, and its overall management processes can be tied in as an integral part of the strategic planning system.
7. Change and organizational innovation are intertwined when viewed from a strategic planning context. What is meant by this statement?
8. What are some strategic choices that an individual faces in his lifetime career planning?

9. Modern organizations tend to operate on the principle that its managers should have both strategic and operating responsibilities. What is the justification for this dual role?

10. Why should professional planners not do the organization's planning? After all, are they not the best equipped people to do so?

11. What are the distinguishing characteristics of a strategic-planning system in an organization? How do these differ from the characteristics of an operational planning system?

12. What are the elements that can be integrated into a consistent structure in an organization to create a strategic-planning system?

13. What role does the value system of a chief executive play in determining the strategic direction of his organization?

14. How might an executive develop his attitude and management skills to deal more effectively with change in his organization?

15. What is the value of explicitly stating strategic planning responsibility in an organization?

16. A strategic planning system is only one of the several management systems in an organization. What are some of the other management systems that are found in an organization?

17. Strategic planning is inherently an ad hoc organizational activity that deals with unique strategic situations; thus there is little place for a formal strategic planning system within an organization. Defend or refute this statement.

18. Distinguish between the mission plan and the development plan of an organization. How do each of these relate to the operational plan?

19. Define contingency planning. Give an illustration that includes the specification of "trigger points."

20. Plans are merely the recorded histories of the planning process. What does this mean?

21. What is meant by a management information system to support strategic planning? Can an organization, have such a system even if it does not have a computer?

22. Explain the idea of "parallel organizations" in terms of the responsibilities and the day-to-day activities that a single manager might have.

23. How can planning be managed? What is meant by the planning management subsystem?

24. What is the traditional view of strategic planning?

25. Identify and define the subsystems that are encompassed in a strategic planning system.

26. The subsystems involved in a strategic planning system are interdependent. What is the nature of this interdependency?

27. The output of a strategic planning process is a system of plans that portrays planning for all organizational activities and all relevant time periods. Describe the nature of the subplans that may be found in such a system of plans.

28. The project plan holds a unique place in the planning subsystem of an organization. Why is this so?

29. Describe the nature of a strategic planning process. What are the relationships, interactions and interdependencies that a strategic-planing process addresses?
30. When initiating strategic planning, it is well to develop a tentative statement of organizational purpose. Why should such a statement be tentative?
31. What are some of the fundamental forecasts that an organization should develop in predicting its future environment? What is the difference between forecasting and planning?
32. What are planning assumptions? What are some examples of planning assumptions? What is the difference between explicit and implicit assumptions?
33. Describe the interrelationships between the selection of objectives and the evaluation of alternatives in the strategic-planning process.
34. The development of implementation strategies is the key to planning success. Why is this so?
35. What is the purpose of managing emerging technological and marketing ideas in an organization? What feedback do such ideas provide in the strategic planning process?

Strategic Questions for the Manager

1. What is the organizational subsystem for doing strategic planning in my organization? How successful has this organizational arrangement been? Why?
2. What are the necessary technical skills reuired to do planning? Are these skills properly placed in the organization to accomplish planning?
3. How are plans presently portrayed in the organization? Are all organizational elements and relevant time periods adequately portrayed in these plans?
4. Do the plans for the organization adequately reflect interrelated and interdependent functions, relevant clientele groups, and organizational interfaces?
5. How are emerging technological and market ideas managed in the organization?
6. What "trigger points" are needed in the organization to put contingency plans into operation? Do key managers understand the nature of these trigger points?
7. What feedback mechanisms are used to measure the efficacy of organizational strategic planning?
8. Can I state my organization's purpose in clear succinct terms? Do key managers agree on this statement?
9. How are future environmental forecasts currently being made?
10. When a strategic decision is made in the organization, is an attempt made to identify and weigh the explicit and implicit assumptions underlying these decisions?
11. Were past strategic decisions made after a thorough assessment of how those decisions would be implemented?
12. How are strategic decisions made in the organization? Are the decisions arrived at through an orderly process or pretty much by "gut feel"?
13. Are major decisions in the organization supported by adequate data bases? Does an information system support these data bases?

References

Ackoff, R. L., and Emery, F. E., *On Purposeful Systems,* Aldine-Atherton, Chicago, 1972.

Amara, R., and Lipinski, A., "Strategic Planning: Penetrating the Corporate Business," Paper P-30, Institute for the Future, Nov. 1974.

Ansoff, H. I., "The State of Practice in Planning Systems," *Sloan Management Review,* Winter 1977.

Baker, C. R., "Behavioral Aspects of Corporate Planning," *Long Range Planning,* Aug. 1976.

Baldwin, H. W., *Strategy for Tomorrow,* Harper and Row, New York, 1970.

Churchman, C. W., *The Systems Approach,* Dell, New York, 1968.

Cleland, D. I., and King, W. R., *Management: A Systems Approach,* McGraw-Hill, New York, 1972.

Clutterbuck, D., "Union Carbide Co-Ordinates Its Planning," *International Management,* May 1975.

Forrester, J. W., *Industrial Dynamics,* MIT Press. Cambridge, Mass., 1961.

Gedrich, S. F., "Business Planning at Sperry Rand," *Long Range Planning,* Apr. 1976.

Glans, T. B., Grad, B., Holstein, D., Meyers, W. E., and Schmidt, R. N., *Management Systems,* Holt, Rinehart and Winston, New York, 1968.

Goggin, W. C., "How the Multidimensional Structure Works at Dow Corning," *Harvard Business Review,* Jan.–Feb. 1974.

Golightly, H. O., "What Makes a Company Successful?" *Business Horizons,* June 1971.

Hollingsworth, A. T., and Preston, P., "Corporate Planning: A Challenge For Personnel Executives," *Personnel Journal,* Aug. 1976.

Kahalas, H. "Long Range Planning: An Open Systems View", *Long Range Planning,* Oct. 1977.

Kano, H., "Managing For the Future in Japanese Industry," *The Future of the Corporation* (H. Kahn, Ed.), Mason & Lipscomb, New York, 1974.

Linneman, R. E., and Kennell, J. D., "Shirt-Sleeve Approach to Long-Range Plans," *Harvard Business Review,* Mar.–Apr. 1977.

Lorange, P., and Vancil, R. F., "How to Design a Strategic Planning System," *Harvard Business Review,* Sept. 1976.

———*Strategic Planning Systems,* Prentice-Hall, Englewood Cliffs, New Jersey, 1977.

McConnell, J. D., "Strategic Planning: One Workable Approach," *Long Range Planning,* Dec. 1971.

Morton, J. A., "A Systems Approach to the Innovation Process," *Business Horizons,* Summer 1967.

Moses, M. A., "Implementation of Analytical Planning Systems," *Management Science,* June 1975.

Nott, Paul C., "An Experimental Comparison of the Effectiveness of Three Planning Methods," *Management Science,* Jan. 1977.

Osgood, W. R., and Wetzel, W. E., Jr., "A Systems Approach to Venture Initiation," *Business Horizons,* Oct. 1977.

Osmond, C. N., "Corporate Planning: Its Impact on Management," *Long Range Planning,* April 1971.

Simmons, W. W., "Strategic Planning Program For Next Decade," *SAM Advanced Management Journal,* Winter 1976.

Tavernier, G., "Swedish Firm Alters Its Approach to Planning," *International Management,* March 1975.

Tilles, S., "The Manager's Job: A Systems Approach," *Harvard Business Review,* Jan.–Feb. 1963.

Wilson, I. H., "How Our Values are Changing," *The Futurist,* Feb. 1970.

PART II

Outputs of the Planning System

Chapter 3

THE OUTPUTS
OF PLANNING—
THE SYSTEM OF PLANS

We begin our detailed treatment of the subsystems of the strategic planning system with *the outputs of the system, the documents called plans, and the choices and resource allocations that they reflect.*

In many organizations, the creation of plans is viewed as the objective of the planning process. Emphasis is placed on the preparation of the documents to such a great extent that the *choices* inherent in developing plans fade into the background. In such instances, the documents called "plans" are primarily made up of financial projections and assessments (the "how much" aspect) with much less attention being devoted to the "how" aspect of planning. The "how" dimension stipulates the way in which anticipated results are to be achieved rather than simply which results are desired or anticipated. To ensure against this predominance of form over substance in planning, Westinghouse Electric Corporation[1] has stipulated in their guidelines for business unit strategic planning that: "The financial data submitted should reflect the realities of the selected strategies, it should not be established as a foundation to which strategies are subsequently tailored."

The documents called plans are simply *records* of the planning process and the choices made. These records are necessary for historical and control purposes. As time goes on, they need to be referred to in order to ensure that the chosen actions are being carried out and that they are achieving the goals being sought. If this is not happening, new choices need to be made and/or new implementation actions taken, i.e., the plan must be revised. Viewed in this way, the plans provide a record of the guides or standards that the organization can use in gauging its progress.

Plans are not the objectives to be achieved through planning. *The objective of the planning process is the establishment of a mission, goals, strategies, programs, and allocations of resources that will enable the organization to best cope with and influence an uncertain future.* Thus, the prime value of the plan

---

[1]*Business Unit Strategic Plan, 1977–1981,* Westinghouse Electric Corporation, Pittsburgh, Pa., March 1976, p. 2, used by permission.

lies not in the document itself, but in the process and choices that have gone into it. The planning decisions that underlie the plan are the very essence of the organization's approach to its future, and if properly conducted, the planning process, which has resulted in the plan, can be of inestimable educational value within the organization.

The idea of a document called the plan as the output of nonmilitary planning was dealt with by Fayol:[2]

> Planning is manifested on a variety of occasions and in a variety of ways, its chief manifestation, apparent sign and most effective instrument being the plan of action. The plan of action is, at one and the same time, the result envisaged, the line of action to be followed, the stages to go through, and methods to use. It is a kind of future picture wherein proximate events appear progressively less distinct, and it entails the running of the business as foreseen and provided against over a definite period.

In this chapter, we seem to better identify these substantive contents of plans as well as the configurations in which the plans may be organized to provide useful guides and standards for organizational development.

The Substantive Content of Strategic Plans

The substantive outputs of strategic planning are *organizational changes,* e.g.,

establishment of new product lines

research and development programs

product diversification

mergers and acquisitions

reorganizations and realignments of authority and responsibility patterns within the organization

divestment and liquidations

designing and building of new facilities

establishment of executive development and other training programs

development of new markets

If the organization is to be effective in the long run, these organizational changes must be *contrived responses to anticipated future environments* rather than conditioned responses to the past and current environmental situations.

---

[2] Fayol, H., *General and Industrial Management,* Pitman, London, 1949, p. 43.

However, since the future environments on which the plans are based are necessarily uncertain, the planned changes must be delineated in a manner that facilitates adaptation, i.e., the plans should be *adaptable* to the evolving circumstances. Viewed in this way, plans are not irrevocable guides from which deviation is sinful; rather, they are adaptive mechanisms that should permit the organization to confidently face an uncertain environment.

This adaptive characteristic is true both of the program changes, such as those listed above, and the revisions in the underlying objectives, strategies, and organizational mission, which underlie the program changes. We shall demonstrate this later in some detail. For now, we pause to treat the significant confusion that exists in the literature of planning concerning the terminology used for the various substantive planning outputs. Words like "objectives," "goals," "missions," and "strategies" are often used synonymously, and even more confusingly, they are often defined in precisely the opposite way by different authors.

Although there is a good deal of semantic confusion in defining these various planning outputs, there is little argument about the necessity for doing so. Every plan must entail the specification of what the organization wants to be in the future and how it plans to get there. To avoid this semantic confusion, we begin, not by giving "correct" definitions of various terms, but rather by simply describing a common set of terminology, adapted from that used by many business firms including the General Electric Corporation. The purpose of this enumeration is to specify and illustrate these various terms, since they represent the outputs of the planning process and the content of the plan. In a later chapter, we will go into more detail concerning their interrelationships and the operational decision process that can be applied to each.

THE ORGANIZATION'S MISSION

The broadest strategic planning choice that must be made by an organization is that of its *mission*. An organization's *mission statement* tells what it is, why it exists, and the unique contribution it can make. To choose a mission is to answer the basic question: "What business are we in?" To some, such questions seem to be idle academic nonsense. To them, their mission (the business that they are in) is clear: "we make widgets," or "we run railroads." During the 1960s, it became increasingly apparent that such thinking was too limited. Many organizations that seemed to know their business have disappeared from the scene. We must therefore recognize that today's business, however bright its growth prospects may appear, may not even exist in only a few years. Although this is difficult for most of us to perceive, the lessons of history are so numerous and so vivid that they cannot be ignored.

Consider the dry cleaning industry, which only a few decades ago was viewed as having unlimited potential.[3] How could a service industry that could offer the low-cost, safe, and quick cleaning of everybody's garments not continue to grow? Yet, synthetic fabrics and modern detergents long ago have reduced significantly the growth prospects of the industry.

Similarly, many movie companies did not survive the advent of television, despite the fact that movies themselves have survived. The companies that did survive turned their expertise to producing movies for TV as well as for theaters and changed the kind of movie that they were making so that they would not be so directly competitive with a medium that they could not conquer. Thus, the surviving movie companies changed their view of their business and began to sell old movies to television as well as to produce new ones for TV. One can only imagine what might have happened had the movie companies viewed TV as an opportunity rather than a threat. The television industry is now larger than the movie industry, and it is easy to surmise that the many now-deceased movie firms might have been corporate giants had they viewed their business as that of "entertainment" rather than of "making movies."

Other examples of mission concepts that led to decline or disaster are legion: the railroads constraining themselves to operating on narrow bands of tracks while the need for passenger and freight transportation grew and was filled by others, food chains whose corner grocery stores were severely damaged by supermarkets, etc.

However, during the 1970s, many of the firms that slavishly followed such expansive views of their mission began to realize that grandiose mission concepts could also lead to serious problems. Broad mission statements can be open invitations to get into new businesses solely on the criterion of *potential profitability*. Such a criterion does not take into account vital factors such as expertise: technological, market, and otherwise; neither does it take account of the uncertainty inherent in *potential* profit.

Many of the companies that got into new "growth" businesses on this basis in the 1960s found themselves in the position of selling off unprofitable ventures in the 1970s.[4] Indeed, *it is as important for an organization to carefully define what it does not do as it is for it to state what it does.* Few modern businesses have stated missions as broad as "transportation" or "entertainment," and any firm that did so broadly identify its mission would be likely to quickly become so diverse that it would have little hope of retaining control and being successful.

---

[3] The ensuing discussion of the dry cleaning and movie industries is based on a similar one in Levitt, T., "Marketing Myopia," *Harvard Business Review,* Sept.–Oct., 1975, pp. 26–44, 173–181.

[4] For instance, see "You Can Be Sure, If It's Industrial—Westinghouse," *Iron Age,* March 3, 1975, pp. 20–25.

The values of a clearly defined mission statement can be illustrated with the business statement of one medium-sized firm:

We are in the business of supplying system components and services to a world-wide nonresidential air conditioning market. Air conditioning is defined as heating, cooling, cleaning, humidity control, and air movement.

Such a statement may at first seem to be the same as "We make widgets." However, it clearly specifies (by exclusion) many things that the firm does not do: it does not supply air conditioning *systems,* rather it focuses on system *components,* it does not address itself to the residential market for air conditioners, etc.

It is both meaningful and necessary for an organization to consciously choose and continually review its mission concept if it is to survive and prosper. This is as true of government as of business, despite the much-discussed perseverance of some bureaucracies past their time of usefulness. This is so if only because a mission statement serves as a guide for the multitude of underlying choices that must be made to guide the organization into the future. However, it is also important in serving to *define the scope of acceptable choice,* as a symbol around which some organizational members can gather, and as a statement from which nonagreeing members can flee.

Of course, there are those that argue that a good mission concept is indeed important, but that is implicit in the mind of the organization's top executives, and need not be thought of as an explicit output of planning. Such an approach might suggest that it is, in fact, an *input* to planning rather than an output of it.

This view ignores the continuous feedback-oriented nature of strategic planning and the value of subjecting tentative choices, whether they be of missions or anything else, to the rigors of discussion, debate, and analysis. In such a process, tentative mission choices are used to guide preliminary lower-level choices of strategies, programs, and goals. These choices are then fed-back to serve as a basis for the possible revision of the higher-level missions and objectives. Through such a continuous feedback process, even such stable entities as the organization's mission may be subjected to objective review. If the underlying strategies and programs are sufficiently worthwhile to warrant a mission change, it can be accomplished in this way.

Ansoff[5] and others have referred to the mission in terms of a "common thread" that binds together the program and activities of the organization. A common thread is a relationship between present and future product markets that permits management to guide the business effectively. To avoid the broad mission concepts that are really not missions at all, a good operational rule is

[5] Ansoff, H. I., *Corporate Strategy,* McGraw-Hill, 1965, pp. 105–106.

that the mission should be perceptible to outsiders as well as to the organization's leaders.

The mission may be built around technology, product characteristics, or product needs. Usually, it is not wise to build a mission around customer *groups* rather than *needs,* since customers are fickle creatures. Thus, the president of a large machinery firm refers to his company's mission as "the business of digging holes" rather than "supplying machinery to the construction industry," because he knows that the need to dig holes will persist long after something called a construction industry (at least in it's present form).

THE ORGANIZATION'S OBJECTIVES

Once the organization's mission has been determined, its objectives, desired future positions or "destinations" that it wishes to reach, should be selected. These destinations may be stated in either quantitative or qualitative terms, but they should be *broad and timeless statements,* as opposed to specific, quantitative goals, or targets.

For instance, among the stated objectives of PPG Industries are:[6]

(1) . . . to bring about consistently increasing earnings per share to attain a satisfactory return on stockholders' book equity on a continuing basis and to provide consistently increasing dividends (the prime objective).

(2) . . . to employ the least number and highest quality of people necessary to accomplish the prime objective and to provide them with the opportunities to develop and apply their fullest abilities.

(3) . . . to have the company accepted—as a dynamic, responsible, professionally managed, profit-oriented corporation engaged in exciting and important fields of business, with the ability to meet successfully the economic and social challenges of the future.

Although such statements may at first appear to be motherhood and sin to some, they say very important things about the company. For instance, the image objective (3) says that it cares greatly how it is thought of in society. This serves to clearly to constrain other choices that must be made in the planning process, e.g., strategies that may be followed to attain the prime objective.

The broad and timeless objectives of the US Government are spelled out in the Preamble to the US Constitution as:

. . . to form a more perfect Union, establish Justice, insure domestic Tranquility, provide for the common defence, promote the general Welfare, and secure the Blessings of Liberty for ourselves and our Posterity. . . .

[6] Excerpted with permission from "Corporate Objectives," PPG Industries, Pittsburgh, Pa., undated, p. 13.

Less enduring, but still broad and timeless objectives have been more recently explicated in the areas of welfare, health, and education[7] as:

. . . eliminating hunger, cleaning up our environment, providing maximum opportunity for human development during the critical first five years of life, maintaining and improving standards of education and medical care, reducing welfare dependency, and making our cities more livable for all.

THE ORGANIZATION'S GOALS

Goals are specific, time-based points of measurement that the organization intends to meet in the pursuit of its broad objectives. Usually, goals are stated as specifically and as quantitatively as possible, the emphasis being on *measurement of progress toward the achievement of objectives.*

For instance, if a firm has an objective of 15% ROI, it might establish a schedule indicating the dollar earnings and investment positions necessary to attain this objective. Additionally, it might establish specific "hurdle rates" (minimum rates of return for new investments) required for the achievement of the stated objectives.

The organization's goals are frequently associated with specific programs and projects intended to be the vehicles through which the organization will achieve its broader objectives. For instance, a program goal might be to achieve, by the end of 1980, a 10% increase in market share through the marketing of specified new products, or a goal might involve achieving cost reductions of 15% through a materials-economy program, a production-efficiency program, and an overhead-reduction program.

THE ORGANIZATION'S STRATEGY

A strategy is the *general direction* in which an objective is to be sought. For instance, if a business firm states its objectives in terms of increased earnings per share, this objective might be sought in a variety of different general directions, e.g., by introducing new products, by acquiring smaller companies, or by selling more of existing products to new market segments. Similarly, an educational institution whose objectives are to survive and to provide opportunities to population segments not now being served might introduce new programs designed to appeal to specific segments, open branch campuses to serve new areas, change admissions standards to increase the likelihood of admitting members of specific population groups, etc. Each of these would be a strategy, or general direction, in which the organization might choose to proceed.

[7] Statement of President Richard M. Nixon, July 13, 1969.

Of course, an organization can utilize complex strategies that are a mixture of these simple ones. In such a case, *a strategy is a combination of the several directions in which the organization will proceed,* e.g., to introduce new products, while at the same time acquiring companies whose products will complement existing ones, and increasing the quality of existing products. For instance, one company's strategy calls for a "low-price, low-cost product achieved through product standardization" together with "the development of new products on a similar basis in a posture of defensive innovation against the technological progress of competitors."

Since strategies are future-oriented and since the future is fraught with risk and uncertainties, a strategy may also be explicated in *contingency terms,* e.g., "if inflation is brought under control, then we will begin introducing new products." [8]

A strategy is a general direction, and *even if the direction cannot be explicated precisely, it is most often greatly beneficial to have even an imprecisely defined general direction rather than none at all.* This is so because even an imprecise, but well-understood, general direction can be translated into tactics or programs to move the organization in that direction. For example, Haggerty,[9] in describing the meaning of strategy in the planning system of Texas Instruments, Inc., notes:

> By strategy I mean the general course of action the responsible executive intends that his organization pursue in achieving company goals. By tactics I mean the specific programs which must be carried out to implement the strategy successfully.

One company has explicated its strategy by saying that it:

> . . . has heavy investment, a good reputation, great skills and experience, a viable organization, and, in some instances, a special situation in the . . . industries.

and that it will:

> . . . exploit these strengths and, . . . not diversify at the present time, into unrelated industries.

A more detailed strategy for another firm includes the following:

> . . . increase U.S. market penetration through the development of a regional manufacturing capability and the development of secondary distribution channels.

---

[8] These multidimensional and contingency views of strategy are consistent with the use of the terms in *game theory.* (Von Neumann, J., and Morgenstern, O., *Theory of Games and Economic Behavior,* Princeton University Press, Princeton, N.J. 1943.) However, despite the fact that this similarity permits the utilization of the strategy idea within the scope of objective analytic frameworks such as that of game theory, there is no need for strategy to be thought of in strictly formal terms.

[9] Haggerty, P. E., "Strategies, Tactics, and Research," *Research Management,* Vol. II 1966, pp. 141–159.

Again, as with a mission statement, the strategy is as important for what it does not say, as what it does say. By excluding numerous possibly valid ways of achieving a stated objective, it ensures a focusing of organizational resources and precludes a scatter-gun approach that is likely to be ineffective and is likely to become the organization's implicit strategy if numerous managers are permitted to make decisions without the specific guidance provided by an explicitly stated strategy.

STRATEGY AND POLICY

The definition of strategic planning used by Anthony et al.[10] states that *a policy is a statement of intended behavior for the organization*. Policies are meant to guide decision making within the organization toward the accomplishment of organizational purposes. Most often, policies tend to limit the scope of alternatives that must be considered in making decisions on the implementation of strategy. For instance, a firm's strategy might entail the dropping of product lines. An implementing policy might spell out the criteria under which a product line is to be considered a candidate for disposition.

Unfortunately, the terms "policy" and "strategy" are often used almost synonymously in the literature and in discussions in the area. This is particularly true in the field of Business Policy, which has for some years been an identifiable area of study in American business schools.

THE ORGANIZATION'S PROGRAMS AND PROJECTS

Programs are the resource-consuming collections of activities that the organization conducts in furtherance of its strategies and in pursuit of its objectives. Often, at the strategic-planning level, these programs involve development, investment, or divestment activities. For instance, a new product-oriented strategy might be furthered by the conduct of a product research program, a product development program, and a product improvement program (since significantly improved products can be considered to be new). A strategy of developing a capability in a particular area of expertise might involve programs of acquisition, merger, personnel development, etc.

These programs would be implemented through specific *projects* (identifiable activities pursuing specific goals with identifiable resources). For instance, a new product development program would normally be supported by a number of development projects, each responsible for a specific product.

The set of programs of a manufacturing business concern are shown in

[10] Anthony, R. N., Dearden, J., and Vancil, R. F., *Management Control Systems,* Irwin, Homewood, Ill., 1965.

TABLE 3.1

Inventory reduction program

Accounts receivable reduction program

Production scheduling improvement program

Distribution channel extension program

Service capability expansion program

Renewal parts distribution program

Key customer program

Negotiation follow system development program

Focused communication program

Sales team development program

New product development program

Product redesign program

Table 3.1 to involve a wide variety of activities and functions of the organization, ranging from inventory, through personnel, customers, products, etc.

THE ORGANIZATION'S RESOURCE ALLOCATIONS

Resources are required to operate programs and *resource allocations* are a basic choice element of planning. If programs are to be carried out, they require facilities, money, people with specialized skills, and other resources. The *levels* of these resource allocations to various programs must be decided as a part of the planning process and stipulated in the plan.

The strategic plan should identify *all* varieties of resources required to accomplish strategic programs. Ultimately all such resources are converted into dollars and expressed in the form of *budgets* and *financial plans*. These elements are of special significance in understanding strategic planning, because they are so important and because they have come, in some organizations, to be identified as *the* outputs of planning. When, this is the case, financial considerations tend to overshadow the true strategic aspects of strategic planning, to the detriment of the organization's planning effectiveness.

Indeed, it is probably not overstating the case to suggest that some organizations do little other than financial planning and budgeting. In such business firms, planning is reduced to a forecasting exercise where estimates of sales to be billed, costs to be incurred, and profits to be realized are made with little or no regard to the strategies used or the alternative opportunities available for choice. To overcome this tendency, one of the nation's top planning companies, General Electric, has divorced the financial aspect of planning from the strategic aspect to ensure that so much emphasis will not be placed on the numbers that the truly strategic elements of planning will be deemphasized.[11]

CONTINGENCY STRATEGIES AND ACTIONS—ADAPTIVE PLANNING

All of the foregoing planning outputs involve choices made by the organization. However, these choices may be based on a single set of forecasts and environmental assumptions that reflect a single "image of the future." Although such single-mindedness may be praiseworthy in some endeavors, it will not facilitate an adaptive approach to planning. Effective planning requires an ability for the organization to *adapt to a changing environment*. If such adaptation is to be accomplished efficiently, contingency plans are required, since economic conditions can change, supply-demand factors can shift, and material and labor costs can fluctutate. Moreover, all of these conditions can change so rapidly as to require a quick response in order to avoid catastrophe.

CONTINGENCY PLANNING. The concept of contingency planning (first prominent in military planning) has come to the forefront of modern business planning as well. The purpose of a contingency plan is to prescribe what actions the organization should take in the event some of the key environmental assumptions on forecasts fail to hold or be sufficiently accurate. Every strategic plan is highly subjective in nature and is based on assumptions, judgments, and predictions, each having varying degrees of risk and uncertainty. The need to think through *what should happen if the key assumptions and forecasts fail to hold* is critical. This concept is well understood in the context of a military commander who prepares a plan for the retreat of his military forces if the campaign does not go as anticipated, but it has not been widely practiced in nonmilitary situations.

Contingency plans specifically deal with the questions: What if things don't go as anticipated? To what extent would such events require modification of the objectives, goals, strategies, and policies? What actions can be taken to put these contingency plans into effect? What are the specific "trigger points" at which contingency actions or strategies should be implemented?

One multinational company which drew up a strategic plan that contained a divestiture strategy for an element of its business also concurrently developed a set of contingencies to deal with the situation if divestiture was not possible. According to this company's contingency plan:

> If current divestiture strategy is not successful in achieving complete divestiture, implement alternative strategies for complete withdrawal from this business through the following strategies:
> 1. Sell segments of the business; or

[11] This is discussed further in Chapter 4.

2. Gradual phaseout of segments that cannot be sold; or
3. Close down segments that cannot be sold or phased out; or
4. If none of the above are achievable at an acceptable cost in the near future, then make whatever management changes and investment required to achieve improved performance until economic and political circumstances change so that we can withdraw at an acceptable cost.

These contingency plans were backed up by strategic data bases that established standards to be used in deciding which contingency plan to follow.

If contingency plans are made a normal part of the overall plan, the organization becomes able to respond quickly and effectively to changes in the environment. Without such contingency plans, environmental changes can create havoc and force the organization into an undesirable choice between doing nothing in the face of impending difficulty or taking major strategic actions on the basis of high-pressure crisis thinking and panic decision making.

Thus, if strategic planning is to be truly adaptive, each of the foregoing planning outputs (particularly those at the lower level of the hierarchy) must be expressed in contingency terms. For instance, when will the organization abandon a strategy and go to another on the basis of real-world events? What program changes will be required if such a strategy shift occurs? What goals will be associated with this revised program structure? Such questions demonstrate that an adaptive strategic plan is really a variety of plans, each applying to specified sets of circumstances.

AN ILLUSTRATIVE PLAN

To illustrate these substantive planning outputs in an integrated real-world context, we illustrate the plan format similar to that utilized by the General Electric Company. GE's myriad businesses are organized for planning purposes as strategic business units (SBUs). A typical SBU plan consists of a series of statements about the business as a whole covering eleven major elements. These major elements are:

1. Statement of the Strategic Business Unit's *Mission*—What it is, why it exists, and the unique contribution it can make to the company.
2. *Key Environmental Assumptions*—These summarize the nature of the external environment in which the business will be working, and the opportunities and threats that the business unit sees in the environment.
3. *Key Competitor Assumptions*—Including estimates of the *strengths and limitations of competitors* and judgments of their probable plans.
4. List of *Constraints*—The forces either from inside or outside the company that may limit the SBU's choice of actions.

5. *Objectives*—The desired future position or destination of SBU wants to attain. These are stated in both qualitative and quantitative terms.
6. *Goals*—The specific time-based points of measurement that the SBU intends to meet in the pursuit of its objectives.
7. *Strategy*—The course of action the SBU intends to follow to achieve its objectives, while meeting goals along the way.
8. *Programs*—Development, investment, divestments, or other programs that are critical to the pursuit of the SBU's strategy.
9. Required *Resources* and sources—The things it takes to do the job, and where they are to be obtained.
10. *Contingencies* and associated *"what if"* contingency plans—Recognition that things might go wrong along the way, the possible cost if they do, and what the SBU plans to do if they do go wrong.
11. *SBU Financial Forecast*—This is the expression in financial terms of the first 10 elements of the strategic plan.

This outline of the content of a SBU plan shows that the plans incorporate all of the output elements discussed previously. However, these plans also incorporate assumptions concerning competition, assumptions and forecasts concerning the environment, as well as the constraints that underlie the choices of strategy programs and the other outputs. These are incorporated because *without such information the plan could not be effectively evaluated or reviewed.*

These competitive and environmental elements are not the direct decision outputs of planning, so they have not been discussed previously in this chapter. However, the decision outputs are made more understandable to higher level management and to the professional planners who will review and evaluate the plans when they are supplemented with explicit statements of underlying assumptions and constraints as well as with statements of the alternatives that were considered but *not* selected.

A System of Plans

If the substantive outputs of planning are to be useful as guides and standards for organizational performance, they must be organized and related to one another in meaningful ways. Reference to "the plan" is misleading, since it suggests a simple one-dimensional document that would be inadequate for most complex organizations.

A basic premise underlying the organization and structuring of the visible output of planning, the planning documents, is that *the plan must be approximately as complex as is the organization and environment with which it is*

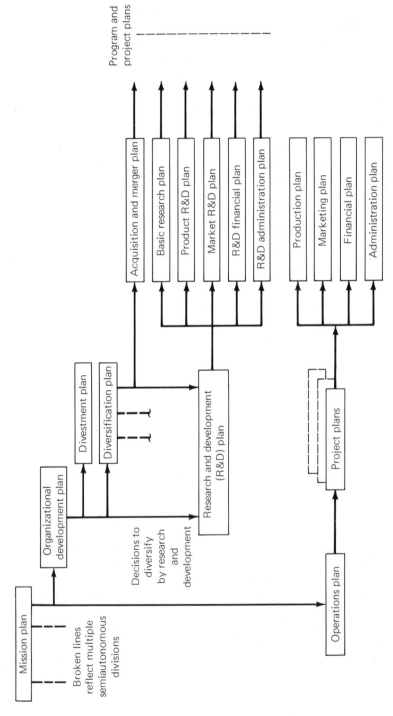

FIGURE 3.1   A System of Plans.*

*Adapted from *A Framework for Business Planning,* Report No. 162, 1963, Stanford Research Institute, Menlo Park, California.

meant to deal. Thus, most complex organizations require complex multidimensional plans. This premise reflects the "Law of Requisite Variety," the well-known control theory result that says that a complex system will necessarily require a complex control mechanism and that complex systems cannot be effectively controlled by simplistic control mechanisms. This control system principle finds its application to planning in terms of the required scope and complexity of the plan, since it is expected to be the control mechanism for the organization's future.

The term "system of plans" is used to describe the complex of interrelated subplans that reflect the missions, objectives, goals, strategies, and other substantive planning elements of the various functional units, divisions, and projects over various time periods.

CONCEPTUAL FRAMEWORK FOR A SYSTEM OF PLANS

A conceptual framework for a system of plans is schematically displayed in Figure 3.1. Much of the terminology used in that figure and the subsequent discussion are directly appropriate to the business firm. However, the functions and purposes of the various plans are appropriate to any organization. Indeed, the authors have themselves applied this system of plans in a wide variety of nonbusiness contexts.

MISSION PLAN

The mission plan of the organization, sometimes referred to as the strategic plan, is at the summit of all the plans; it outlines the broad mission of the organization and the objectives and strategies that the organization wants to pursue. It includes the answers to such questions as:

What are the broad missions and roles of the organization? What objectives are to be sought?

What strategy is required to move from today's position to the position desired in the future?

What image does the organization want to portray in the greater system (social, economic, political) of which it is a part?

What are the major policies under which lower-level decisions are to be made?

The mission plan is important because it becomes a standard for deciding what direction the subsidiary plans in the organization should take. It is the overall document used to determine the organizational compatibility of the other plans. The mission plan guides and constrains the organization in deci-

sions involving changes in current products and markets and the future generation of products and markets.

ORGANIZATIONAL DEVELOPMENT PLAN

The next echelon in the system of plans is the *organizational development plan,*
which determines the activities necessary for a new generation of products or
services. At the same time, the organizational development plan maps in
greater detail the route toward the future position of the organization that has
been specified by the mission plan. The development plan answers such questions as:

> What will the future environment consist of in terms of demand for our
> goods or services? What will be expected of our organization in that future
> time period?
>
> What favorable conditions must be created within the organization so that
> new products and new markets can be conceived and defined?
>
> What techniques will be used to screen out poor investments and products
> and high-risk ventures?
>
> What are the expected resources available for the new products or ser-
> vices?

The organizational development plan provides the guidance for three succeeding plans.

DIVESTMENT PLAN This plan deals with the divestiture of major elements of the
organization. These elements can consist of products, services, property, or organizational entities.

DIVERSIFICATION PLAN This plan describes the development of new products,
services, and markets to join or replace the current generation of products. It
selects new product areas and determines when entry should be made by acquisition of other organizations that possess required capabilities, by merger with
another organization, or by conducting in-house research and development
which builds on existing competence.

RESEARCH AND DEVELOPMENT PLAN This plan specifies actions oriented toward the creation of new products or processes for existing demand or a new
market for existing products or services. It is through this plan that the organization does research to advance the state-of-the-art of what it has to offer. This
plan cuts across all elements of the organization to include products, markets,
finance, and administration.

PROGRAM AND PROJECT PLANS

Program plans are the basic building blocks of the system of plans in Figure 3.1. Each echelon of plans receives guidance from prior plans and further specifies such direction by focusing on groups of activities having a common purpose. Program plans support higher-level plans; for example, the corporate development plan is supported by a complex of program plans covering the details of undertakings reflected in it. In such a case, program plans might be developed to sustain and guide the following types of actions:

1. Developing and installing of a new management information system
2. Developing and producing a new product
3. Building and activating a plant
4. Effecting a corporate merger or acquisition
5. Redesigning the organizational structure
6. Moving on organization from one location to another.

Program plans are supported by specific *project plans*. Thus, program plans can have short-, intermediate-, and long-range implications. What makes the project plan unique is its concern with an identifiable effort having cost, schedule, and technical parameters.

OPERATIONS PLANS

The operations plan (sometimes called the "business plan" or "profit plan") is focused toward the activities through which the current generation of products and services serves existing markets. Normally of 1 to 2 years duration, the operations plan is supported by plans in each functional area: marketing, production, finance, etc.

Although the development of the operations plan is not a part of the strategic planning process, it must be coordinated with the strategic plan. This book deals little with the operations plan other than emphasizing that such coordination must exist. The principal methods by which this can be achieved are through the planning process and the planning organization, both discussed in later chapters.

RELATIONSHIPS AMONG SUBPLANS IN THE SYSTEM OF PLANS

Figure 3.2 shows the system of plans in a slightly different context than Figure 3.1. The previous figure emphasizes the various subplans. Figure 3.2 emphasizes the *relationships among the various different kinds of plans* in the system, together with *typical time horizons* and the *specific foci of the various plans*. The terminology used in Figure 3.2 is applicable to the planning process for a

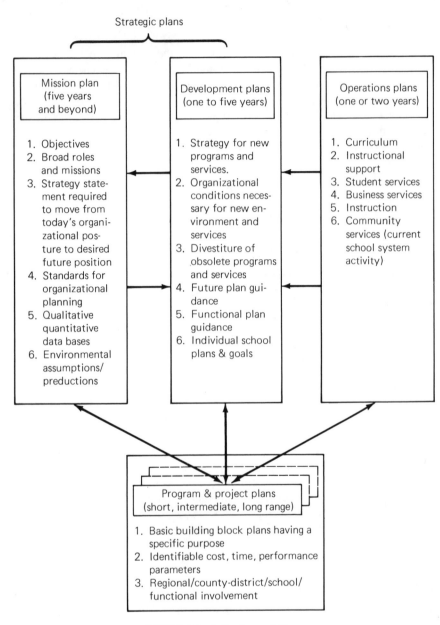

FIGURE 3.2 A System of Plans.

school system rather than for a business firm to emphasize the broad applicability of the strategic-planning process beyond the business organization.

Figure 3.2 shows that operational plans focus on a 1- or 2-year horizon and existing resources and programs. Development plans can involve a 1- to 5-year horizon in an organization like a school, or in many businesses, and emphasize new programs and resources. The mission plan guides the others in that it focuses on objectives, roles, missions, and strategy for the organization as well as on the underlying standards, assumptions, and data bases, many of which will involve a longer time horizon. All of these plans are supported by program/project plans that may have various time horizons.

PLANNING OUTPUTS AT VARIOUS LEVELS OF THE ORGANIZATION

Vancil[12] has characterized the interrelationships among planning outputs in a fashion that emphasizes three levels of organizational managers: corporate level, business unit and activity, or program managers. Table 3.2 shows how illustrative objectives, policies, and goals at the three hierarchical levels differ in nature, in the terms in which they are stated, and in their level of specificity. At the lower levels, goals are shown to be shorter in range than at the higher levels. At the corporate level, objectives are also less tangible than are objectives at the other levels.

CRITERIA FOR A SYSTEM OF PLANS

A system, according to Rappaport,[13] is a "bundle of relationships." A system of plans is also a bundle of relationships portraying the intended future strategies of the organization. The interrelationships among the plans require assessment as do the specific subplans.

A system of plans may also be thought of as an integrated set of guidelines prescribing how organizational resources are to be allocated in support of goals and objectives. The system of plans:

1. Establishes strategies and programs for resource allocation for various organizational levels and time periods.
2. Provides guidelines for establishing priorities in the allocation of resources.
3. Delineates objectives and goals for all organizational elements.
4. Postulates competitive and environmental forecasts and assumptions in addition to organizational constraints affecting strategic purposes.

[12] Vancil, R. F., "Strategy Formulation in Complex Organizations," *Sloan Management Review,* Winter 1976, reprinted with permission.

[13] "General Systems Theory," *International Encyclopedia of the Social Sciences,* Vol. 15, p. 452.

TABLE 3.2 Objectives, Policies and Goals at Various Managerial Levels

LEVEL IN THE HIERARCHY	OBJECTIVES	CONSTRAINTS AND POLICIES	PLANS AND GOALS
Corporate Managers	Stated in terms for: stockholders other identifiable constituencies society at large. Examples: Financial performance of the corporation Corporate citizenship and "personality" characteristics	Financial policies (debt structure dividends, diversity of risk, etc.) Specific industries to be in, or characteristics of appropriate industries Criteria for approving new resource commitments to businesses.	Prospective magnitude of discretionary resources to be utilized by the corporation. Prospective distribution of resources in order to affect the future mix of businesses. Performance expectations for the corporation and for each business over the next 5–10 years.
Business Managers	Stated in terms for: corporate management Examples: Financial performance of the business Position of the business in the industry	Definition of niche in the industry; relative importance of, and interrelationships between each activity. Priorities for changing the relative contribution from each activity.	Prospective patterns of resource allocation intended to affect the future contribution from each activity. Performance expectations for the business and for each activity over the next 3–7 years.
Activity Managers	Stated in terms for: business management. Examples: Contribution of the activity to the business Position of the activity in the industry	Delineation of limits on the scope of the entire activity. Criteria for optimizing the use of resources available to the activity.	Prospective sequence of resource utilization intended to affect the future contribution from the activity. Performance expectations for the activity and for each subactivity over the next 1–3 years.

5. Constructs contingency strategies which recognize that things might go wrong and what strategies to pursue if they do go wrong.
6. Develops a financial forecast—expressing goals, objectives, and strategies in financial terms of reflecting resource allocation within the organizational context.
7. Provides coordinative mechanisms for integrating short-term, medium-term, and long-term organizational purposes.
8. Establishes standards for evaluating organizational progress.

Summary

The outputs of planning, the plans, are records of the assumptions and choices that have been made in the planning process. Plans are important to planning, but the plans themselves are not the goals to which planning is addressed. These goals are rather the choices and resource allocations which are reflected by the plans. Plans are made up of the organizational missions, objectives, strategies, goals, programs, and resource allocations which have been selected and decided on in the planning process. Each of these elements must be incorporated into a planning system, despite the fact that different sets of terminology may be used in various circumstances.

The organization's mission delineates the business that it is in. Its objectives are the broad timeless things that it is trying to achieve within the framework of its mission.

The organization's strategy states the general direction in which it will pursue its objectives. Programs are the specific focused activities through which strategies are implemented, and goals are specific measurable quantities that are used as standards for judging whether the strategy and programs are leading toward the desired objectives.

All of these elements comprise the system of plans: the complex of interrelated elements through which multiple subunits seek diverse goals in various time frames. The system of plans relates these many elements into an integrated whole that ensures consistency, sufficiency, and efficiency. Only such a complex system of plans will be adequate for a complex organization if it is to truly influence its future environment.

Chapter 3—Questions and Exercises

1. What is a strategic plan? Describe the essential features of a strategic plan.
2. What is the organizational development plan? How is it related to the strategic plan? the divestment plan? the diversification plan? the project plan?

3. What is the operations plan? How is it related to the other plans in the organization?
4. What are the two basic plans that directly support the strategic plan? Generally describe their salient differences.
5. What is the significance of project plans in terms of the long-term future of the organization? In light of this relationship, how should the strategic plan and the research and development plan of the organization be related?
6. Relate strategic, development, operational, and project plans (a) schematically, (b) in illustrative relative-time horizons, and (c) in terms of content.
7. "Plans are important. How they are developed is more or less irrelevant. The important thing is the product that planning produces." Critique these statements.
8. "The best laid plans of mice and men . . ." Complete this old adage and relate it to planning in organizations.
9. Plans are the documents that reflect the objectives and goals of an organization. The substantive outputs of strategic planning are organizational changes. What are examples of these changes?
10. How would you describe the mission of a university?
11. How are an organization's objectives and mission related?
12. Differentiate between an organization's objectives and its goals.
13. How are programs and projects related to the strategic direction of an organization?
14. Ultimately all strategies are expressed in financial terms. Defend or refute this statement.
15. What is contingency planning? How is contingency planning related to the implementation of strategy in an organization?
16. The plan format used by the General Electric Company consists of a series of statements about the business as a whole covering eleven major elements. What are these major elements? Do these major elements reflect a systems awareness?
17. Define a system of plans.
18. The development of the operations plan is usually not a part of the strategic planning process. Why is this so?
19. Why might a business firm rationally choose not to enter a new business area despite the fact that they predict the potential for great profits in the area?
20. Why is it important for an organization to state what business it is *not* in?
21. What is a "common thread" as it relates to an organization's mission?
22. Every business firm has one and only one objective, to make a profit. Is this so? Why or why not? Can you give a counter example?
24. Give illustrations of the nature of the objectives that might exist for managers at various levels in a business firm.

Chapter 3—Strategic Questions for the Manager

1. What "system of plans" do you currently have in your organization? Do these plans portray a set of guidelines for the organization's future?
2. Identify the key changes that have occurred in your organization in the past several years. Were these changes reflected in planning documents?

3. Are objectives, goals, missions, and strategies explicitly defined in the organization? Is there a thorough understanding of the meanings of these words in the organization?
4. Is the organization's mission defined in such a way that it describes the *unique contribution* the organization can make in its market environment?
5. Are objectives defined in broad and timeless statements that express a desired future position or destination?
6. Are organizational goals defined so that quantitative and qualitative progress toward them can be measured?
7. Are organizational strategies defined in such a way that overall guidance is provided as to how goals and objectives will be achieved?
8. Are *programs* (integral resource consuming activities) established for furthering strategies in pursuit of organizational objectives? Are identifiable *projects* evident in these programs?
9. Does strategic planning in the organization consist principally of financial and budget considerations, to the neglect of strategic elements of the organization?
10. What contingency plans have been developed for the organization? Do these plans provide alternative objectives, goals, and strategies if things don't go as anticipated?
11. Does a management development plan exist in the organization for facilitating an orderly strategy for executive succession?
12. Does the existing system of plans provide guidelines for establishing priorities in the allocation of resources?
13. Are organizational mechanisms (policies, procedures, strategies, etc.) in operation which bring about an effective coordination of short, intermediate, and long-term considerations?
14. Considering the results obtained in the marketplace, do my organizational plans seem to be better than my competitor's? Why or why not?

References

Andrews, K. R., *The Concept of Corporate Strategy,* Dow Jones–Irwin, Homewood, Ill., 1971.

Argenti, J., *Corporate Planning—A Practical Guide,* Dow Jones–Irwin, Homewood, Ill., 1969.

"At Potlatch, Nothing Happens Without a Plan," *Business Week,* Nov. 10, 1975.

Cleland, D. I., and King, W. R., *Systems Analysis and Project Management,* (2nd Ed.) McGraw-Hill, New York, 1975.

Drucker, P. F., *The Age of Discontinuity,* Harper and Row, New York, 1968.

Friedman, Y., and Segen, E., "Horizons For Strategic Planning," *Long Range Planning,* Oct. 1976.

"GE's Jones Restructures His Top Team," *Business Week,* June 30, 1973.

Hobbs, J. M., and Heany, D. F., "Coupling Strategy to Operating Plans," *Harvard Business Review,* May–June 1977.

Hussey, D., *Corporate Planning: Theory and Practice,* Pergamon Press, New York, 1974.

Lamson, N. W., "Plots Thicken for Corporate Planners," *New York Times,* April 13, 1975.

Nagashima, Y., "Response of Japanese Companies to Environmental Changes," *Long Range Planning,* Feb. 1976.

O'Connor, R., "Corporate Guides to Long-Range Planning," *The Conference Board,* Rep. 687, 1976.

Ramsey, J. E., "A Framework for the Interaction of Corporate Value Objectives, Corporate Performance Objectives, and Corporate Strategy," *Journal of Economics and Business,* Spring-Summer 1976.

Rush, K., "Business Planning at Union Carbide," *Long Range Planning,* Dec. 1968.

Smalter, D. J., "Anatomy of a Long Range Plan," *Long Range Planning,* March 1969.

Vancil, R. F., "Strategy Formulation in Complex Organizations," *Sloan Management Review,* Winter 1976.

Wheelwright, S. C., "Reflecting Corporate Strategy in Manufacturing Decisions," *Business Horizons,* Feb. 1978.

Woodie, P. R., "From PPBS to Program Strategies," *Governmental Finance,* Aug. 1976.

PART III

The Planning Process

Chapter 4

THE STRATEGIC-PLANNING
PROCESS

The institution of a formal strategic-planning process into an organization has simple and straightforward values such as ensuring that strategic considerations will be applied to the analysis of contemplated actions and that the best analytical tools that the organization possesses will be applied to its strategy. A formal process can also have many less-obvious benefits, such as the general management "education" that it can provide to middle managers who are given the opportunity to participate in a level of strategic thinking that their operational jobs may not provide to them.

Of course, these benefits do not accrue from all formal planning processes. Unfortunately, a planning process has, in some organizations, come to mean a process whereby numeric estimates of sales, billings, and profits are entered in the appropriate places on a series of forms by division, group, and profit center executives. These projections are then reviewed as to reasonableness at the top organizational level by the planning staff and, after adjustment, aggregated into the overall organization's plan.

Often, during this process, much less attention is paid to the *strategic* element of planning (missions, strategies, objectives, etc.) than is paid to the *dollar consequences,* such as projections of sales and profits. Thus the critical "What to do" and the "How to do it" questions of planning somehow become subordinated to the question of "What results are expected?"

This deficiency of some planning processes may be a consequence of the overoptimism of the 1960s and early 1970s, which was the expression of an optimistic and expansionary interpretation of what was meant by the question: "What business are we in?" During that era, many companies seem to have concluded that the only valid answer to that question was one which led to a broader definition of their business. Indeed, many came to so broadly define their business that their definition became "anything that is potentially profitable." As previously noted, this total emphasis on *potential* profitability led many companies to overextend, to go beyond the bounds of their expertise, often with results varying from terrible to disasterous!

This expansionary "potential profit-to-the-exclusion-of-everything-else" philosophy may naturally have led to planning processes that overemphasized projected sales and profits and underemphasized the *strategies* required to achieve those objectives. However, most organizations who made this sort of error have now recognized it and have taken action to develop a broader, more meaningful planning process. Indeed, even companies that have developed successful planning processes, such as General Electric, have separated the financial and strategic aspects of the process so that the easier numerical aspects would not overshadow the strategic ones.

Structure of the Organizational Planning Process

Figure 4.1 shows a simple and highly abstract organizational planning process structure that is in use in many modern organizations. This process is a simple feedback loop activated at the top level, that of the chief executive and the corporate planning staff, through the preliminary promulgation of missions,

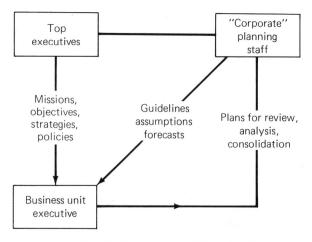

FIGURE 4.1   Basic Organizational Planning Process.

objectives, strategies, and policies by the top executive level, and planning guidelines, assumptions, and forecasts, by top-level planners. These are the *tentative* top-level elements of the organization's strategic plan which are to serve as guides for lower-level first-stage planning activities.

Business unit executives use this guidance in their preparation of plans, which are then reviewed, analyzed, and consolidated by the top-level planning staff and passed on to the top executives for review. The chief executives may approve the plans or recycle the process by returning them with guidance for revision. Alternatively, the tentative plans may cause top-level management to alter some aspect of the tentative assumptions and strategies that have served as guidelines for business unit planning. In any case, the feedback cycle continues until satisfactory plans have been developed for all business units and for the organization as a whole.

Of course, a real-world organizational planning process is much more complex than the simple structure of Figure 4.1. Each business unit executive is likely to have his own planning staff to fulfill a similar function as does the corporate planning staff. Large organizations are composed of a number of different levels that must develop plans for themselves, as well as contribute to the overall planning process. Also, groups of managers may perform various of the planning tasks rather than individuals as implied in the figure.

Despite the many complexities of the real world, the somewhat more complex hierarchical description of Figure 4.2 is a useful description of the structure of the organizational planning process. It depicts a process for several levels of management and incorporates planning staffs at the various levels. Each level of line management works with his staff planners, analyzes the guidance provided by higher levels, interprets and decomposes as necessary, and provides guidance to lower level managers. Then, after plans have been prepared at lower levels, each manager considers them in the light of the analysis, review, and consolidation that has been provided by his staff planners, and produces plans for his own level for subsequent review at higher levels.

The uninitiated may view this as a complex and time-consuming process. In fact, as conducted in most organizations, it is even more complicated than the figure implies in terms of the number of people who are involved and the number of elements that are considered, but it is, in fact, much less tedious than may be inferred from Figure 4.2. Once the process has been initiated, many of its elements may be conducted in parallel rather than in strict sequence.

Figure 4.3 shows a variation of this process that is in use in the Westinghouse Electric Corporation. Although the diagram does not show it, the process does begin with the promulgation of guidelines. This figure focuses on the *preparation and review of plans,* which begins, after the corporate strategic guidelines are received, with each business unit preparing a 5-year

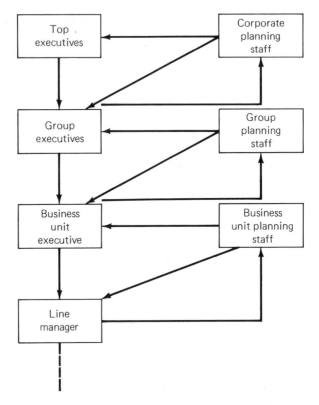

FIGURE 4.2   Hierarchical Planning Process.

strategic plan. This involves interactions with the component divisions where profit and loss responsibility rests. Each business unit has staff planners to aid in the formulation of the strategic plan for the business unit. Each of the strategic plans follows a standard format determined by the business unit manager under general corporate guidelines.

The book of plans is submitted via the company president to the top management committee for review; the management committee is provided with advice and counsel on the business unit strategic plan by a corporate review team. These corporate review teams are composed of both line and staff people who have outstanding credentials in their respective fields. Once the corporate review teams have analyzed the business unit strategic plan, the book of plans is then returned to the business unit manager with appropriate comments and criticism. After modifying or justifying the plans, the business unit manager then resubmits them through the company president, and the plans become part of the corporate strategic plan.

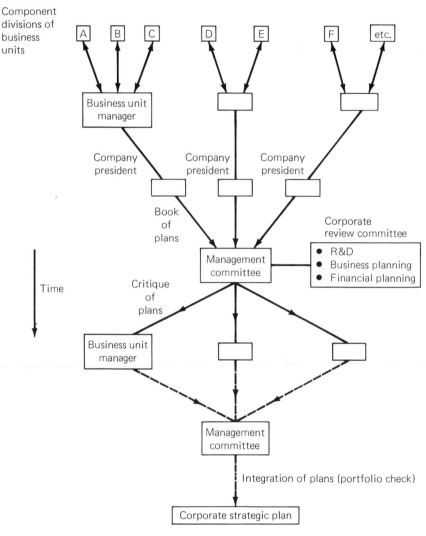

FIGURE 4.3 Westinghouse Strategic Planning Process.

Substance of the Planning Process

A simple concept of the substantive issues to be considered in a strategic-planning process involves the development of answers to four basic questions:

1. What is our current situation?
2. What do we want the future situation to be?

3. What might inhibit us?

4. What actions should we take to achieve our objectives?

The process is not greatly different than any problem-solving or decision-making process, except that, as applied to planning, it must be sufficiently broad to encompass choices of missions and objectives and the analysis of opportunities, rather than just "problem solving."

Figure 4.4 shows some of these substantive elements of the planning process. It reflects various "strategic data bases" that address the initial planning phase: the situation assessment question. The figure also shows choice

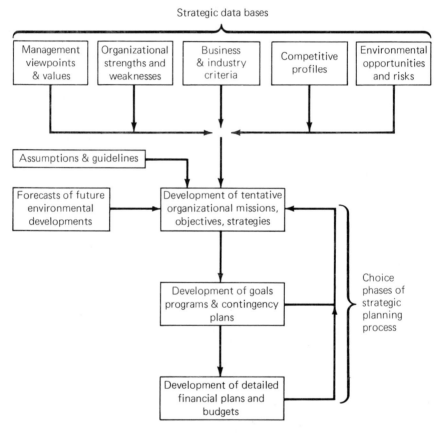

FIGURE 4.4   Substantive Strategic Planning Process.*

*This diagram draws on ideas from Grant, John H., "Corporate Strategy: A Synthesizing Concept for General Management, unpublished paper, University of Pittsburgh, 1975.

phases involving the selection of missions, objectives, strategies, and the other decision elements of strategic planning.

This process of Figure 4.4 is an operational one, despite its apparent simplicity and the apparent motherhood and sin nature of some of the strategic data bases. We shall make this clear by describing in detail in the next chapter, both the content of and process for developing the strategic data bases, assumptions, and forecasts that are shown as the initial elements of the overall process in the figure. For now, it is sufficient to briefly describe the role of one of these elements, which has not been previously alluded to—the strategic data bases.

STRATEGIC DATA BASES

Strategic data bases are concise statements of the *most significant* strategic items related to various clientel or environments that affect the organization's strategic choices. As such, they are primary mechanisms through which the first substantive issue of planning, the current situation assessment, is addressed. The strategic data bases shown in Figure 4.4 reflect the influence of the environment, competitors, top management, as well as the status of the organization itself (in terms of its strengths and weaknesses).

These strategic data bases can be made to be important parts of the substantive strategic planning process, rather than just informational inputs to it. We shall deal with the process for developing strategic data bases, as well as the other informational inputs to the planning process (assumptions and forecasts) in Chapter 5 which treats the initiation phase of the planning process in detail.

AN ILLUSTRATIVE CORPORATE PLANNING PROCESS

The process elements of Figures 4.2 and 4.4 are illustrated by the more complex real-world planning process similar to that used by the General Electric Company and other sophisticated planning firms. The process is described in a time sequence to illustrate the magnitude of the various activities and to emphasize the continuous nature of the planning process.

ENVIRONMENTAL ASSESSMENT. In January of each year, the Corporate Strategic Planning Staff presents overall environmental assessments to the top-level Corporate Policy Committee.

IMPLICATIONS TO SBUs. In February, a second meeting serves to focus attention on the implications of the overall environmental assessment to each of the Strategic Business Units (SBUs). The output of these discussions are guidelines for each SBU to follow in preparing its strategic plans. Such guidelines may involve such things as:

1. Specific ideas or trends to be considered by the SBU
2. Relevant corporate policies, e.g., regarding liquidity or cash flow
3. Strategic issues to be addressed in the development of plans
4. Specific contingencies for which contingency plans should be prepared
5. Analyses to be included in the documentation of the plan, e.g., trade off analysis between income growth and investment

PLAN PREPARATION. During the February-to-June period, SBUs work on their plans. Executive Boards, which are made up of high-level executives, serve as "working boards of directors" to informally review planning progress and the tentative plans as they are being developed.

FORMAL REVIEW BY PLANNING STAFF. When plans are completed in June, they are reviewed by the Corporate Planning Staff in the fashion described in Figures 4.1 and 4.2.

FORMAL EXECUTIVE REVIEW. After the planning staff review, formal reviews are conducted by the Corporate Policy Committee and the relevant Executive Board, meeting together. Each SBU manager presents his plans for review and critique by the planning staff and top corporate executives. The output of this review is recommendations for change as suggested in the feedback loops of the process model of Figures 4.1 and 4.2.

SECOND REVIEW BY PLANNING STAFF. After plans have been revised, they are submitted to the Corporate Planning Staff for further review—a second time around the feedback loop.

ALLOCATION OF RESOURCES. After SBU plans have been again reviewed, top management makes resource allocations that serve as guidelines for the development of detailed operating plans and budgets by the SBUs. These top-level allocation choices are made in September.

FINAL REVIEW OF PLANS AND BUDGETS. In October, the Executive Board for each SBU reviews final plans and budgets.

COMPANY BUDGET REVIEW. Finally, in November, the overall corporate budget is reviewed by top management and the implementation of plans is approved.

Comparison of this process with the organizational process of Figures 4.1 and 4.2 and the substantive process of Figure 4.4 will reveal great consistency. Although the process descriptions in these figures were developed as composites of experiences in a variety of organizations, the substantive process conforms to them rather well. Of particular note are the institutionalized feedback loops, at least two being required around the topmost loop of Figure 4.2, the participation and involvement of top-level management, and the utilization of strategic data bases at the corporate level as well as at the business unit level.

Planning processes may be conducted within a formalized organizational framework with only top executives performing the review function, as literally described in Figure 4.1, or within a GE-like context where an Executive Board of managers is established to provide informal guidance and review prior to formal review. Such participative approaches can be effective, and as well provide motivation and learning for the managers who participate. Since training for general management is one of the least understood areas of managerial education, these secondary benefits may be of longer term impact than the direct consequences of improved planning.

A CORPORATE PLANNING PROCESS

The structure and substance of the planning process may be combined into an overall corporate planning process in terms of the four-cycle process in Figure 4.5. This process, which is an adaptation of various actual processes in use in a number of companies, is stated in terms that are consistent with the General Electric process just described. Figure 4.5 shows a first cycle in which environmental assumptions and planning process guidelines are communicated directly to the SBU by staff. During this phase, these assumptions are also used to develop preliminary corporate strategy by top management. This strategy is also promulgated to the SBU level during the first phase along with substantive strategy guidance. The second cycle involves the submission of strategy alternatives (a preliminary SBU plan) to top management. This is amended and approved first by the "executive board" and then by the chief executive officer before being returned to the SBU with instructions and guidelines for preparing the final plan. The third cycle is that in which the final strategic plan is submitted for approval. When it has been acted on, it is returned with guidance for translating it into a short-range operations plan. The fourth cycle involves the submission of the operations plan to the executive board for approval.

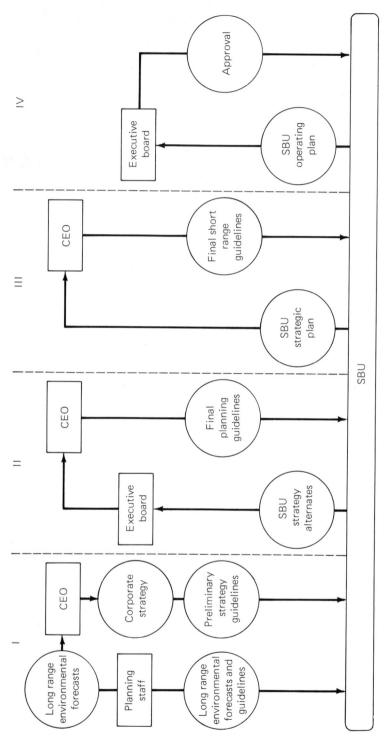

FIGURE 4.5   A Four-Phase Corporate Strategic Planning Process.

Conceptual Basis for a Strategic Planning Process[1]

Among the most striking features of the planning processes described thus far in this chapter are the feedback loops, the broad scope of the informational inputs to the process (as defined by the strategic data bases), and the fact that the process can extend down into the organization to a level where managerial concerns are primarily tactical, rather than strategic. These uncommon features suggest that these processes are founded on a set of operational requirements and a conceptual base that are different from those most organizations have used in the past.

THE SYSTEMS APPROACH TO STRATEGIC PLANNING

The planning processes described in this chapter inherently view the organization in terms of a *systems viewpoint*. This viewpoint involves a perspective of the organization as a conglomerate of interrelated and interdependent parts. No one of the parts (subsystems) can perform effectively without others, and any action taken on (or by) one will have effects that can be traced *throughout the organization and throughout the complex environment in which the organization exists*.

Indeed, the expression that "everything depends on everything else" is perhaps the best way of thinking about the systems viewpoint. Although that thought is not a calming one, it does enable us to raise ourself above the level of provincialism to see the whole problem, however complex it may be.

Moreover, not only does everything depend on everything else, but these relationships exist in ways that set up *chains of effects* throughout the organization and its environment. For instance, technological innovations by business have produced both direct and indirect benefits, and at the same time, have created new problems. The automobile is a good illustration. The immediate impact of the invention of the automobile was the creation of a nuisance that frightened horses and created confusion. Those with foresight could readily see that the potential benefit of this device for transportation was great, but few could have foreseen the scope of the impact created by the new industry on the nation's economy and on the day-to-day lives and habits of its people. It is apparent that the profound problems created or amplified by the automobile, e.g., traffic congestion and air pollution, were not envisioned by anyone in the early days of its use. Thus, the new invention set up a complex series of events, initially negative, then positive, then again negative, that have directly influenced the life of every living American in rather significant ways.

---

[1] The remainder of this chapter treats the conceptual basis for the strategic planning process. It may be skipped on first reading without loss of continuity.

Other technological advances have triggered similar chains of events. The development of indoor plumbing made high-rise office buildings and apartments feasible. This led to center-city congestion and parking problems, which, in part, motivated an exodus to the suburbs for both business and personal housing. This, in turn, led to problems in the suburbs similar to those that had been experienced in the center cities.

Within the organization, similar phenomena occur. An executive order issued to managers eventually creates impact on the lowest-level workers. An order affecting one department changes that department's behavior in dealing with other departments. This induces changes in them as well, and, in turn, their behavior affects those with whom they deal. The ultimate effect may be far-reaching.

Despite the generality of this systems viewpoint, it is important to recognize that the complex organizational system, which may be perceived by viewing an organizational chart, is not the whole system that must be considered by the strategic planners.

Among the elements that the organizational chart does not show, but that must be considered in an organizational systems model are:

1. The organization's relationships with environmental elements— suppliers, stockholders, local governments, regulatory agencies, etc.
2. The nature of the claims of each of these stakeholders on the organization.
3. Informal relationships among internal organizational elements.
4. Flows of information among organizational elements and between the organization and other environmental organizations.

Thus, a systems view of the organization depicts it as an organism whose life depends on *symbiosis,* the mutually beneficial living together of dissimilar organisms. This concept, the antithesis of functionalization, has been argued to be central to modern management. In fact, Tilles has defined the role of the general manager as one of presiding over these dissimilar systems as they seek to achieve symbiosis.[2]

THE IMPORTANCE OF BEING GENERAL

There are few people who would question the critical significance of strategic planning to every organization. However, as noted earlier, some would ques-

[2] Tilles, S., "The Manager's Job: A Systems Approach," *Harvard Business Review,* Jan.– Feb. 1963, p. 77.

tion the real value of the systems view of strategic planning by arguing that it is idealistic, nebulous, and too general.

To understand the importance and practicality of "being general," one must recognize the basic nature of strategic decision making. It inherently involves: (a) a concern with the overall effectiveness, as opposed to the efficiency, of the organization, and (b) a balancing of the *conflicting objectives* of organizational subunits. Thus, whereas many organizational subunits may have goals related to their unit's efficiency, the *objectives of the overall organization are both broader and of a different nature* in that they are stated in *effectiveness* terms.

Perhaps both of these points are best illustrated by considering the corporate viewpoint involved in the "simple" decision involving which products are to be produced and in what quantities. The production department of the enterprise would undoubtedly prefer that few products be produced in rather large quantities so that the number of costly machine setups necessary to convert from production of one product to production of another is minimized. Such a policy would lead to large inventories of a few products. Sales personnel, on the other hand, desire to have many different products in inventory so that they may promise early delivery on any product. Financial managers recognize that large inventories tie up money that could be invested elsewhere, hence, they want low total inventories. The personnel manager desires constant production levels so that he will not constantly be hiring new workers for short periods of peak production and laying them off in slack periods. One could go on to identify objectives of almost every functional unit of an organization relative to this simple tactical decision problem. As demonstrated, these objectives each conflict to some greater or lesser degree: low inventory levels versus high inventories, many products versus few products, etc. Moreover, these subunit objectives are not even stated in the same terms as are overall corporate goals, e.g., profit, since they tend to reflect efficiency considerations rather than effectiveness.

Of course, the same variety of situations can exist at every other level of the enterprise. The production department must constantly balance the speed of production with the proportion of rejects and the proportion of defective products not detected. The marketing function becomes involved when defective products cause complaints and lost sales. Indeed, wherever the labor has been divided in an organization, the management task of effectively integrating the various elements is paramount, and this can only be effectively accomplished by the manager adopting the broad *systems viewpoint* for the system that is his domain.

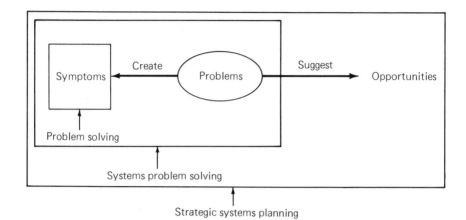

FIGURE 4.6   Three Varieties of Planning and Problem-Solving.

PROBLEMS AND OPPORTUNITIES IN THE PLANNING PROCESS [3]

Figure 4.6 shows the conceptual relationship between two kinds of problem-solving and strategic systems planning in terms of relationships between problems, problem-symptoms, and opportunities. The first variety of management planning activity, termed "traditional problem solving," emphasizes the scientific problem-solving approach of cutting the problem down to size by simplifying it and treating only its salient features. Although this is a necessary approach to the ultimate solution of any problem, it operationally suffers from its implicit assumption that the correct or whole problem has been identified. Often, this is not the case and the traditional mode of problem solving may lead to solving the wrong problem.[4] Indeed, the domain of traditional problem solving is shown in Figure 4.6 to be largely that of dealing with *symptoms*, since the parochial nature of the managerial process and of the organizations that deal with problems are such that only narrow viewpoints are taken of most problem contexts.

Of course, many may view this drawing of a correlation between problem solving and symptoms as an exaggeration, but within the context of society, there are few problems that get dealt with at anything other than a symptomatic level, even when the processes required to do so is at purely the level of simple logic rather than insight or clairvoyance. For instance, consider the American city that spent years in debate over an airport extension of the existing public transit system, and on finally building the system, found itself

[3] Some of the material in this section is adapted from the author's paper, King, W. R. and Cleland, D. I., "A New Method for Strategic Systems Planning," *Business Horizons,* Aug. 1975.
[4] Mitroff, I. I., and Featheringham, T. R., "On Systemic Problem Solving and the Error of the Third Kind," *Behavioral Science,* Vol. 19, Nov. 1974.

faced with a proposal for a relocation of the airport based on a forecast of early inadequacy and the high cost of expansion at the existing site. Such a sequence of events clearly indicates the restrictions placed on problem solving both by our traditional analytical methods and by organizational constraints that do not motivate people to look beyond the bounds of the problem, as presented, or beyond the scope of their own organization and personal responsibilities.

Figure 4.6 also shows *systems problem solving* in terms of a focus on the broader domain of symptoms *and* problems. This has been the concern of systems-oriented managers and strategic planners in recent years, and it is a clear improvement in problem solving over nonsystematic approaches.

However, as the figure shows, the domain of problems can be further extended to encompass opportunities in the *strategic systems planning* process. For instance, a major fast-food chain is faced with a peakload problem of tremendous magnitude. Its facilities are stretched to the breaking point at the lunch and dinner hours, and there is plenty of slack time at other hours. This problem of unused resources is viewed as an opportunity to introduce new items on its menu that will have special appeal at nonpeak hours: breakfast items, snack items, and nighttime specialities. Another company uses the major problems of society and business, consumerism, pollution control, etc., as a basis for a formal study of market opportunities that may be related to these phenomena. From this study, it concluded that it has the expertise to make a profit in several lines of business that will aid society and simultaneously reduce the image of business as a creator, rather than a solver, of societal problems.

In the former case, a single creative mind *could have* turned the problem into an opportunity. In the latter case, substantial study, data gathering, and analysis was required beyond the capacity of any individual. In both cases, the likelihood of achieving the transition from problem to opportunity was greatly enhanced by an operational process of applying systems ideas to planning.

An example of the failure to plan in the *strategic systems* context is reflected in the planning by Egypt for the Aswan Dam.[5] In that project, the evidence seems to indicate that the only real advantage that Egypt is getting from the dam is power generation. What has been absent was planning on a *total systems basis* to determine how the Dam would fit into the total Egyptian system, economic, social, agricultural, what its adverse side effects might be, and what strategies might be developed for alleviating these side effects.

Some total systems effects that apparently were not adequately evaluated were the following:

1. An excessive use of water by the farmers that has caused a water logging of much of the farmland.
2. With a greater exposure of water surface to the atmosphere, salts have

[5] Adapted with permission from *The Wall Street Journal*, Sept. 24, 1976, pp. 43 and 46.

built up in the soil through increased evaporation, and because the dam itself has ended the Nile River's annual floods that help to flush out the salts from the land.

3. The still waters of the reservoir and the irrigation canals have become fertile breeding ground for insects that cause intestinal diseases and malaria.

4. The surplus water resulting from too much irrigation will have to be carried away by some artificial draining system; an expense of massive proportion for Egypt.

5. Certain nutrients are being denied to the soil because the Nile no longer floods each year. This requires replacement with commercial fertilizers; the cost of commercial fertilizers has gone beyond the wherewithal of the farmers even with government subsidies.

Some of these problems would be solved if the excessive irrigation by the farmers could be reduced. But this would be difficult to bring about for such a change would require a massive reorientation of social tradition; for centuries the waters of the Nile have been regarded as a divine gift and their free use as a basic right in the culture of Egypt.

The total *systems effect* of the Aswan Dam may lead to a long-term degradation of the soil at the expense of a short-range power-generation capacity. Were these total systems effects taken into account when the planning and decision making for the Dam was carried out? The evidence suggests that the concepts of strategic systems planning were indeed not well implemented.

OPERATIONAL REQUIREMENTS FOR STRATEGIC PLANNING PROCESSES

Taken in its broadest sense, *planning* is an activity consciously programmed into an organization's continuing activities and having as its focus *the objective consideration of the future*. Whether the organization be a company, a public agency, a nation, or humankind, there is both a need and place for such activity, and there are evolving methodologies for effectively and objectively dealing with future-oriented activities in a fashion that heretofore was considered by many to be within the province of the occult.

This is not to say that crystal balls or astrology charts should become a part of the organizational planner's milieu. Rather, there should be a recognition that *since present actions necessarily reflect implicit anticipations and assumptions about the future, these anticipations and assumptions should be made explicit* and should be subjected to the same sort of analysis as is commonly carried out for less nebulous, and consequently often less important, immediate issues.

This expansive view of planning is intended to remove it from the constraints of a pure problem-solving reactive mentality to the larger domain of proactive thinking and acting. In accomplishing this, one is moving against a well-ingrained philosophy of our society, since reactive problem solving, i.e., "define the problem and solve it," is a cornerstone of much of our scientific and technological thinking.[6]

There are a number of operational requirements that must be fulfilled by a comprehensive planning process. First, such a view requires that the organization extend its attention beyond the boundaries of the immediately controllable to encompass those environmental aspects that are influenced by organizational actions, as well as to those elements of the environment that must simply be accepted as facts of life. To do this in a more than peripheral way requires the conscious consideration of environmental influences that are foreign to the day-to-day activities of most managers. Hence, a *systems model,* one defining the organization as a subsystem of a larger system, is necessary for performing comprehensive planning. Such a model may well be qualitative and descriptive. However, it is essential to developing the understanding required for effective planning.

Second, a comprehensive view of strategic planning that usefully encompasses such divergent activities as "futurism" and organizational financial planning must relate these various activities in some logical way. Therefore, a strategic-planning process must adopt the systems framework as an effective device for considering the myriad interrelationships and feedback loops inherent to such a unification.

Third, any view of planning that extends deeply into the environment of the organization almost inevitably results in the consideration of chains of effects and second-order social consequences. Chains of effects have been previously described as phenomena that are analogous to atomic reactions. Second-order social consequences may be best illustrated as described by Bauer,[7] who in turn, paraphrased Sharp,[8] who described the problems created by the missionary-induced replacement of stone axes with steel axes as the primary cutting tools of the Australian Yir Yorunt aborigines.

But stone axes played important functions in Yir Yorunt life beyond that of cutting wood. The men owned the stone axes, which were symbols of masculinity and of

[6] Of course, there is no converse intention to decry the utility of classical scientific problem solving as a part of the overall concept of planning. Indeed, there is need for more, not less, formal analytical activity in the management of organizations. The key to success in the modern view of *planning* put forth here is to *integrate futuristic thinking with careful analysis.* Indeed, this simple statement well reflects the objectives of our entire treatment of planning.

[7] Bauer, R. A., *Second-Order Consequences,* MIT Press, Cambridge, Mass., 1969, p. 15.

[8] Sharp, L., "Steel Axes for Stone Age Australians," *Human Problems in Technological Change* (E. H. Spicer, editor), Russell Sage Foundation, New York, 1952, pp. 69–92.

respect for elders . . . The missionaries had distributed the steel axes to men, women, and children without discrimination. But the older men, having less trust of missionaries, were not as likely to accept the steel axes. Soon elders of the tribe, once highly respected, were forced to borrow steel axes from women and younger men. The previous status relationships were thoroughly upset. . .

Finally, the organizational strategic planning process must give attention to *both* the long and the short run in a perspective that allows neither to dominate the other. Among strategic planners, and increasingly among managers, it is commonly recognized that the short run can appear to be so important that it precludes consideration of the long run. However, not so widely recognized is that exactly the opposite can occur. Such an illustration of short-run unimportant phenomena becoming important in the long run is described by Toffler in *Future Shock*[9] in terms of the "time skip" phenomenon. He argues that phenomena that are rather limited in their impact when they occur may, by virtue of the simple passage of time and natural processes, have effects that are amplified far beyond the original impact.

. . . the Peloponnesian War deeply altered the future course of Greek history. By changing the movement of men, the geographical distribution of genes, values, and ideas, it affected later events in Rome, and through Rome, all Europe. Today's Europeans are to some small degree different people because that conflict occurred.

In turn, in the tightly wired world of today, these Europeans influence Mexicans and Japanese alike. Whatever trace of impact the Peloponnesian War left on the genetic structure, the ideas, and the values of today's Europeans is now exported by them to all parts of the world. Thus today's Mexicans and Japanese feel the distant, twice-removed impact of that war even though their ancestors, alive during its occurrence, did not. In this way, the events of the past, skipping as it were over generations and centuries, rise up to haunt and change us today.

Thus, the cumulative effect of things that affected a small number of people in the past can today affect everyone, just as a recently discovered arithmetic error by a debtor in failing to pay a small sum to one's ancestor can, through the magic of compound interest, make his estate worth millions today![10]

Of course, the planner must consider "time skip" not only in historical perspective, but also in a proactive way. What consequences, so minor as to now warrant being ignored, may grow through natural processes into major problems in the next decade? Are there population segments, which if unsatisfied today, will create more costly demands in the future?

Thus, an organizational strategic-planning process must utilize a systems model, feedback loops, and the consideration of chains of effects and second-

---

[9] Toffler, A., *Future Shock,* Bantam Books, New York, 1971, pp. 17–18.

[10] Of course, we ignore here statutes of limitations and the possible effect of time skip and "natural" processes on the number of heirs who are due a part of the fortune.

order consequences. In doing this, it has the potential to balance the short run and the long run in an appropriate way.

BASIS FOR A STRATEGIC-PLANNING PROCESS

These operational requirements for a strategic planning process emanate from a conceptual basis that has been well described by Jantsch[11] as the salient "dimensions of integration in a systems approach." The dimensions Jantsch defines can be interpreted as being those that define the strategic-planning process. They are termed "horizontal," "vertical," "time and causality," and "action."

HORIZONTAL DIMENSION OF STRATEGIC PLANNING. The *horizontal* dimension exemplifies the need in planning for continuous interaction and *feedback* from general to particular and back again, i.e., between aspects of systems that require description in terms of many interrelated measures and those that are best treated in terms of one, or a few, such measures. For instance, the strategic planner is constantly aware that it is necessary to look at the "big picture" by considering the social, cultural, economic, static, dynamic, psychological, technological, and other impacts of contemplated actions on contemplated systems designs. Yet, in doing so, a monster described in complex multidimensional terms is created.

To deal with this monster, the strategic planner then may proceed on the time-honored problem-solving approach of cutting the problem down to size by considering only a smaller set of measures, combining various measures into a lesser number of indices, or by concentrating on the most important consequence. In doing so, the dimensionality of the system is reduced, making it manageable. Yet, once conclusions have been reached on the basis of this restricted version of the system, the planner must return to the more complex description of the system to investigate the impact of the abstraction and to ensure that the search for a manageable model has not ignored reality.

VERTICAL DIMENSION OF STRATEGIC PLANNING. The second dimension requiring integration and *feedback* in strategic planning is the vertical dimension, which involves a hierarchy of planning levels. Various authors have proposed taxonomies to describe this hierarchy. Jantsch[11] uses an adaptation of a structure proposed by Ozbehkan,[12] which sees three critical levels: the "ought to," "can," and "will" aspects of strategic decision making. At the highest level,

[11] Jantsch, Erich, "Forecasting and Systems Approach: A Frame of Reference," *Management Science*, Vol. 19, Aug. 1973.
[12] Ozbehkan, H., "Toward A General Theory of Planning," *Perspectives of Planning* (E. Jantsch, editor), OECD, Paris, 1969, p. 153.

the salient measures are the *objectives* of the organization, expressed as enduring concepts of dynamic behavior (e.g., profit maximation) rather than as specific quantitative goals to be achieved. At the next level, *goals* (in terms of specific outputs of functional outcomes) are the salient measures. This is the level
of strategic choice that takes the objectives as given and seeks to make optimum choices among strategic alternatives.[13] At the *operational planning* level
(the third level), activity is aimed at fixed attainable *targets*. As such, it is input
oriented in that it focuses on the allocations and arrangements of inputs to
achieve fixed targets.

Just as with the horizontal dimension, the key to this dimension of systems
planning is the continuous interaction and feedback among the levels that make
up the dimension in question. Objectives guide the development of goals,
which, in turn, determine targets. Yet, the input arrangements *necessary to the
achievement* of specific targets reverberate upward to necessitate the rethinking
of goals and sometimes, objectives. Moreover, general objectives, once finally
defined, must be translated into a set of mutually consistent goals, which in
turn must be defined in terms of a set of specific targets. Or, alternatively, one
may think in terms of the achievement of several targets that must logically
aggregate to constitute movement toward a goal, several of which must, in
turn, be logically equivalent to the achievement of an overall objective.

TIME-AND-CAUSALITY DIMENSION OF STRATEGIC PLANNING. The planning dimension called "time and causality" involves continued feedback and interaction between *exploratory forecasting and normative forecasting*. This distinction is between the process of plotting alternative paths into the future and the
structuring of courses of action on the normative basis of *desired* future states.

In the case of exploratory forecasting, various sets of assumptions are
made concerning future developments. For instance, Kahn and Wiener[14] have
adopted the technique of writing *scenarios* based upon paradigms, i.e., explicitly structured sets of assumptions definitions, typologies, conjectures, analyses, and questions,[15] to develop *alternative* futures likely to come about under
the stated conditions. Thus, the scenario is an explication of *possibilities* in the
manner of exploratory forecasting rather than a specification of a desired state
or a "point estimate" of what the future *will* hold.

Of course, such alternative futures become inputs into the strategic decision-making process where specific choices must be made; but it is important
that they be made within the context of a range of objectively defined alterna-

---

[13] In this book, *both* of the topmost two levels are encompassed by the term "Strategic Planning."

[14] Kahn, H., and A. J. Wiener, *The Year 2000*, Macmillan, New York, 1967.

[15] Bell, D., "Twelve Modes of Prediction—A Preliminary Sorting of Approaches in the
Social Sciences," *Daedalus*, Summer 1964, p. 865.

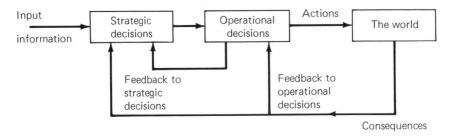

FIGURE 4.7 Planning Feedback Process.

tives rather than in a vacuum. Without such guiding information, strategic decisions tend to be based on one of two extreme modes of forecasting, simple *extrapolations* and *normative modes* of forecasting. A systems framework can prevent these extremes from being unthinkingly chosen, thus leading to more effective strategic planning.

ACTION DIMENSION OF STRATEGIC PLANNING. The *action* dimension of strategic planning refers to the interaction of planning and action. The entire focus of planning is a learning feedback process where plans depend on the consequences of action just as intrinsically as do actions reflect the results of planning.

The simple diagram of Fig. 4.7 describes this *feedback* process in terms of mutually supportive strategic and operational decision making, which results in actions. These actions influence "The World" and produce consequences which are fed back to provide the capability for revising strategic decisions. As shown by the inner feedback loop, the influence that this basic information has on operational decisions also provides part of the feedback data, which are provided to support potential changes in strategic decisions.

Summary

The strategic-planning processes may be thought of in terms of the roles to be played by various managers, the sequences in which they perform these roles, and the schedule that guides the processing of various planning information throughout the organization.

The substance of any planning process involves the development of analytical answers to the questions:

1. What is our current situation?
2. What do we want the future situation to be?

3. What might inhibit us?
4. What actions should we take to achieve our objectives?

Adequate answers to these questions require that a broad range of environmental information be analyzed and that the knowledge and experience of many organizational managers be marshalled and utilized. Such a broad and comprehensive process intrinsically requires that a systems viewpoint be adopted and that a systems—oriented process be implemented. A systems-oriented process is one that focuses an overall organizational effectiveness within the context of conflicting subunit objectives. It also motivates "strategic systems planning," in which the real, or underlying causes of symptoms are identified, and the identification of the opportunities, which are often suggested by organizational problems.

Chapter 4—Questions and Exercises

1. A formal planning process is important to the development of strategy for an organization. There are additional benefits that accrue to the organization through carrying out a planning process. What are some of these benefits?
2. Describe in schematic terms a strategic-planning process. What is the significance of the feedback loop in such a process?
3. What should be the role of the headquarters planning staff in the strategic planning process?
4. There are certain basic questions concerning an organization's future that the strategic planning process attempts to answer. What are these questions?
5. What is the role of strategic data bases in the strategic-planning process?
6. Take the schematic in Figure 4.4 and identify some specific data that could fit into each of the blocks in that schematic.
7. How might management viewpoints and values affect the strategic direction of the organization? Give some examples.
8. An important part of the strategic planning process is the manner in which the plans for the organization are reviewed. How might a review process be designed so that checks and balances are brought into play in the organization?
9. Why should assumptions and anticipations about an organization's future be made explicit?
10. What is the systems viewpoint as it applies to planning?
11. The organizational strategic-planning process should give attention to *both* the long and the short run in a perspective that allows neither to dominate the other. What is meant by this statement?
12. What is meant by "time skip" in the strategic sense?
13. What is the "horizontal dimension" of strategic planning?
14. Describe the "action dimension" of strategic planning. What is the value of this concept to the manager?

15. Implicit assumptions play an important role in the strategic planning process. Why is this so?
16. What are "second-order consequences" in the context of strategic planning? What are some examples of second-order consequences drawn from contemporary times?
17. If a manager does not do strategic planning for his organization someone else will do it for him. What is meant by this statement?
18. What is systems problem solving? How is it different from strategic systems planning?
19. Explain the second-order consequences concept in the context of the Aswan Dam example given in the chapter.
20. What is a scenario? How can it be used in planning?

Chapter 4—Strategic Questions for the Manager

1. Does a formal planning process exist within the organization? What are the strengths and weaknesses of this process?
2. Do the desired financial results tend to dominate the planning process to the neglect of dealing with truly strategic questions?
3. Have mechanisms been developed between top managers, staff planners, and subordinate line managers and planners to provide feedback on the efficacy of the planning process?
4. When was the last time these individuals got together to discuss such questions as: What's right and wrong about our planning process? How could the process be improved? Is the process understood and accepted by all parties concerned?
5. What strategic data bases are required in the organization? To what degree do these data bases exist?
6. In each of the elements of the strategic data bases (e.g. environment, competitor, organizational strengths and weaknesses, etc.), can the chief manager(s) identify and articulate the five or six key elements? Can the key planners do likewise?
7. Have historical records been developed that can serve as informational inputs to the planning process? Are these historical data bases available in a systematic way to decision makers?
8. What is the timetable for the strategic-planning process in the organization? Is this timetable complementary to short-term profit planning in the organization?
9. What techniques exist for making planning assumptions as explicit as possible?
10. Does the organizational culture exist for encouraging "futuristic" thinking as well as rigorous analysis in the planning process?
11. Can the "chain of effects" of several recent organizational strategic decisions be postulated?
12. What feedback loops exist in the organization to relate strategic and operational decisions?

References

Ansoff, H. I., and Stewart, J. M., "Strategies For a Technology-Based Business," *Harvard Business Review,* Vol. 45, Nov.–Dec. 1967, pp. 71–83.

Bauer, C. R., "Behavioral Aspects of Corporate Planning," *Long Range Planning,* Aug. 1976.

Branch, M. C., *The Corporate Planning Process,* American Management Association, Inc., New York, 1962.

"Corporate Planning—A Sometimes Thing," *Commercial and Financial Chronicle,* Aug. 25, 1975.

"Corporate Planning: Piercing the Future Fog," *Business Week,* April 28, 1975, pp. 46–54.

Drucker, P. F., *Management: Tasks, Responsibilities, Practices,* Harper and Row, New York, 1973.

Engster, Carl, "Corporate Planning in an Unstable Environment," *Futures,* Dec. 1971.

Helms, E. W., "The OST System for Managing Innovation at Texas Instruments," Address to the Armed Forces Management Association, Washington, D.C., April 7, 1971.

Hobbs, J. M., and Heany, D. F., "Coupling Strategy to Operating Plans," *Harvard Business Review,* May–June 1977.

Koontz, H., "Making Strategic Planning Work," *Business Horizons,* April 1976.

Linneman, R. E., and Kennell, J. D., "Shirt-sleeve Approach to Long-Range Plans," *Harvard Business Review,* Mar.–Apr. 1977.

Steiner, G. A., *Comprehensive Managerial Planning in Contemporary Management, Issues and Viewpoints* (J. W. McGuire, Editor), Prentice-Hall, Englewood Cliffs, N.J., 1974.

Steiner, G. A., *Top Management Planning,* Macmillan, New York, 1969.

van de Ven, A. H., and Koenig, R., Jr., "A Process Model for Program Planning and Evaluation," *Journal of Economics and Business,* Spring–Summer, 1976.

Wheelwright, S. C., "Reflecting Corporate Strategy in Manufacturing Decisions," *Business Horizons,* Feb. 1978.

INITIATING THE
PLANNING PROCESS—
STRATEGIC DATA BASES,
ASSUMPTIONS, AND FORECASTS

The planning process model of Figure 4.4 shows that the initial steps of the planning process involve informational inputs referred to as "strategic data bases," "assumptions," and "forecasts." The development of these inputs can be more than an analytic information collection and processing task. *If performed properly, these informational functions can be an important part of the planning process itself.* More significantly, they can ensure that the remainder of the process will be performed by informed and highly motivated managers at all levels in the organization.

Strategic Data Bases [1]

The first strategic question that must be addressed in a strategic planning process is related to the current situation: "Where are we?" Such a question can be regarded as either foolish, since the answer is well-known to all, or as being adequately answered only by collecting voluminous data on all of the many aspects of the organization's status. Despite the widely disparate positions that can be taken concerning this question, there is widespread agreement among managers and planners on the need for some critical informational inputs to the planning process.

Among these informational inputs are assessments of the organization's strengths and weaknesses, competitive information, and environmental opportunities and risks. Although general agreement exists in the literature and among planning professionals concerning the need for such informational inputs to strategic planning, in real organizations such information is often either not explicitly gathered and evaluated, or it is gathered, but not made a substantive part of the strategic choice process. Thus, while all planners, and most managers, appear to pay lip service to the idea that these informational inputs

---

[1] Portions of this section are adapted from King, W. R., and Cleland D. I., "Information for Strategic Planning," *Long-Range Planning,* Feb. 1977 with permission of the publisher.

are critical parts of the overall strategic planning process, there is little evidence that they actually play such a role.

For instance, one company employed two staff people for 6 months to develop a "competitive data base" to be used in the planning process. When their efforts reached fruition, they had created a room full of carefully cross-filed documents that were made no use of in planning because the data was too voluminous and too difficult to use. Subsequent evaluation of these competitive data resulted in the production of a very thick loose-leaf book that was put to little use for the same reasons.

In this section, we seek to illustrate an entity, referred to as a strategic data base (SDB), which can be developed in a form that makes it useful for directly supporting the strategic planning process. In doing so, we also describe the process through which SDBs are developed. These SDB-development processes thereby become intrinsic parts of the overall planning process. The specific SDBs and processes described here are largely taken from actual experience with business firms, although the illustrations are disguised and simplified for security and expositional purposes.

DEVELOPING STRATEGIC DATA BASES

SDBs are concise statements of the *most significant* strategic items related to various clientele/or environments that affect the organization's strategic choices. As such, they are the mechanisms through which the current situation and future opportunities are assessed. The SDBs shown in Figure 4.4 reflect the influence of various forces on the strategic options that are available, including the environment, competitors, top management, the business in which the organization operates, as well as the organization itself.

The approach adopted here emphasizes the development of SDBs—*objective collections of manageable, and therefore useful, data in the planning process*. These SDBs represent the *major conclusions regarding the environment and the organization's clientele,* which have been evaluated to be the *most important* such informational inputs to be considered in the planning process.

The evaluations of the vast quantities of data that form the raw input for the development of SDBs should be performed by task forces or teams of managers representing diverse interests within the organization. *In this way, the organization can be assured that the evaluation does not represent one narrow point of view or only the parochial viewpoint of analysts.*

These teams of managers, supported by staff, may be charged with arriving at *conclusions* concerning a *specified number* (usually from 10 to 15) of the *most important* factors affecting the future of the organization in each specified area. The development of conclusions on such things as the 10 to 15 most important organizational strengths and weaknesses can be a difficult task, when it involves managers representing various organizational interests and points of view. *Developing a 20-page list of strengths and weaknesses could be accomplished relatively easily, but a list of the 10 to 15 most significant ones involves significant analysis and negotiation.* This is so because of the judgments involved, the potential organizational impact that such a list can have through the strategic choice process, and the vested interests of the various participating managers.

ALTERNATIVE APPROACHES TO DEVELOPING PLANNING INFORMATION. It is useful to contrast this participative process for developing strategic inputs to the planning process with those that are more commonly used to prepare the informational inputs to planning. One common approach relies on staff analysts who gather data and prepare documents to serve as background information supporting planning activities and choices. Because the planners and analysts who perform these tasks often have neither the managerial expertise nor the authority to make the significant choices involved in any information evaluation process, the typical output of such an exercise is a document prepared on the basis of not leaving anything out.

Such an emphasis on ensuring that nothing relevant is omitted rather than on attempting to distinguish the most relevant information from the mass of less relevant and the irrelevant serves only to perpetuate the existing state of affairs regarding the informational support provided to managers at all levels: the manager is deluged with irrelevant information, whereas, at the same time, he or she is unable to find elements of information crucial to his or her function.[2]

Another approach to developing planning information, such as a strength-weakness analysis, is through charging the responsible managers with identifying their own organization's strengths and weaknesses. However, managers are not motivated to point out their organization's weaknesses in a honest and unbiased manner since doing so focuses attention on them and suggests that they may be responsible for the weaknesses, or at least, responsible for not remedying them.

Indeed, organizational budget processes often ask line managers to identify their weakest activities. This is especially prevalent in public agencies that are being subjected to budget cutbacks. The manager who is a ''gamesperson'' and who wishes to preserve his or her domain is likely to identify ''weaknesses'' that are not, in fact, among the weakest activities. In particular, if any activities

---

[2] For a full exposition of this situation, see Ackoff, R. L., ''Management Misinformation Systems,'' *Management Science*, Dec. 1967, pp. B147–B156. Vol. 14, No. 4.

are especially appealing to upper-level management, the manager will identify those as the weakest in the knowledge that top management would least like to cut these activities from the budget.

This "tell them only what they want to hear" philosophy is exemplified by Rohr Industries' experience in the late 1960s.[3] During this period Rohr changed from a subcontractor for aircraft power-plant assemblies into a producer of ground transit equipment. In one large contract, Rohr submitted a bid that was 23% below the customer's own estimate, and $11 million under the next lowest competitive bid. The program manager on this contract felt that this estimate was too low, but did not argue against it because he "didn't want to express a sorehead minority view when I was in charge of the program." Other executives reported that the daily staff meetings held at Rohr precluded any negative or pessimistic report. Such reports would provoke open and sharp criticism from the chief executive. These executives reported that problem areas were glossed over; the positive was emphasized in order that the chief executive would be pleased.

Despite the fact that the Rohr of this era may be an extreme case, the point is clear that the responsible people may not be the best ones to assess their own weaknesses, either because of their own objectives or what they perceive as the wishes of top management.

THE STRATEGIC DATA BASE DEVELOPMENT PROCESS. Contrary to both of these approaches, the SDB concept incorporates a process involving task forces of managers each of whom represents his own parochial area of interest or sub-unit. These task forces are charged with the responsibility for gathering and evaluating the data in each of a number of areas and *choosing* (through the consensual process that guides most task-force decision making) the most important to the development of the organization's strategy.

Thus, the SDBs represent "information" rather than "data" in the sense that large quantities of data have been evaluated and condensed to a form that can feasibly be used in the strategic planning process. With the SDB approach, there is a greater likelihood that some of the information universally regarded as being important to strategic planning will actually become an integral part of the strategic-planning process.

Moreover, a secondary benefit that is invariably realized from the SDB approach must not be overlooked. The participative process of developing SDBs will usually involve a variety of middle-level managers from each of the organization's functional units. The SDB development process is thereby a way of involving middle managers in the strategic thinking of the total organization long before they might normally become so involved by virtue of their op-

[3] As reported in *The Wall Street Journal,* Nov. 5, 1976.

erational job responsibilities. Thus, the SDB approach serves as a *training ground for the development of those elusive strategic thinking abilities* that are so necessary to successful top-level management.

To further elucidate the idea of strategic data bases, we shall elaborate on the contents and processes for development of those strategic data bases (SDBs) shown in Figure 4.4:

Strength-and-Weaknesses SDB

Business-and-Industry-Criteria SDB

Competitive SDB

Environmental-Opportunities-and-Risks SDB

Management-Viewpoints-and-Values SDB

These SDBs are somewhat generic in nature and have been useful to the authors in their consulting activities. Others may also prove to be useful in specific organizational situations.

Strength-and-Weakness Strategic Data Base

A strength-and-weakness SDB is a candid and concise statement of the most significant strengths and weaknesses of the organization. Although most planners would agree in principle that such a data base should importantly guide strategic choice, there is little evidence to suggest that many organizations have explicitly developed strength-weakness data bases or made effective use of them. For instance, a major electrical manufacturer that became involved in the public housing and land development businesses might have been deterred from doing so if the organization's weakness in the basic skills necessary for success in that area had been explicitly enumerated for all to see.

Table 5.1 shows a strength-weakness SDB for one business unit of a major conglomerate. This summary list was displayed on the first page of a strength-

TABLE 5.1 / Illustrative Strength and Weakness Data Base

MAJOR STRENGTHS	MAJOR WEAKNESSES
Technical expertise in centrifugal area	Low market share
International sales force	Lack of product standardization
Heavy machining capability	Poor manufacturing nonfragmented product
Business systems	line
Puerto Rico facilities	Poor labor relations
Technically superior image among	Weak domestic distribution network
customers	High price image (?)

and-weakness planning guidebook that was prepared for use in the planning process. The remainder of the book contained exhibits that explained and elaborated on these conclusions.

Some of the items in Table 5.1 might be thought of simply as items describing the status of the firm or as problems that need be corrected, rather than weaknesses. However, in the firm's detailed explanations of these areas in their planning guidebook, they were treated as weaknesses that must guide strategic decisions, rather than merely as problems to be overcome. For instance, the details relevant to the low-market-share weakness emphasized the strategies that were precluded as a result of low market share rather than emphasizing low market share merely as a deficiency to be corrected. In this way, attention was directed toward the *strategic implications of each strength and weakness* rather than to the familiar sort of exhortations for the firm to "do better by increasing market share."

Two of the entries in the strength-weakness table refer to the firm's "image." These indicate that the firm believes that its customers perceive it positively in terms of its technical superiority and (perhaps) negatively in terms of the relatively high price of its products. Such image assessments are commonly incorporated into statements of corporate objectives as well as into strength-weakness analyses. Yet often, as in this instance, the firm is to some degree uncertain of just how it is perceived. In this instance, the company was not certain if its high technical quality was perceived as justifying its relatively higher price.

Such a resolution of the image situation in a state of partial uncertainty is a common, and valuable, variety of outcome of SDB development efforts. It points up the need for information that is more detailed and specific than that which the firm currently possesses. This result can lead to an ad hoc study or to the development of a more detailed information system to provide the firm with the answers and the understandings that it needs to do effective strategic planning.

The key difference between SDBs and the more detailed data bases that are important to information systems can now be made clear. Data bases such as that of Table 5.1 require significantly more *evaluation* in their preparation than do information systems data bases. Table 5.1 is the result of an evaluative process that began with the compilation of a long list of potential strengths and weaknesses and proceeded to reduce these to a concise list of those most important to the organization. Such a list is both valuable and practically useful in the later stages of the strategic-planning process.

Business-and-Industry-Criteria Strategic Data Base

One informational input to planning that is widely recognized to be important but rarely made into an explicit element of the planning process is the key element of *what it takes to be successful in this business.* There are critical elements of business sense in any activity, and, even though key executives may have a good feel for these elements, a rational planning process will make the elements explicit and available to all planning participants. Such planning inputs help to guide the choices that are made just as do the strength and weakness analyses.

For instance, the business criteria that might be specified as being the keys to success in the weapons system industry might be as follows:

1. A strong research and development capability;
2. A commitment to using project management systems;
3. A strong field marketing effort closely tied in with customer organizations;
4. An ability to deal effectively with a relatively few knowledgeable customers;
5. An ability to identify and track emerging technological and market opportunities over long periods leading to consummation of sales;
6. Willingness to commit substantial company resources to study and prepare bids on government proposals.

In a consumer-oriented industry the requirements for success might include such factors as standardization of product line components, high volume production runs, highly dispersed marketing and service centers; low technology; and development of a recognized brand name.

The Business-and-Industry-Criteria SDB may be developed by a team in much the same fashion as discussed previously. Their work will probably involve more interviewing of top executives and less formal data gathering than will the work of the developers of the strength-weakness data base, but ultimately data will have to be developed to substantiate, if possible, the beliefs of top executives about the factors that are critical to success.

The format used by one company to present all of their data bases is appropriate here as well: a one page summary of the data base along with substantiating details in the form of a booklet.

Competitive Strategic Data Base

Competition is the most-apparent, and probably least-understood element of the organizational environment. Analyses of competition, their status and likely strategies, is so important that we have chosen to separate it from other environmental elements in later chapters. This separation emphasizes not only the importance of the area, but the generally unrecognized feasibility of discovering a great deal about competition that can be greatly useful in the planning process. Here, we merely seek to illustrate the broad insights concerning competition that can be used as guidance for the planning process in the form of a SDB.

For instance, competitors who are identified to be out-performing the organization can be identified and their significant actions and strategies can be cataloged and analyzed. Several major issues must be addressed with regard to competition:

1. Who are the several most threatening competitors?
2. What are the strengths and weaknesses of the competition?
3. What is believed to be the strategy (and associated risk postures) of the competition?
4. What resources (financial, plant and equipment, managerial know-how, marketing resources, and technical abilities) are at the competition's disposal to implement their strategies?
5. Do any of these factors give the competition a distinctly favorable position?

The evaluation of competition is, in a sense, a mirror image of the strengths and weaknesses of the organization itself. The competitor's ability to innovate and to implement has to be evaluated. This evaluation should concentrate on his products and their design, as well as on his ability to innovate in the creation, production, and marketing of his products. Evaluation of a competitor's resources must be done in a fashion that emphasizes what each can reasonably be expected to accomplish rather than solely on the resources available.

Environmental-Opportunities-and-Risks Strategic Data Base

A wide variety of other-than-competitive environmental invormation can provide valuable inputs to the strategic choice process. Every organization has environmental opportunities and risks related to customers, government agencies, and other regulators of the organization. Profiles of some important organizational clientele can be input to planning in a fashion similar to that done for competitors. This idea is particularly valuable in the case of major customers, who may be viewed in much the same way as a competitor for analytic and informational purposes.

Often, environmental risks and opportunities may be reduced to a series of specific questions and, hopefully, answers that can guide planning. Amara and Lipinski[4] have illustrated such questions as shown in the left column of Table 5.2. Illustrative answers to the strategic questions about the environment are

---

[4] Amara, R., and Lipinski, A., "Strategic Planning: Penetrating the Corporate Business," Institute for the Future, Paper P-30, Nov. 1974, p. 3.

TABLE 5.2 / Environmental-Opportunities-and-Risks Strategic Data Base

STRATEGIC QUESTIONS	ANSWERS
Will there be widespread nationalization of industry?	Rail transport (both freight and passenger) is likely to be fully nationalized by 1985; all other industries (including energy-related) will remain in private hands. Financial services (insurance, banking, securities) and consumer goods industries will undergo the greatest regulatory changes.
What is the possibility of the development of large industry/government cartels in the United States, particularly with respect to foreign markets?	Any major shift toward industry/government cooperative arrangements (as in Japan) is highly unlikely in the near future.
What dominant changes are likely to take place in the attitudes of the labor force, both supervisory and nonsupervisory?	Workplace discontent will intensify considerably. Much of this will be due to the entrance into the labor force of the baby bulge of the late 1950s and the peculiar set of problems associated with this age group. Work incentives in the future will emphasize greater freedom of choice regarding surroundings, dress, and a decision-making role in forming teams and structuring work functions. This change involves democratization to some degree, but not of business decisions. A reversal of economic prosperity will markedly reduce the importance of psychologic rewards to employees.
Is consumerism a fad? And, if not, what directions is it likely to take in the next decade?	Consumerism is not a fad. The scope of consumer-protection measures will widen in the next few years; mandatory product performance guarantees are quite possible, and regulation requiring industry-wide common performance indicators and detailed reporting of product testing results is very likely.
In what ways may the activities of multinational corporations be subject to increasing regulation?	The rate of growth of multinational corporations will slow somewhat in the next decade, and multinational corporations can anticipate more international controls, both from regional codes and from global organizations. However, it is unlikely that capital controls will be bothersome to multinational corporations.

shown in the right column in a concise form that marks them useful in the planning process.

The environmental data base can, as well, entail a section dealing with general areas of opportunity that are perceived to emanate from the environment. For instance, in a business related to recreation, the increasing availability of leisure time, which can be projected from a temporal analysis of union contract provisions regarding the length of the work week and vacation durations, might well be identified as a basic environmental opportunity for consideration.

The risks associated with these "opportunities" should be delineated so that they are not viewed with the proverbial rose-colored glasses or treated as established facts subsequently in the planning process. For instance, increased vacation durations among blue-collar workers might translate into increased sales of paints and other home-repair items long before it affects sales of vacation homes.

Management-Viewpoints-and-Values Strategic Data Base

It is well understood that top management's viewpoints and values play an important role in guiding the organization. Although this is completely proper, it is often not explicitly spelled out in the organization's strategic-choice process. This is not to say that a management-viewpoints-and-values guidebook be provided in the same fashion as might be done for strengths and weaknesses, environmental opportunities, and risks and business criteria, and the other SDBs, but it is also important that the organization not be misled into considering alternatives that have little chance to be viewed positively by top management. Participative strategic planning is a time-consuming activity and clearly the effort should be focused in directions that satisfy the practical constraints and reflect top management views, as well as more formal resource and legal constraints. If these constraints become apparent only *after* the planning process has been conducted, it will have been wasteful and the negative effect on managerial morale will be severe. There are few more disheartening situations for a manager than to feel that he is involved in high-level decisions regarding the future of the organization only to discover that recommendations on which he has spent considerable time and effort have been rejected because they violate constraints that he was not told about.

Ackoff[5] has used the term "stylistic objectives and constraints," to refer or describe this sort of qualitative statement about what the organization will and will not do. He illustrates stylistic constraints as (paraphrased):

[5] Ackoff, R. L., *A Concept of Corporate Planning*, Wiley, New York, 1970, pp. 28–29.

1. The company is not interested in any government-regulated business.
2. The businesses into which we may go must permit entry with modest initial investments but eventually permit large investments to be made.
3. The technology of any new businesses should be directly related to that used in current businesses.

However, the idea of management values and viewpoints clearly is broader than implied by these examples. For instance, it includes the *social responsibility* viewpoint of top management. Do they feel that the organization should pursue a broad multifaceted social purpose, or do they believe that the broad social good is best served if each institution seeks only a narrow range of objectives that best suits its expertise? If, in the case of a business firm, top management believes that profit seeking does create the greatest social benefit that the firm itself can feasibly produce,[6] this belief must be translated into operational terms to guide the strategic planning process.

The general aggressive-versus-defensive posture of the organization is another guide to the planning process that can only be specified by top management. If the posture is to be defensive, much time can be wasted in considering aggressive strategies that will ultimately be disapproved by top-management review. If the general posture is stated in advance, it serves to make the planning process more efficient and more productive.

Some top executives might be reluctant to spell out their personal ideas in such a way that they will formally constrain the planning process. Their fear in doing so reflects an unwillingness to appear to be making the organization into their personal image. However, most managers recognize the appropriateness of having the personal philosophy of top management play a role in guiding the organization's direction. Indeed, most experienced managers realize that chief executives often have as a major personal objective the making of *a distinctive personal impact* on the organization.

If strategic planning were solely the function of top management, this would not be a problem, but this is not the case. Therefore, it is important that the initiation of the planning process, as described in Figure 4.1 by the vertical arrow extending from the chief executive to the business unit executive, be performed explicitly and clearly. A memo or letter from the chief executive that serves as a cover letter for the other planning guidance materials can often serve as a good device to go into some detail concerning constraints and emphases that are to play a role in the planning process. In this fashion, a happy medium may be struck between the extremes of burying such guidelines in the

---

[6] See Drucker, P. F., *The Age of Discontinuity,* Harper and Row, New York, 1968, and the writings of many conservative economists, such as Milton Friedman, for the rationale for this viewpoint.

minds of top managers and requiring that they be spelled out in the formal terms that are suggested for the other strategic data bases.

ANALYTICAL INPUTS TO STRATEGIC DATA BASES

The analytic processes that have thus far been suggested for strategic data-base development have been subjective and consensual in nature. It is also feasible to utilize objective analysis as a basis for developing some of the SDBs. One approach to such analysis is through a model, called PIMS, which is available to U.S. business firms.

PIMS MODEL. PIMS is a statistical model (multiple regression) used to analyze data on business characteristics and performance that are submitted by U.S. firms to the Strategic Planning Institute. In return for their contribution of data and for a fee, SPI will provide statistical comparisons of the firm's businesses with other businesses in the data bank. No direct comparisons are made and all data are scaled to protect confidentiality.

The overall PIMS model has as its goal the answering of two basic questions: What factors influence profitability in a business, and how much? How does return on investment (ROI) change in response to changes in strategy and market conditions?[7] PIMS reports show how a firm's performance measures up to a "PAR" profitability level based on its market, industry, environment, competitive position, capital structure, etc.

The businesses also are provided with information concerning the major characteristics influencing ROI, both positively and negatively. For instance, one such report indicated that a business's ROI was being negatively influenced by (in order of importance) the degree of vertical integration, market position, product quality, and "sales direct to end users."

These factors, which are statistically determined to be the most significant ones in negatively affecting the business's ROI as compared with other similar businesses, are obvious candidates for designation as major weaknesses of the business. Of course, these analyticaly results like any others, cannot be taken too literally because the model is only a partial description of reality.[8] Thus, the statistical result should be taken to be suggestive of potential strengths and weaknesses. Informed analysis by managerial task forces are still required to substantiate these suggestions.

[7] Paraphrased from Schoeffler, S., Buzzell, R. D., and Heany, D. F., "Impact of Strategic Planning on Profit Performance," *Harvard Business Review,* March–April, 1974, p. 139.

[8] For instance, PIMS does not account for the effect of patents or trade secrets on profit performance. See Schoeffler et al., p. 145.

Developing Assumptions for Strategic Planning

In addition to the SDBs, it is necessary to input specific planning assumptions into the planning process at an early stage. Some of these planning assumptions are provided by the strategic data bases, but since their emphasis is on a relatively *small number of critical elements* to guide the planning process, they do not provide the extensive data that may be needed as the elements of the planning process progress.

Thus, in beginning to discuss assumptions, we recognize that they are not necessarily distinct from the information contained in the strategic data bases, nor the forecasts that are also important inputs to the process. One important distinction that does exist is that of comprehensiveness. Although concise SDBs are necessary to focus planning and to *guide* the planning process, more comprehensive statements of assumptions are necessary to *control* the planning, e.g., to ensure that tentative choices are not made for the wrong reasons or on the basis of invalid implicit assumptions.

Another, but nonetheless equally incomplete, distinction between assumptions and forecasts has to do with their qualitative-subjective versus quantitative-objective nature. Certainly forecasts can, and should, be made of qualitative future environmental factors; however, there is a tendency for forecasting to concentrate on future elements that can be foreseen using objective forecasting tools. Such factors tend to be numerical in nature. Thus, assumptions about the future can fill in the gap left by forecasts.

In this regard, General Electric uses assumptions that reflect anticipated institutional and attitudinal factors for the future, e.g.,

> All organizations will be operated less and less by the dictates of administrative convenience, more and more to meet the wants and aspirations of their membership.[9]

Such assumptions serve to guide the development of both product and market strategies for the future.

NEED FOR EXPLICIT ASSUMPTIONS

Planning assumptions are always present, whether explicit or implicit. The strategic planner must realize that the shape of policies and future plans can be determined, even unknowingly, in the implicit judgments that a manager integrates into his planning process. In this respect, Boettinger[10] cautions us:

---

[9] Wilson, I. H., "How Our Values are Changing," *The Futurist*, Feb. 1970, pp. 5–7.

[10] Boettinger, H. M., "Corporate Planning—Its Importance for the Individual Manager," presented to the British Institute of Management, London, 1970.

When a manager selects the means to get to the end (aim, objective, goal) he wants, if his assumptions about causes and effects operating in the problem are valid, then no harm is done and he will probably succeed. However, if his choice is based on an 'understanding' rooted in hunch, whim, myths, or wishful thoughts, he will set up intolerable conditions for his people and a crisis for his company.

Thus, despite the difficulty in making assumptions explicit, one must recognize that the only alternative is to have them be implicit, for one can never avoid making some assumptions in any choice process. If they are not made explicit, some or all of the following are likely to occur:

1. Assumptions are implicitly made in developing the plans, but, since they are not brought to the surface, top managers are unaware of these bases for the plans.
2. Different assumptions are made by planners in various business units, so that the plan becomes a hodgepodge in which the business units are betting with one another about the future.
3. The assumption is implicitly made that the future will be the same as, or a simple extrapolation of, the past.

Assumptions and forecasts therefore cannot be avoided in planning; they can only be hidden below the surface.

The role of implicit assumptions might be further illustrated by drawing on some recent examples in government experience[11] to illustrate the point:

In McNamara's management of the Department of Defense policy was understood as a derivative of technical processes and technical rationality. Yet in fact policy was determined in the implicit judgments contained in the assumptions used by the analysts. 'It's better to recognize that Defense policy is inherently political and to make your political and intuitive judgments out in the open.' "

"In the 1960's '. . . those who cared about better education, health, and social services . . . thought the main problem was under-financing.' "

These statements by Rivlin and Roherty make it clear that the failure to consider implicit assumptions may pre-empt policy choice or constrain the range of available strategies.

FEASIBILITY OF MAKING ASSUMPTIONS

Some managers react to requests that they participate in processes for the development of assumptions by stating that they are not clairvoyant about the future. They say that should be left to the forecasters. This issue of clairvoyance in both assumptions and forecasts is an important one, since most of us—planners

---

[11] Quotes from Alice M. Rivlin, and James M. Roherty, as reported in, "On the Limits of Rationality," *Wall Street Journal*, Sept. 10, 1971.

and nonplanners alike—feel inadequate when we attempt to foresee the future. Many, therefore, view the making of assumptions and forecasts to involve the never-never land of clairvoyants and seers.

The facts are that a great many forecasts and assumptions that are of significance and value to strategic planning can be developed on the basis of simple analyses. Although we cannot often accurately predict the future, we can analyze the current situation and its trends and use this information as a basis for communicating expectations to guide organizational planning.

For instance, one firm made an analysis of its cost structure and developed simple projections of future costs *based on known, or extremely likely, changes to occur over the next five years.* It took into account recent trends in material costs as well as uncontrollable future wage increases dictated by union contracts, cost-of-living escalators in contracts, anticipated changes in statutory Social Security contributory requirements, and a variety of other "hard" bases for projecting the future. The aim was to merely *analyze those cost changes that could be reasonably anticipated on the basis of current "knowns"* rather than to creatively forecast the future on statistical or other formal bases.

The results of this analysis were startling to the top managers of the firm. In his memo to division controllers explaining the results, the corporate controller said, "I am sure that you and your general manager will be shocked, as we were, with the financial impact of these factors." One can readily see the reason for his surprise from Table 5.3, particularly when it is recognized that *they are based solely on known or readily foreseeable changes and not on speculations about future happenings.*

When such data are provided to business unit planners with guidance on adjustments that should be made because of various materials mixes and other differential factors, they provide a solid basis for the development of plans. Moreover, they ensure that plans will be developed by various business units on a consistent basis.

Consistency, of course, does not mean that the assumptions must be rigidly adhered to; indeed, one of the basic assumptions of an adaptive planning process is that contingencies and alternative assumptions need to be considered. However, if a given plan is to be meaningful, it must be based on a common set of assumptions. Contingencies can then be considered as they relate to this basic plan. To do otherwise is to compare apples and oranges without even realizing that one is doing so.

ASSUMPTIONS AND FORECASTS

The line of demarcation between assumptions and forecasts is blurred at best. For instance, Table 5.4 shows a statement of environmental assumptions made by a firm for one of its businesses. These assumptions are clearly broad ranging

TABLE 5.3 / Illustrative Assumptions and Forecasts of Cost Element (Percent Increases for the coming 5-Year Period)

	YEAR 1	YEAR 2	YEAR 3	YEAR 4	YEAR 5
Labor	12	8	14	8	15
Material	10	10	10	10	10
Social Security	43.3	10.5	10.8	10.5	10.5
Pension	6	100	6	6	20
Employee Insurance	10	12	10	10	12
Workmen's Compensation	10	10	10	10	10
Auto Liability	5	5	5	5	5
General Liability	10	9	8	8	7
Taxes	10	20	10	10	10
Research and Development Rates	8	14	8	8	10
Holidays and Vacations	20	10	20	10	20

and encompass many generalizations or conclusions that result from more detailed forecasts. Thus, viewed in this way, some environmental assumptions may be viewed as integrated summaries of the most important results of forecasts.

Forecasts as Inputs to Strategic Planning

The third generic informational input to strategic planning, as shown in the process model of Figure 4.4, is "forecasts." Forecasts of the future environment are the variety of informational inputs most commonly associated with strategic planning. In fact, Warren has suggested that many people view planning to be synonymous with forecasting.[12]

TRADITIONAL BUSINESS FORECASTING

Businessmen have long had to forecast future demand and prices for their goods in order to make good strategic choices concerning what to stock, where

[12] Warren, E. K., *Long-Range Planning: The Executive Viewpoint,* Prentice Hall, Englewood Cliffs, N.J., 1966, p. 17.

TABLE 5.4 / Basic Environmental Assumptions Over Next Five Years

1. The general economy will have little real growth.

2. The location of demand from new buildings will continue shifting toward the south and southwest U.S. and internationally in several selected countries. However, the demand for service will change geographically much slower and for the next five years remain pretty much as we can now see it.

3. Construction activity will tend to have the following characteristics:
   a. More emphasis in the south, southwest, and in suburbs of older market areas where land area is not so critically short.
   b. Be restricted by changing values against "skyscrapers" and resistance to too much development.
   c. Energy-materials influences in building design, size of projects, and rate of construction.
   d. Housing trends will increase demand for low- and medium-rise apartments.
   e. Transit-related construction may increase dramatically.

4. Inputs to our business will tend to have the following characteristics:
   a. Labor
      i. Managerial-professional personnel will be harder to attract;
      ii. Pressure toward higher field labor costs will continue through union activities and scarcity of skilled labor.
   b. Materials' costs will continue up and their availability will be a problem.
   c. Transportation costs will become more serious as distribution of demand gets further from plant sites.
   d. Basic technology for our business is already pretty much in place.

5. Competition for the next few years will remain keen since the industry has an over-capacity and construction will remain slow. However, attrition should remove some of the weaker competitors.

to locate their businesses, and when to purchase their inventories. Until late in the past century, most such forecasting was done intuitively, an innate ability, which served to separate the successful businessman from the failures. With the increases in business complexity that occurred in the late 1800s, the need for "more scientific" forecasting became apparent.

The early scientific approaches to business forecasting were borrowed from the natural sciences. Quantitative economic time series were analyzed with regard to secular trend and cyclical and seasonal patterns. It was generally assumed that the regularities of behavior found in the natural sciences would also be displayed by these business data.

These techniques and their more sophisticated derivatives are in widespread use today in business forecasting of individual economic indicators or performance measures such as the Gross National Product, sales, or disposable income. The primary techniques are treated in various texts on business forecasting, so it is not our intent to deal with them here.[13] Although many of these forecasting techniques are commonly used to provide forecast inputs to strategic planning, their use is not well understood. The most interesting and innovative uses of forecasting in strategic planning have come in less structured areas such as technologic and social forecasting. In these areas, one of the most widely used approaches is the Delphi technique.

DELPHI FORECASTING

The Delphi-forecasting approach was developed as a method of eliciting expert opinion about the future in a systematic fashion. Such opinion forecasts are familiar and valuable inputs to strategic planning. For instance, McGraw-Hill surveys of businessmen's plans for making expenditures on plant and equipment are published regularly in *Business Week* and are widely used as forecasting bases. Other forecasts are made by obtaining the collective judgments of groups. However, forecasts based on composites of group opinions have often been found to represent *compromises* rather than *consensuses,* since such things as the prestige or personality of individuals can inordinately influence the judgment of a group.

The Delphi technique enables a group of experts to contribute to one another's understanding and to refine their opinions as a result of interaction with other experts.[14] Delphi physically separates the experts, however, so that some individuals and their rationales do not become submerged in the overt activities of a group.

Delphi involves a series of steps:

1. Predictions by each expert.
2. Clarification by a neutral investigator.
3. Requestioning of experts combined with feedback from other experts.

The process of requestioning is designed to eliminate misinterpretation and to bring to the attention of each expert elements not known to all.

A typical Delphi session might involve an initial round in which each participant is asked to predict when a technological development is likely to occur. The data from the various participants are tabulated and clarified and fed back to the participants in a second round. They are asked to review their first predictions in the light of those of the other participants. Those who made extreme assessments (in the upper and lower 25% of responses in the first

---

[13] For instance, see Wheelwright, S.C., and Makridakis, S., *Forecasting, Methods for Management,* New York, 1973, or Gross, C. W., Boston, and Peterson, R. T., *Business Forecasts,* Houghton Mifflin, Boston, 1976.

[14] Delphi and Delphi derivations used by TRW, Inc., are reported in "New Products: Setting a Timetable," *Business Week,* May 27, 1967, pp. 52–56.

round) are also asked to *explain* these extreme positions. The process may go on through a number of rounds in which each participant is given the opportunity to reassess his forecast in the light of those made by others and their rationales. Sometimes this results in a concensus developing around a well-rationalized initially extreme position. At other times, the extremists moderate their forecasts. In any case, the difficulties of face-to-face forecasting are avoided, whereas the benefits of expert judgement are realized.

Modifications to the basic Delphi are too numerous to detail. However, almost all modified Delphis are designed to achieve three attributes that are believed to contribute to authentic consensus and valid results: anonymity of respondents, statistical response, and iterative polling with feedback.

Turoff[15] identified several possible uses for Delphi:

1. To determine or develop a range of possible alternatives.
2. To explore underlying assumptions or information leading to differing assumptions.
3. To correlate informed judgments on topics spanning a wide range of disciplines.
4. To educate respondents to the diverse and interrelated aspects of a topic.
5. To generate consensus.

Despite these significant benefits and potentials for Delphi, after more than 25 years of use, Delphi is increasingly being criticized, tested, and evaluated for use in a variety of strategic-forecasting situations.[16]

SOCIOPOLITICAL FORECASTING

Perhaps the least understood and potentially most useful variety of forecasting for strategic planning involves qualitative social and political phenomena. Political and social scientists have dealt with forecasting in these environments for many years, but only recently have such forecasts begun to play major roles in organizational planning.

The social and political turbulences of the late 1960s and early 1970s demonstrated conclusively to public agencies and business firms that they needed improved capabilities for developing proactive strategies based on forecasts of social and political phenomena. In 1967, General Electric established sociopoli-

[15] Turoff M., "The Design of a Policy Delphi," *Technological Forecasting and Social Change,* Volume 2, 1970, pp. 149–171.

[16] See Sackman, H., *Delphi Critique,* Lexington Books, 1975, and Dalkey, N.C., *Studies on the Quality of Life: Delphi and Decision Making,* Lexington Books, 1972, as well as basic texts such as Martino, J. P., *Technological Forecasting for Decision Making,* American Elsevier, New York, 1972.

tical forecasting as a separate organizational entity to meet this challenge.

One of the outputs of sociopolitical forecasting at General Electric is given by Wilson[17] in the form of a profile of significant value changes between 1969 and 1980. A version of his values profile is shown in Figure 5.1 in terms of contrasting values (e.g., war versus peace or work versus leisure) which are held by trend setters in the general population.

FUTURISTIC FORECASTING

The emphasis in the last two decades on futurism has led to increasing attempts to integrate futuristic forecasting into organizational strategic-planning activities. There is evidence that these efforts have not yet had major impact, but that the potential is assessed to be great.

Narayanan[18] has reported on a survey of the utilization of futurism by the organizations of business, government and consulting professionals who are knowledgeable in the field of futurism. He concludes that:

1. Futurism has had an impact on the thinking and policy making of various social entities and on broadening their perspective, though it has not necessarily resulted in enlarging the time frame of reference. Specifically, futurism has aided in getting these social entities seriously involved in specific consideration of social and ecological issues.

2. The methodologies employed in futurism are restricted to those that facilitate adaptive behavior of systems rather than inventive behavior. The latter have not yet been integrated into practicing futurist's regular 'tool kit.'

3. Despite its perceived utility, futurism was not regarded so overwhelmingly important as to necessitate a major deployment of resources.

The best known varieties of futuristic forecasting are the large-scale simulation models such as those reported on by Meadows et al. in *The Limits to Growth*.[19] These models depict the world as a system incorporating consideration of population and technological, industrial, natural resources, and other interacting subsystems. These models project the consequences of current growth rates into the future and permit the analysis of the impact of global growth policies. The initial and widely publicized study reported on in *The Limits to Growth* indicated that if the world did not moderate industrial and population growth, the system might well collapse within fifty years.

---

[17] Wilson, I. H., General Electric Company, reprinted with permission.

[18] Narayanan, V. K., "Role and Status of Futurism: An Empirical Study," unpublished research paper at the Graduate School of Business, University of Pittsburgh, 1976.

[19] Meadows, D. H., Meadows, D. L., Randers, J., and Behrens, W. W., III, *The Limits to Growth: A Report for the Club of Rome's Project on the Predicament of Mankind*, Universe Books, New York, 1972.

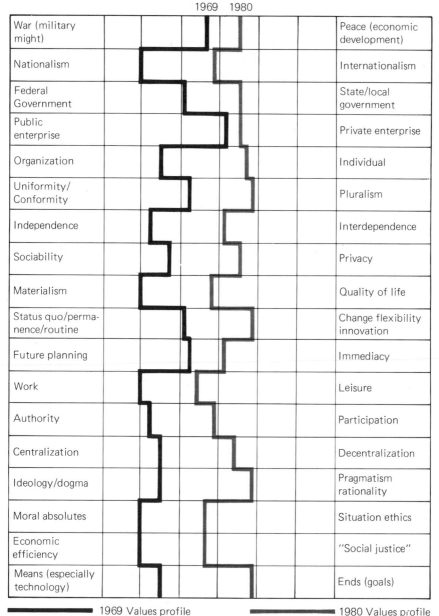

Profile of significant value-system changes: 1969–1980
as seen by General Electric's Business Environment section

	1969	1980	
War (military might)			Peace (economic development)
Nationalism			Internationalism
Federal Government			State/local government
Public enterprise			Private enterprise
Organization			Individual
Uniformity/Conformity			Pluralism
Independence			Interdependence
Sociability			Privacy
Materialism			Quality of life
Status quo/permanence/routine			Change flexibility innovation
Future planning			Immediacy
Work			Leisure
Authority			Participation
Centralization			Decentralization
Ideology/dogma			Pragmatism rationality
Moral absolutes			Situation ethics
Economic efficiency			"Social justice"
Means (especially technology)			Ends (goals)

▬▬▬▬▬ 1969 Values profile   ▬▬▬▬▬ 1980 Values profile

FIGURE 5.1   Values Profile.

Subsequent studies[20] have altered this bleak outlook to some degree. However, the various forecasts have had great impact, if only in the psychological sense, on the general populace and on organizational strategic planning. In general, large-scale simulation models of the world economy have great potential for providing important informational inputs to the strategic planning of business firms and government agencies.

ECONOMETRIC FORECASTING MODELS

Another variety of large-scale model used by corporate strategic planners is the large-scale econometric model. Several firms[21] operate such models and provide model forecasts and other services to business and other organizations on a fee basis. These econometric models depict the national economy in terms of hundreds of statistically estimated equations. The equations are based on economic theory as well as empirical evidence and they are used to test the economy's likely response to national policy changes, such as tax cuts or reform, tighter monetary policy, or higher energy prices.

At the level of the business firm or other nonfederal policy organization, the various firms operate industry input-output models in addition to econometric models that forecast special production indices or segments of the economy.

The organizational strategic-planning activity can use these forecasts in a variety of ways:

1. To develop a set of consistent forecasts for a variety of different products or markets.
2. To evaluate the impact of different scenarios on the economic performance of various markets.
3. To evaluate the market segments which will significantly contribute to future growth.

Although such models are often spoken of in the terminology of "what if" questions, this use of the term is different from the use of the term in this book. *Aggregate econometric models have no capability for assessing the future impact of actions taken by a single organization.* This is the sense in which the "what if" question is usually used, e.g.: "What would happen if we changed our prices?" The "what if" question capability of econometric models operates at the aggregate level of national policy scenarios, e.g.: "What would happen if taxes were cut by 10%?" Although the latter sort of scenario can be a

---

[20] Mesarovic, M. and E. Pestel, *Mankind at the Turning Point: The Second Report to the Club of Rome,* E. P. Dutton, New York, 1974.

[21] Data Resources Inc., Chase Econometric Associates Inc., and Wharton Econometric Forecasting Associates Inc., are the best known of these firms.

useful guide to corporate planners, these models will not provide "what if" answers to corporate strategy issues.[22]

Summary

The informational inputs to planning should be developed to integrate into the planning process. Indeed, the processes for the development of informational inputs may be the first stages of a planning process.

SDBs are concise statements of important underlying phenomena that must be assessed if the organization is to do effective planning. These data bases may be viewed as planning tasks to be performed by managerial task forces in the early stages of a planning cycle. When viewed in this way, the development of strategic data bases is made an integral part of the overall planning activity of the organization rather than being viewed as a special study activity to be performed by staff specialists.

This is important because the development of such planning information directly involves *choices* that cannot be readily made by staff specialists. For instance, an assessment of the most important organizational strengths and weaknesses, if it is to be useful in planning, must necessarily result from discussion, negotiation, and argument among representatives of various interest groups within the organization. If a strength-weakness assessment is not so accomplished, it is likely to have little impact.

Assumptions and forecasts are other important elements of planning information that must be integrated into the planning process. In most situations, the simple process of making assumptions and forecasts explicit will have great value. Of particular importance in planning are some of the less well understood forecasting tools such as Delphi, sociopolitical forecasting, futuristic forecasting, and econometric forecasting models. All have their place in a comprehensive planning process, but none can take the place of managerial judgement as the prime element of strategic decision making.

Chapter 5—Questions and Exercises

1. Who should be involved in developing strategic data bases for an organization?
2. Who should be responsible for analyzing the significance of the strategic data bases in an organization?
3. What can a manager do to prevent being deluged with strategic information?

[22] For a discussion of the various econometric models which are available to subscribers, see Golden, S., "Forecast: Profits for Prophets," *New York Times*, Oct. 19, 1975.

4. What role might the participative process of management play in an organization in the development of strategic data bases?
5. How should a manager go about developing a strength-and-weakness strategic data base for his organization? What are the advantages of doing so?
6. Select a particular industry and develop a business-and-industry criteria strategic data base.
7. What are the several key questions that a manager should ask and have answered about his competition?
8. Once a competitive data base has been developed, what should be done with it?
9. How might a first cut of environmental-opportunities-and-risks strategic data bases be developed for an organization?
10. How might one go about determining the management viewpoints and values that the chief executives of an organization hold?
11. Strategic planning is too important to be left to the chief executives of an organization. What is the significance of this statement?
12. What is the value of the PIMS Model in the analysis of strategic alternatives for an organization?
13. What role do assumptions play in strategic planning? What are some examples of such assumptions?
14. Differentiate between planning and forecasting.
15. What is the Delphi process of forecasting? Does it have any pragmatic value to the strategic planner?
16. What value does sociopolitical forecasting play in the strategic planning process?
17. How might strategic data bases be used as educational material in an organization's executive development program?
18. What is the role of the strategic data base in management devèlopment?
19. Does the making of good assumptions or forecasts of the future require clairvoyance? Does it require a level of insight into the future that few of us possess?

Chapter 5—Strategic Questions for the Manager

1. What major conclusions can be reached regarding the organization's environment and clientele?
2. What are the *current* strengths and weaknesses of the organization? What are the *expected* strengths and weaknesses when the current long-range strategies come to fruition?
3. What is the organization's image with respect to its clientele? Is there any difference between the image held by clientele and what the organization's managers believe that image to be?
4. If there are deficiencies in the image held by clientele, what strategies should be developed to change these perceptions?
5. What counts for success in my industry? What distinctive competence does the organization have to match the industry-success criteria?
6. How does the competitor's distinctive competence match up to what counts for success in the industry?

7. Which competitors are out-performing this organization? Why?
8. What are the strengths and weaknesses of the organization *vis-a-vis* the competitors?
9. What are the major environmental opportunities and risks faced by this organization?
10. Have key managers made a practice of attending industry association meetings to facilitate building a data base for the strategic question: What counts for success in the industry?
11. Do the key manager(s) have any views or value systems that might influence their strategic decision? What are the key elements of these viewpoints or value systems?
12. Can measures be taken to recognize explicitly the influence of these viewpoints and value systems in the decision process?
13. Have implicit assumptions been dealt with adequately and clearly in the organization's strategic planning?
14. Do you wish to make a distinctive personal impact on your organization? What strategic implications does that have for the organization's stakeholders?
15. Have past strategic decisions been adversely influenced by implicit assumptions?

References

Anshen, M., "The Management of Ideas," *Harvard Business Review,* July-Aug. 1969.

Baldwin, H. W., *Strategy for Tomorrow,* Harper and Row, New York, 1970.

Baughman, J. P., Lodge, G. C., Pifer, H. W., *Environmental Analysis for Management,* Irwin, Homewood, Ill., 1974.

Delombre, J. and Bruzelius, B., "Importance of Relative Market Share in Strategic Planning—A Case Study," *Long Range Planning,* Aug. 1977.

DeSalvia, D. N., and Gemmill, G. R., "An Exploratory Study of the Personal Value Systems," *Academy of Management Journal,* Vol. 14, June 1971, p. 227.

England, G. W., "Personal Value Systems of American Managers," *Academy of Management Journal,* Vol. 10, March 1967, p. 53.

Ericson, R. F., "Organizational Cybernetics and Human Values," *Academy of Management Journal,* Vol. 13, March, 1970, p. 49.

Fahey, L., and King, W. R., "Environmental Scanning for Corporate Planning," *Business Horizons,* Aug. 1977.

Gechele, G. B., "Evaluating Industrial Technological Forecasting," *Long Range Planning,* Aug. 1976.

Guth, W. D. and Taguri, R., "Personal Values and Corporate Strategy," *Harvard Business Review,* March–April 1959, and Sept.–Oct. 1965.

Hofer, C. W., "Toward a Contingency Theory of Business Strategy," *Academy of Management Journal,* Dec. 1975.

King, W. R., *Quantitative Analysis for Marketing Management,* McGraw-Hill, New York, 1967.

King, W. R., "Systems Analysis at the Public-Private Marketing Interface," *Journal of Marketing,* Jan. 1969.

Learned, E. P., Dooley, A. R., and Katz, R. L., "Personal Values and Business Decisions," *Harvard Business Review*, March–April 1959.

Mangulies, W. P., "Making the Most of Your Corporate Identity," *Harvard Business Review*, July–Aug. 1977.

Marquis, D. C., "The Anatomy of Successful Innovations," *Innovation*, Vol. 1, Nov. 1969.

Pekar, P. P., "Typology for Identifying Risk," *Managerial Planning*, Sept. 1976.

Sikula, A. F., "Value and Value Systems: Relationship to Personal Goals," *Personnel Journal*, Vol. 50, April 1971, p. 310.

Simmonds, W. H., "Planning and R&D In a Turbulent Environment," *Research Management*, Nov. 1975.

Stevenson, H. H., "Defining Corporate Strengths and Weaknesses," *Sloan Management Review*, Spring 1976.

Tannenbaum, R., and Davis, S. A., "Values, Men and Organizations," *Industrial Management Review*, Vol. 10, Winter 1969, p. 67.

Telling-Smith, G., "Medicines in the 1990's: Experiences With a Delphi Forecast," *Long Range Planning*, June 1971.

Wheelwright, S. C., and D. G. Clarke, "Corporate Forecasting: Promise and Reality," *Harvard Business Review*, Nov.–Dec. 1976.

PART IV

The Planning Decision Subsystem

Chapter 6
STRATEGIC CHOICE

Attention in the planning literature is so often devoted to the process and procedural aspects of planning that the decision-making aspects are deemphasized. At its essence, *planning is decision making,* and the level of attention and formalism devoted to planning processes and procedures should at least be equalled by that devoted to the "decision subsystem"—the set of decision processes, models, and procedures used in making strategic choices.

This is not to say that the choices of such things as missions, objectives, and strategies, which are the essence of planning decisions, can be reduced to equations and numbers. All human decision making is inherently subjective, and this is particularly so in areas of *strategic choice* since such decisions involve a variety of different elements, many of which cannot be objectively measured. However, if that subjective judgment can be guided and focused, the quality of the strategic choices that are made will be enhanced. The decision subsystem, the planning subsystem that can guide and provide structure for strategic choice, is the subject matter of this chapter. The various approaches that may be taken to the selection of missions, objectives, strategies and resource allocations are treated in detail in subsequent chapters. Here, the purpose is to discuss the nature of strategic choice and the inherent interdependencies among these strategic choice elements.

The Need for Strategic Choice

Although the need for strategic choice in any organization is clear, the need for *explicit* choice, with delineated alternatives, formal evaluation of alternatives, etc., is not nearly so clear. Many argue that such things as missions, objectives, and strategies are best kept implicit, or at least, undisclosed.[1]

The variety of participative strategic-planning process being put forth here

---

[1] For instance, see Wrapp, "Good Mangers Don't Make Policy Decisions," *Harvard Business Review,* Sept.–Oct. 1967.

obviously makes any such nebulousness or secrecy difficult. Indeed, this is so because there are real needs for such disclosure and significant values to be gained from it.

THE VALUE OF BEING EXPLICIT

The explicit delineation of *missions, objectives,* and *strategies* in the strategic choice process is designed to accomplish the following:

1. To ensure unanimity of purpose within the organization.
2. To provide a basis for the motivation of the organization's resources.
3. To develop a basis, or standard, for allocating organizational resources.
4. To establish a general tone or organizational climate, e.g., to suggest a businesslike operation.
5. To serve as a focal point for those who can identify with the organization's purpose and direction and as an explication to deter those who cannot from participating further in the organization's activities.
6. To facilitate the translation of objectives and goals into a work-breakdown structure involving the assignment of tasks to responsible elements within the organization.
7. To provide a specification of organizational purposes and the translation of these purposes into goals in such a way that the *cost, time, and performance* parameters of the organization's activities can be assessed and controlled.

These "objectives for having objectives" suggest the need for an explicit framework of missions, objectives, strategies, goals, programs, etc., as outlined in Chapter 3. Without such a framework, the complex organizational system is virtually incomprehensible to any individual, however bright he may be. If one just attempts to vaguely think about the organization's purpose and direction, he is likely to become muddled, to neglect important areas of opportunities, and to fail to foresee important reactions of competitors, governments, or pressure groups.

In addition, if purposes and directions are not made explicit, there is likely to be misunderstanding and inconsistency of action among organizational managers and other personnel. Many complex organizations have discovered that the absence of explicit objectives and missions has nurtured a process whereby various managers develop conflicting strategies and programs; in effect, putting the organization into competition with itself.

However, and perhaps most importantly, *without explicit objectives, strategies, and goals, measurement of performance, and hence control, are impossible.* Thus, with no such statements of purpose and direction, one literally could not tell where the organization was going or how fast it was getting there. Since such assessment of progress is a critical element of management, it cannot be overlooked on the basis of unnecessary complexity and excess formality as some would try to do.

Of course, there are those who will argue that even though these rationales may hold for goals, i.e., specific measurable achievements to be attained in a specified time period, they do not necessarily hold for the broader levels of missions, objectives, and strategies. The arguments over this point will undoubtedly continue to rage. However, one thing does seem to be clear: *the curse of multidimensionality,* which is endemic to modern organizations, creates the need for explicit statements of those broader elements of organizational purpose and direction.

THE CURSE OF MULTIDIMENSIONALITY

The curse of multidimensionality simply means that an organization that attempts to achieve one simple objective will probably unknowingly also achieve others that have not been made explicit. Of course, since they have not been made explicit, progress toward or away from them will not be monitored. These implicit objectives only become apparent when a critical point is reached. For instance, many firms that neglected to establish a liquidity goal found themselves in a critical cash-short situation in the mid-1970s. Similarly, those firms that stated profit was the "only and obvious" objective found that its pursuit led to reactions from government, pressure groups, and stockholders that required a reexamination and formal statement of objectives.

Indeed, even the simple profit measure is itself multidimensional. Profits can accrue in both the long and short run, and profit-oriented decisions inevitably trade off profit at one time for profit at another. Moreover, most organizations have multiple *claimants* or *stakeholders* (as opposed to stockholders), individuals and groups outside the organization who have a claim on it. Such a claimant-oriented view of the organization implies a multiplicity of objectives, since each claimant has different, and often conflicting, objectives; for instance, speculators have different objectives than do the proverbial widows and orphans, yet all may be stockholders.

ECONOMIC AND NONECONOMIC PLANNING MEASURES

There is a school of antiplanning thought that emphasizes the indisputable fact that "we will all be dead in the long run." "So," say these antiplanners, "why should one do long-range planning?" At another level, antiplanners might argue on an economic basis. If one looks far enough into the future, the costs and benefits that lie far away on the time horizon become insignificant compared to today's costs and benefits and those to be attained in the near future. Thus, in discounted, or present-value terms,[2] these costs and benefits would not seem to be important to today's strategic choices.

Of course, this quantitative *economic* argument is valid. However, it neglects the qualitative and noneconomic aspects of strategic choice as well as the *processes* through which costs and benefits are accrued. For instance, even though the economic costs and benefits associated with a newly developing technology may well be 20 years from realization and costs and benefits that are to be realized that far in the future are small in present-value terms, strategic choices may be necessary now to ensure that they will be attained then, and not 40 years hence, or never. Logical and technological sequences of choices and events comprise the process of technology development, and despite the fact that costs and benefits may accrue far in the future, the organization may be forced to take strategic action today if it is *ever* to realize some of its objectives, e.g., to be a predominant force in a given area of technology.

In such a situation, the strategist is faced with a dilemma, since certain choices which may reflect his or her best judgment relative to the organization's objectives, may be irrational from the standpoint of pure economics. In such a case, the strategist must recognize the multidimensional nature of objectives, economic objectives being only one kind of objective in a broader array of objectives.

Moreover, if the strategist is clever enough, strategic choices can be made that will satisfy both economic and noneconomic objectives in a synergistic fashion. For example, the business could embark on incremental technological developments that have the prospect of providing interim benefits along the way toward a major technological breakthrough. If, for instance, a new product can be marketed based on some incremental technological development that is primarily viewed as a step along the way to a major breakthrough, a steam of benefits may be generated justifying the overall effort on grounds of pure economics as well.

There are therefore real logical and behavioral reasons for making explicit choices of missions objectives and strategies (the broader more comprehensive elements of strategic choice) as well as for making such choices among programs, goals, and resource allocations (those elements of strategic choice for which these needs are more generally recognized). If these explicit choices are made in an environment of secrecy by one individual or by a small group of individuals, they are unlikely to achieve these benefits. Hence, along with explicit choices goes openness and candor with regard to the chosen missions, objectives, and strategies.

[2] See any text on finance or capital budgeting for a discussion of "discounting," and "present values," e.g., Bierman, H., Jr., and Smidt, S., *The Capital Budgeting Decision: Economic Analysis and Financing of Investment Decisions,* Macmillan, New York, 1966.

The Essence of Strategic Choice—Alternatives

Formalized decision models and techniques, such as those associated with operations research and mathematical modeling, have proved to be of limited value in strategic choice. The expectations and hopes of practitioners in those fields who expected successful application of models in tactical and operational settings to be inevitably followed by similar successes at strategic level have not been borne out.

There are undoubtedly many reasons for this. However, one important reason seems to be that most models presume that the available alternatives are prescribed in advance. In effect, they are *pure choice* models, those involving the selection of the best, or a good, alternative from a *previously defined* set of alternatives.

The essence of choice in many real-world situations, and in *most* strategic choice situations, is the *development or generation of alternatives.* For instance, the multiple objectives and interests of an organization serve to suggest many possible strategies. With regard to the pricing strategy for a new product, Oxenfeldt[3] suggests some of the more commonly considered strategies:

1. Get as much profit as you can, as soon as you can.
2. Set a price that will discourage the advent of competitors.
3. Recover your development costs within a specified period.
4. Set a price that will yield your 'regular' rate of return.
5. Set a price that will win speediest acceptance of the product.
6. Use the product to enhance the sales of the entire line rather than to yield a profit on itself.

Clearly, if any one of these strategies is not considered in the choice situation, and this unconsidered strategy best incorporates an important *strategic factor,* such as the discouragement of competitors or the relationship to the rest of the line, a poor outcome may result. In such a case, the reason for the poor result of the choice is not that the choice process itself was bad, but rather that it failed to consider important alternatives.

Any pure-choice model or procedure is only as good as the set of predefined alternatives on which it operates. In tactical and operational choice situations, this is not so critical because the range of all possible, or feasible alternatives is not difficult to develop. Despite the fact that a production scheduling problem may be extremely complex and may involve a large number of alternative schedules, there are no qualitatively different alternatives that need to be considered to ensure good results. The entire range of alternatives is

[3] Oxenfeldt, A. R., *Developing a Product Strategy,* American Management Association, New York, 1959, p. 338.

specified by the many possible combinations of products, machines, and sequen-ces. *Strategic choice situations are invariably different from tactical and opera-tionsl situations in that the range of alternatives is not predefined.* Creativity, and the process of developing and specifying alternatives, therefore, plays a much more important role in strategic choice.

It is unlikely that anyone, even the strongest proponent of mathematical modeling, would take issue with this characterization of the relatively greater importance of developing alternatives, as opposed to choosing among prede-fined alternatives, in strategic choice situations. However, such modeling ad-vocates would undoubtedly validly argue that this does not in itself preclude the use of models; rather, it simply says that one must spend time and attention on developing strategic alternatives *before* using the model to guide choice.

This may be true; however, most good strategic-planning processes operate in a manner that prevents the simple separation of the two phases of alternative development and choice among alternatives. In effect, *the processes of devel-opment and choice go on concurrently.* They are not readily separable as two distinct phases of an overall decision process.

We illustrate this practical interdependence between alternative develop-ment and choice throughout this and succeeding chapters. At this point, we merely say that effective real-world strategic choice processes often have such interdependence, despite the theoretic niceties that permit one to conceptually separate the two.

This importance of alternative development in any choice process, coupled with the interdependence of alternative development and the pure-choice pro-cess in strategic situations, thus serve as partial explanations for the failure of many promising decision models to have significant impact on real-world *stra-tegic* planning.

The Complexity of Strategic Choice and the Strategic Choice Process

In addition to the complexity inherent in strategic choice because of its mul-tidimensional nature and the concurrency of the processes of developing and choosing strategies, strategic choices are the most complex of those with which an organization is faced. Primarily, this is because of the long time horizons in-volved, their typically ill-defined nature, their inherent lack of definition and structure, the difficulty in obtaining relevant information to support strategic choice, and the difficulty in defining that critical time when a choice is best made.

THE TIME HORIZON OF STRATEGIC CHOICE

One of the most important features of strategic situations is that they involve the long-range future, whereas many other planning approaches, such as "management by objectives," tend to emphasize the nearer term (usually one year hence). The questions of the appropriate time dimension for strategic choice has been much discussed in the classic literature of planning. For instance, most literature cites three to five years as the most common long-range planning term. However, if one considers the problem of determining a corporate long-range planning period, it is easily concluded that the span of an overall planning period might well be determined as any of the following:

1. The average planning period for the various functional areas of effort.
2. The longest single period of functional-area long-range planning.
3. The time period required to provide for the amassing of necessary resources.
4. An arbitrary period that in the judgment of the executive group best fits the long-range objectives of the organization.
5. A period that encompasses the most critical areas of long-range planning within the organization.
6. A period that provides for the best market advantage in terms of economic cycles and long-term growth

The above list suggests a "multi-horizon" for strategic choice. The precise period of time is less important than the determination of the *ability of the organization to realize a return on the resources that have been committed in the strategic choice process.* According to Koontz and O'Donnell:[4]

There should be some logic in selecting the right time range for company planning. In general, since planning and forecasting that underlie it are costly, a company should probably not plan for a longer period than is economically justifiable; yet it is risky to plan for a shorter period. The logical answer as to the right planning period seems to lie in the 'commitment principle,' that planning should encompass the period of time necessary to foresee (through a series of actions) the fulfillment of commitments involved in a decision.

Thus, pulp, paper, and lumber companies are required to plan in terms of a 40-year horizon, whereas a cosmetics manufacturer would have no need for such a long time frame.

Amara[5] has proposed another view of the time horizon for planning, which

---

[4] Koontz, H., and O'Donnell, C. J., *Principles of Management,* McGraw-Hill, New York, 1974, p. 87.

[5] Amara, R. C., "Some Features of the World of 1994," *The Futurist,* June 1974, pp. 129–130.

regards the future in terms of three planning periods, referred to as "inertia," "choice," and "uncertainty." For most organizations, the inertia period extends out from the present to a point that may be as many as 5 years away. This is the period over which the current situation can be extrapolated rather readily and during which change is rather difficult to effect. At least, the *impact* of *strategic choice* may have had little opportunity to be felt during this inertia period. The subsequent time period is that referred to as the period of choice. In this period, which may extend out as far as 20 years in the future, the organization's projected trajectory becomes vague, and current strategic choices will have their primary impact. The farthest out period, often extending beyond 20 years into the future, is that of greatest uncertainty. For this uncertainty period, projections are most difficult, and the impact of strategic choice is difficult to determine.

Thus, the time dimensions of strategic choice may realistically be viewed as neither entirely foreseeable nor controllable. Of course, so too is it viewed as something other than inevitable. Perhaps the best way of viewing it is in terms of our ability to *influence* the future through strategic choices made in the present.

THE TIMELINESS OF STRATEGIC CHOICE

An important aspect of strategic choice is the timeliness associated with the *choice* (as opposed to the time horizon over which the choice will have taken effect and have impact). Elsewhere, we have distinguished between time-sensitive and knowledge-sensitive decisions.[6] Time-sensitive decisions are those quick and accurate choices that are often thought of as the forté of military commanders. In such situations, there is great value to be gained from "doing something" and relatively less to be gained from making the "best" choice. When one is standing in the middle of the street with a speeding car bearing down on him, he is best advised to move, with the direction of movement being less important than the taking of the action in a timely fashion. Stragegic choices are generally knowledge-sensitive: the worth of the result is usually more dependent on the quality of the choice than on its timeliness.

The very nature of strategic systems thinking, with its emphasis on opportunities rather than problems and the future rather than the present, also means that strategic choice situations need not be addressed at a specific time. Tactical decisions often have a critical time: they must be made before the end of the month or before any action can be taken. Strategic decisions, on the other hand, often are made under no such time pressure.

---

[6]Cleland, D. I., and King, W. R., *Systems Analysis and Project Management* (2nd Ed.), McGraw-Hill, New York, 1975, pp. 64–65.

However, strategic decisions are highly uncertain in nature. They involve the (sometimes distant) future. Enough information is never available to ensure that the right choice is made. Therefore, there is every rationale for delay and procrastination until more information can be gathered and the problem or opportunity more clearly understood. Thus, the very characteristic of strategic choice that gives the planner the opportunity to decide with some leisure may be a great burden to him, since it may encourage him to delay decision pending receipt of more information. Also, since there is never enough information in the nebulous context of organizational strategic choice, this opportunity for delay can have the devastating effect of ensuring that strategic choices are not made.

Of course, the alternative of no choice is, in reality, a choice itself, a selection of the status quo or of the inevitable future from the range of available alternative strategies. Thus, the strategist who procrastinates has made a passive choice just as surely as has the one who actively chooses, since it is just as binding and plays just as great a role in influencing the future.

THE DIFFICULTY IN DEFINING AND SOLVING STRATEGIC PROBLEMS

The inherent difficulty that exists in defining and solving strategic problems is made clear by Rivlin[7] in the context of strategic social programs. To make informed strategic decisions concerning social programs, she says we need to answer such questions as:

1. How do we define the problems and how are they (the problems) distributed? Who is poor or sick or inadequately educated?
2. Who would be helped by specific social action programs, and how much?
3. What would do the most good? How do the benefits of different kinds of programs compare?
4. How can particular kinds of social services be produced most effectively?

In effect, Rivlin says that in social programs (and in much of strategic choice) the issues to be decided are not themselves well defined and that the distribution of the costs and benefits that result from strategic choices to various clientele groups is difficult to determine. Moreover, even when we know what the problems are and how the benefits and costs might be apportioned to interest groups for the various available alternative choices, it is difficult to compare across programs and to develop and choose among alternatives.

[7] See Rivlin, A. M., *Systematic Thinking for Social Action*, The Brookings Institution, Washington, D.C., 1971, pp. 6–7, and her many references.

These observations clearly hold true for social programs, those in which a public body attempts to alter the behavior or status of various social groups. In those situations, myths have been created about what the real problems are and how various clientele groups might be affected by social programs under consideration. Perhaps the classic case of this is the myths dealing with the poor, who they are and what their motivations may be. Some people believe that the poor, or welfare recipients as the case may be, are shiftless people who have no desire to work and are using welfare and other social programs to live in comfort without working. Under this description of the problem, increases in welfare may simply stimulate more people to collect checks and not work, the result being an overall decline in the work ethic and our nation's moral fiber. Moreover, under this view, increases in welfare benefits are drunk up by shiftless parents rather than translated into food for needy children or improved education or other worthy things.

Another view of the problem sees the poor as being largely composed of disabled, hard-core unemployed, mothers with dependent children, etc. This view of the problem may lead to a quite different analysis of the distribution of benefits from welfare programs. Under this view, increases in welfare lead to healthier children, opportunities for enrichment, and other things that are desirable for society as well as for the individuals who are aided.

These two stereotypical extremes are suggested to indicate the depth of difficulty that is indeed involved in identifying the problem in strategic-choice situations, as well as the distribution of costs and benefits that would accrue to various parties of interest.

At the next lowest level of strategic choice, it is extremely difficult to compare predicted actions *across programs,* even if one is able to obtain a clear definition of what the problem is and how benefits and costs might be distributed from various social-program alternatives. For instance, how does one compare the educational benefits predicted to result from an educational program with the mortality decreases that might result from a highway-safety campaign or a speed-limit change? Moreover, how does one compare the same educational benefit, in the one case, to a teenager and in the other case to a golden-ager? Is a new level of education of the same worth in both cases?

Much has been written and discussed concerning these problems in the social program area. However, *these general characteristics are true of many strategic choice situations* in business, industry, and other not-for-profit contexts as well. The difficulty in identifying the problem is often just as great for a business. Is the problem the lack of sales of a new product, is it the advertising theme that is the real problem, is it the product design that is being rejected by the consumers, or is it any one of the many other things that might be significantly influencing sales?

The authors recently participated as consultants in a high-level meeting of executives and staff people from a major United States corporation which was called to develop the recommendation to the board of directors on the strategy to be adopted for a subsidiary firm whose performance had been below par for some time. During this meeting, strategies ranging from outright sale of the subsidiary to cut losses through a variety of product-change strategies, to a simple cost-cutting strategy were proposed and championed by various managers. Such a range of strategies suggested that even at the late date when a final choice was being faced, many of those who had participated in lengthy studies and discussions did not agree on what the problem was. Thus, in the business field, where everything is supposed to be much simpler than in social areas, the same lack of definition of the problem prevailed.

Even in the area of comparisons across programs, the bottom-line profit measure of business is often not a greatly simplifying factor. The diverse clientele, not all of whom are seeking profit, ensures that the business strategic choice situation is as complex as are social-change contexts.

Strategic Choice Elements and Their Relationships

The simple conceptual model of Figure 6.1 shows the critical elements of organizational purpose and direction and their relationship as they were defined in Chapter 2, and as they are used in this book. The figure represents an operationally useful way of defining the various elements of organizational purpose

FIGURE 6.1 Relationship of Strategic Choice Elements.

and direction. These elements of strategic choice and their interrelationships are important to developing an understanding of the complexity of strategic choice and the need for a planning system for dealing with this complexity.

Since detailed definitions and illustrations of each of the elements of the figure have previously been given, we shall primarily confine ourselves here to the *relationships among these elements* and the need for explicit delineation of each. In subsequent chapters, we deal with operational decision processes for explicating and choosing among alternative strategic choice elements, whether they are alternative mission concepts, alternative objectives, alternative strategies, or alternative allocations of resources.

At the apex of the pyramid in Figure 6.1 is the organization's *mission,* its basic purpose and the definition of the business that it is in. Within the scope of the mission, broader and more comprehensive *objectives* must be developed. These objectives specify the positions or "destinations" that the organization desires to reach in fulfilling its mission. Based directly on these objectives the organization chooses its strategy (general direction), goals (specific targets), and programs (objective- or goal-focused collections of activities). Figure 6.1 shows that objectives are directly based on the chosen mission. In turn, strategies, goals, and programs are derived from objectives. A strategy may be oriented toward the accomplishment of a single objective, or an array of objectives. Goals are more detailed and specific states to be achieved within the framework of objectives and strategy. Programs may relate to goals or objectives or both.[8]

Figure 6.2 shows a more detailed version of the triangular format of Figure 6.1, with illustrative entries representing the strategic elements for a business firm.

MISSION AND OBJECTIVES. At the top of the hierarchy is the mission, illustrated in Figure 6.2 in terms of an air-conditioner-system components producer. Underlying this mission statement are objectives in three areas that this firm has chosen to emphasize, return on investment, dividends, and image. The ROI objective is stated quantitatively (14.5%), but without a time dimension. The other objectives are stated qualitatively ("more" and "nondecreasing"). In the case of the dividend objective, the index, or measurement that reflects the objective is clear, "dollars per share of dividends"; in the other case, image, the index is not specified.

STRATEGY. Supporting the base of the triangle are strategies, goals, and programs. The firm's strategies are stated in terms of a three-phase approach. First, the company will concentrate on achieving its objectives through existing

[8] Granger, C. H., "The Hierarchy of Objectives," *Harvard Business Review,* May–June 1964, provides a more detailed delineation of the various levels of organizational purpose and direction.

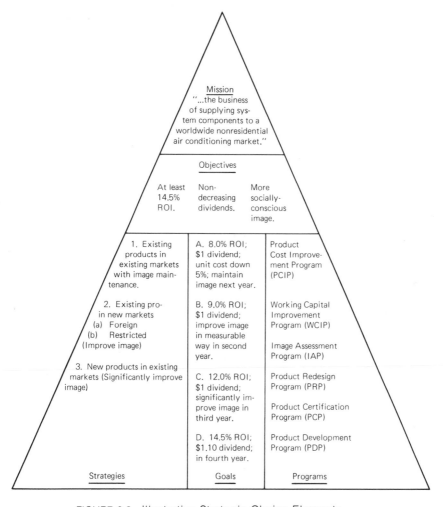

FIGURE 6.2 Illustrative Strategic Choice Elements.

products and markets while maintaining its existing image. Then, it will give attention to new markets for existing products, foreign and restricted,[9] while improving the company's image. Finally, it will focus on new products in existing markets while *significantly* improving its image.

Clearly, this is a staged strategy, one that focuses attention first on one

---

[9] "Restricted" markets may be thought of as those that require product-safety certification before the product can be sold in that market.

thing and then on another. This staging does not imply that the first strategy element is carried through completely before the second is begun; it merely means that the first element is given primary and earliest attention, then the second and third in turn. In effect, the first element of the strategy has its implementation *begun* first. This will be made more clear in terms of goals and programs.

PROGRAMS. At the right base of the triangle, a number of the firm's *programs* are identified. Each of these programs is made up of a variety of projects or activities. Each program serves as a focus for various activities having a common goal. For instance, in the case of the Product Cost Improvement Program, the associated projects and activities might be as follows:

Quality Control Project

Production Planning Improvement Project

Production Control System Development Project

Plant Layout Redesign Project

Employee Relations Project

All of these projects and activities are focused toward the *single* goal of product cost improvement.

In the case of the Working Capital Improvement Program, the various projects and activities might include a "terms and conditions" study aimed at revising the terms and conditions under which goods are sold, an inventory reduction project, etc. Each of the other programs would have a similar collection of projects and activities focused on some single well-defined goal.

GOALS. The goals are listed in the middle-lower portion of the triangle in Figure 6.2. Each goal is stated in specific and timely terms related to the staged strategy and the various programs. These goals reflect the desire to attain 8.0% ROI (a step along the way to the 14.5% objective) next year, along with a $1 dividend (the current level), a unit cost improvement of 5%, while maintaining image. For subsequent years, the goals reflect a climb to 14.5% ROI, a steady and then increasing dividend, and an increasing and measurable image consistent with the staged strategy that places image improvements later in the staged sequence. This is also consistent with the program structure, which includes an "Image Assessment Program," a program designed to develop methods and measures for quantitatively assessing the company's image.

RELATIONSHIPS AMONG THE STRATEGIC CHOICE ELEMENTS

Figure 6.3 shows the same elements as does Figure 6.2, with each being indicated by number, letter, or acronym. For instance, the block labeled 1 in Figure

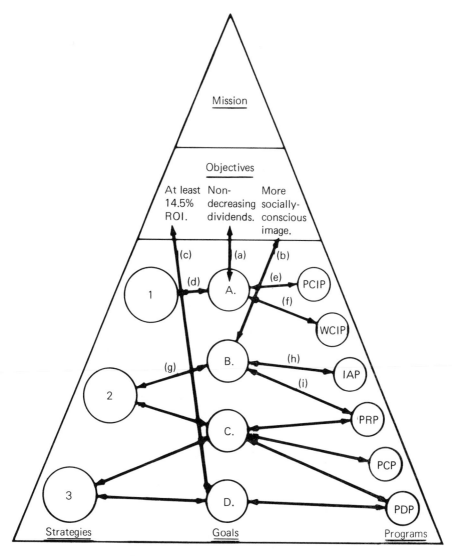

FIGURE 6.3 Relationships Among Illustrative Choice Elements.

6.3 represents the first stage of the strategy in Figure 6.2, the letter A represents next year's goals.

The arrows in Figure 6.3 represent *some* illustrative relationships among the various objectives, programs, strategy elements, and goals. For instance, the arrows a, b, and c reflect direct relationships between specific timely goals and broad timeless objectives:

    a. A, next year's goals primarily relate to the objective of nondecreasing dividends

    b. B, the second year's goals relate to the "more socially conscious image" objective

    c. D, the quantitative ROI figure is incorporated as a goal in the fourth year

Of course, each year's goals relate implicitly or explicitly to all objectives. However, these relationships are the most direct and obvious.

Similarly, arrow d in Figure 6.3 relates the first year's goals to the first element of the overall strategy in that these goals for next year are to be attained primarily through the strategy element involving "existing products in existing markets." However, arrows e and f also show that the Product Cost Improvement Program (PCIP) and the Working Capital Improvement Program (WCIP) are also expected to contribute to the achievement of next year's goals.

The second year's goals will begin to reflect the impact of the second strategy element (existing products in new markets) as indicated by arrow g in Figure 6.3. The effect of the Product Redesign Program (PRP) is also expected to contribute to the achievement of these goals (arrow i) as is the Image Assessment Program (IAP) expected to provide an ability to measure image by that time. The other arrows in Figure 6.3 depict other rather direct relationships whose interpretation is left to the reader.

From this figure, relationships among the various strategic decision elements can be seen:

1. Goals are specific steps along the way to the accomplishment of broad objectives.
2. Goals are established to reflect the expected outputs from strategies.
3. Goals are directly achieved through programs.
4. Strategies are implemented by programs.

Thus, the picture shown in Figure 6.3 is that of an interrelated set of strategic factors that demonstrate both *what* the company wishes to accomplish in the long run, *how* it will do this in a sequenced and sensible way, and *what performance levels* it wishes to achieve at various points along the way.

In subsequent chapters, we shall investigate the strategic choice process in terms of each of these critical elements (missions, objectives, strategies programs, and goals) and the allocations of resources that reflect the final output of the strategic choice process.

Summary

Planning inherently involves strategic decision making. Hence, it requires that strategic choices be made. Such choices will be made by every organization in either an explicit or implicit manner. Formalized planning merely ensures that they will be dealt with in an explicit fashion so that unanimity of purpose can be achieved, personnel can be motivated, and the other lower-level decisions of the organization can be guided in a direction that best suits the organization's purpose.

Strategic choice differs from other levels of choice in that it does not generally involve only the selection of one alternative from a set; rather, it simultaneously involves both the development and selection of alternatives. Thus, strategic choice is inherently complex. However, other elements of strategic choice, such as the long time horizons that may be involved, the lack of clear definition of the problems and issues, and the nebulous nature of the time at which choices are best made, serve to make such choices even more complex.

The interrelationships of the various strategic choice elements (missions, objectives, strategies, programs, and goals) also serve to heighten the difficulty of strategic choice. These relationships demonstrate why an overall strategic systems planning approach is vital if consistent choices are to be made for the various inter-related elements of strategic purpose and direction.

Chapter 6—Questions and Exercises

1. Planning is described in this chapter as decision making. What is the justification for this statement?
2. What arguments could one present to keep organizational missions, objectives, and strategies implicit rather than explicit?
3. What are some of the values that can accrue to an organization by going through an explicit delineation of missions, objectives, and strategies?
4. How are explicit objectives, strategies, and goals in an organization related to the control system of the organization?
5. What is meant by the "curse of multidimensionality" in dealing with organizational objectives?
6. Most organizations have multiple clients or stakeholders. What is a client or stakeholder? Select an organization of your choice and identify the multiple clients that are associated with it.
7. Certain strategic choices may dictate that criteria rather than the economics of a situation be considered. Defend or refute this statement.
8. What is the value in developing or generating several alternatives to consider in making a strategic choice?
9. Select an organization of your choosing and identify some of the strategic choices that the organization faces.

10. What should be the appropriate time horizons of strategic choices for an organization? What are some criteria to use in determining the time horizon of a strategic choice?
11. What is the distinction to be drawn between time-sensitive and knowledge-sensitive decisions? What are some examples of each type of decision?
12. There is never enough information available to a decision maker who is dealing with an organizational strategic choice. Why is this so?
13. Explain the model for a hierarchy of organizational purpose and direction. Explain the interrelationships of the elements in this hierarchy.
14. In your life experience can you identify some choices that faced you that were implicit in nature? Explicit in nature?
15. What is the value to having organizational purposes, missions, objectives, goals, strategies, etc., made in such a way that maximum participation of the people in the organization is involved?
16. What criteria might be used by a planner to determine if the right problem has been identified in his management of the organization?
17. How can it be argued that even the simple measure "profit" is itself a multidimensional performance measure?
18. What are some alternative product pricing strategies that a firm might consider? What are some of the product quality strategies that it might consider? How would each of these be related to various different objectives that the firm might have?
19. Start with any program in Figure 6.2 and trace the relationships to each other element of that diagram that you can reasonably infer.
20. Start with the ROI objective in Figure 6.2 and trace the relationships to each other element as in Question 19.

Chapter 7—Strategic Questions for the Manager

1. In the experience of your organization, have historical choices that have emerged been mostly *implicit* or *explicit?* Why?
2. Is there any evidence that suggests opportunities have not been exploited or problems have been ignored because of management's failure to state objectives, goals, strategies, and programs in explicit terms?
3. Have organizational objectives been stated in multidimensional terms?
4. Considering the proprietary factor, have organizational purposes, missions, objectives, goals, strategies, and programs been made in sufficient openness and candor that management participation in realizing these purposes can be facilitated?
5. What has been the success (or failure) of formal decision models and techniques in the organization? Why?
6. Is strategic choice as practiced in the organization accompanied by a range of predefined alternatives?
7. Does the "organizational culture" help to encourage the development of alternatives as a prerequisite to strategic choice?
8. What is the appropriate time horizon for strategic choice in the organization? What is the basis for this time horizon?

9. What criteria do I use to help me to determine if the right problem has been identified in the management of my organization?
10. Do the key managers understand the relationships among the key strategic choice elements in their organizational responsibilities?

References

Ansoff, H. I., "Managing Strategic Surprise by Response to Weak Signals," *California Management Review,* Winter 1975.

Cornelissen, J. A., "Corporate Strategies in the Eighties," *Long Range Planning,* Oct. 1977.

Haggerty, P. E., "Strategies, Tactics and Research," *Research Management,* Vol. IX, 1966.

Hammerton, J. C., "Management and Motivation," *California Management Review,* Vol. XIII, Winter 1970.

Hargreaves, D., "Corporate Planning: A Chairman's Guide," *Long Range Planning,* March 1969.

Hobbs, J. M., and Heany, D. F., Coupling Strategy to Operating Plans," *Harvard Business Review,* May–June 1977.

Hussey, D. E., "Strategic Planning in International Business," *Long Range Planning,* June 1972.

Kahn, H., and Wiener, A. T., *The Year 2000,* Macmillan, New York, 1967.

King, W. R., "Human Judgment and Management Decision Analysis," *Journal of Industrial Engineering,* Vol. 18, Dec. 1967.

Leyshon, A. M., "Marketing Planning and Corporate Planning," *Long Range Planning,* Feb. 1976.

Mockler, R. J., "Theory and Practice of Planning," *Harvard Business Review,* March–April 1970.

Prahalad, C. K., "Strategic Choices in Diversified MNCs," *Harvard Business Review,* July–Aug. 1976.

Toffler, A., *Future Shock,* Random House, New York, 1970.

Rutenberg, D. T., "Planning for a Multi-National Synergy," *Long Range Planning,* December 1969.

Schoeffler, S., Buzzell, R. D., and Heany, D. F., "Impact of Strategic Planning on Profit Performance," *Harvard Business Review,* March–April 1974.

Wind, Y., and Clycamp, H. J., "Planning Product Line Strategy: A Matrix Approach," *Journal of Marketing,* January 1976.

ESTABLISHING
ORGANIZATIONAL
MISSIONS AND
OBJECTIVES

The questions and issues relating to organizational missions and objectives are among the most discussed and argued areas of strategic planning. On the one hand are those who argue that the organization's missions and objectives are obvious and that great time and attention need not be paid to explicating them. "We build widgets," or, "The clear and sole mission of business is to make a profit," are often-heard. Another viewpoint says that organizations don't even have objectives: individuals have objectives.[1] Those with still another viewpoint would attempt to prescribe what the objectives of various organizations *ought* to be, e.g., "Business should be socially responsible." These diverse illustrative views, involving the highly connotative terms "obvious," "nonexistent," and "ought," suggest the diversity of opinion concerning organizational missions and objectives.

In this chapter and in succeeding ones, the various strategic decision elements are treated within the context of strategic choice as developed in Chapter 6; namely, that insofar as possible, missions, objectives, strategies, goals, programs, and resource allocations should be chosen explicitly and objectively.

In these several chapters, the various strategic decision elements are treated hierarchically, beginning here with the broadest levels—missions and objectives. However, since the various strategic choice elements are so interdependent, they cannot readily be considered separately. This means that the methods or techniques that we discuss in each chapter are not limited in their applicability to the particular level of choice under which they are discussed.

Developing and Choosing the Organization's Mission

The broadest choice that the organization must make is the choice of its basic purpose, the business that it is in. Although little in the way of a formal procedure for such a choice can be prescribed, and despite the fact that the organization should not redefine its basic mission on nearly so frequent a basis as its

---

[1] See Cyert, R. and March, J., *A Behavioral Theory of the Firm*, Prentice-Hall, Englewood Cliffs, N.J., 1963.

strategies, the primary mistakes that have been made by organizations in their selection of a mission have been in treating their basic purpose as being obvious or predetermined. The discussion of missions in Chapter 3 has provided illustrations of this.

So, although mission choice is of obvious importance and among the most highly unstructured decisions that an organization must make, it should be dealt with explicitly, rather than implicitly, if strategic errors in business definitions are to be avoided. The critical question is: "How can this be done?" There is, of course, no simple answer to this question, but one proposition appears to be clear. *Organizations that do not discuss their basic mission and purpose will inevitably lose whatever consensus may have once existed among its members as to their common purpose.*

This is so because of personnel turnover as well as environmental changes that serve to subtly divert an organization from a previously chosen direction. For instance, a graduate-level educational institution discovered that it had not discussed and debated its mission, its underlying educational philosophy, and its allowable scope for over a decade. Few people in the organization had been present 10 years earlier and it had become obvious that a series of new programs, changes in existing programs, as well as subtle changes in technique and emphases made by individual faculty members had cumulatively served to alter the mission and direction of the organization. When this became apparent, a series of discussion sessions was planned to ensure that the organization's mission would be the result of conscious choice and that the result of this choice process would be known to all participants.

Thus, the first precept of mission choice is that *the alternatives should be openly developed and discussed among organizational participants.* If this is done in some formal way, it can serve both to vitiate the effects of personnel changes and to permit the organization to consciously consider alternatives and thereby modify its mission through explicit, rather than implicit, choice.

Of course, this does not mean that unanimity or consensus is to be expected; indeed, such a result may be impossible to achieve. It does not even mean that some democratic choice procedure is necessarily to be followed. Rather, it indicates that *alternatives* are to be made explicit, evaluated, and discussed within the organization and that participants will be given a hearing in terms of their personal expectations and beliefs about what "their" organization should be.

If, when a mission choice is made, all do not agree, no one should be surprised. *One of the primary values of explicit statements of mission and objectives is that they provide a rallying point for those who can ally themselves with them and a clear indication to those who cannot that they might wish to consider alternative organizations as the source of their economic and psychic satisfactions.*

Several approaches to the structuring of mission-related organizational discussions have proved to be useful. Among these are techniques known as "brainstorming," "focus groups," "alternative futures and scenarios," and "Policy Delphi." None of these approaches are useful only at the mission level of strategic choice. Indeed, such techniques as the use of scenarios usually involve both the development and use of a combination of organizational missions and strategies.

BRAINSTORMING

One technique that has been used successfully in generating new alternatives is known as "brainstorming." In a brainstorming session, a group is called together and encouraged to discuss possible new alternatives, e.g., new missions for the organization.

The focus of a brainstorming session is the creation of new ideas, so that out-of-the-blue thinking aloud is encouraged. No critical analysis of idea is permitted, although it is hoped that each wild idea may lead to another and perhaps eventually to a radical idea that has merit. The interaction of the individual members of the group is believed to have a stimulating effect. Often during later analysis, although most of the recorded ideas put forth in the brainstorming session are discarded as impractical, a few ideas that merit study are uncovered. Some who have participated in apparently fruitless sessions have felt that, at the very least, the sessions served to open new avenues of thought in the minds of individuals who might later produce meritorious ideas.

Pseudosophisticates may consider the technique of brainstorming to be old hat. Indeed, there is no scientific evidence that it really is a valid methodology, particularly at the level of generality of organizational mission definition. Nonetheless, the pragmatist will find that the basic idea is both useful and used (although the term "brainstorming" may not always be applied). A good illustration of its utility is the important role it has played in the operations of the Van Dyck Corporation, which specializes in devising new products for clients such as Olin Mathieson, J. C. Penney, and Textron. *Business Week* describes Van Dyck's brainstorming session as follows[2]:

> The staff bats around ideas, and scrawls them down on scraps of paper, which are tossed into a huge fishbowl. . . . Any idea goes in if it has aroused even a glimmer of response from the group. Later on, a two-man team—always one engineer and one industrial designer—cull out the most promising candidates.

Other brainstorming approaches may also be effective in developing alternative missions for organizational consideration. Focus groups often make use of edited tape recordings or some other medium so that the key elements of the

[2]*Business Week,* July 2, 1966, pp. 52–54.

brainstorming sessions of one group can be displayed to a second group before it begins its session. In this way, each group is able to build on the thoughts of the prior groups and to get into the spirit of the brainstorming concept more readily. It also enables the group administrator to identify common threads that run through the various groups.

In the context of mission definition, brainstorming represents one model that can be used for group invention of alternative organizational missions. If it is complemented with subsequent evaluation sessions, it can serve as a vehicle for introducing mission-oriented debate into the organization.[3]

ALTERNATIVE FUTURES AND SCENARIOS

The idea of "alternative futures" is associated with the area of "futurism." Although this field is sometimes viewed in a way that suggests a combination of astrology, mysticism, and fakery, it is a valid area of inquiry, which has produced concepts and techniques that have been useful to a wide variety of organizations.

The concept of alternative futures is broader than that of scenarios since scenarios, or "future histories," are but one way of generating alternative futures for later discussion and analysis. However, for our discussion here, a focus on scenarios will serve to fulfill the purpose of demonstrating how both the concept and the technique may be applied.

Scenarios are attempts to describe in detail a sequence of events that could plausibly lead to a prescribed end state or alternately, to consider the possible outcomes of present choices. Usually, scenarios are heavily qualitative, but nonetheless detailed. Their particular advantage is to permit the integrated consideration of many diverse factors. For instance, a specific corporate mission and its associated strategy and programs may be explored in terms of a scenario involving societal change, competitive reactions, regulatory change, etc. Thus, the scenario becomes a structured way of considering the overall system in a way that no abstract technique can hope to do.

The best known use of scenarios is undoubtedly the work of Kahn and Weiner who applied them on a worldwide scope.[4] Scenarios have been used in organizational planning to explore the consequences of current choices of missions, objectives, strategies, and programs as they will impact on, and be impacted by, a complex environment. Zentner[5] reports that a search of English language business literature over a five year period resulted in 33 articles dis-

---

[3] See Rosenstein, A. J., "Quantitative—Yes Quantitative—Applications for the Focus Group, or What Do You Mean You Never Heard of 'Multivariate Focus Groups'?" *Marketing News,* May 21, 1976, p. 8.

[4] Kahn, H., and Weiner, A. J., *The Year 2000,* Macmillan, New York, 1967.

[5] Zentner, R. D., "Scenarios in Forecasting," *C & E News,* Oct. 6, 1975, pp. 23–24.

cussing applications of scenarios involving such diverse issues as the future of the actuarial profession, government agricultural policy, the role of management in dealing with governmental intervention, the seizure of Arab oil, bank assets and liabilities, the pulp and paper industry, and world energy systems. Since most uses of scenarios by business firms are proprietary in nature, they appear less frequently in public literature,[6] but firms such as General Electric, Monsanto, and Shell Oil are known to use the approach in planning.

Although scenarios may be useful for consideration of environmental factors only, their use in mission development and selection is enhanced if they are developed to integrate organizational mission and strategy choices with uncontrollable forces. In this way one is able to deal with details, dynamics, and subjective considerations; a level of richness and complexity that is difficult to achieve with other structured approaches. The scenario approach to alternative futures for the organization thereby has the advantages of objectivity and structure without the disadvantages of high degrees of abstraction.

If used appropriately, scenarios can serve to focus attention on missions and strategies that will *not* be fruitful, particularly those that may seem to be good in the short run while producing poor second-order consequences. For instance, a business firm's scenario might show that the long run effect of not being in a particular business could be the stimulation of competitors who would be likely to develop capabilities that would in turn make them viable potential competitors for other businesses in which the firm currently engages.

The concept of *alternative* futures implies that more than one scenario will be developed. Through the development of at least several credible and understandable scenarios, the organization can begin to see the impact of various missions and strategies as they interrelate with each other and with the environment. Of course, if the missions and strategies to be used involve many different dimensions, a large number of scenarios may be required. However, since scenario development is valuable as a learning device as well as for the output produced, and since the ongoing utility of scenarios to managers may be inversely related to their number, a few would appear to be adequate to begin with. After the technique has become accepted and found to be strategically useful, a wide range of scenarios can be introduced into the planning process.

POLICY DELPHI

The Delphi approach, which has previously been discussed in Chapter 5 in terms of its use in forecasting, can also be used in a *normative* framework to aid the organization in establishing its mission and objectives. The Delphi

[6] For instance, see Noland, et. al., "The Computerization of the ABC Widget Company," *Datamation,* April 1974, p. 71.

approach was developed in the context of forecasting numerical variables and most uses of the approach have indeed involved the forecasting of dates, quantities, and other numerical entities.

However, the normative uses of the approach are concerned with group choice of *desirable,* rather than probable, future states.[7] The mechanics of the "Policy Delphi" approach are largely the same as when it is used in the exploratory forecasting mode: participants are chosen for their expertise, they respond anonymously to questionnaires, statistical results and supporting arguments are recycled, and eventual consensus is sought.

The Policy Delphi is an organized way of correlating different viewpoints and information pertaining to a mission or policy area. The participants can, as with any Delphi, assess and react to the views of others. The approach can be used to ensure that feasible missions are not overlooked, to estimate the future consequences of various mission alternatives, or to assess the desirability and organizational acceptability of proposed missions.

Turoff[8] has described a Policy Delphi in terms of six phases:

1. Formulation of the issues. What is the issue that really should be under consideration? How should it be stated?
2. Exposing the options. Given the issue, what are the policy options available?
3. Determining initial positions on the issues. Which are the ones everyone already agrees upon and which are the unimportant ones to be discarded? Which are the ones exhibiting disagreement among the respondents?
4. Exploring and obtaining the reasons for disagreements. What underlying assumptions, views, or facts are being used by the individuals to support their respective positions?
5. Evaluating the underlying reasons. How does the group view the separate arguments used to defend various positions and how do they compare to one another on a relative basis?
6. Reevaluating the options. Reevaluation is based upon the views of the underlying "evidence" and the assessment of its relevance to each position taken.

When Delphi is used for establishing organizational missions or objectives, it represents a formalized approach to the process of negotiating and consensus-

[7] For instance, see Uhl, N. P., "Encouraging Convergence of Opinion Through the Use of the Delphi Technique in the Process of Identifying an Institution's Goals," Educational Testing Service, Princeton, N.J., 1971.

[8] Turoff, M., "The Policy Delphi," *The Delphi Method: Techniques and Applications* H. A. Linstone, and M. Turoff, (editors), Addison Wesley, Reading, Mass., 1975.

seeking that Cyert and March[9] found to be descriptive of the way organizations informally operate. Thus, the Delphi process may well enhance the efficiency, effectiveness, or equity in that process, since it, in effect, simulates the informal processes that already take place.

Of course, consensus on missions or objectives does not ensure that they are wisely chosen. This is a problem with Delphi, as it is with every other approach to mission determination and objective setting.[10]

Concepts of Business Objectives

A review of some of the concepts that relate to appropriate objectives for one familiar kind of organization, the business firm, will facilitate consideration of appropriate processes and methods for selecting objectives for any organization.

PROFITABILITY AS A BUSINESS OBJECTIVE

The concept of profit, or profitability (return on resources), is basic to most people's idea of business objectives, but it is generally agreed to be of limited usefulness, particularly with regard to long-range planning. Profit in any particular time period is a product of an accounting system and is readily manipulable by accountants using various accounting approaches. Despite the auditor's use of the term "generally accepted accounting principles," which laymen take to mean that the right, or correct, accounting principles have been applied, most managers know that there are a wide variety of accounting approaches that may be used by any firm. These various approaches are likely to produce quite different overall results in any given year. Thus, when a new corporate leader promises the stockholders an immediate return to profitability, knowledgeable people view the situation with possible alarm, precisely because they know that he may well accomplish his goal through accounting changes. Such changes often can lead to improved near-term results at the expense of the long-run.

If profit, or profitability, is allowed to become the sole objective of the firm, it will almost inevitably lead to the deterioration of the firm over the long run. Emphasis will be placed on the sales of existing products using existing resources, and concern with investment for future returns will be minimized.

---

[9] Cyert, R. M., and March, J. G., *A Behavioral Theory of the Firm*, Prentice Hall, Englewood Cliffs, N.J., 1963, Chapter 3.

[10] See Sackman, H., *Delphi Critique*, Lexington Books, New York, 1975; also Weaver, W. T., "Delphi: A Critical Review," EPRC Research Rept. RR-7, Educational Policy Research Center, Syracuse University Research Corporation, Syracuse, N.Y., 1972.

Thus, while profit, or profitability, must be a prime objective of business firms, it must be only one of an array of performance measures in terms at which objectives are stated and against which progress is measured.

THE ROLE OF ORGANIZATIONAL CLIENTELE IN BUSINESS OBJECTIVES

A basic foundation of many more sophisticated concepts of objectives is the clientele groups, claimants or "stakeholders," of the organization.[11] Even the most parochial of business firms would agree that it has responsibilities to its stockholders, managers, and employees. Beyond these groups are the contractual arrangements that exist with suppliers, distributors, and supporting service organizations such as advertising agencies. Some would argue that such ties are purely legal and limited, as spelled out in the written contract, but they are nonetheless real, and must be considered by the organization in selecting its objectives and strategies. Moreover, they are in fact not strictly limited in many instances, as in the case of a firm's moral obligations to a supplier for whom one has been the single dominant customer for many years.

The claims of various interest groups, public agencies, and the public at large, all somewhat difficult to make explicit, are nonetheless very real to those business firms that have experienced delays, legal battles, picketing, and the "harassment" of government agencies as a consequence of their failure to explicitly consider these clientele.

If the diverse objectives of various claimants are to be considered by the business firm, or any organization, in determining their own objectives, some methodology is essential. Otherwise, consideration of clientele may be reduced to vague musings about "what they want to get out of us." Later in this chapter, we shall present such a methodology.

INDIVIDUAL VALUES IN BUSINESS OBJECTIVES

Another dimension of the diverse clientele idea has to do with the individuals who comprise the organization. The notion of organizational participants, each with different personal values and motivations, is pervasive.[12] Cyert and March[9] and others argue that *organizational* objectives are not really meaningful except as they reflect some consensus among the different personal objectives of organizational participants. The idea of the *interdependence of personal and organizational values* is basic to their "behavioral theory of the firm."

---

[11] Among those who have taken this viewpoint are Churchman, C. W., *The Systems Approach,* Dell Publishing Co., New York, and McConnell, J. D., "Strategic Planning: One Workable Approach," *Long Range Planning,* Dec. 1971, p. 3.

[12] For instance, Galbraith, J. K., *The New Industrial State,* Houghton-Mifflin, Boston, 1967.

One might sum up these multiple clientele notions with a gross simplification suggesting that organizational objectives must be thought of to be complex. No simple notion of profit, or anything else, will adequately describe the objectives of any very complex organization, and no simple notion will probably be adequate to prescribe what an organization's objectives *should* be.

THE COMPLEX SYSTEM OF OBJECTIVES

In recognizing the need for a sophisticated collection of organizational objectives in order to adequately respond to a complex environment, many management theorists have suggested appropriate objectives to subsume or complement profitability. Survival or growth are often mentioned as basic objectives of business as well as other organizations. These are usually coupled with the idea of a *minimum acceptable level of earnings*.[12] Others suggest *gross earnings* as opposed to the classic net earnings, as an appropriate measure in which objectives are, or should be stated. Organizational size, in terms of number of personnel, is a related growth-oriented measure.[13]

If one considers the various members of the organization as individual clientele, their individual objectives become of primary concern. Since individual objectives may be diverse, theorists have focused on *processes* for translating individual objectives into organizational objectives. For instance, Galbraith,[12] Cyert and March,[9] and others have focused on the processes of *identification* (the process by which individuals adopt the group's goals as one's own) and *adaptation* (the process by which the individual attempts to influence the organization's goals). Cyert and March[9] have described a bargaining process involving coalitions of individuals and "side payments" among individuals to assure support as indicative of the manner in which organizational purposes are actually determined.

Whatever view one takes of proper organizational objectives, it becomes increasingly clear that only a complex system of objectives will suffice for even the simplest organization. Moreover, even though the clientele concept must be central to such a system, other organizational objectives must also come into play.

A Systems Model of Organizational Objectives

The recognition that any organization must either implicitly or explicitly operate with a complex framework of purposes leads one to think in terms of a *systems model of organizational objectives*. Such a model can provide insight

---

[13] Churchman, C. W., *The Systems Approach*, Dell, New York, 1968.

into the array of objectives, their interrelationships, and an operational process for explicating objectives and measuring progress toward their achievement.

Such a systems model is shown in Fig. 7.1. There, the organization is depicted in the central rectangle. The horizontal arrows indicate the organization's role as a *processor,* or transformer, of inputs into outputs. Whether these inputs are materials, information, energy, or all three, any organization can be viewed as a black box in this fashion.

In addition to the primary purpose of satisfying clientele, every organization must choose objectives with regard to the efficient utilization of these inputs and in terms of the output that it produces. For instance, "product cost" as related to some standard is a basic measure of the efficiency of input utilization, and "product mix" and "price" are measures related to the output objective.

Figure 7.1 also shows objectives related to the "acquisition of resources" and to "organizational development." Measures related to the desired levels of acquisition of capital, people, equipment, etc., reflect the former, whereas measures such as "retained earnings" and "personnel training expenses" reflect investments in the organization's future.

The organization itself is shown to have the objective of "behaving rationally." This means that in addition to the other more specific objectives, or-

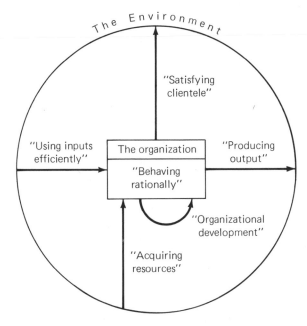

FIGURE 7.1 Systems Model of Organizational Objectives.

ganizational personnel generally wish to feel that they are observing laws and regulations, using good management techniques, and up-to-date technologies. Such an abstract model may be useful for developing an understanding of the complex of organizational objectives and for ensuring completeness in one's consideration of objectives.

However, something more is obviously needed to turn the systems model of Figure 7.1 into an operational guide. In subsequent sections of this chapter, we shall provide such an operational spproach, beginning with the basic objective of satisfying clientele.

Establishing Organizational Purposes and Directions

The concept of organizational clientele is basic to the establishment of specific statements of organizational purpose and direction. However, most discussion of the organization's clientele is at the motherhood and sin level which abounds with pontifications about the importance of considering the myriad clientele groups. Here, we seek to provide an operational framework within which the organization can analyze its clientele structure and incorporate this analysis into its strategic planning.

This operational framework is made up of a number of steps:

1. Identification of claimants and their claims.
2. Refining the basic claimant definitions.
3. Assessing claims.
4. Using the claimant analysis in establishing objectives.

IDENTIFICATION OF CLAIMANTS AND THEIR CLAIMS

The first step in the utilization of a claimant approach to establishing organizational purposes and directions is the identification of claimant groups. *Claimants are individuals, groups, or institutions who have a demand for something due from the organization.*

Ordinarily at most a few individuals need be considered explicitly. For instance, a primary stockholder or a retired chief executive may be of such influence that it will be propitious to identify the individual and to explicitly consider his claim. Normally, claimant groups, *groups of individuals who are relatively homogeneous with regard to the demands that they place on the organization,* will be of prime concern.

Table 7.1, shows a first cut at identifying significant claimant groups and the nature of their claims on the business firm. Such a claimant model may be of direct use in planning in that it can serve as a checklist for managers to use in testing and evaluating proposed objectives or actions. Although this may

TABLE 7.1 / Business Firm Claimant Structure[a]

CLAIMANT TO THE BUSINESS FIRM	GENERAL NATURE OF THE CLAIM
Stockholders	Participate in distribution of profits, additional stock offerings, assets on liquidation; vote of stock, inspection of company books, transfer of stock, election of board of directors, and such additional rights as established in the contract with corporation.
Creditors	Participate in legal proportion of interest payments due and return of principal from the investment. Security of pledged assets; relative priority in event of liquidation. Participate in certain management and owner prerogatives if certain conditions exist within the company (such as default of interest payments).
Employees	Economic, social, and psychological satisfaction in the place of employment. Freedom from arbitrary and capricious behavior on the part of company officials. Share in fringe benefits, freedom to join union and participate in collective bargaining, individual freedom in offering up their services through an employment contract. Adequate working conditions.
Customers	Service provided the product; technical data to use the product; suitable warranties; spare parts to support the product during customer use; R & D leading to product improvement; facilitation of consumer credit.
Supplier	Continuing source of business; timely consummation of trade credit obligations; professional relationship in contracting for, purchasing, and receiving goods and services.
Governments	Taxes (income, property, etc.), fair competition, and adherence to the letter and intent of public policy dealing with the requirements of "fair and free" competition. Legal obligation for businessmen (and business organizations) to obey antitrust laws.
Union	Recognition as the negotiating agent for the employees. Opportunity to perpetuate the union as a participant in the business organization.
Competitors	Norms established by society and the industry for competitive conduct. Business statesmanship on the part of contemporaries.
Local communities	Place of productive and healthful employment in the local community. Participation of the company officials in community affairs, regular employment, fair play, local purchase of reasonable portion of the products of the local community, interest in and support of local government, support of cultural and charity projects.
The general public	Participation in and contribution to the governmental process of society as a whole; creative communications between governmental and business units designed for'reciprocal understanding; bear fair proportion of the burden of government and society. Fair price for products and advancement of the state-of-the-art in the technology which the product line offers.

[a] Adapted from Cleland, D. I., and King, W. R., *Management: A Systems Approach*, McGraw-Hill, New York, 1972, p. 104, with permission of the publisher.

seem to be an innocuous use of such a formidable-sounding entity as a claimant model, many firms decisions do not consider the possible consequences of their actions or its diverse clientele, simply because of the diversity and man's notorious inability to think of everything.

Undoubtedly, illustrative of this was Bristol-Myers Company's 1975 strategy of introducing a non-aspirin pain remedy called "Datril" on the basis of the product being equally effective but lower priced than the established product "Tylenol." While Tylenol maker Johnson & Johnson reacted with price cutting, deals, and aggressive sales promotion, Datril's price and novelty-factor advantages were rapidly overcome. Failure on the part of Bristol-Myers to foresee these reactions of the competitive claimant led to an upsetting of the market and a lack of anticipated success for the new product.[14]

REFINING THE BASIC CLAIMANT MODEL

Once the basic claimant structure has been developed, it can be refined on the basis of the relative homogeneity of various groups incorporated into the model. The claimant groups should be identified in terms of the homogeneity of their outlook, claims, and perceptions, rather than on their common legal status. For instance, although all stockholders of a given class have the same legal claims they do not behave homogeneously. Investors, e.g., the proverbial little old widow who holds her stock to pass it on to her children, and speculators have very different planning horizons with respect to their claim on the firm. One is looking at the long term and the other at the short term, and this leads them to desire very different things of the corporation.

Similarly, customers and potential customers do not behave uniformly; nor do they respond uniformly to corporate sales strategies. This has been recognized in the concept of a *market segment,* which is widely used as a basis for marketing strategy development. Each of the wide array of different autos produced by Detroit is targeted toward a particular market segment that is relatively homogenous with regard to the needs fulfilled by a car.[15] Similar customer market segments can be defined to refine the basic claimant structure of Table 7.1.

ASSESSING CLAIMS

Of critical importance to the utilization of a claimant structure as anything more than a general guide or checklist is the *definition of measures, direct or proxy, for the claims of claimant groups.* Indeed, measurability is one of the important

[14] See "A Painful Headache for Bristol-Myers," *Business Week,* Oct. 6, 1975, pp. 78–80.

[15] Of course, this targeting does not always work. For instance, American Motors' introduction of the Pacer in 1975 resulted in initial sales to a significantly different market segment, older, more affluent, and better educated, than that which had been targeted.

keys to the development of useful objectives in any situation, since measures permit the assessment of progress toward the accomplishment of objectives.

Each of the claims specified in the refined claimant structure should be analyzed with a view to defining objective measures of that claim. Some of these measures are straightforward; dividends, the time pattern of dividends, and the proportional payout of earnings may measure the stockholders' claim of participating in the distribution of profits for instance.

However, some measures are much less apparent. Many organizations state objectives in terms of the way in which they wish to be perceived. For instance, one of PPG Industries' objectives was seen in Chapter 3 to be

> . . . to have the company accepted (*by the general public*) as a dynamic responsible professionally managed corporation . . .

This suggests a claim of the general public, but how can it possibly be measured? The answer, of course, is that it cannot be measured in the same sense that earnings or dividends can be. However, the tremendous strides in *attitude measurement* [16] in recent years provide the basis for the objective assessment of attitudes on numerical scales that can be traced over time to indicate whether progress is being made in achieving desired objectives of public image.

The same approaches can be used with the customers (for firms who do not sell to individual consumers) and other clientele groups. For instance, one firm conducted an image survey of its primary customers in terms of a variety of dimensions related to customer perceptions of the firm's product, prices, personnel, practices, etc. This survey led to significant changes in the firm's organization, assignment of duties, and procedures for preparing proposals for customer review when it was discovered that customer perceptions differed greatly from what was anticipated. The impact of these and other strategic changes was monitored over time with additional surveys to assess progress toward changing customer perceptions.

Other *proxy measures* will also be appropriate to measure progress toward some organizational objectives. For instance, Ackoff[17] suggests that an improved employee relations, or morale objective should be assessed in terms of "attrition rate," "absenteeism," and "productivity" as proxies. If such objective proxies are complemented with *attitude measures*, a very complete picture of progress toward the achievement of a morale objective may be obtained.

USING THE CLAIMANT ANALYSIS IN ESTABLISHING OBJECTIVES

It can reasonably be argued that every objective of an organization must necessarily be related to one or more of the objectives of the organization's clientele.

---

[16] For instance, see Summers, G. F., *Attitude Measurement*, Rand McNally, New York, 1970.

[17] Ackoff, R. L., *A Concept of Corporate Planning*, Wiley, New York, 1970, p. 30.

If the clientele analysis is comprehensive, it encompasses all of those who have a claim on the organization, and it thereby reflects all that the organization is about and all that it should be seeking.

In effect, under this view, an organization's objectives are derived from the diverse objectives and claims of its clientele. Of course, since the objectives and claims of various clientele groups are in conflict, choices must be made, and priorities must be applied to the broad array of claims.

The clientele analysis provides basic data that are required for any rational choice process concerning objectives. In the absence of such an analysis, important claimants are likely to be overlooked or misunderstood, thus leading the organization to adopt objective and strategies that may cause unforeseen difficulties.

ESTABLISHING NONCLIENTELE OBJECTIVES

Although it can reasonably be argued that *every* organizational objective should be related to the satisfaction of *some* clientele group, it may be artificial and inefficient to carry the clientele analysis beyond the point just described. The basic purpose of any explication of objectives is to ensure that we know where we are going and what we are about, and the primary criterion to be applied to the explication process is completeness. The systems model of Figure 7.1 provides a guide to the explication of tentative objectives that complement those developed through the client model.

INPUT AND OUTPUT CONSIDERATIONS. The input and output process shown in Figure 7.1 involves implicit objectives that may be explicated for both the short and long run. A measure of profitability, such as return on investment sums up both input and output considerations for the short run, but it must be complemented with measures of the *rate* of sales, earnings, and market share growth as well as with output mix and output quality measures if the long-run is to be adequately represented.

ACQUIRING RESOURCES. The acquisition of resources class of objectives includes those developed to ensure the capability of survival and the achievement of other objectives. Financial and human resources are of primary concern, although most organizations delineate objectives related to facilities as well.

Human skills, labor, management, research, etc., along with financial resources, are the primary capitals of the organization.[18] Objectives must be

---

[18] The field of "Human Resource Accounting" has been developed to provide similar treatment to human capital as is provided to financial capital in organizational accounting. See, for example, Flamholtz, E., *Human Resource Accounting,* Dickenson Publishing Company, Encino, Calif., 1974.

established to ensure that they will be acquired in appropriate quality and quantity.

ORGANIZATIONAL DEVELOPMENT. In addition to satisfying clientele, the organization must satisfy itself. Of course, the organization develops through the acquisition of resources and the satisfaction of clientele, but it should also delineate specific objectives for participants and for the organization as a whole. In effect, it must choose to invest something in itself.

One dimension of the idea of investments of the organization in itself recognizes that, although the organization may acquire resources from external sources, it must also internally develop some of its own resource base. Business firms may do this from retained earnings. However, objectives and policies must be established to guide the nature, amount, and timing of earnings retention.

Another dimension of this developmental element is the training and education of organizational participants. Skills may be developed as well as acquired, and since the way in which they are obtained may well affect the rationality with which the organization operates (e.g., morale), objectives should be stated for people development.

Indeed, the organization can have objectives that delineate the basic characteristics it wishes to display. Does it, for instance, wish to be open and participative? It is only through such objectives that organizations are likely to change in predictable and desired ways.

BEHAVING RATIONALLY. There are many dimensions to the concept of an organization's "rational behavior." One important aspect of this concept is *adaptability*. Since the future is inherently unpredictable, the organization should remain adaptable to changing circumstances. (Indeed, in earlier chapters, we have characterized the output of strategic planning to be "adaptive" plans.)

Adaptability is achieved, however, not only by the nature of the plans that the organization produces, but also through *diversification and liquidity of resources*. Diversification in this sense may be measured by the portfolio of customers, products, markets, and technologies, and their balance in terms of reactions to the business cycle, social change, and political upheaval.

Another aspect of diversification relates to the opportunities that the organization has for participating in the changes that inevitably will occur in society. For instance, a strong research and development effort enhances the likelihood of the development of new products and processes, and involvement by the organization in planning increases the likelihood that it will be able to influence the changes that will be of consequence to it.

Liquidity characterizes the organization's ability to *respond* to change. Although it seeks to *influence* change, it is inevitable that it will, at times, be in a position of response. The liquidity concept is usually applied to resources through measures such as debt/equity ratios and fixed/current asset ratios.

However, the liquidity notion applies equally well to the skills of the organization and to the responsiveness of its members to change. Toffler[19] has described *future* shock as

> . . . the distress, both physical and psychological, that arises from an overload of the human organism's physical adaptive systems and its decision-making processes . . . the human response to over stimulation.

If organizational participants suffer future shock, the organization will not respond well to change, whatever may be its resource liquidity.

A variety of other dimensions of rational behavior may be of import to the organization. For instance, stability, through the reduction of fluctuations in sales, earnings, and work levels, worker morale and attitude, innovativeness, and the utilization of the best in technology and management techniques all may well be elements of an organization's unique definition of behaving rationally.

Strategic Planning and "Management by Objectives"

"Management by objectives" (MBO) is a widely-known organizational tool which one might take to involve the development of organizational objectives. In fact, most MBO applications take the overall objectives of the organization as given and strive to foster the development of objectives at the middle management level. Thus, these MBO applications are really not related to the development of organizational objectives and hence, are not an important element of strategic planning.

Haines[20] has recently proposed a scheme for incorporating the development of organizational objectives into the overall MBO process. His model relies heavily on the use of an outside consultant, managerial working groups and stakeholder claims as discussed in this chapter. Except for the use of a consultant, the approach essentially involves the integration of the ideas of this chapter with the task force planning approaches discussed (in the context of strategic data bases) in Chapter 5. These approaches will be elaborated on later in Chapters 12 and 13.

[19] Toffler, A., *Future Shock,* Bantam Books, New York, 1971, p. 326.
[20] Haines, W. R., "Corporate Planning and Management by Objectives" *Long Range Planning,* Aug. 1977, pp. 13–20.

Summary

Missions and objectives are the highest level, most important, and least understood of the strategic choice elements. Missions and objectives are often viewed to be well understood by organizational participants. However, examples are legion of organizations that have lost their sense of mission and those that have misallocated their resources in the seeking of too many diverse objectives.

Organizations that do not discuss their basic mission and purpose will inevitably lose whatever concensus may have once existed among the members. This is so because people are replaced and the environment changes. If the organization does not change in a variety of ways, it will not prosper and it may perish.

Of course, an organization cannot change its basic mission and objectives frequently. However, it *must* eventually make even such basic changes and it cannot do so if it does not have a planning process that provides methodologies for the invention, discussion, and evaluation of alternative missions and objectives. Among the methodologies that may be so employed are brain-storming, focus groups, alternative futures and scenarios, and the Policy Delphi.

The diverse array of objectives that are reasonable for a business firm serve to suggest the need that every organization has for considering a complex array of objectives rather than a single simple objective such as profit. A general systems model of the objectives for any organization, such as that in Figure 7.1, can be suggestive of objectives that may be considered in a planning process.

An operational approach to the establishment of objectives must begin with the identification of organizational claimants and the nature of their claims. Once the claims have been refined, they should be assessed and used as a basis for the establishment of organizational objectives that relate to the objectives of the organization's clientele groups.

Chapter 7—Questions and Exercises

1. What is the justification for spending organizational resources in a discussion of an organization's missions and objectives?
2. One viewpoint says that organizations don't have objectives; only individuals have objectives. What do you think? If this is so, what implications does it have to organizational strategic planning.
3. Is an organization's mission usually predetermined?
4. What role does a consensus type of decision making play in the determination of an organization's mission? What should be the strategy within an organization if it

wishes to seek a consensus type of approach to the determination of the organization's objectives?

5. What is brainstorming? What is the value of such a technique? What are some of the factors to be considered in setting up a brainstorming activity in an organization?

6. What is the concept of alternative futures in strategic planning? How does this relate to scenarios in the strategic planning context?

7. Can you give an illustration of an organization that may have lost its sense of purpose, its mission?

8. Why might a knowledgeable stockholder view a corporate executive's promise of immediate gains in profitability with alarm?

9. What is meant by the idea of the clientele groups of an organization?

10. Select an organization of your choosing and describe the clientele groups that claim something of value from the organization.

11. There can be assumed that many other organizational objectives can be identified that subume or complement profitability. What are some of these objectives?

12. What are the key elements of a systems model of organizational objectives? How would such a systems model operate?

13. What is the purpose in considering the claims of the clientele group in developing future strategies for the organization?

14. Why is it important for an organization to have an explicit mission statement?

15. What is the "Policy Delphi?"

16. Distinguish between identification and adaptation in terms of individual and organizational objectives.

17. How may one try to make operational the claims of various clientele groups as they relate to organizational objectives?

Chapter 7—Strategic Questions for the Manager

1. What is the general attitude in your organization concerning its missions and objectives? Are the existing objectives clearly stipulated? Are they measurable?

2. Are the organization's mission and objectives established through a "consensus" type of approach? Do key members of the organization have the opportunity to debate missions and objectives in both an adversary and friendly context?

3. Do the explicit statements of missions and objectives provide a rallying point for motivating people in the organization?

4. Does the cultural ambience of the organization provide suitable opportunities for brainstorming, organizational development, and such related techniques?

5. Have any team building activities been carried out in the organization, particularly with respect to developing a strategic sense of direction for the organization?

6. Have I identified my organizational claimants?

7. Have the claims of the organizational claimants been identified? To what degree are these claims being satisfied? How is this known to be so?

8. What is the organization's image from the perspective of each of these claimant groups?

9. Are any claimants currently dissatisfied with the level of satisfaction of their claims? Why?
10. What changes will the long-range future bring about in the claimant's needs? Have strategies been developed to deal with these changes?
11. Is profit the sole objective of the organization?
12. How do the value systems of key executives affect organizational objectives?
13. Can a systems model of organizational objectives be built?

References

Argenti, A. J. A., "Defining Corporate Objectives," *Long Range Planning*, March, 1969.

Breech, E. R., "Planning the Basic Strategy of a Large Business," *Planning the Future Strategy of Your Business* (E. C. Bursk and D. H. Fenn, Jr., editors), McGraw-Hill, New York, 1956.

Cleland, D. I. and King, W. R., *Systems Analysis and Project Management* (2nd Ed.), McGraw-Hill, New York, 1975.

Edmonds, C. P., III, and Hand, J. H., "What are the Long-Run Objectives of Business," *Business Horizons*, Dec. 1976.

Granger, C. H., "The Hierarchy of Objectives," *Harvard Business Review*, May–June 1964.

Haggerty, P. E., "Long-Term Viability—The Business Problem," *IEEE Student Journal*, Sept. 1968.

Haggerty, P. E., "Strategies, Tactics, and Research," *Research Management*, Vol. 9, 1966.

Haines, W. R., "Corporate Planning and Management by Objectives," *Long Range Planning*, Aug. 1977.

Helms, E. W., "The OST System for Managing Innovation at Texas Instruments," presented to the Armed Forces Management Association, Washington, D.C., April 7, 1971.

Idiorne, G. S., *Management By Objective*, Pitman, New York, 1965.

Koontz, H., and O'Donnell, C. J., *Principles of Management*, McGraw-Hill, New York, 1974.

Krynen, H. G., "Formulating Corporate Objectives and Strategies," *Long Range Planning*, Aug. 1977.

Mertin, D., "Planning and the Corporate Philosophy," *Managerial Planning*, Sept. 1976.

Migliore, R. H., "Planning and Management Objectives," *Long Range Planning*, Aug. 1976.

Morton, J. A., "A Systems Approach to the Innovation Process," *Business Horizons*, Summer 1967.

Reddin, W. J., *Effective Management by Objectives: Three D Method*, McGraw-Hill, New York, 1971.

Simon, H. A., "On the Concept of Organizational Goals," *Administrative Science Quarterly*, Vol. 9, p. 23.

Smalter, D. J., "The Influence of D-O-D Practices on Corporate Planning," *Management Technology,* Vol. 4, Dec. 1964.

Tilles, S., "How to Evaluate Corporate Strategy," *Harvard Business Review,* July–Aug. *1963.*

Wademan, V., "Setting Corporate Objectives," Financial Executive, Jan. 1976.

Warner, W. K., and Havens, A. E., "Goal Displacement and the Intangibility of Organizational Goals," *Administrative Science Quarterly,* Vol. 12, p. 539.

Chapter 8

CHOOSING THE ORGANIZATION'S STRATEGY

The choice of the organization's strategy is the heart of any strategic planning process. This is so because, despite the importance of mission and objective choices, they are much more enduring entities than are strategies. Organizations may have their missions under continuing review and discussion, but they will not normally make frequent substantial changes in their mission. Some organizations have retained a single mission concept over many decades, whereas most alter their missions in major ways no more often than once a decade. Thus, when compared to mission and objective selection, strategy choice is the most important activity that has the prospect of significant and continuing change.

Conversely, when one contrasts this combination of great significance and opportunity for change inherent in the selection of a strategy with the lower elements in the strategic choice hierarchy, such as goals, programs, and of resource allocations, it is apparent that they are not nearly so significant and enduring as are strategies. Programs and goals may be more readily altered if the environment changes or if they are viewed as not producing the desired results. Strategies define the general direction in which the organization is proceeding and, as such, are more enduring and less often changed.

Thus, the strategy-selection level in the hierarchy of strategic choice processes is the keystone in the sense of the combination of significance, opportunity for choice, and enduring nature of the consequences of choice that it entails. Indeed, there are some organizations that operate with either so fixed or so implicit an interpretation of their missions and objectives that strategy choice is the highest level decision making which ever explicitly takes place.

The Strategy Choice Process

The process of strategy choice can be thought of as consisting of three elements: strategy *development, refinement,* and *evaluation.* Although these elements are not separate and distinct, the various phases of strategy choice draw on different organizational capabilities and represent different levels of analysis. Strategy *development* involves the creation, or invention, of strategies suited to the achievement of the organization's objectives. Strategy *refinement* involves the elaboration of basic strategies to the point where they adequately reflect the diversity and complexity of organizational objectives. Strategy *evaluation* may be thought of as the culmination of a filtering process in which proposed strategies are subjected to close scrutiny and in which alternative strategies are compared in terms of the degree to which each is anticipated to achieve organizational objectives.

A Basic Strategy Concept

The simple chart of Table 8.1 suggests a basic strategy concept that may be used to develop general strategies that can then be refined in more specific terms. Although the table reflects a business orientation, it is readily translatable into appropriate terms for public sector and other not-for-profit strategy-choice contexts that do not specifically involve traditionally defined products and/or markets.

In the table, both products and markets are thought of in terms of those that currently exist and those that do not currently exist.[1] Each element of the table defines a basic strategy element for the organization. For instance, the element A suggests a strategic focus on existing products and markets—a "do better those things that we are already doing" strategy. Many organizations who adopt this strategy explicate it as a "tight ship" or cost-conscious approach. The strategy element B suggests an emphasis on developing new markets for existing products, and C emphasizes the development of new products for currently existing markets. The implications of these two strategies are quite different. In case B, new *market development* is emphasized, whereas C emphasizes research and new *product development* as the general direction in which the organization will seek its objectives. Situation D in the figure is the most innovative strategy. It emphasizes new products for new markets. It is therefore the riskiest of the four basic strategic alternatives.

Of course, an organization need not select only one of these four alternatives as its strategy. An overall strategy may involve a combination of these strategic alternatives that are given priority to suggest relative importance and sequence. An illustration used previously was as follows:

1. Primarily, emphasize existing products in existing markets to achieve short-term improvements in ROI, maintain dividends, and maintain existing image.

---

[1] This simple idea can be applied in a variety of ways. For instance, see Cravens, D. W., "Marketing Strategy Positioning," *Business Horizons,* Dec. 1975, pp. 53–61.

TABLE 8.1 / Product-Market
Strategy Space

	MARKETS	
PRODUCTS	EXISTING	NEW
Existing	A	B
New	C	D

2. Then, put emphasis on existing product sales into new markets, particularly foreign and restricted markets, in a manner that positively affects safety consciousness image.
3. Then, emphasize broadening product line to achieve increasing ROI and increased dividends while maintaining improved image.

This strategy involves a combination of the three strategic alternatives labeled A, B, and C in Table 8.1. The alternatives are grossly given priority through the use of the words "primarily" and "then," and they are sequenced in terms of those words, as well as in the way that they are to influence the various objectives related to return on investment (ROI), image, and dividends, e.g., as indicated by the terms "short term," "maintain," "improve," etc.

Developing and Refining Strategies

Strategies may be initially thought of in terms of the strategic product-market space of Table 8.1. Then they may be further refined and elaborated in a variety of ways, through the strategic data bases described in Chapter 5, through application of the organization's previously-stated objectives, through strategic "normative propositions," through the development of strategic inferences from assumptions and forecasts, through organizational development methodologies, or through analytic models that reflect organizational strengths, weaknesses, and opportunities for improvement.

USING STRATEGIC DATA BASES IN STRATEGY DEVELOPMENT

Strategic data bases were discussed in Chapter 5 in the context of a set of activities that could be used to initiate the planning process. These strategic data bases are of obvious implicit use in the phases of the planning process that involve the selection of missions and objectives, but they may also play a very direct and explicit role in the refinement of strategy.

The strategic data bases discussed in Chapter 5 are:

1. Business and industry criteria (what it takes to be successful in this business and industry).
2. Organizational strengths and weaknesses.
3. Competitive profiles.
4. Environmental opportunities and risks.
5. Management viewpoints and values.

To use these strategic data bases in strategy refinement, one must determine the relationship between the strategic factors that they entail and the elements of the strategy space of Table 8.1. What is the relationship between business and industry factors, organizational strengths and weaknesses, and the elements of the strategy space of Table 8.1? What does this relationship suggest about the strategy that may be selected? For instance, if a strong field marketing force has been identified as a strategic business factor as well as a major strength of the organization, a strategy that emphasizes market development (B in the strategy space) is strongly suggested. This is so because of the nature of the strategic data bases; field marketing has been identified as one of the most significant things that the organization can do to be successful and it is also an organizational strength that should be used to advantage.

On the other hand, if strong field marketing is a strategic business factor but also is a current organizational *weakness,* a more conservative, (A), strategy may be all that is feasible. If the mangement-viewpoints-and-values data base suggests that aggressiveness is to be emphasized, a product development (C), or even diversification (D), alternative may become the focus of attention.

The other strategic data bases can also serve in a similar fashion to aid in qualitative strategy refinement. A diversification strategy involves some risks that are greater than those inherent in other elements of the basic strategy space. The data base that encompasses competitive advantages or disadvantages can serve in helping to assess the significance of this as can the environmental data base. For instance, a strategy of penetrating newly perceived markets, which markets are thought to have been brought into being by great current governmental emphasis on product safety, might be poor if the strategic environmental data base suggests that concern with such niceties as safety are likely to be overshadowed by the basic product performance and economic concerns that are the predicted result of a current poor economic climate. A diversification strategy might be similarly refined, through the use of a strategic data base, to incorporate the effects of government regulation and intervention in the industries of interest.

The importance of using strategic data bases in this way is made apparent by considering that they encompass *a small number of the most important strategic factors for each relevant area,* e.g., competition, strengths, weaknesses, etc. Since the strategic data bases are so important, they, in fact, represent one of the primary operational tools for strategy development and refinement.

THE USE OF OBJECTIVES IN DEVELOPING STRATEGY

The organization's objectives play two major roles in the process of strategy development. First, *objectives determine or suggest the measures to be used to assess the relative value of various strategies.* If the organization's only objective involves profitability, a strategy that is predicted to achieve a better ROI is dictated *by that objective* to be superior to one that is expected to produce less, despite the fact that the lesser-ROI strategy may involve greater market penetration. If there is more than one objective, as is usually the case, each plays a similar role in determining performance measures, although, of course, such a simple ranking of strategies will not generally be feasible when multiple performance measures are involved.

A second major role for objectives lies in the development and refinement of strategies. In this regard, objectives play a role similar to that of the strategic factors that make up the various strategic data bases. For instance, a set of objectives incorporating adaptability and flexibility will probably tend to lead the organization away from A-type strategies (see Table 8.1). Indeed, if flexibility is a major aspect of the organization's objectives, a diversification strategy (D) may be indicated. At the very least, an emphasis in the objectives on flexibility and adaptability would lead one to question whether a broader range of products, a broader range of markets, or both, would most readily achieve this objective. On this basis, a market development and/or product development (B or C) strategy might be given prominence.

Thus, the organization's objectives can be made to serve a strategy development and refinement function in much the same fashion as strategic data bases can be used. As in virtually all of the strategic planning processes, feedback from this strategy refinement stage may be used to develop and refine the objectives. This is so because it will be recognized in this step that if the previously stated objectives do not significantly aid in strategy refinement, the objectives are probably too broad or nonspecific. With the specific questions that are brought up in the strategy refinement process in mind, the objectives can themselves be reviewed and refined.

NORMATIVE PROPOSITIONS TO REFINE STRATEGIES

A great deal of research in the area of business policy has focused on the development of normative propositions to guide strategy under various environmental conditions and sets of organizational traits. Various sets of normative

propositions have been proposed, some very general in nature like the principles that formed the core of traditional management theory, e.g., Katz's
universal propositions[2]:

1. Always lead from strength.
2. Concentrate resources where the company has (or could readily develop) a meaningful competitive advantage.
3. The narrowest possible product-market scope should be selected for
   each unit consistent with unit resources and market requirements.
4. A unit whose future earning power (discounted at the company's current cost of capital) is less than its liquidation value should be sold as
   quickly as possible.

Other strategic propositions are more specific and contingency-based, e.g.,

For dominant firms in an industry, the best strategies (in order) are innovation, intense marketing (fortification); the least are persecution and con-
frontation.

Acquisition strategy is best when the company has little knowledge of the
product, when speed is vital, or when other companies own key patents or
control key resources.[3]

Such normative propositions, either general or situational, can be helpful in
the initial testing and refinement of strategy. Of course, no universal propositions, or contingency-based propositions, have been conclusively demonstrated
to be valid. This means that all such normative propositions should be used
with a healthy tongue-in-cheek attitude on the part of the strategic manager.

STRATEGIC INFERENCES FROM ASSUMPTIONS AND FORECASTS

The assumptions and forecasts developed in the early stages of the planning
process may be used in the strategy refinement phase. This can be accomplished through the drawing of *strategic inferences* from the information
that is entailed in the previously evaluated and accepted assumptions and forecasts.

For instance, Bridgewater et. al.[4] describe a food manufacturing firm that
developed the strategic implications shown in Table 8.2 on the basis of the
listed assumptions. The arrows in the table reflect the inferential process that

---

[2]Katz, R., *Cases and Concepts in Corporate Strategy,* Prentice-Hall, Englewood Cliffs,
N.J., 1970.

[3]Glueck, W., *Business Policy: Reality and Promise, Proceedings of the National Meeting of
the Academy of Management,* August, 1972.

[4]Bridgewater, B. A., Jr., Clifford, D. K., Jr., and Hardy, T., "The Competition Game Has
Changed," *Business Horizons,* Oct. 1975.

TABLE 8.2[a] / Strategic Implications Derived from Assumptions

ASSUMPTIONS	STRATEGIC IMPLICATIONS
Consumer will put premium on convenience range of choice, and diversity	Emphasize value-added products
Volume gains possible through new products	Enrich mix via new forms, sizes, varieties, products, private label lines
	Emphasize marketing and distribution
	Open more and bigger stores
Spending on nonfood items will rise sharply	Stimulate volume through promotion
	Broaden mix with nonfood lines
	Diversify into other consumer goods and services

[a] Adapted from Bridgewater et. al.,[4] p. 11.

led to the specification and refinement of the aggressive strategy depicted on the right.

Another compamy, manufacturers of capital goods, developed a strategy oriented toward emphasizing increasing sales levels in the *service* segment of their business on the basis of a process of drawing inferences from assumptions and forecasts dealing with both external phenomena and internal considerations. The plan describing this inferential process is stated in part:

Underlying Assumptions and Rationale

A. External

1. *Shifts in the geographic source of demand for new construction (south, southwest, and international becoming more important), while the service base shifts more gradually.*

2. *Competition will remain keen for at least a few years because the industry has an overcapacity and the economy will remain basically a nongrowth one. Attrition should eventually soften the competitive pressure.*

3. *Construction is slowing.*

4. *Service is the most profitable part of the industry.*

B. Internal

1. *We have previously limited our service market to our own equipment design. Removing this restriction opens a vast service market opportunity to us.*

> 2. *We have been profitable in service with the present organization despite the fact that it has not been a subject of primary organizational responsibility. Therefore, a focusing of our attention on it should yield even better results.*

ANALYTIC MODELS IN STRATEGY REFINEMENT

In Chapter 5, the PIMS model,[5] operated and maintained by the Marketing Science Institute, was discussed as a basis for developing inputs for the development of the strength/weakness strategic data base. If so used, it indirectly impacts strategy formulation through that data base. However, some of the results from analytical models such as PIMS may also be directly useful in strategy development and refinement.

PIMS is a statistical model that permits the analysis of a wide variety of business factors as they affect a business' ROI. Data on more than 600 diverse businesses are incorporated into the data bank and individual companies who supply their own business data are provided with diagnostic reports that statistically compare their business and market characteristics with other businesses in terms of the way in which they relate to relative profitability.

For instance, one business was provided with four major factors that negatively affected ROI (in one business area) as compared with a "par" ROI for all businesses in the PIMS data bank. These factors were numerically scaled in terms of their relative impact:

Vertical Integration	−7.9
Market Position	−7.4
Product Quality	−3.9
Sales Direct to End users	−2.2

These factors obviously suggest potential weaknesses and are therefore useful in developing a strength/weakness strategic data base as discussed in Chapter 5.

However, an analysis of the manner in which each element affects relative ROI can serve beneficially in strategy refinement as well. For instance, PIMS analyses for the firm in question showed that, on the basis of their position vis-a-vis other firms in the data bank, one could conclude that ROI is highest at the beginning and end of the product life cycle (for a business such as this one, which had low relative market share). This understanding led the firm to reconsidering the *timing* of the product research and development

---

[5] Schoeffler, S., Buzzell, R. D., and Heany, D. F., "Impact of Strategic Planning on Profit Performance," *Harvard Business Review,* March–April 1974, pp. 137–145.

strategy element and the *pricing* strategy for products that were then in the early and late phases of the product life cycle.

The same firm incorporated the PIMS delineation of sales direct to end users as a major detriment to achieving par ROI in their strategy refinement by identifying probable explanations, e.g., the relatively high cost of selling directly to many end users and the higher costs of performing associated inventory and accounting functions. This led them to consider a secondary distribution strategy for existing products as well as to the incorporation of such considerations into the design of a distribution strategy for new products.

The use of PIMS-defined factors in strategy development and refinement can go beyond those few factors that suggest major structural strengths or weaknesses and have probably already been incorporated into the strength/weakness strategic data base. For instance, one firm determined, by analyses that were suggested by PIMS results, that ROI in one business could not be improved without a significant improvement in market share. Despite the fact that improved ROI was a major overall objective of the firm, a "market position" strategy was adopted, including elements of product development and market development, to build market share at the recognized cost of short-run ROI for this business. The model had suggested to them that ROI in the long run could be achieved only through some sacrifices of ROI in the short-run.

BUSINESS SCREEN STRATEGY ASSESSMENT

Table 8.3 shows a "business screen" used by General Electric and other firms as a basis for evaluating their various businesses in terms of the potential attractiveness of the industry in which the business is competing and the position of the business unit within that industry.[6] In this simple illustration, the organization's businesses and their related industries are shown to be qualitatively evaluated as to high, medium, or low levels of penetration and attractiveness.

Of course, these qualitative evaluations must be made on the basis of significant quantitative analyses of the market, industry, and business profitability, etc., but at the strategy choice level, these numerical evaluations are aggregated into qualitative categories as shown in Table 8.3.[7] Such qualitative strategic assessments are advantages in that they also permit the incorporation

---

[6] This idea has been depicted in a number of different ways in various publications. Many adaptations are possible. For instance, see "General Electric's 'Stoplight Strategy' for Planning," *Business Week,* April 28, 1975, p. 49.

[7] In practice, some firms that have used this form of analysis have found that it is more effective to use more than three categories. Here, the three-category version reported in the literature is primarily used for simplicity of explanation.

TABLE 8.3 / Business Screen

INDUSTRY ATTRACTIVENESS

BUSINESS UNIT POSITION	HIGH	MEDIUM	LOW
High	①		④
Medium		③	
Low	②		⑤

of qualitative factors such as employee loyalty, industry volatility, and technological position into the strategy assessment process.

Assessments of various businesses are shown in Table 8.3 as represented by the circled numbers. A business such as 1 is evaluated to have a strong position in a highly attractive growth industry, and as such might be given high priority for resource allocation. At the other extreme is Business 5, which has a weak position in an unattractive industry and is probably therefore a candidate for divestment. Business 2 has a weak position in a highly attractive industry. A potential strategy for this business may be to move it up the leftmost column to a better position. Business 3 is clearly in a never-never land which suggests no clear strategy. Business 4, on the other hand, is a leader in an unattractive, perhaps mature, industry and should probably be harvested, i.e., primarily used to develop profits and cash flows from previous investments rather than having significant new investments made. If such assessments are made on the basis of objective analysis (quantitative and qualitative) and with the participation of top executives and business unit executives, they comprise a useful aid in the development of strategy as well as a foundation for subsequent resource allocation decisions.

ORGANIZATIONAL DEVELOPMENT

Organizational development (OD) is a term applied to a variety of behavioral methodologies for systematically attempting to bring about organizational change. Most approaches to OD focus on both the enhancement of organizational effectiveness and the participant's opportunity to develop his individual potential in an organizational setting.

A variety of methodologies fall within the general category of OD. Among them are team building, laboratory learning exercises, and transactional analysis. The most useful of these methodologies for planning are those that focus group attention of the development of organizational strategy and strategies for the implementation of organizational strategy. This latter element, conscious concern with the design of mechanisms for implementing organizational strategy, is one of the most important dimensions of OD as it relates to strategic planning.

Of course, many OD approaches concentrate exclusively on process rather than substance. Such approaches may be useful in other contexts, but not in planning. Thus, while the use of OD in planning is not a well-developed field, it has great potential. This is made clear by considering the relevance of OD "values" as outlined by Margulis and Raia.[8]

1. Providing opportunities for people to function as human beings rather than as resources in the productive process.
2. Providing opportunities for each organization member, as well as for the organization itself, to develop to his full potential.
3. Seeking to increase the effectiveness of the organization in terms of *all* of its goals.
4. Attempting to create an environment in which it is possible to find exciting and challenging work.
5. Providing opportunities for people in organizations to influence the way in which they relate to work, the organization, and the environment.
6. Treating each human being as a person with a complex set of needs, *all* of which are important in his work and in his life.

When one compares these underlying values of OD with the basic premises set out for the development of strategic planning systems in this book, he notices a great similarity. Indeed, many of the processes described here for performing effective planning are similar to those exercises that are an important aspect of OD. The primary difference between the two approaches would appear to be the emphasis of OD on process and team building as a *primary* output, whereas the processes discussed here, e.g., the use of managerial task forces to develop strength/weakness strategic data bases, have focused on *strategic output* while relegating process values to a secondary role.[9]

One of the primary observations that the authors can make from their experience in applying the ideas of this book in a variety of industrial and government contexts is that the OD values of Margulis and Raia do indeed seem to be achieved in large measure. Participation by managers of various levels in such group processes as mission development, strength-weakness data base development, etc. (all strategic organizational activities that extend the range of the typical manager's activities beyond that of his legal job description and normal operating responsibilities) certainly do, in fact, produce these benefits or values.

---

[8] Margulis, W. and Raia, A. P., *Organizational Development: Values, Process and Technology,* McGraw-Hill, New York, 1972.
[9] We shall have more to say about these "process values" in Chapters 12 and 13.

This idea has just begun to be perceived and applied, and little in the way of answers is yet available. However, it is clear that an organization should view its strategic-planning activities as an opportunity area for the achievement of broad organizational goals as well as for producing formal planning outputs such as organizational strategies. The techniques of organizational development may be helpful in answering some of the practical "how to" questions associated with doing this.

The Time Dimension of Strategy

One of the essential elements of any strategy is the time dimension. Every strategy involves perhaps implicitly, a *sequence* of elements. For instance, even a radical diversification strategy would probably be staged so that the impacts, both costs and benefits, would be absorbed over time. A natural approach would be to first take diversification actions that are expected to have short-run impact, say cash flow, which may help to finance investments in longer payout activities.

Indeed, when we recognize the simple concept of an "idea whose time has come," we become aware of the importance of considering the time element to be a necessary part of any strategy. Technological developments may not lead to viable products as soon as they are achieved. Their acceptance, in the form of a marketable product may depend on societal and cultural factors and on the resolution of problems associated with distribution and maintenance.

For instance, lightweight parts for autos were not of major concern to the auto industry until energy problems led to public awarenes of fuel economy. Yet, even when lightweight parts became of great concern, products such as aluminum radiators still were not widely introduced because of the specialized equipment and training necessary for their repair. The timing of the intoduction of aluminum auto radiators thus became dependent on both societal factors (energy problems) and maintainability considerations, despite the fact that the technology and cost aspects of the product would have allowed it to be placed on the market much earlier. If this had been done, the product would probably have been evaluated to be premature, failed, and been relegated to the scrap heap, perhaps to lie there forever disregarded.

LIFE-CYCLE CONCEPTS

Other strategic timing considerations, such as the life-cycle concept, must enter into the refinement of strategy. The life-cycle concept, which applies to any system or product, is the simple recognition that there is a dynamism to pro-

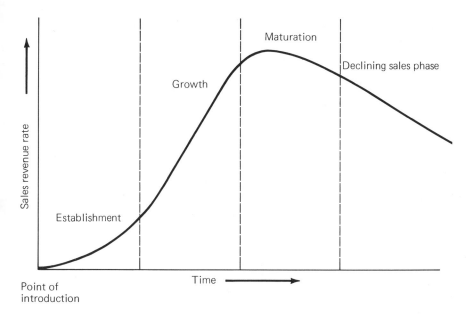

FIGURE 8.1   Product Sales Life Cycle.

ducts and systems reflected in different benefits being produced and different mixes of resources being required at different stages of the development and maturation of a product or program.

This life-cycle concept is expressed in a variety of ways in different environments. For instance, the concept of a product *sales life cycle* in marketing[10] is often described by a sales revenue rate graph such as that of Figure 8.1. This figure shows the rate of generation of sales revenue slowly rising after a product is introduced (the establishment phase), rising rapidly thereafter (the growth phase), reaching a plateau (the maturation phase), and finally decreasing (the declining sales phase). Every product displays such dynamic characteristics, although some, such as novelty items, may be through the various phases very rapidly, and others, such as established commodity-type products, may stretch out the life cycle over many decades.

In research and development efforts, life-cycle concepts have been institutionalized to ensure that varying resources will be made available during different stages of the life cycle and that appropriate analyses will be made of research and development efforts at the various stages. The *systems-development life cycle,* as developed in NASA (National Aeronautics and Space Ad-

[10] See King, W. R., *Quantitative Analysis for Marketing Management,* McGraw-Hill, New York, 1967, p. 113.

ministration) and DOD (The U.S. Department of Defense) is often described in terms of five phases:[11]

Conceptual Phase

Definition Phase

Production or Acquisition Phase

Operational Phase

Divestment Phase

The *conceptual phase* is that in which an idea is generally evaluated in terms of its potential benefit, cost, and the resources required for further development. In the *definition phase,* these assessments are refined to the level of detailed specifications, resource requirements, detailed plans for development, schedules, etc. In the *production phase,* the production, acquisition, or installation of the system is begun. Such things as initial performance testing and the development of support and/or marketing plans are also begun in this phase. The *operational phase* involves the use of the system by the intended user or customer. This phase of the systems development life cycle encompasses much of the marketing sales life cycle of a product as described earlier. The *divestment phase* is the one in which the organization gets out of the business represented by the system in question. Since every system—be it a product, a weapons system or a management system—has a finite lifetime, the organization must make objective analyses and choices about divesting itself of the system just as it made such choices about developing and acquiring it.

STRATEGIC IMPLICATIONS OF LIFE CYCLE CONCEPTS

Life-cycle concepts have direct bearing on overall organizational strategy as well as the strategy for managing individual products and programs.

LIFE CYCLE STRATEGIES. The idea of an overall life-cycle strategy is illustrated for products by Figure 8.2. This figure shows the anticipated revenue streams from three products over an eight-year period. In Figure 8.2, Product B is expected to begin producing revenues in 1983 and to be entering the declining sales phase of its life cycle after 1986. Product A is already in the midst of a long declining sales phase. Under current plans, Product C is expected to be introduced in 1985.

The total revenue (the top curve in Figure 8.2) is predicted to go through a brief decrease in 1986 under this product life cycle strategy. If this is not con-

---

[11] Adapted from Cleland, D. I. and William R. King: *Systems Analysis and Project Management* (2nd Edition), McGraw-Hill, 1975, pp. 185–190.

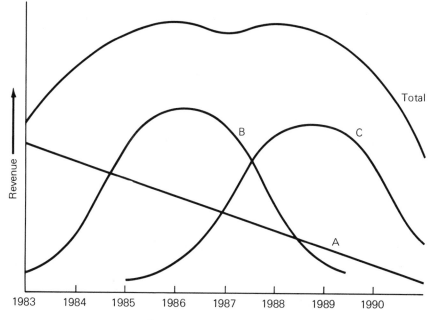

FIGURE 8.2 Sales Life Cycles for Several Products.

sistent with the organization's objectives, as it would not be if the firm has the objective of constantly growing revenues, Product C's development may be speeded up. Alternately, another new product may be considered for introduction about 1985. Or, it may be necessary to go beyond the domain of new product development to design a strategy that will achieve the revenue objective; for instance, acquisitions may be considered.

The same variety of analysis can be carried on in terms of resource requirements as well as revenues (benefits). Such analyses help to refine strategies in the sense that they serve to distinguish the feasible from the infeasible.

THE SEQUENCE DIMENSION OF LIFE CYCLE STRATEGIES. The aspect of the life cycle strategy concept which has just been discussed has solely to do with timing. Another important aspect is *sequencing,* in the sense that many products can have their life cycles planned. Such a planned life cycle is different from those described for products in Figure 8.1, since it was presumed there that the life cycles were largely determined by uncontrollable market and technical factors, e.g., when the product was developed and introduced and the demand level was found to exist.

A product life cycle may be made more controllable and extended in duration through a sequence of planned changes in the product. These changes can be thought of in product terms, market terms, or both, i.e., developing variations of the basic product that will enhance the likelihood of additional sales to existing customers or developing new product uses and appeals that will increase the likelihood of demand by new customers. These two approaches are well illustrated by two photographic giants, Kodak and Polaroid, and the product-market strategies they have used. Kodak's introduction of refined versions of their pocket cameras, such as one that has a built-in telephoto lens, is an example of product sequencing, whereas Polaroid's introduction of lower-cost versions of its instant cameras is an illustration of market sequencing. In the Kodak case, the new version of the camera is designed to create additional customer satisfaction and value by widening the potential use of pocket cameras, thus making the new versions appealing even to people who already own an earlier model. Polaroid, on the other hand, has usually followed a strategy of introducing the top of the line camera first and then successively introducing lower-cost versions in an attempt to appeal to new customer groups who could not afford the earlier versions.

The essence of both of these varieties of strategy is a planned sequence of product refinements which will maximize the benefits obtained from the basic product. In effect, what such a strategy does is extend the life cycle, as shown in Figure 8.3, through the addition of increments to the sales pattern as the basic product life cycle is in its maturation and declining sales phases.

Of course, an overall life-cycle strategy should involve single-product life-cycle planning (as in Figure 8.3) and multiproduct planning (as in Figure 8.2),

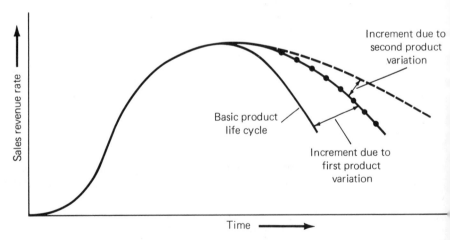

FIGURE 8.3   Single Product Life Cycle Strategy.

as well as acquisitions and other strategy elements that focus on the achievement of objectives through life cycle analyses.

PRODUCT STRATEGIES BASED ON LIFE CYCLES. Within the scope of a single program or product, effective strategy is also dependent on life cycle phases. For instance, such factors as product design strategy, pricing, promotional and advertising strategy, distribution policy, and the intelligence gathering focus of the organization are all strategy elements that must vary throughout the life cycle.

Wasson[12] has suggested that overall product strategy should evolve through a series of phases that are roughly equivalent to the phases of the life cycle:

1. To develop widespread awareness of product benefits and obtain trial by early adopters.
2. To establish a strong market and distribution niche.
3. To maintain and strengthen consumer and trade loyalty.
4. To defend the position of a brand against competing brands and the product category against other products, and to promote even tighter dealer relationships.
5. To milk the offering dry of all possible profit.

Similarly, promotional objectives and media strategy should vary in a sequence of steps throughout the life cycle:

1. To create a general awareness of the product and its benefits. To stimulate trial by early adopters. Maximum use of personal sales, sampling, and publicity, plus moderately heavy introductory advertising.
2. To create brand preference among trade and final users. Heavy emphasis on mass media.
3. Maintain consumer franchise and strenthen dealer ties. Mass media plus increasing dealer-attracting sales promotions.
4. Maintain consumer and trade loyalty, with strong emphasis on the dealers and distributors. Intensification of use frequency, if possible, by getting the fullest use of all use systems. Optimum use of mass media plus dealer-oriented sales promotions.
5. The minimum expenditure necessary to just sustain that distribution which is profitable. Phase out rapidly and let product coast.

Product life-cycle strategic analysis therefore represents a "normative propositions" approach to the development and refinement of strategy. Levitt[13]

[12] Wasson, C. R., *Product Management: Product Life Cycles and Competitive Marketing Strategy*, Challange Books, St. Charles, Ill., 1971, pp. 195–196.

[13] Levitt, T. "Exploit the Product Life Cycle," *Harvard Business Review*, Nov.–Dec. 1965.

suggested this in the mid 1960s. Subsequently, Michael[14] suggested that the declining phase of the product life cycle may be different for various products.

The strategy elements inferred from the life cycle are not solely marketing in nature. Fox[15] has provided "hypotheses" about appropriate strategies to follow in various functional areas throughout the life cycle. For instance, in a series of life-cycle phases ranging from "precommercialization" to "decline," he suggests that the personnel strategy should involve a sequence of phases:

1. Recruit for new activities; negotiate operational changes with unions.
2. Staff and train middle management; stock options for executives.
3. Add suitable personnel for plant; many grievances; heavy overtime.
4. Transfers; advancements; incentives for efficiency, safety and so on; suggestion system.
5. Find new slots; encourage early retirement.

Synergy Considerations in Strategy Choice

Much of the previous discussion has implicitly viewed the organization's activities, be they businesses, products, or projects, as independent entities. This abstraction is useful for analyzing strategic alternatives, but it is not an accurate description of reality.

The activities of an organization are generally interdependent. This is the case if only because they draw, to some extent, on a common resource base within the organization. However, this interdependence is often reflected in other ways as well. For instance, the introduction of a new product may take sales away from an existing one. This is often the case with functionally related products, e.g., the lower-cost models of Polaroid's cameras obviously were bought by some people who had delayed their purchase but who would have eventually made a purchase of the more sophisticated version.

Since this interdependence of organizational activities exists, it must be accounted for in strategy development. Indeed, if strategic planning is to truly be the positive force that it can be, *these interdependencies must be planned for and used to advantage.*

The concept of *synergy* (that the combined performance of several entities can be greater than the sum of the contributions independently made by individual entities) can be used to advantage in various ways to create market, cost, technology, and management synergy.

[14] Michael, G., "Product Petrification: A New Stage in the Life Cycle," *California Management Review,* Fall 1971.

[15] Fox, H., "A Framework for Functional Coordination," *Atlanta Economic Review,* Nov.–Dec. 1973, pp. 10–11.

Market synergy reflects such things as tie-in sales within a product line. This can be achieved through joint promotion or retail display as well as through a product strategy. The branding of a new product in a way that takes advantage of the name of a well-known brand or firm is a market synergy element of an overall strategy.

Cost synergy uses common product facilities, distribution channels, sales personnel, etc., for a variety of products to achieve overall lower costs than could be achieved separately by the individual products.

Technological synergy results from the transfer of technology developed for one purpose to applications in a different field. The term "technology transfer" has been popularized as a result of the U.S. space program and subsequent transfers of NASA space technology to commercial applications. The best known such example is Teflon (Dupont's coating material), which was originally developed to facilitate atmospheric re-entry by space vehicles.

Such technological synergy has often formed a strategic foundation for corporate strategy. For instance, the combining of North American Aviation and Rockwell Manufacturing into North American Rockwell[16] was largely predicated on the potential for technological synergy, the marriage of North American's aerospace technology with Rockwell's access to civilian markets that might be responsive to products developed using aerospace technology.

Management synergy is a much-discussed, but less well-understood, strategy element that is often reflected in acquisition or merger strategies. The idea that effective management in one business can be transformed to other businesses is often an important rationale for such arrangements, although there are probably as many examples of failures as there are of successes in this strategy. The seeking of management synergy is sometimes based on a naive belief in the universality of management, the idea that those things that lead to management success in one environment will also produce success in another.

This principles approach to management, that which views management to be the application of some basic principles, has been recognized to be anything but universal.[17] However, this does not debunk the idea of management synergy; it merely suggests that potential synergy of this variety must be carefully defined and made explicit if it is to be a strategy element. Wishful thinking is no more a sound basis for strategy in achieving management synergy than it is in any other area; yet, so often this seems to have been the basis for personnel changes that are expected to achieve synergistic impacts.

At the level of *general management,* there is almost certainly great potential for synergy. There is a well-recognized shortage of effective general man-

[16] This company has subsequently changed its name to Rockwell International.
[17] See Cleland, D. I. and King, W. R. *Systems Analysis and Project Management,* McGraw-Hill, New York, 1975, Chapter 1.

agers, as well as a deficiency in the processes used in public organizations, business firms, and educational institutions in educating and preparing managers for general management responsibilities.[18] This suggests that a merger or acquisition strategy that seeks to achieve management synergy through the acquisition of talented people at the general management level may sometimes be well founded.

Synergy, in all of its various dimensions, is an important element of strategy choice and refinement. The various synergistic elements should be made explicit and quantified if possible. Since this process is closely related to such things as strength/weakness analyses discussed earlier (see Chapter 5), we shall not go into detail as to the format in which this may be done. The particular format chosen is much less important than are two characteristics of the process of synergistic analysis—*explication and participation.*

By explication, we mean the making explicit of the anticipated detailed elements of synergy as well as the development of tactics for achieving potential synergy. Synergy, however great its potential, will not just happen; it must be planned for and caused to happen. This can only be achieved if it is defined and explicated so that plans can be rationally developed. Rockwell International, for example, took nearly ten years before it was able to achieve the level of technological synergy on which the North American-Rockwell merger had been predicated.

The participative aspect of synergistic analysis is much the same as that previously discussed for the development of strategic data bases. Synergy is so ephemeral that a single individual is almost never able to explicate and foresee completely. The analysis of the synergy aspects of strategy therefore can only effectively be accomplished in a participative group environment. Since synergy is extremely complex, its achievement requires the successful bringing together of many different elements, whereas a failure to achieve synergy can be brought about by the exclusion or failure of one, or a small number, of these elements. Since knowledge of all of the required elements is not generally in the possession of any individual, the assessment of synergy requires more than consideration of almost everything. The single bit of knowledge that one person may possess may be the critical factor that permits or precludes the achievement of synergy, and the only way to determine this is to bring together knowledgeable people to participate in synergy assessments.

Formalized processes, such as the Delphi approach (see Chapter 7) may be used to achieve this end. However, formalized approaches are not necessary to the achievement of participative explication of the elements of synergy. A simple group discussion focused toward the development of a specific list of

[18] See Andrews, K. R., *The Concept of Corporate Strategy,* Dow Jones-Irwin, Homewood, Ill., 1971, Chapter 1.

synergy elements, along with an evaluation of the likelihood of achieving each and the impediments to doing so, may be all that is required to demonstrate that some synergy elements are of that common variety that should be devoutly sought and hoped for, but not counted on. When such realities are brought into the strategy choice process, they can serve to deter the wishful thinking that has so often characterized synergy-based strategies.

Corporate Models for Strategy Evaluations

The process of developing and refining strategies is necessarily somewhat loosely structured because it importantly involves elements of creativity and insight. The process of strategy *evaluation* must be more highly structured, since it is in the evaluation phase that strategies are to be stringently assessed in terms of their potential contribution to the achievement of organizational objectives.

Of course, many of the development and refinement approaches discussed earlier have evaluative aspects. Similarly, the corporate models to be discussed here may be used at the strategy refinement level. However, the principal reason for developing a corporate model is usually strategy evaluation.

THE PURPOSE AND USE OF MODELS

Any management model has a purpose of *predicting the consequences of proposed actions*. These consequences are predicted in terms of measures that are dictated or suggested by organizational objectives, e.g., market share, profit, ROI. This is so whether the model is a sophisticated computerized one or a "mental model" that exists only in the mind of a top executive. At either extreme, and throughout the range between, models are *abstractions of reality that are used to predict the consequences of actions or strategies that are being considered for use in the real world.*

Thus, when considering a price increase, the anticipated consequence is always first predicted in terms of additional revenues, lost sales, customer reaction, competitor reaction, etc. Whether this prediction is done formally or informally, it is done through the use of a *model,* an entity that considers the *most important* aspects of the process in question and their relationships to each other. Even if this process is solely a mental one, it nonetheless involves a model, since the considerations are abstract and selective (i.e., they do not involve the myriad complexities of the real world).

All human choice processes must therefore involve models. Strategy choice in organizations almost always involves formal models of some variety,

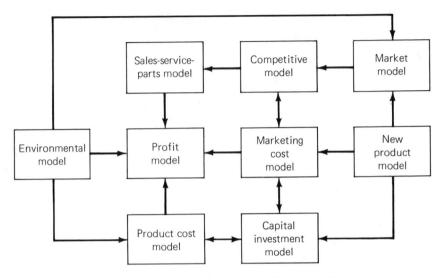

FIGURE 8.4 Conceptual Outline of Corporate Model.

even if they are only of a financial variety such as projections of the stream of costs and revenues to be expected from proposed strategies.

CORPORATE MODELS

"Corporate model" is the term used to describe the broadest variety of formal model applied to the strategy choice process. Such models depict the entire organization in abstract terms. Because of their breadth, they are particularly well suited to the selection of strategies (general directions) for the organization.[19]

Figure 8.4 shows the conceptual outline of a corporate model developed by the authors for a business firm. The profit model module is the calculational core of the overall model. It takes the interrelated outputs from four varieties of models and projects the volume, profit, and profitability consequences for various sets of conditions. The four general inputs to the profit model are from:

1. Market oriented models
   a. Sales-service model
   b. Market model
   c. Competitive model

---

[19] Other models that are more appropriate to program evaluation and resource allocation choice levels will be treated in the next chapter.

2. Marketing cost model
3. Product cost model
4. Environmental model

The first of the three market-oriented submodels depicts sales and service relationships in the business in question. The business involves the sale of capital equipment and the subsequent sale of parts, service, and service contracts. This model utilizes historic patterns to project the distribution of future service and maintenance revenues to be anticipated because of sales of capital equipment. It also uses inputs from the market and competitive models to project future service revenues to be expected on competitive equipment based on competitor's sales projections.

The other two market-oriented submodels are the market and competitive models. The market submodel projects the market for this variety of equipment based on data on construction activity patterns in a variety of geographic areas and construction types. The competitive model uses past and projected competitive practices and patterns in the industry to predict how the total market will be divided among the competitors.

The profit model also processes the outputs of the marketing and product cost models, which project these cost elements under various conditions, and an environmental model, which primarily involves inflationary and other uncontrollable economic forces.

The other submodels in Figure 8.4 (capital investment and new product) are used to analyze specific strategies involving either or both of these elements, e.g., a process investment intended to reduce production cost or a new product. The outputs of these models are fed into the overall profit model through other submodels as shown by the arrows in the figure.

The uses of such corporate models are manifold. The particular model of Figure 8.4 was used for three general purposes:

1. The *testing of proposed strategies* through the posing of "what if" questions.
2. The *analysis of the sensitivity of overall business performance* to changes in various factors.
3. The *forecasting* of business performance.

To illustrate each of these uses, consider the three statements below, each of which is an actual request by management for a model run, one for each of the above categories.

1. What would happen if we went out of the X segment of our business over the next two years and began producing for the Y market as soon as possible?

2. How important is the combined effect of our improved warranty and the anticipated improvement in our parts and service sales generating capacity?
3. Suppose that we forecast the following changes in construction over the next few years, what would be the effect?
   Family dwellings down 10% per year
   Apartments up 15% next year and 10% per year thereafter
   Government building down 5% per year

The model of Figure 8.4 presented "answers" for each of these questions in terms of financial projections of revenues, income, and ROI on a year-by-year basis in both actual dollars and present dollars (corrected for inflation). These projections are made for various business lines for both domestic and international markets.

When the projected consequences of any question such as those above are compared with a *base case,* a projection which has been agreed to represent a "surprise free" projection, or a "business as usual" scenario, the potential value of such a model becomes clear. For instance, "what if" strategy questions serve to directly evaluate proposed strategies. Even if one is unwilling to use the model as the final basis for choice, such projections often serve to delineate poor strategies (thus saving further evaluative effort) and to highlight potentially good strategies for further analysis.

Sensitivity questions like the previous question 2 serve to define what is important and what is relatively less important. This seemingly simple thing is, in fact, one of the primary values of corporate models, because analyses conducted in other ways cannot so readily isolate single factors, pairs of factors, etc., in terms of their relative importance. For instance, in the company involved in the model of Figure 8.4, a study group presented a report to top management that resulted in a morning-long discussion concerning various strategy elements, production cost improvements, material utilization, and the potential sale of a production facility. At lunch, the chief executive said, "Let's see what the model says about this!" Various runs of the model were made over the lunch break, with the result that all three of the strategy elements that had consumed the entire morning's discussion were shown to have relatively small strategic impact on the firm's long-run future! The identification of *high impact* variables, strategies, and sets of variables and strategies and of relatively low impact strategies is an important use of such models.

Corporate models can also be used in the forecasting, as illustrated by the third question above. In the company in question, this use of the model provided insights that resulted in a regional strategy for the company's marketing effort. Such a strategy had never been contemplated until the differential construction activity forecasts for various construction segments in various parts of the country, coupled with a marketing and distribution cost analysis, showed that a uniform nationwide strategy would be clearly inferior to one that emphasized different products in various geographical areas.

These uses of the specific corporate model in Figure 8.4 generally reflect the uses to which models have been put by a survey conducted by Gershefski.[20] That survey resulted in the following list of most frequently mentioned ways in which corporate models are used to aid management:

1. Evaluate alternative operating or investment strategies.
2. Provide revised financial projections rapidly.
3. Assist in determining feasible corporate goals.
4. Analyze the effect of interacting items.
5. Determine the sensitivity of earnings to external factors.
6. Develop a documented projection of financial position.
7. Allow management to consider more variables when planning.
8. Determine the need for long-term debt.
9. Validate manually prepared projections and existing procedures.
10. Develop a corporate data base or information system.
11. Assist in the evaluation of capital investment proposals.

APPROACHES TO CORPORATE MODELING

Corporate models may be constructed to emphasize various aspects of the organization. Indeed, since the task of building a corporate model is of significant magnitude, such models should be constructed in modular fashion with the early modules being those most related to the priority strategy choices facing the organization.

The overall model of Figure 8.4 was constructed in such a fashion. Each phase of model development allowed for restricted use of the model while subsequent modules were being developed.

Other corporate models have been constructed to emphasize various aspects of the overall enterprise. For instance, Kotler[21] describes an approach emphasizing the marketing sector of the business. Boulden and Buffa[22] describe a computerized approach that emphasizes production relationships in an overall corporate model. In each case, the segment of the business being em-

[20] Gershefski, G. W., "Corporate Models: The State of the Art," *Management Science*, Vol. 16, Feb. 1970, pp. B303–B312. See also, Naylor, T. H. and Schauland, H., "A Survey of Users of Corporate Planning Models," *Management Science*, May 1976, pp. 927–937.

[21] Kotler, P., "Corporate Models: Better Marketing Plans," *Harvard Business Review*, July–Aug. 1970, pp. 135–149.

[22] Boulden, J. B., and Buffa, E. S., "Corporate Models: On-Line, Real-Time Systems," *Harvard Business Review*, July–Aug. 1970, pp. 65–83.

phasized is treated in detail, whereas other segments are treated at a high level of aggregation and abstraction. A model such as that of Kotler therefore, permits the analysis of alternative *marketing* strategies in some detail, but it is not an effective vehicle for analyzing nonmarketing strategies.

In a later chapter dealing with information systems to support strategic planning, we shall return to the question of how corporate models and other management decision support systems can be developed to enhance the quality of strategic choice.

Summary

The selection of the organization's strategy is the keystone of strategic planning. This is so because strategy is extremely important, yet it is not so firmly cast that it cannot be reviewed and altered if it is inappropriate. This means that the strategy choice level represents a unique combination of significance and of opportunity for choice. Strategy selection may be thought of as a three-stage process of development, refinement, and evaluation. Although these stages are not necessarily distinct, they are useful ways of conceptualizing the strategy choice process.

A basic strategy concept distinguishes between both products and markets in terms of whether they are currently in existence. A market development strategy, for instance, focuses on existing products in new markets, whereas a product development strategy focuses on new products in existing markets.

Once a basic strategy concept has been selected it may be refined and elaborated using any of a variety of methods such as through the application of organizational objectives and strategic data bases, through the use of normative propositions, through the use of organizational development techniques on using the results of analytic models. The business screen approach of General Electric may be applied to this refinement function in an organization which is involved in many diverse businesses.

Timing sequencing and synergy considerations are important elements of strategy refinement. A strategy's impact may be importantly affected by *when* it is put into effect, and its substantive and sequential relations with other strategies and actions. Thus, strategies may not be evaluated independently; they may require analysis within a portfolio of actions to be implemented.

In the strategy evaluation phase, corporate models may be used to predict the consequences of proposed strategies. Such models may also be useful to explicate the relatively high-impact elements of strategy and to provide forecasts of the future.

Chapter 8—Questions and Answers

1. Strategies have been defined as the general prescription that gives direction to the organization's future; such strategies tend to be more or less enduring. Defend or refute this statement.

2. It is possible for an organization to develop a strategic direction that is a reflection of implicit strategies rather than explicit strategies. What is meant by this statement?

3. The process of strategy choice can be thought of as consisting of three elements. Identify and define these three elements.

4. What is the purpose in using strategic data bases in the development of strategy? What are some of the strategic data bases that can be used in strategy development?

5. What role do objectives play in the process of strategy development? How does a strategic planner deal with a number of objectives in selecting strategy?

6. What is the role of feedback in the refinement stage of strategy dvelopment? What sort of feedback should the strategic planner seek to identify?

7. What is a normative proposition which provides guidance in strategy development? What are some principles of management that can provide a point of departure in developing normative propositions to refine strategies?

8. Select a business organization with which you are familiar and develop some normative propositions that you feel would support the existing strategy of that organization.

9. Strategic inferences may be drawn from assumptions and forecasts. Apply this idea to an organizational situation of your choosing.

10. What is the purpose of using the results from such analytical models as PIMS in strategy development and refinement? What is PIMS?

11. Describe the conceptual nature of the General Electric business screen.

12. At what organizational level should a model such as the General Electric business screen be developed? Who should have the responsibility for developing such a screen? Who should use the business screen and for what purposes?

13. The time dimension of strategy is relevant in developing a sense of direction for an organization's future. What is the conceptual thinking behind the development of a product sales life cycle?

14. Using the systems development life-cycle concept developed by NASA (National Aeronautics and Space Administration), portray a systems life cycle for the writing of a research report for a class.

15. What is the meaning of synergy? How does synergy relate to the matter of strategy choice? What are some types of synergy that can be applied to a business organization?

16. What is the purpose of a management model? If management models are indeed abstracts of the world of reality, what value do such models hold for the manager?

17. Explain the "Product-Market Strategy Space" in Table 8.1. How can it be used in strategic decision making in a business firm? Does it relate to the strategy of a public agency as well?

18. What is the potential role of PIMS in strategy refinement?
19. What is the sequential aspect of the time dimension of strategy?

Chapter 8—Strategic Questions for the Manager

1. Considering existing organizational mission, objectives, and goals, how supportive is the existing strategy of these ends?
2. Do existing strategies define the general direction of the organization? Do these strategies provide enduring guidance for the organization?
3. Does a distinct understanding exist on the part of key executives concerning the need for strategy *development, refinement,* and *evaluation?*
4. Have basic strategies been developed that deal with products/markets that currently exist and those that do not currently exist?
5. Can the existing strategic data bases (Chapter 6) in the organization be *directly* related to the refinement of strategy in the organization? Why or why not?
6. What feedback has been developed to evaluate objectives? Can this feedback be measured and verified?
7. Would there be any advantage for the organization to participate in the *PIMS* model of the Marketing Science Institute?
8. How appropriate is the timing for the product research and development strategy? What is the basis and justification for that timing?
9. When was the last time the market position strategy, to include product development and market development, was reviewed?
10. Have any attempts been made to understand the time dimension of the organizational strategy? Has the *sequence* of elements in that strategy been identified?
11. Have proposed technological developments of the organizational products been evaluated for acceptance in terms of societal and cultural factors?
12. What is the typical life cycle for organizational products? Does a study of this life cycle suggest any strategies that might enhance the organization's competitive position?
13. Have the synergistic elements of the organizational strategy been evaluated?
14. Have any organizational models for evaluating strategy been considered?

References

Anderson, C. R., and Paine, F. T., "PIMS: A Re-examination," Presentation to the Academy of Management, Orlando, Florida, Aug. 1977.

Ansoff, H. I., "The Firm of the Future," *Harvard Business Review,* Vol. 43, Sept.–Oct. 1965.

Ansoff, H. I., and Leontiades, J. C., "Strategic Portfolio Management," *Journal of General Management,* Vol. 4, No. 1, Autumn, 1976.

Berg, N., "Strategic Planning in Conglomerate Companies," *Harvard Business Review,* Vol. 43, May–June 1965, pp. 79–92.

Boulden, J. B., and Buffa, E. S., "Corporate Models: On-Line, Real-Time Systems," *Harvard Business Review,* July–Aug. 1970.

Channon, D. F., "Strategy Formulation as an Analytical Process," *International Studies of Management and Organization,* Vol. VII, No. 2, Summer, 1977.

Clifford, D. K., Jr., "Managing the Product Life Cycle," *McKinsey Quarterly,* Vol. I, Spring 1965, pp. 48–60.

Corey, E. R., and Starr, S. H., Organization Strategy—A Marketing Approach, Division of Research, Graduate School of Business Administration, Harvard University, Boston, 1971.

Cox, W. E., Jr., "Product Life Cycles as Marketing Models," *Journal of Business,* Vol. 40, Oct. 1967, pp. 375–388.

Dhalla, N. K., and Yuspeh, S., "Forget the Product Life Cycle Concept!" *Harvard Business Review,* Jan.–Feb. 1976.

"General Electric's Stoplight Strategy for Planning," *Business Week,* April 28, 1975.

Gershefski, G. W., "Corporate Models: The State of the Art," *Management Science,* Vol. 16, Feb. 1970.

Gluck, F. W., Foster, R. N., and Forbis, J. L., "Cure For Strategic Malnutrition," *Harvard Business Review,* Nov.–Dec. 1976.

Haggerty, P. E., "Strategies, Tactics, and Research," *Research Management,* Vol. 9, 1966.

Hall, W. K., "Strategic Planning Models: Are Top Managers Really Finding Them Useful?" *Journal of Business Policy,* Vol. 3, No. 3, Spring 1973.

Hedley, B., "A Fundamental Approach to Strategy Development," *Long Range Planning,* Dec. 1976.

Kano, H. "Managing For the Future in Japanese Industry," *The Future of the Corporation* (H. Kahn, editor), Mason and Lipscomb Publishers, New York, 1974.

Kinnunen, R. M., "Hypothesis Related to Strategy Formulation in Large Divisionalized Companies," *Academy of Management Review,* Oct. 1976.

Kotler, P., "Corporate Models: Better Marketing Plans," *Harvard Business Review,* July–Aug. 1970.

Lusch, R. F., Udell, J. G., and Larzniak, G. R., "The Future of Marketing Strategy," *Business Horizons,* Dec. 1976.

McDonald, J., "The Use of Management Science in Making a Corporate Policy Decision—Charging for Directory Assistance Service," *Interfaces,* Nov. 1976.

Murdic, R. G., "The Long-Range Planning Matrix," *California Management Review,* Vol. 7, Winter 1974, pp. 35–42.

Naylor, T. H., and Gattis, D. R., "Corporate Planning Models," *California Management Review,* Summer 1976.

Naylor, T. H., and Schauland, H., "A Survey of Users of Corporate Planning Models," *Management Science,* May 1976, pp. 927–937.

Payne, B. *Planning for Company Growth: The Executives Guide to Effective Long Range Planning,* McGraw-Hill, New York, 1963.

Perutz, P., "Implications of Qualitative Growth For a Business," *Long Range Planning,* Oct. 1976.

Prahalad, C. K., "Strategic Choices in Diversified MNC's," *Harvard Business Review,* July–Aug. 1976.

Rapaport, L. A., and Drews, W. P., "Mathematical Approach to LRP," *Harvard Business Review,* May–June 1962.

Rumelt, R. P., *Strategy, Structure and Economic Performance in Large American Industrial Corporations,* Harvard University Press, Cambridge, Mass., 1974.

Schoffler, S., Buzzell, R. D., and Heany, D. F., "Impact of Strategic Planning on Profit Performance," *Harvard Business Review,* March–April 1974, pp. 137–145.

Smalter, D. J., "The Influence of Department of Defense Practices on Corporate Planning," *Management Technology,* Vol. 4, Dec. 1964.

Springer, C. H., "Strategic Management in General Electric," *Operations Research,* Nov.–Dec. 1973.

Tersine, R. J., and Riggs, W. E., "Delphi Technique: A Long Range Planning Tool," *Business Horizons,* April 1976.

Vancil, R. F., "Strategy Formulation in Complex Organizations," *Sloan Management Review,* Winter 1976.

Weber, J. A., "Planning Corporate Growth With Inverted Product Life Cycles," *Long Range Planning,* Oct. 1976.

Webster, R. E., "New Product Adoption in Industrial Markets," *Journal of Marketing,* Vol. 33, July 1969.

Williams, R. E., "Top Management Ferment at Koehring," *Business Week,* Jan. 19, 1976.

Wills, G., Ashton, D., and Taylor, B. (editors), *Technological Forecasting and Corporate Strategy,* Bradford University Press, Crosby Lockwood, 1969.

Woodruff, R. B., "A Systematic Approach to Market Opportunity Analyses," *Business Horizons,* Aug. 1976.

Chapter 9

SELECTING PROGRAMS,
SETTING GOALS, AND
ALLOCATING RESOURCES

The "action" level of planning comes at the point where specific programs and projects are instituted and resources are allocated to them. Although this is the lowest level of decision making in the hierarchy of strategic decisions, it is equally as important as the higher levels, because of the old cliche concerning the "best laid plans of mice and men . . . ."

In other words, the best mission, soundest objectives, and most brilliant strategy will go for naught unless they are translated into action programs that implement the strategy and serve to fulfill the objectives and mission. This requires the translation of organizational objectives into *organizational goals:* specific, measurable, timely levels of accomplishment that can serve both as motivators of action and as standards of performance against which actions can be evaluated. It also requires that these programs and projects are supported by resources of a quantity, quality, and mix, which permit the achievement of the goals, since even the most carefully conceived programs are doomed to failure if they are inadequately supported with resources.

This motherhood and sin emphasis on the importance of program and project selection, goal setting and resource allocation in strategic planning may be brought into sharp focus if one observes the large number of firms and other organizations that have expended significant resources on planning, only to find that the output, the plan, is filed on a shelf and has little discernible impact on the organization. These many failures of planning are not so at all; they often represent a failure to *implement* the plan through effective program and project selection, goal setting, and adequate allocations of resources to programs.[1]

Basic Program and Project Concepts

The term *program* is used in various ill-defined ways. The term, as used here, refers to a collection of activities, or *projects,* that are addressed to the achieve-

---

[1] In a subsequent chapter, we shall discuss an overall approach to the successful implementation of *planning* in organizations. Here, the emphasis is on the implementation of the *plan* through program and resource decisions.

ment of a specified purpose or set of purposes. For instance, a "cost reduction program" has a clearly implied purpose. Such a program may itself be a collection of activities, or it may subsume a set of well-defined *projects,* each of which is itself a collection of activities. In either case, these activities are directed toward the achievement of some well-defined purpose.

Usually the program or project's purpose is such that it is both clearly definable and explicitly achievable, e.g., "to reduce costs by 10% before January." Thus, *programs and projects normally have a finite life.* Unlike strategies and missions, which may go on forever, programs begin at a point where a purpose is specified and resources are allocated and end at a point when the purpose is achieved, or when a decision is made to terminate the effort and reallocate the resources.

The idea of a program in a public organization is exemplified by the following excerpt from a U.S. Bureau of the Budget directive that established basic PPBS (Planning-Programming-Budgeting System) procedures in the federal government.

> Programs . . . are groups of agency . . . activities or operations . . . which serve the same broad objective . . . Succinct captions or headings describing the objective should be applied to each such grouping. Obviously, each will contain . . . (activities) . . . which are complementary or are close substitutes in relation to the objectives to be attained. For example, a broad . . . objective is improvement of higher education. This would . . . contain programs aiding undergraduate, graduate and vocational education including construction of facilities, as well as such auxiliary Federal activities as library support and relevant research programs." [2]

Thus, an objective, or set of objectives may be sought through a strategy that is implemented through a series of programs. The programs are *output oriented;* they directly relate to the achievement of some organizational purpose. They are *not,* as organizational units often are, defined in terms of the input resources (people, equipment and funds) that they utilize.

This characteristic distinguishes programs and projects, (sometimes called the horizontal organization), from departments and functional units, (some times referred to as the vertical organization). The accounting department is defined as a collection of accounting resources (people, machines, etc.) that represent inputs to the organization's activities. A program is defined, on the other hand, in output terms of *something to be achieved,* regardless of which resources may be devoted to it.

This distinction between inputs and outputs and vertical and horizontal organization is described in Figure 9.1, which shows a program structure (set of programs) for a corporation. The various programs cut across both the operating units and staff functions of the firm. For instance, the "plant nutrition"

---

[2] *U.S. Bureau of the Budget Bulletin* 66-3, Oct. 17, 1965, p. 4.

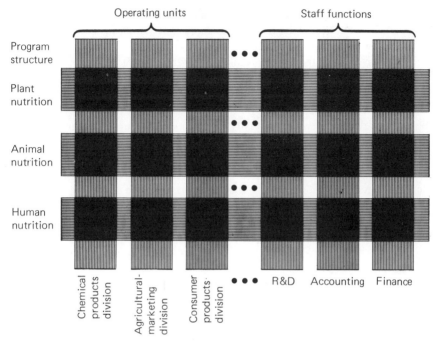

FIGURE 9.1 Corporate Program Structure.

program involves inputs from the chemical products division as well as the agricultural marketing and consumer products divisions (which may wish to sell plant nutrition products to the farmers and consumers respectively). The program also draws on research and development, accounting, and other service departments for support.

A government agency such as the Department of Defense has similar output-oriented programs such as "air defense" and "strategic retaliatory." Each of these programs is horizontal in that it utilizes inputs from various services (Army, Navy, Air Force) and various staff support functions (research and development, procurement, etc.).

Each such program may involve a number of *projects*. For instance, a project at the University of Pittsburgh that has the purpose of designing a new curriculum in strategic planning may be one part of an overall government program to improve graduate education. Another project at UCLA may be a part of the same program, but it may be quite different in content. For instance, it might involve the development of a new computerized teaching machine. The projects are different in their objectives, technologies, locations, and resource requirements, but they complement one another in facilitating the achievement of a broader (program) purpose.

Of course, all of the programs and projects that might make sense in an organization are not strategic in nature. For instance, a large order from a customer might be "projectized" by having a project manager assigned to the job of seeing that the order is filled on time and within cost and quality specifications. However, this would normally be considered as an "operating project" rather than a "strategic project."

Strategic programs and projects are directly and importantly related to basic organizational objectives and strategies. Such a strategic program might be "new product development." This program would be supported by product development projects involving specific new product ideas. Another strategic program might be "acquisitions." This program could involve projects in which various acquisition candidates are being analyzed, perhaps differentiated by industry, if the organization's objectives are to diversify through acquisition into several different fields.

Sometimes, major internal system development projects may well be strategic in nature. For instance, one firm stated its strategy to be one that involved direct head-to-head competition with several other firms that had dominated a particular market. To do this, it developed new product development programs, cost reduction programs, etc., but it also included a program of competitive intelligence gathering under this strategy. A competitive business intelligence systems development project thereby became directly supportive of a major business strategy and was considered as a part of the set of strategic programs. Other system development projects that existed in the organization and that had objectives related solely to the more efficient operation of the organization were not so designated.

The Hierarchy of Goals

Organizational goals are best thought of in terms of a hierarchy of those things which the organization, as an entity and as a collection of subunits and individuals, is trying to attain. A useful hierarchy might be:

Mission
Organizational Objectives
Organizational Goals
Program Goals
Group, Project or Subunit Goals
Individual Goals

Of course, individuals and groups also have objectives, longer range broader things that they are trying to attain, but within the structure of the formal organizational planning system, their goals are most significant.

This hierarchy shows that organizational objectives must be *translated* into terms that are more specific and timely (organizational goals) and then *disaggregated* into sets that are appropriate to the organizational level involved: programs, projects, groups, subunits, or individuals.

This process of translation and disaggregation must be accomplished to assure *goal congruence,* the logical aggregation of one set of goals into the other goals sets and then, into the objectives. For instance, the goals delegated to individuals must fit together to produce a project goal. Various project goals must similarly mesh to form a program goal. Various program goals are related to organizational goals, which in turn must, in combination, and over time, logically specify the accomplishment of overall organizational objectives. *Thus, each level of goals is derived from, and in turn supports the accomplishment of, the next highest level in the hierarchy.*

ORGANIZATIONAL GOALS

Figure 6.2 shows this relationship between organizational objectives and organizational goals quite clearly for a business firm. Among the most common measures in terms of which business goals are stated are:

Percentage market share (by product and/or country).

A ratio, such as return on sales.

An absolute figure for sales.

A minimum figure for customer complaints.

A maximum figure for hours lost in industrial disputes.

A labor productivity ratio.

Total number of employees.

A maximum employee wastage rate.

A standard cost.

A cost reduction target.

A date by which a particular event must take place (e.g., new product launch).[3]

An obvious point concerning objectives and goals is often missed by managers, viz., they are the common denominators of the management process and

[3] List suggested by Hussey, D., *Corporate Planning: Theory and Practice,* Pergamon Press, New York, 1974, p. 112.

can provide the basis for developing the organizational structure, performance evaluation, control, and coordination. Thus goals can be translated directly into programs or projects, (e.g., a cost reduction program), and have a part of the organization itself revolve around the goal (since a project is an organizational entity).

PROGRAM AND PROJECT GOALS

Goals have been treated in this book as specific, measurable, and timely things that are to be sought or attained. Every program and project naturally involves three generic kinds of goals, *cost, time, and performance*. *Cost* refers to the resources being expended. One would want to assess cost sometimes in terms of an expenditure rate (e.g., dollars per month) and sometimes in terms of total cumulative expenditures (or both). *Time* refers to the timeliness of progress in terms of a schedule that has been set up. Answers to questions such as "Is the project on schedule?" "How many days must be made up?" etc., reflect this dimension of progress.

The third dimension of project progress is *performance;* i.e., how is the project meeting its objectives or specifications? For example, in a product development project, performance would be assessed by the degree to which the product meets the specifications or goal set for it. Typically, products are developed by a series of improvements that successively approach a desired goal, e.g., soap powder with the same cleaning properties but less sudsiness. In the case of an airplane, certain requirements as to speed, range, altitude capability, etc., are set and the degree to which a particular design in a series of successive refinements meets these requirements is an assessment of the performance dimension of the aircraft design project.

MANAGEMENT BY OBJECTIVES

The popular term "management by objectives" (MBO) refers to a process of administering the organization through a participative goal-oriented process. Although the term "objective" is used, MBO is really more related to "goal" as the term is used here.

The purpose of MBO is the clear definition and communication of goals to each organizational level responsible for accomplishing them. People who are operating under management by objectives programs stand a better chance of knowing exactly what is expected of them and how they are to be evaluated for their performance. The management by objectives approach assumes that an individual performs more effectively when he has developed his own objectives and has more opportunity to control his own behavior. At the heart of the MBO concept is a set of beliefs about the value system that the people hold and how they pursue their organizational duties.[4]

Strategic Program Evaluation and Selection

Program evaluation and selection cannot really be dealt with independently of the decisions regarding the choice of goals and the allocation of resources since goals, resources, and the worth of a program or project are intrinsically interdependent. That this is so is made clear by the following illustrations:

> Different goals can be achieved at various levels of resource commitment—e.g., we can complete the project one month ahead of schedule but it will cost $10,000 more and we will need to have an extra engineer.

> A project's worth depends on the goals associated with it, e.g., having this product developed by January is useless to us, because we need it for the Christmas season.

Thus, it is never really possible to first decide which program is to be implemented, then decide on goals for it and on the resources to commit to it, since worth depends on goals and goals depend on resources. We shall idealize the strategic choice process to suggest that this can be done, however, since that is the way that it is usually done in practice.

The practical process involves the specification of alternative proposed strategic programs and projects, each with associated goals and assumed resource commitments. These alternatives form the pool from which an initial selection of programs is made. This selection process may involve the redefining of some of the tentative goals. Then, resources are allocated to various programs. When programs are not sufficiently high priority to be fully funded, they may be discarded, held in abeyance, or partially funded. If partial funding is the choice that is made, program goals must be redefined.

Thus, at the level of program evaluation and selection, one assumes that the program goals are correct and that funding is available. Subsequently, both of these assumptions may be modified.

PRELIMINARY PROGRAM EVALUATION AND SELECTION

At the initial phase of program evaluation and selection, the primary requirement is for a filtering process that permits the selection of those strategic programs and projects that will subsequently be subjected to intensive economic

---

[4]See Idiorne, G. S., *Management by Objective,* Pitman, New York, 1965, Reddin, W. J., *Effective Management by Objectives: Three D Method,* McGraw-Hill, New York, 1971 and the discussion in Chapter 7 of MBO as it may be related to strategic planning.

analysis. Thus, at this preliminary level, the judgments of managers and technical experts play an important role. This judgment may simply be directly expressed in an unstructured fashion, or it may be formalized to one of a number of different degrees, depending on the level of sophistication that is warranted.

To illustrate, consider the product selection decision faced by a firm that has adopted a new product development and introduction strategy. Product ideas come to the firm from a variety of sources (research and development, marketing, outside brokers, etc.) in a variety of different forms, (e.g., ideas and mockups). The first thoughts that come to the mind of a manager faced with evaluation of the worth of such a new product idea are:

1. Can the present production facilities be utilized to manufacture this product?
2. Can present raw materials be utilized?
3. Can it be priced competitively?
4. Is there an existing demand?
5. Does it make use of the know-how of our present organization?
6. Can the product be distributed through the present organization?

Unfortunately, there are no simple good or bad answers to such questions. What is needed is a logical way to approach the questions systematically and consistently so that all project ideas get equal treatment. In this way they can at least be compared with each other to identify those that should be picked for development, even if precise measures of their real worth cannot be obtained.

If a large number of product or project ideas are available, it may be desirable to reduce the evaluative workload by eliminating as many bad ideas as possible through a preliminary screening step as illustrated in Figure 9.2. This figure shows the use of some basic selection criteria in a "go-no-go" fashion to "separate the wheat from the chaff." It is important to note that this type of elimination process cannot be accomplished arbitrarily. The decision rules for elimination must be consistent with organizational objectives, strategies, and policies. If there is any doubt about eliminating a project idea, it is best to keep the idea and subject it to further analysis along with the good ones. This preliminary screening process results in a pool of programs, projects, or products that merit further evaluation.

CRITERIA FOR STRATEGIC PROGRAM EVALUATION

The most critical aspect of any scheme for a strategic program or project evaluation is in the determination of the criteria against which proposals will be judged. It is in this dimension that the strategic choice applications of program selection are meaningful.

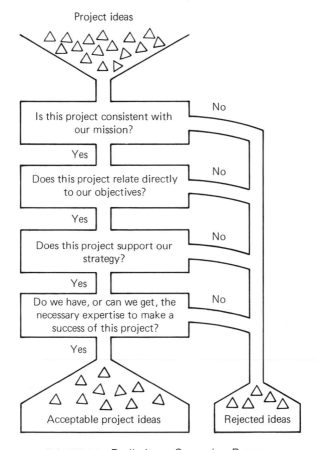

FIGURE 9.2 Preliminary Screening Process.

The simplest thing that can be said in this regard is that *these criteria must directly reflect the organization's previously chosen missions, objectives, strategies, and goals.* Thus, if a new product development program is under consideration, it must first be consistent with the mission, the kind of business that the organization is in. Then, it must fit with the strategy and the objectives that have been established.

For instance, a new product idea that required new production and distribution facilities would probably not be consistent with a "tight ship" strategy, but these might be necessary attributes for a product idea that would fit into a diversification strategy.

Thus, *the criteria to be used to judge the worth of a program must be stra-*

tegic criteria that emanate directly from the organization's mission, objectives, strategies, and goals. Those programs that are highly rated under one set of objectives, strategies, and goals might not be highly rated under another set. There are, therefore, no such things as good and bad programs. Rather, there are only programs that are good and bad relative to a given set of strategic criteria.

Of course, one might argue that the preliminary criteria related to mission, objective, and strategy consistency in Figure 9.2 are too rigid and do not allow for creative changes in established organizational missions, objectives, and strategies. We have, however, emphasized throughout that the hierarchical process of establishing missions, then objectives, then strategies, then programs, and finally goals is an iterative one involving feedback loops. This means that strategies, once chosen, can be changed, either because it is found at the program level that they cannot be implemented, or because other programs not supporting the strategy are found to be so good that they dictate a strategy reconsideration. Indeed, this may lead to a revision of objectives and even, though not often, a revision in the mission of the organization.

However, this "bottoms up" approach must not be the norm. Rather, if programs are to influence the choice of higher level elements in the hierarchy, they must be so outstandingly meritorious as to warrant a deviation from the standard "top-down" approach. If this is not the case, the organization may well find itself involved in a collection of unrelated programs, each good in its own right, but without any synergy, economy of scale, or focus. Such a situation has led to the downfall of many organizations when they eventually found that they could not control, much less effectively operate, a wide diversity of such programs.

Thus, a preliminary screening process such as that in Figure 9.2 is a rational extension of the top-down strategic decision process that has been discussed in this and the previous chapters.

PROJECT SELECTION METHODS

There are a wide variety of project selection methods that have been developed for various situations, such as marketing and research and development, and that have been made use of in the selection of strategic programs. Here, we briefly review a number of general classes of methods to provide a basis for the selection of an appropriate level of sophistication to suit a particular situation.

The many varieties of selection methods may be categorized as:

1. Qualitative project evaluation schemes
2. Simple project scoring schemes
3. Probabilistic project scoring schemes

4. Sophisticated project scoring models
5. Economic project selection models

As one proceeds sequentially through these general classes, he is moving from the simple to the complex, from small data requirements to large ones, and from easily-understood schemes to sophisticated approaches that may not be readily understood by managers.

The stage of strategic choice may determine which level of sophistication is appropriate. In the initial screening stage, a simple low-cost method is probably preferred. Later, when more stringent evaluation is necessary, precise dollar estimates should be incorporated into an economic model. In even later stages, the manager may be concerned with models that consider the project mix and trade-offs between various projects. The sequence of presentation here is in general consistency with this view. The initial models are most appropriate for screening. Subsequent models introduce precise economic estimates and consideration of the mix of projects and programs.

QUALITATIVE PROJECT EVALUATION SCHEMES. After project ideas pass the preliminary screening stage, they must be compared with each other and ranked in order of relative attractiveness according to the previously chosen criteria. A simple checklist shown in Table 9.1 can give a decision maker an overall picture of project worth with very little effort. As can be seen, the first project is obviously better than the second one. However, if the profiles are less extreme, a ranking judgment would be more difficult to make. It would then be necessary to introduce some quantitative technique.

SIMPLE PROJECT SCORING SCHEMES. The simplest method of quantifying the preceding checklist approach is to assign numbers to the criterion factors as follows:

1. Rank the various criteria in order of their relative importance to the decision maker and assign "weights" to indicate that ranking. This can be accomplished simply by asking managers to distribute 100 points among the various criteria to reflect their relative importance in the overall decision. Such weights are shown in Column A of Table 9.2 (on a decimal basis). For instance, these weights reflect the conclusion that "Similarity to major business" is only one-half as significant as "Effect on present products" in the judgment of managers.
2. Numerically judge the relative importance of the ratings—very good, good, etc. This can be done subjectively by describing each level in detail and then applying judgment. For instance, the "very good" level of the "Similarity to major business" factor might be described as follows: "A project in this category will totally require existing facilities

TABLE 9.1 / Qualitative Project Evaluation Scheme

Case A: A Generally Favorable Pattern

	RATING				
	VERY GOOD	GOOD	FAIR	POOR	VERY POOR
Similarity to major business	✓				
Technical opportunity	✓				
Value added	✓				
Effect on present products		✓			
Patent protection		✓			
Threat of competition				✓	
Probability of success			✓		

Case B: A Relatively Less Favorable Pattern

	VERY GOOD	GOOD	FAIR	POOR	VERY POOR
Similarity to major business	✓				
Technical opportunity					✓
Value added				✓	
Effect on present products					✓
Patent protection	✓				
Threat of competition		✓			
Probability of success			✓		

and expertise. No additional competences or equipment will be necessary to embark on it."

Other ratings for the various factors would be similarly described and subjectively evaluated to obtain the weights shown across the top of Table 9.2. There, for simplicity, it is assumed that all factors have the same set of rating weights. In general, this need not be the case.

To score a project on this basis simply involves the *summing of the products* of the weights that correspond to the pattern of checkmarks. Projects can then be ranked based upon their appropriate scores. The higher the score, the better the project, and vice versa.

This method has an advantage over the previous one in that the subjective impression derived from looking at a pattern of checkmarks is quantified. However, there is still a major weakness in that the weights are all based upon subjective judgment. For this reason, the project scores cannot be interpreted as absolute fact. For example, a project with a score of 0.37 cannot be said to be definitely superior to one with a score of 0.34, *but* there would be good reason to believe that both of them would be superior to one that received a ranking of

TABLE 9.2 / Basic Project Scoring Scheme

PROJECT EVALUATION FACTOR	(A) RELATIVE WEIGHT	(B) FACTOR RELATIVE VALUES					RATING (A x B)
		1.0 VERY GOOD	0.75 GOOD	0.5 FAIR	0.25 POOR	0.0 VERY POOR	
Similarity to major business	0.10	√					0.10
Technical opportunity	0.15	√					0.15
Value added	0.10			√			0.05
Effect on present products	0.20		√				0.15
Patent protection	0.05	√					0.05
Threat of competition	0.20		.			√	0.00
Probability of success	0.20				√		0.05
Total	1.00						0.55 [a]

[a] Project score.

0.19. In other words, this scheme is designed to aid in the systematic judgment of project intangibles, not to replace judgment.

PROBABILISTIC PROJECT SCORING SCHEME. The basic project scoring scheme can be made a little more precise by adding in probability judgments. Since it is often quite difficult to decide whether or not some factor will be precisely "good," "fair," or even "very poor," with respect to a specific project, provision is made for the decision maker to hedge a little bit.

Table 9.3 illustrates a probabilistic scoring scheme in which a third set of numerical factors has been added to the previous scoring scheme: the probabilities in the body of the table. These probabilities describe the decision-maker's opinion concerning a particular program proposal. For example, the table may be interpreted as saying that the likelihood that the particular project idea in question will positively affect present company products is almost certain (as reflected by the 0.9 entry for "very good") and that it has some chance (as denoted by 0.1 for "good") to have a modest positive effect. It is assessed to have no chance of having a bad effect on present products (as denoted by zero entries for "fair," "poor," and "very poor").

The weights in Table 9.3 have been changed from decimals to illustrate that any arbitrary, but consistent, set of numbers will serve the desired purpose.

The overall project score can be derived under this scheme by multiplying the factor weight, the weight attached to a particular rating level, and the probability of achieving that level and summing across all factors and levels. We may view this in two steps. First, we obtain an expected level weight for each factor, which is independent of the importance of the factor, by multiplying

TABLE 9.3 / Probabilistic Project Scoring Scheme

PROJECT EVALUATION FACTOR	RELATIVE WEIGHT-	LEVEL					EXPECTED LEVEL WEIGHT	CONTRIBUTION TO TOTAL EXPECTED SCORE
		VERY GOOD (10)	GOOD (8)	FAIR (6)	POOR (4)	VERY POOR (2)		
Similarity to major business	10	0.2	0.2	0.4	0.2	0.0	6.8	68.0
Technical opportunity	15	0.0	0.0	0.2	0.4	0.4	3.6	54.0
Value added	10	0.0	0.1	0.5	0.2	0.2	5.0	50.0
Effect on present products	5	0.9	0.1	0.0	0.0	0.0	9.8	49.0
Patent protection	20	0.2	0.4	0.2	0.1	0.1	7.0	140.0
Threat of competition	20	0.9	0.1	0.0	0.0	0.0	9.8	196.0
Probability of success	5	0.8	0.1	0.1	0.0	0.0	9.4	47.0
Personnel necessary	10	0.8	0.1	0.1	0.0	0.0	9.4	94.0
Raw materials necessary	5	0.6	0.2	0.2	0.0	0.0	8.8	44.0
Total	100							742.0[a]

[a] Project score.

each level weight and probability and summing across the five levels. This expected level weight is given in the next-to-last column of Table 9.3. The calculation for the first factor is:

$$10(0.2) + 8(0.2) + 6(0.4) + 4(0.2) + 2(0.0) = 6.8$$

The contribution of each factor to the total expected score may then be incorporated by multiplying its importance weight by the expected level weight and summing over all factors. These individual contributions are given in the last column of Table 9.3 as the factor's "contribution to total expected score." The project score is the sum at the lower right. The probabilistic project scoring scheme is about as complex as a project selection method can become without getting into some mathematics.

SOPHISTICATED PROJECT SCORING MODELS. Sophisticated project scoring models involve economic criteria and scores determined from assessments of temporal distributions of costs and benefits. For instance, representative income streams are given different scores and a project is rated as being "like" one of these representative streams. Table 9.4 illustrates such a model in which five criteria are used:

1. Likelihood of success.
2. Total project income.
3. Total project cost.
4. Timing of the stream of income payments.
5. Timing of the stream of cost payments.

For each of these five criteria, nine categories are set up with related scores from 1 to 9. For instance, the "probability of success" criterion has categories ranging from a lowest (with a score of one) where the likelihood of success is rated below $(u - 1.75\ \sigma)$. The $(u - 1.75\ \sigma)$ designation may be better understood from the diagram in Figure 9.3 which shows a normal (bell-curve) distribution of the factor "likelihood of success." The point u represents the average likelihood of success for projects. The point $(u - 1.75\ \sigma)$ can be seen from the figure to be at a point significantly below the average likelihood of success. Other points can be seen from the figure to represent various levels of success likelihood.[5]

The evaluator is merely asked to judgmentally select a category for each of the first three criteria. Since each category has an associated score, by doing so, he is scoring the project in terms of each of the criteria.

For the two criteria involving streams of payments, the various categories

---

[5] Of course, probabilities may be inserted in Figure 9.3 to better enable judgments to be made, but we have found that the approach shown in the figure is adequate for most purposes.

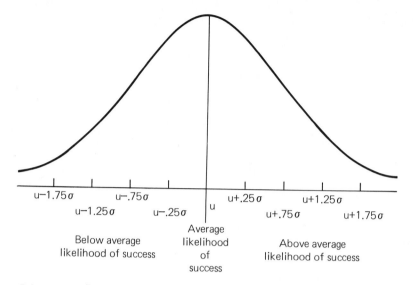

FIGURE 9.3   Distribution of Projects in Terms of Likelihood of Success.

merely represent increasingly valued payment streams.[6] Again, as with the previous criteria, the valuation is asked to match his anticipations for the income and cost streams with one of the illustrations.

The total score for each project may then be developed as the sum of the scores for each of the five criteria. As with previous scoring models, small differences in the total scores of two projects would probably be ignored, but the score provides a basis for ranking projects for further evaluation.

ECONOMIC PROJECT SELECTION MODELS. Ultimately, most organizations will require that stringent economic analyses be conducted of a strategic program before it is adopted. However, because of the impreciseness in assessing future costs and revenues, the greater sophistication and precision that seems to be associated with economic models may be more apparent than real. In the business environment, a measure of profitability such as return on investment, calculated on a discounted basis or on an annual basis projected into the future, is the measure most commonly applied to such assessments.

Also included in this broad category are optimization and simulation selection models that emphasize economic considerations. Although these models are more sophisticated than the others described here, they are less applicable to strategic choice situations than to the selection of engineering and research

[6] Established on the basis of "present worth" calculations.

TABLE 9.4 / Sophisticated Scoring Model

CRITERION	RANGE OR FORM					SCORE
(A) Likelihood of project success	Under $u-1.75\ \sigma$					1
	$u-1.75\ \sigma$ to $u-1.25\ \sigma$					2
	$u-1.25\ \sigma$ to $u-0.75\ \sigma$					3
	.					.
	.					.
	.					.
	Over $u+1.75\ \sigma$					9
(B) Total project income	Under $u-1.75\ \sigma$					1
	$u-1.75\ \sigma$ to $u-1.25\ \sigma$					2
	.					.
	.					.
	Over $u+1.75\sigma$					9
(C) Total project cost	Over $u+1.75\ \sigma$					1
	$u+1.75\ \sigma$ to $u+1.25\ \sigma$					2
	.					.
	.					.
	.					.
	Under $u-1.75\ \sigma$					9
(D) Income stream timing						

FORM	YEAR 1(%)	YEAR 2(%)	YEAR 3(%)	YEAR 4(%)	YEAR 5(%)	
A	0	20	40	30	10	1
B	20	25	25	20	10	2
C	40	20	15	15	10	3
.	.	.	.	.	.	.
.	.	.	.	.	.	.
.	.	.	.	.	.	.

(E) Cost stream timing

FORM	YEAR 1(%)	YEAR 2(%)	YEAR 3(%)	YEAR 4(%)	YEAR 5(%)	
A	40	30	10	10	10	1
B	30	20	20	20	10	2
C	10	25	35	20	10	3
.	.	.	.	.	.	.
.	.	.	.	.	.	.
.	.	.	.	.	.	.

and development projects. In these cases, economic projections are more meaningful.

Moreover, as is the case with any model, the validity of simulation and optimization models (e.g., linear programming) depends intrinsically on the quality of input data. Since most applications tend to either rely on hard (rather than subjective) data, or to assume that the judgmental data that they use are in fact objective data, great care must be taken in assessing the credibility of the model's results. This is particularly so at the level of strategic choice, because so many important strategic considerations are difficult to explicate in the simple quantitative terms that such models require.

Resource Allocation

The final choices to be made in the planning process are those of resource allocation, the allocation of funds to the various strategic programs and projects. It should be recognized that although some organizations do not choose to distinguish between the operating and strategic budgets of their various divisions and departments in the sense that they deal with them as a whole and concurrently, our focus here on strategic choice means that we will not devote attention to the allocation of operating funds.

Some organizations have gone to great lengths to distinguish between operating and strategic funds to avoid the difficulties inherent in the natural law that the short-run will drive out the long-run in periods of budget cutting. Eugene Helms of Texas Instruments has said of this distinction: [7]

> All of our investments at TI are classified either as 'operating' or 'strategic.' By 'operating,' we mean investments or expenses which are necessary for current operations. That means, for one thing, that we could choose not to do them. Theoretically at least, we could terminate all strategic investments with essentially no effect on current operations, although the long term results would surely be disastrous. So these are the investments which are related to growth. By nature they are always avoidable or postponable, and they are undertaken primarily to maximize long term results.

USING THE BUSINESS SCREEN TO ESTABLISH
ALLOCATION PRIORITIES

The highest level of strategic resource allocation is to organizations, business units and divisions, that are essential to the execution of the organization's

---

[7] Helms, E. W., "The OST System for Managing Innovation at Texas Instruments," presented to the Armed Forces Management Association, Washington, D.C., April 7, 1971.

TABLE 9.5 / Business Screen Used to
Establish Funding Priorities

INDUSTRY
ATTRACTIVENESS

BUSINESS STRENGTH	High	Medium	Low
High	B		
Medium	↑		
Low	A		C

strategy. For instance, using the business screen model of General Electric, as discussed in previous chapters and displayed in Table 9.5,[8] a corporate strategy might involve or require the movement of a particular business currently rated in the A position in the table to the B position, as indiated by the arrow. Such a strategy would probably require that additional funds be allocated to this business unit in order that this strategy be feasible.

When contrasted with a business unit which is evaluated to be situated at "C" in Table 9.5, the priority for fund allocation of "A" (in order to achieve a move to "B") would be higher.

In general, one may broadly categorize the three left uppermost and shaded squares to be of potential highest priority, the three lowermost and right shaded squares to be of least priority, and the three unshaded diagonal squares to be of intermediate priority for resource allocation.[9]

Of course, this general priority scheme would be modified depending on the particular strategy adopted. Moreover, the actual resource allocations to be made on the basis of these modified priorities would be made for specific purposes on the basis of a plan developed by each business unit for implementing the overall strategy that is seen to be the best approach to moving it toward its objectives.

USING PROJECT EVALUATIONS TO ALLOCATE RESOURCES

Any of the ranking schemes discussed in the previous section for evaluating projects may be used as a basis for resource allocation. Indeed, when a specific business unit is seen from the standpoint of a strategic movement as de-

[8] Channon, D. F., "Strategic Planning Portfolio Models: Practical Problems and Problems in Practice," Manchester Business School, 1976 uses the term "directional policy matrix" to describe a similar model in use by the Royal Dutch Shell Group.

[9] As discussed by General Electric's Allen, M. G., "Strategic Problems Facing Today's Corporate Planner," Academy of Management, Kansas City, Aug. 1976.

picted for A in Table 9.5 this planned move becomes equivalent to a project or program. The business unit has a specific goal in terms of its projected position on the business screen grid. This goal can be stated numerically in terms of sales, profits, or market share, and a plan can be developed that estimates the resources required to achieve this move.

Thus, the business may be thought of from this strategic point of view as another project or program, and it can be ranked along with others that may be of narrower scope, such as a new product to be developed or a specific acquisition to be made.

THE STRATEGIC RESOURCE ALLOCATION PROCESS

The total resources to be devoted to strategic programs should be tentatively set by top management on the basis of the general economic outlook, market trends, and capital situation of the organization as a whole. This tentative strategic budget should then be allocated to the various strategic programs on the basis of requests made up at lower levels for each program.

This allocation process may be accomplished in any of a variety of ways. The simplest allocation procedure allocates the necessary resources, as indicated by the program plan or budget request, to the highest ranked programs until the funds are exhausted. Those good programs that are not funded are put into a "hold" category for the next round of allocations, for additional funds that may become available, or for consideration should funded programs be cut back. This simple allocation procedure is perfectly sound so long as programs have been carefully defined and program budget requests have been audited to ensure that they are realistic.

The need for careful definition of programs is not so obvious as it might first appear. *The interdependencies of programs and projects can easily be overlooked* if such interdependencies are not explicitly considered in the allocation process. Thus, if one project's greatest value can only be achieved if a second project is also successful, and if the first project is rated more highly than the second, it is possible that a simple resource allocation process will fund the first, but not the second, thus ensuring that the first will not achieve its full potential. At the program level, the omission from consideration of such interdependencies is less likely, since programs are broad objective-oriented sets of activities within which project interdependencies have already been considered.

This simple, but effective, allocation process makes use of a combined top down and bottom up approach since strategies and overall budgets are established in a top-down fashion and program plans and resource requirements are established from the bottom up, i.e., by those people who will be called upon to execute the plan. In this way, the aspirations of the organization, the availability of funds and the realities of what it will take to accomplish programs all come together in the resource allocation process.

THE TIME DIMENSION OF RESOURCE ALLOCATION

Just as the importance of the timing was stressed in discussing strategy in Chapter 8, it must also be stressed in this consideration of resource allocations. Indeed, one view of strategy is as a sequence of conditional resource commitments. This view takes cognizance of the fact that strategy is translated from abstract to real terms through resource allocations, so that in effect, *the resource allocations are the strategy.*

Although this is only one way of conceptualizing strategy in concrete terms, this view does emphasize the importance of *timing.* Few strategies or programs are so simple that one-time allocations are sufficient to accomplish them and few proceed to accomplish their associated goals and objectives without requiring that changes be made in planned commitments. Thus, the timing and sequencing of resource commitments are crucial.

RISK ANALYSIS IN RESOURCE ALLOCATION

Associated with the timing dimension of resource allocation is the issue of risk and uncertainty. Even though the degree of risk can readily be factored into the program selection processes discussed earlier, the interrelationship of timing and risk often becomes an important consideration in strategic allocation decisions. This interrelationship of timing and risk can be illustrated through a variety of questions such as:

1. Should we undertake this strategic project now or delay it until the situation becomes more clear (and less risky)?
2. Would an investment now be warranted on the grounds that this activity will itself help to resolve the uncertainty?

These questions suggest the direct relationship between timing and risk. Timing delays may reduce uncertainty, but they may also result in lost opportunities. On the other hand, investments in high-risk programs will, by definition, sometimes result in failure and economic loss. However, small investments may be made with the objective of gaining better information which will reduce the risk associated with further larger investments.

Many companies have approached this relationship between timing and risk with a resource allocation approach that complements their major resource allocation activity. This secondary resource allocation process focuses on new, innovative, high-risk alternatives for which risk capital is made available.

By proposal to a committee charged with administering these funds, an individual or unit can obtain modest funds for exploration of a new technical area, product opportunity, or business venture. These small investments are meant to foster creativity while stringently controlling expenditures on high-risk activities. In effect, the small investments are made in order to collect further information about an idea before funds are invested on a larger scale.

When such a secondary resource allocation activity is implemented on an objective basis in an organization, it can accomplish much in balancing timing and risk. Such a procedure means that ideas do not have to await that point when they are so obviously perceived to be worthwhile that all possible timing advantage is lost. At the same time, the organization's scarce resources may be effectively used in reducing risk and limiting the likelihood of substantial investments in infeasible or unprofitable ventures.

ZERO-BASE BUDGETING

Zero-base budgeting has received much attention by business and government in the mid 1970s. While it was first applied as early as 1969,[10] great public attention to the idea is largely the result of President Carter's references to applications in the state of Georgia during his tenure as governor and his subsequent applications of the ideas at the federal level.

Zero-base budgeting (ZBB) requires management to analyze all proposed budget items for the coming period as though the budgetary starting point were zero. This includes both proposed new programs and activities as well as ongoing ones. Like its predecessor PPBS, (Planning Programming & Budgeting Systems),[11] the ZBB approach requires that all programs be assessed on a cost-benefit basis at several levels of funding (service), usually one below the proposed or present funding level and one above it. Management then makes resource allocation decisions by ranking activities at various levels of service and cost.

The conceptual foundation of ZBB is unassailable. It requires that every resource-consuming activity be compared against all others and that several activity levels be considered for each. However, despite the claims made for it in both government and industry, it is still unproven, particularly at the level of *strategic* resource allocation.

---

[10] Pyhrr, Peter A., *Zero-Base Budgeting: A Practical Management Tool for Evaluating Expenses,* John Wiley, New York, 1973.

[11] See Cleland, D. I. and W. R. King, *Systems Analysis and Project Management* (2nd ed.), McGraw Hill, 1975 for a discussion of PPBS.

Summary

Organizational goals and programs are the action elements of strategic choice. Programs are combinations of activities focused toward a specific purpose. Goals are the identifiable and specific things to be achieved. Programs, and the projects that comprise them are normally of finite duration. They represent the horizontal strategic work of the organization, whereas its vertical functional units focus on operations activities.

Program and project goals always involve cost, time, and performance parameters. These project dimensions must be established as a consequence of the strategic choice process and then controlled to ensure that planning choices are being effectively implemented.

Program and project evaluation and selection represent critical choices in the planning process. For instance, a new product development strategy must incorporate mechanisms for the selection of particular new product ideas and concepts to be pursued. These mechanisms may be formal or informal, but the wide variety of existing simple techniques for explicating subjective judgment and bringing it to bear in an organized fashion suggests the feasibility of using formal approaches. These formal models serve to tie selection decisions in with the overall objectives of the organization in a fashion that is difficult to otherwise achieve.

Resource allocations are the final decisions to be made in the strategic choice process. A business screen model may be used to make broad allocation decisions among business units. At the program level, the priorities developed in the selection phase serve to guide, but not uniquely determine, allocation decisions.

Chapter 9—Questions and Exercises

1. What is meant by the action level of strategic planning? Give an example.
2. Define a program. What are projects in the program context?
3. The authors state that programs and projects normally have a finite life. What is meant by this?
4. Programs are output oriented; they directly relate to the achievement of some organizational purpose. Explain what this means.
5. Projects and programs exist in a horizontal organizational context. What does this mean? Give an example of a project or program?
6. Build a program structure for an organization with which you are familiar similar to Figure 9.1, "Corporate Program Structure."
7. Strategic programs and projects are directly and importantly related to basic organizational objectives and strategies. Why is this so?
8. Programs and projects typically involve three generic kinds of goals. What are these

goals? Demonstrate by example that you understand the interdependence of such goals.

9. What is the significance of management by objectives in the context of strategic planning?
10. What is meant by program evaluation and selection? What are some criteria that can be developed for evaluating strategic programs and projects?
11. There are many varieties of project selection models. Identify and briefly define several varieties.
12. What is the objective in developing scoring schemes for project selection?
13. What is the value of developing a probabilistic project scoring scheme?
14. Identify some more-sophisticated scoring models. What are the forms of such models? Is it possible that such models are so complex that they lose value in the real world application?
15. What are the final strategic choices that have to be made in the planning process?
16. Using the General Electric business screen concept, describe how allocation priorities might be established in a diversified business firm.
17. Describe what is meant by the time dimension of resource allocation.
18. What is goal congruence? Why is it important in an organization?
19. How does goal congruence relate to the hierarchy of goals in an organization?
20. How should the criteria that one uses for the evaluation of projects and programs relate to the organiztion's objectives?
21. In Table 9.3, clearly distinguish between those elements that are fixed for all projects and those that are different for each project that may come under consideration. In other words, which constitute the evaluation framework and which describe the specific project?
22. Suppose that a project under consideration using Table 9.3 had been evaluated on the basis of the certainty assumption of Table 9.2 (and with identical ratings). What would the overall score be? Would this project be preferred to the one in Table 9.3?
23. Explain the reason for the preferences reflected in the scores that are associated with various income and cost streams in Table 9.4.
24. Explain the logic underlying the scores associated with various likelihoods of project success, total project incomes, and costs in Table 9.4.

Chapter 9—Strategic Questions for the Manager

1. Can specific programs and projects be identified in the organization?
2. Are organizational program and project goals specific and measurable? Do these goals serve as motivators of action and standards of performance?
3. What failures of planning in the organization have occurred in the past? Why?
4. Have *strategic projects* (those whose output will affect the long-term future of the organization) been chosen, along with suitable management systems? Have managers of these programs and projects been designated?
5. Have cost, performance, and schedule goals been established for organizational projects? How often are these goals reviewed by the key organizational managers?

6. In the selection of organizational programs and projects, are alternative programs and projects considered?
7. What is the process that is used to select programs and goals? What techniques are used to complement executive judgment in this process?
8. Can the preliminary screening process described in Figure 9.2 be adopted by the organization? Who should participate in this preliminary screening process?
9. What criteria have been used in the past to evaluate and select strategic programs and projects. Have these criteria been relevant to organizational missions?
10. Do key manager preferences, expressed through personal value systems, tend to dominate the program and project selection process? What influence have these preferences had on organizational effectiveness?
11. Have peer groups, particularly in research and development projects, particpated in the evaluation and selection of projects?
12. What project selection process methods are most appropriate for the organization? What organizational element should manage this process?

References

Ackerman, R. W., "Influence of Integration and Diversity on the Investment Process," *Administrative Science Quarterly,* Vol. 15, No. 3, Sept. 1970.

Anderson, T. A., "Coordinating Strategic and Operational Planning," *Business Horizons,* Vol. 8, Summer 1965, pp. 49–72.

Bower, J. L., *Managing the Resource Allocation Process: A Study of Corporate Planning and Investment,* Harvard Business School, 1970.

Carter, E. E., and Cohen, K. J., "Portfolio Aspects of Strategic Planning," *Journal of Business Policy,* Summer 1972.

"Flexible Pricing: Industry's New Strategy to Hold Market Share Changes the Rules for Economic Decision Making," *Business Week,* Dec. 12, 1977.

Gedrich, S. F., "Business Planning at Sperry Rand," *Long Range Planning,* Apr. 1976.

George, W. W., "Task Teams for Rapid Growth," *Harvard Business Review,* March–April 1977.

Groves, D. L., Kahalas, H., and Lamb, F., "Planning—Satisfaction and Productivity," *Long Range Planning,* August 1976.

Higgins, R. B., "Reunite Management and Planning," *Long Range Planning,* August 1976.

Harrison, F. L., "How Corporate Planning Responds to Uncertainty," *Long Range Planning,* Apr. 1976.

Linneman, R. E., and Kennell, J. D., "Shirt Sleeve Approach to Long Range Plans," *Harvard Business Review,* March–April 1977.

Migliore, R. H., "Planning and Management By Objectives," *Long Range Planning,* August 1976.

Moose, S. O., and Fanon, A. J., "Frontier Curve Analysis as a Resource Allocation Guide," *Journal of Business Policy,* Spring 1972.

Osgood, W. R., and Wetzel, W. E., Jr., "A Systems Approach to Venture Initiation," *Business Horizons,* Oct. 1977.

Payne, B., "How to Set Realistic Profit Goals," *Harvard Business Review,* Sept.–Oct. 1958.

Stonich, P. J., *Zero-Base Planning and Budgeting,* Dow Jones-Irwin, Homewood, Illinois, 1977.

Suver, J. D., and Brown, R. L., "Where Does Zero-Base Budgeting Work?" *Harvard Business Review,* Nov.–Dec. 1977.

PART V

The Strategic–Information Subsystem

Chapter 10

INFORMATION FOR
STRATEGIC PLANNING

Most complex organizations have developed sophisticated information systems to support their decision-making and other managerial activities. Indeed, the term "management information system" (MIS) has become so pervasive that it is now used to describe a wide variety of data processing systems, some of which are only indirectly related to the management process. Usually such systems, even the ones that support management decisions, are almost exclusively concerned with the control function as applied to the operational activities of the organization; few are directly focused on the planning function or the strategic decisions that are so critical to the organization's future.

The emphasis on operations rather than planning has resulted in the creation of sophisticated systems for collecting, processing, and disseminating internally generated information for control purposes such as costs, inventories, and personnel data, whereas relatively unsophisticated systems suffice for coping with critical planning-related information. For instance, if one investigates the MIS development efforts of many firms, he finds that these efforts have begun by emphasizing cost and financial data systems and have evolved to incorporate other varieties of internal data. Usually only after these internal systems have been rather fully developed is attention given to the systematic collection and utilization of external information. Even then this function is usually performed in a narrow sales context that may not significantly encompass the wide variety of relevant environmental information that is potentially of critical value to the organization's strategic planning.

In this chapter and the two succeeding ones, we seek to develop a concept of strategic planning information to demonstrate the feasibility and importance of developing such information in a variety of contexts, and to provide an outline of the wide range of approaches that may be used to collect, analyze, and utilize strategic information.

The Nature of Strategic Information

Strategic decisions are the ultimate output of the strategic planning process. These strategic decisions provide responses to changes or anticipated changes in future organizatonal, environmental, and competitive conditions. All effective strategic decisions must be based on appraisals of factors and forces in the organization and its environment: timely information concerning the economic, political, social, legal, and technological forces affecting the ability of the organization to compete and prosper in the future.

The organization needs a way of identifying, collecting, and analyzing a wide conglomeration of data that can have a potential effect on its future. As well, it needs a system for disseminating information to those who are able to use it. And, this must be done in a timely and efficient fashion that produces accurate and reliable information as a basis for strategic decision making.

Illustrative of important classes of strategic information already been alluded to or utilized in previous chapters are as follows:

Information on the environmental system (political, technological, legal, social, economic)
Information on the market
Information on the competition
Information on the strengths and weaknesses of the firm
Information on the contingencies
Information on past performance
Information on current problems and opportunities
Information on the risks and uncertainties of the current strategies

Strategic Data and Strategic Information

Of critical importance to the understanding of strategic planning information systems is an understanding of the difference between strategic *data* and strategic *information*. As these terms are used by computer and information scientists, "data" refers to *unevaluated* available symbols, whereas *"information" refers to data which have been evaluated for some particular application or use.*

In the case of *strategic data* and *strategic information,* the particular use for which data must be evaluated in order to create strategic *information* is, of course the strategic decision making of the organization. Thus, *strategic information represents data that have been evaluated to be of specific and identifiable use in the strategic planning process.*

Even though the wide variety of information enumerated previously is indeed related to strategic planning, it has not yet been comprehensively evaluated for use in that process. Thus, all of the elements in that list do not necessarily warrant the appellation "information."

A Conceptual Framework for Strategic Information

The process of separating strategic information from data is one of filtering the wide range of economic, cultural, political, competitive, and organizational data that might be argued to be *relevant* to the strategic choices of the organization into that set of strategic *information* that has been evaluated for specific and direct use in the strategic planning process. The first step involved in filtering the data must be the development of a relationship between sets of information and the tasks that must be performed in the strategic planning process.

Table 10.1 is such a conceptual linkage between stages of the strategic planning process and questions whose answers represent *strategic information*. The left column of that table describes a simple and abstract generic strategic planning process beginning with a situation assessment and proceeding sequentially through the choice of objectives, the identification of constraints, and the selection of strategies.

The right side of the table shows a set of basic questions related to each step in the strategic planning process. The answers to these questions represent a gross-level definition of the *strategic information requirements* of the organization. This is so because the salient answers to those questions must be developed if an effective strategic planning process is to be carried out.

Fulfilling Strategic Information Needs

The information needs shown in Table 10.1 in the form of answers to questions may be fulfilled in a variety of ways. Some of those ways have already been treated in past chapters and others will be developed here and in succeeding chapters.

Figure 4.4 has shown a substantive strategic planning process, which emphasizes the use of strategic information in planning. We shall begin by relating the elements of this planning process diagram to the concept of strategic information.

STRATEGIC DATA BASES REVISITED

One of the most useful approaches to the development of strategic information has already been dealt with in Chapter 5 in the discussion of the use of strategic data bases in initiating a planning process. In that chapter, we defined five strategic data bases dealing with organizational strengths and weaknesses, business and industry criteria, competitive and environmental factors, and management viewpoints and values. These topics are directly related to those questions labeled with an asterisk in Table 10.1.

TABLE 10.1 / Strategic Information Needs[a]

STAGES OF THE STRATEGIC PLANNING PROCESS	STRATEGIC INFORMATION
Situation Assessment (What is our current situation?)	What have been our past missions, objectives, strategies, goals and programs? What are we selling? (# and $) Where are we selling it? (geography and product mix) What do we own? (facilities, inventories, etc.) Where is it? (locations) What are we producing? (production schedules) What are our costs? What is our image among our clientele?
Objective Development (What do we want our future to be?)	What opportunities can we use to advantage? (*) What future products can we produce and sell? Which markets offer the best potential? What are the strengths on which we wish to build? (*)
Constraint Identification (What constraints might inhibit us?)	What future environmental conditions might affect us? (*) What competitive actions might affect us?* What commitments do we have that will affect the future? What governmental actions or laws might affect us? What business and industry constraints exist? (*) What weaknesses do we have? (*)
Selection of Strategies (What should we do to achieve our objectives?)	What consequences can be anticipated for various strategy alternatives? What can we do to assure that our choices have the anticipated impact?

[a] Asterisks refer to those questions which may be addressed by strategic data bases.

Chapter 6 also describes a process for evaluating data and reducing the broad range of data in each of these areas to a concise list of those data elements most salient and critical to the strategic choice process. These concise lists of evaluated data are the, so called, strategic data bases.

In developing these strategic bases, we are, in effect, converting *data* into strategic *information,* i.e., evaluating data for a specific use in a strategic planning process. That use is described in Figure 4.4. Thus, strategic data bases are, in fact, information, not data![1]

ASSUMPTIONS AS STRATEGIC INFORMATION

Chapter 5 has also treated the role of assumptions as informational inputs to the strategic planning process. Since explicit assumptions are nearly always made through a process of evaluation, they clearly qualify as strategic information in the sense used here.

Assumptions may be appropriately used as responses to a variety of the questions in Table 10.1. For instance, in Table 5.3, we illustrated cost assumptions. Assumptions might also be made about future governmental actions, laws to be enacted, competitive actions, etc.

One view of the informational input provided by assumptions sees their role as similar to that of forecasts. In effect, assumptions are a kind of forecast. Usually forecasts are founded on more explicit data or, at least, on a more formalized process for transforming data into projections of the future. Thus, assumptions may be thought of as ways of dealing with our need for future projections in those instances and for those variables where formalized forecasts are not available.

Assumptions are also inherent in the strategic data base concept. For instance, the managment-viewpoints-and-values strategic data base may be thought of as a set of guidelines reflecting the attitudes of managment about how the business will be operated. As such, these guidelines become *assumptions* that underly the subsequent development of plans for the organization.

Of course, a variety of different assumptions may be utilized in the strategic planning process. This process has been described in Chapter 9 in terms of the use of corporate models in assessing strategy. There, a process of sensitivity analysis is described as one of testing the sensitivity of organizational performance to changes in the inputs.

This process can directly be one of testing the sensitivity of projected per-

---

[1] We have selected the terminology "data base" in full awareness that we are creating a semantics problem, because strategic data bases represent "information" and not "data." However, we have found the term to be useful in communicating to managers that this variety of information is just as important, useful, and valid as are the data bases contained in their computerized information systems.

formance to changes in the assumptions underlying the choice process. For instance, a model may be exercised under various sets of assumptions for future material costs to determine the impact of this assumption on overall performance. If, as might well be the case in some industries, it were determined that a wide range of different assumptions concerning materials costs did not lead to great changes in overall profitability, less attention might be paid to the specific materials cost assumptions that are input into the strategic planning process. Other assumptions to which overall performance is more sensitive would correspondingly be given greater weight.

FORECASTS AS STRATEGIC INFORMATION

Another important variety of strategic information was also treated in Chapter 5. Forecasts of the future environment are an important informational input to the strategic planning process. Indeed, forecasting is sometimes thought of as being equivalent to, or at least, the essence of, planning.[2] In fact, forecasts are only one of the important international inputs to planning. Thus, good forecasts in some form are necessary to, but not sufficient for, good planning.

As noted earlier, the distinction between forecasts and assumptions is not always clear. A forecast, when evaluated and accepted, can be used as a basic assumption in planning. Moreover, forecasts of the variety of simple cost extrapolations such as those shown in Table 5.3 do indeed represent anticipations of the future, despite the fact that they may not be based on any forecasting technique other than that of assessing future events, such as the implementation of existing contract provisions certain to occur in the future.

Forecasts are indeed information since every sensible forecast represents evaluated data. Forecasts that do not have this characteristic, such as those produced by mystics, have not proved to be of great use in organizational planning.

Forecasts, like assumptions, may typically be made for a variety of the questions posed in Table 10.1. Certainly those related to future costs, markets, and environmental conditions may be addressed through forecasts. At least, the numerical aspects of all of these are the basic grist of the forecaster's mill.

STRATEGIC MANAGEMENT INFORMATION SYSTEMS

The comments made in the introduction to this chapter concerning the potential for the development of strategic-planning MISs should not be taken to refer exclusively to computerized information systems. The processes of developing

---

[2] For instance, see the discussion of this misconception provided by Warren, E. K., *Executive Long-Range Planning*, Prentice-Hall, Englewood Cliffs, N.J., 1968.

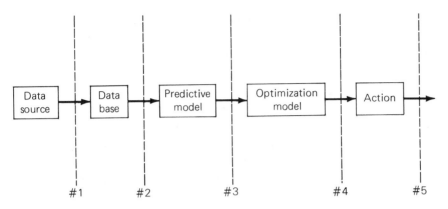

FIGURE 10.1 Information-Decision Process.

forecasts, assumptions, and strategic data bases, if formalized and executed on a continuing systematic basis, represent part of an overall strategic planning information system just as validly as do the kind of computerized approaches, which are more commonly associated with the term "information systems." (Indeed, many of the negative references to the concept of "strategic information systems" seem to refer largely to computerized systems.)

Despite the broader definition of a strategic-planning information system, which we are using here, there is a role for computerized systems as well as the noncomputerized strategic information processes that are implicit in the continuing use of such strategic informational inputs as strategic data bases.

Perhaps this range of systems can be best illustrated by the diagram of Figure 10.1, adapted from Mason,[3] which shows a decision-making process described in information and model terms. It shows a data source that provides information to a data base (a storehouse of data). The data are then used in predictive models and optimization models before action is taken. Predictive models are used to predict future events, whereas optimization models serve also to evaluate and select a best course of action on the basis of predictions of the future. Thus, a formal predictive model might result in sales forecasts, whereas a linear programming petroleum refinery scheduling model that produces the best production plan is an optimization model.

It is important to recognize that the decision process described in Figure 10.1 is valid even if the models and data base employed are not formal ones. Every decision is based on some set of data selected from the broader set of all

[3] Adapted from Mason, R. O., Jr., "Basic Concepts for Designing Management Information Systems," AIS Research Paper #8, Graduate School of Business Administration, University of California, Los Angeles, Oct. 1969.

that is available, the data base, and every decision involves the use of some abstract model, even if it is of the mental model variety, to make predictions of the future and choices of actions. Thus, whether or not the entities in Figure 10.1 are formal and explicit ones, they must exist and form a part of every decision process.[4]

Many of the differences between various types of information systems and individual concepts of MIS may be explained by the man-machine interfaces (represented by the numbered dotted lines in the Figure 10.1).

For each of the five *alternative* interfaces in Figure 10.1, the machine portion of the system is presumed to occupy those activities to the left of the interface, and the manager is presumed to deal with those to the right. For instance, if the man-machine system interface of a particular MIS is at the point labeled 1, the MIS is simply an information collection system; all of the data and all of the models used in the decision process, if any, are stored in the mind of the manager.

At the interface designated as 2, the data base is a part of the machine system, but all of the critical decision-making mechanisms are handled by the manager; he is simply provided with reports that summarize and aggregate data. In situation 3, the manager also is provided with the output of predictive models, such as sales forecasts and forecasts of GNP. In situation 4, the manager is provided with the recommended courses of action as determined by optimization models. He might, for instance, be provided with the new product opportunity that is selected as best according to some criterion from among a set of available opportunities. He could then evaluate this recommendation in the light of his knowledge of the model and of those things that the model omits. In the last situation, 5, we have automated decision making, since the machine system even goes so far as to perform the action.

There are two important aspects of the various interfaces in Figure 10.1. First, recognize that it is common practice to use the term "management information system" to describe systems that have their sole or major interface at 2, 3, 4, and sometimes even 5. Thus, two people may find themselves agreeing on MIS procedures, only to find that they are each using different MIS definitions, depending on their own concept of the interface.

Second, any modern information system should simultaneously include many of these interfaces. For instance, an MIS might allow for the collection of information for unique, high-level, subjective decisions such as those involving the identification of who will be the real governmental decision maker for a weapons system contract. In such a case, the manager would be provided with basic information insofar as possible, but the decision would revolve about his experience, and knowledge of governmental organizations and operations.

---

[4] See King, W. R., and Cleland, D. I., "Manager-Analyst Teamwork in MIS Design," *Business Horizons*, April 1971.

At the other extreme, the same MIS might include a capability for automated routine decision making. For instance, a computerized model for monitoring stock levels and placing orders where stock levels have reached prescribed levels is operational in many companies.

At the level of a strategic MIS, this multi-interface system must be the concept employed, for many strategic decisions will be so ill-structured that they will have to be made with a level of informational support such as that represented by 1 in Figure 10.1, whereas other informational support can be provided at least at the level of interface 3 and possibly even at 4. Illustrations of the former variety of strategic choice are easy to develop. Forecasts as informational inputs illustrate interface 3, the use of corporate models *approaches* interface 4, whereas the use of a computerized resource allocation model or program selection model would represent interface 4.

Environmental Information Systems to Support Strategic Planning[5]

The best understood and most adequately developed element of any information system, be it strategic or tactical, is that which focuses on internally generated information, i.e., that information desired from data sources *within* the organization itself. Thus, costs, inventory levels, personnel data, and other elements of information are routinely available for the support of strategic decisions. However, little attention has often been devoted to the more difficult task of systematically developing externally oriented information systems, *environmental information systems*. This bias in favor of internally oriented systems is natural and easily understood. First, internally generated data are easier to obtain. Indeed, they have routinely been produced by organizations since time immemorial. Moreover, internal data are necessarily collected in a systematic fashion since they must be reported to government agencies and to satisfy disclosure laws.

However, the most important reason for the bias toward internal information concerns an understanding of what is meant by good management. In an era when good management meant the efficient administration of the organization, the avoidance of waste and the maintenance of good clear internal information designed to permit the assessment of "how the organization was doing" was adequate.

However, today's concept of good management is quite different. No longer is efficient administration adequate. Now, good management is measured in terms of opportunities lost or used to advantage, advanced planning for

[5] This section is adapted in part from the authors' paper: King, W. R., and Cleland, D. I, "Environmental Information Systems for Strategic Marketing Planning," *Journal of Marketing,* Oct. 1974.

the future and the contrivance, at least in part, of the organization's future, rather than the simple reaction to evolving circumstances.

In such a milieu, environmental information becomes of paramount importance, for most opportunities are generated externally and the identification and evaluation of those opportunities require information. Moreover, an organization's strategic planning effort is aimed at providing a sense of direction when approaching an uncertain future, the nature of which will only in part reflect the organization's own goals and choices. Forces in the environment, will also play an important role in determining the organization's future, so that effective strategic planning must operate to permit the organization to assess the environment, to forecast it, to develop strategies for taking advantage of it, and, to the degree possible, to alter it.

Environmental information is, therefore, critical to effective strategic planning. However, most organizations base their strategic planning more on judgment, intuition, partial data, and *ad hoc* studies than on objective systematic information routinely collected and analyzed for strategic purposes. This is the case, in part, because they have justified information systems largely on the basis of cost efficiencies rather than on increased organizational effectiveness and, in part, because of the conceptual and practical difficulties inherent in the definition of systems designed to support strategic decision making.

ENVIRONMENTAL INFORMATION SUBSYSTEMS AND THE PLANNING PROCESS

In much the same way that Wrapp[6] has argued for the avoidance of structure in strategic planning, it is possible to rationally argue that truly strategic decisions are of such a unique and unstructured nature that it is not cost-effective to develop an information system to support them. Although this may be true to some degree, the authors will attempt to demonstrate here that it is feasible, and even cost-effective, to develop formal information systems to support strategic planning processes (as opposed to individual strategic decisions).

The emphasis of this presentation is, therefore, on the informational support of a strategic planning process through the gathering of information from generically defined sources. The methodology proposed is the development of interrelated information subsystems. Table 10.2 extends the framework of Table 10.1 to depict a strategic planning process in terms of a number of key sources of environmental information, and gives descriptive names to a number of environmental information subsystems that will be described in this chapter. The context used in this table and the illustrations which are based on it is the busi-

---

[6] Wrapp, "Top Managers Don't Make Policy Decisions," *Harvard Business Review*, Sept.–Oct. 1967.

ness firm. However, similar subsystems would be appropriate in a wide variety of non-business organizations.

The classically structured strategic planning process of Table 10.2 is very general, but adequate to identify the four basic questions that must be asked in any strategic planning process, "Where are we?" "Where do we want to go?" "What will tend to prevent us from getting there?" and "What should we do to get there in the face of these obstacles?"

The answers to each of these planning questions depend on adequate information, and, although there is no unique relationship between the information sources and questions on any given row of Table 10.2, there is a primary relationship that is so identified. For instance, the assessment of "Where we are?" depends primarily on internally generated data and on data concerning *existing customers*. Since this chapter does not deal with internally oriented information subsystems, only customers are identified in the first row of the table as being information sources that are primarily related to this strategic question. This is true also of the linkage between potential customers and the second strategic question. Although information concerning existing customers will hopefully play a role in the answer to this question, the major opportunities for the organization are represented by it's potential customers. In the same vein, competitors and government serve to constrain the organization's future, as depicted in the third row of the table. In the last row, the deciding aspect of planning depends on all information sources.

TABLE 10.2 / Information Subsystems Relating Information Sources To The Planning Process

STRATEGIC PLANNING PROCESS	ENVIRONMENTAL INFORMATION SUBSYSTEMS	STRATEGIC INFORMATION SOURCES
Situation Assessment (What is our current situation?)	Image subsystem Customer subsystem	Customers
Objective Development (What do we want our future situation to be?)	Potential customer subsystem	Potential customers
Constraint Identification (What constraints might inhibit us?)	Competitive subsystem Regulatory subsystem	Competitors Government
Selection of Strategies (What actions should we take to achieve our objectives?)	Critical intelligence subsystem	

ENVIRONMENTAL INFORMATION SUBSYSTEMS

The design for an environmental information subsystem of an overall strategic planning system will be outlined here in terms of the informational subsystems delineated in Table 10.2. However, before describing these subsystems, two caveats are in order. First, the various informational subsystems to be described need not be developed as computerized information systems. The term "system" is also used here to describe a systematic, continuous, and formal set of activities that provide decision-related information. Second, no inference should be drawn that it is necessary, or even feasible, for a single firm to develop the total system described here. The framework of Table 10.2 will be explained in subsequent sections in terms of specific systems, all in industrial contexts, in whose development the authors have participated. However, no single firm has, in fact, implemented all of these subsystems, and it may well not be cost-effective for any single firm to do so. The industrial systems described here are illustrations of the kinds of environmental information systems that may prove to be useful and cost-effective to any given firm.

IMAGE INFORMATION SUBSYSTEMS. The most basic assessment made by the managers of an organization is summed up in the question, "Where are we now?" To function effectively, every organization must continually assess its status relative both to its history and its environment. Such an assessment requires objective and subjective measurements. At the objective level, the necessary information is readily obtainable from internal sources: data on profits, costs, financial status, and, in general, historical performance data produced by the internal accounting and financial information systems. These objective data can be readily complemented with subjective judgmental data from internal sources. Whether this is done formally [7] or informally, internal judgments are often biased by the influence of the readily-available objective data. More importantly, internally generated judgmental data do not provide critical information concerning the firm's external image as it is projected to and perceived by the customers and potential customers on whom the firm depends for its success.

The authors' experience suggests that there are great discrepancies between a firm's image of itself and the image held by its customers. Often these discrepancies are less significant in their impact on the firm's current operations

---

[7] See King, W. R., "Human Judgment and Management Decision Analysis," *Journal of Industrial Engineering.* Vol. 18, Dec. 1967, pp. 17–20, for an assessment of using formal assessments of human judgment in management; and King, W. R., "Intelligent Management Information Systems," *Business Horizons,* Vol. 16, Oct. 1973, pp. 5–12, for a description of the incorporation of human judgmental data into information systems.

than in terms of their potential impact in the future. For instance, the firm that sees itself as technically superior in an era when cost is becoming more significant may find that its image of being high priced is more important to its future success than is presumed quality image.

A firm's image may be assessed in two general areas: product image (price, quality, reliability, etc.) and organizational image (quality of personnel, responsiveness, integrity, etc.). The basic techniques to use in a formal image assessment are structured and unstructured personal interviews of key customer personnel. A questionnaire to serve as a guide for the conduct of these interviews can be developed and initially tested *within* the organization. This in-house testing can be used as a basis to define and operationally describe the important dimensions of the product and organizational characteristics that are deemed to be important to the seller's image. For example, in one such survey conducted by the authors, the customer interviews centered around an evaluation of the following product and organization characteristics areas:

1. General characteristics.
2. Personnel image.
3. Ability to communicate with customers.
4. Project management skills and capabilities.
5. Ability to meet normal customer requirements.
6. Responsiveness to customers' special requirements.
7. Negotiating skills.
8. Special capabilities.
9. Product characteristics.

Table 10.3 shows the way that some of the data for the "Personnel Image" category was collected and displayed in terms of the degree to which survey respondents agree or disagree with the statements on each side of the table. These data were sufficient to suggest to the firm that it had potential problems with the degree to which top management was interacting with the customer and the freedom given to project managers in selecting staff personnel.

Overall, the survey developed an image that was surprising to the executives of the sponsoring organization. It depicted an honest and technically competent organization that lacked marketing aggressiveness. This lack of aggressiveness was reflected in the customers' perceptions of virtually all aspects of customer contact, from the bureaucratic lack of responsiveness to customer inquiries to the lack of contact of top management with customers. Such specifics as the failure to communicate to customers about key personnel changes in the organization and deficiencies in the technical proposals presented to customers were also pointed out. The seller's products were rated high in terms of operating characteristics (performance, reliability, and ease of maintenance), but cus-

TABLE 10.3 / Personnel Image Survey Responses (Numbers are Percentages)

	VERY	QUITE	SLIGHTLY	NEUTRAL	SLIGHTLY	QUITE	VERY	
Their managerial staff seems to have a high degree of technical competence	34	52	10	3		4		Their managerial staff is not highly qualified technically
Their program managers are good business managers	20	40	12	20	4			Their program managers are poor business managers
They seem to have competent personnel handling projects for us	23	48	19	10				They do not seem to have competent people on our programs
Their top executives get together with ours just to see how things are going	11	28		50	11			We seldom see their top executives with ours for any reason
Their project manager makes an effort to attend our program review meetings when invited	65	26		9				Their project manager although invited seldom attends our program review meetings
Their project people seem to have sufficient authority to get things done	21	58	10	10				Their project people seem to lack the authority to get things done
Their project manager seems to have a free hand in selecting his staff people	11	11		78				Their project manager does not seem to be able to control the makeup of his own staff
We can usually always contact someone who has answers	53	40	3		3			We generally seem to get the run around
honest and open in their dealings with us	66	28	6					are not candid with us

234

tomers raised serious questions about the seller's overall capability to manage a technical product development effort and still maintain cost and schedule credibility.

The image survey was also conducted internally by querying personnel within the sponsoring company. The contrast between customer perceptions and internal personnel perceptions led management to take a number of specific actions designed to have a short-run impact on the image as well as to formalize the incorporation of image considerations into the strategic planning activities of the firm. *This led, for the first time, to specific concern with the image that the company wished to project and the strategies that it could take to reach this image goal.*

Such incorporations of image information as an integral and continuing part of the strategic-planning process require that some type of formal information subsystem be established. In the case in point, the economic impracticality of continuing large-scale surveys led the firm to integrate the continuing image–monitoring activities into other information subsystems where image-related surrogate measures were monitored and assessed. In this firm, the overall image assessment is to be updated at two-year intervals.

This example serves to illustrate a number of important points concerning information and the strategic planning process. First, subjective judgmental data can be incorporated into the planning to complement more readily available objective information. Second, the collection analysis and dissemination of such information can be performed systematically on a continuing basis, rather than on the one-time special study basis, to which analyses of such data are normally confirmed.

Further, image objectives can be objectively established and explicitly incorporated into the objective array of the organization. As discussed earlier objectives and goals must, at some level be translated into measurable terms, and image information of the form of that is displayed in Table 10.3, is directly measurable and assessable.[8] Of course, purists might argue that image is only a means to an end and not an objective of the organization. However, every organization is sometimes forced to use proxy measures for its objectives, as in the case where advertising effectiveness is assessed in terms of consumers contacted rather than sales generated.

CUSTOMER INFORMATION SUBSYSTEM. In most firms, the area of customer information is the best developed of all of the environmental information subsystems. However, much of the existing customer information is not systematically used for any decision purposes, much less for strategic planning.

---

[8] Indeed, if strategic goals are established to change the distribution of responses in one of the rows of Table 10.3, statistical tools such as chi-square analysis can be employed to assess the significance of changes that have occurred. See any basic statistics text.

Two types of customer information are most useful for strategic planning: aggregate information and trend information. Thus, whereas data on a specific customer may be useful in the short-term decisions of the sales manager, long-range decision making requires that sets of customers who form important market segments be identified and analyzed. Such segments are made up of customers who are homogeneous in some sense that is relevant to strategic planning, for example, a common industry, common behavior, common responses to changes in the business cycle, and the like.

Trend information, both in terms of individual customers and for market segments, is also important to strategic planning. For instance, is a given market segment likely to increase or decrease in importance in the future? Will a given segment be changing so that a different strategy will be required to retain them as customers? These are questions related to strategic planning that can only be answered through analyses of aggregates and trends.

The keys to creating customer information subsystems that are supportive of strategic planning are twofold: first, new varieties of information in the form of aggregates and trends and, second, a built-in analytic capability that permits the objective analysis of the strategic customer information. Even though many customer information systems are in existence, few have significant capabilities in these areas.

POTENTIAL CUSTOMER INFORMATION SUBSYSTEMS. Although most organizations have some form of organized information about current customers, few have similar information on *potential customers*. Yet, such information is of equal importance for the development of strategic goals, since potential customers represent the opportunities that will ultimately determine the organization's future. Information on potential customers permits the organization to make rational choices concerning its *future* products, services, and markets.

The development of a potential customer information subsystem is not a straightforward task for most organizations. The list of potential customers is infinite, so some rational culling of this list must be performed. This may be begun by using a criterion that reflects the *potential* of a particular segment of the overall market. For instance, one commercial bank determined that many small manufacturing firms in the local area could avail themselves of a variety of bank services. They began to construct a data base using commercially available services such as *Dun and Bradstreet's State Sales Guides*[9] and those provided by various manufacturers' associations. They then assessed the potential of various segments of the market through personal contacts made on a test basis.[10]

---

[9] Published for various states by Dun and Bradstreet, Inc., New York, N.Y. 10008.

[10] See King, W. R., "Estimating Market Potential, *"Marketing Research Handbook* (R. Ferber, editor), McGraw-Hill, New York, 1975, Section IV, Part A, Chapter 1, for a treatment of various approaches to assessing potential.

Another firm, after having built the data base and having identified high potential firms, developed a "clipping service" for collecting and assembling published references to these potential customers. In this way, a great deal of intelligence information concerning the performance, plans, new products, finances, and the like, of other organizations was obtained. Although this approach may seem naive to the uninitiated, it is the essence of any good intelligence function, and those firms that have tried it have often found it to be of surprising significance.

We shall delve more into the details of such subsystems in Chapter 11, which focuses primarily on the competitive information subsystem. The reader will immediately see that the information systems ideas which are put forth there in the context of competitors are really applicable to customers as well. Indeed, the subsystems developed for these two may easily be physically combined in some situations. For instance, an industrial products manufacturer who sells to other industrial firms may choose to integrate the competitive and potential customer subsystems, since each deal with business firms and since similar information would be required for both varieties of firms.

COMPETITIVE INFORMATION SUBSYSTEM

Few organizations have a great deal of nonhearsay information about competitors. Often the limited hearsay information that is available is misleading and, in any case, such unsystematic competitor information usually does not provide a sound basis for strategic planning.

One of the most useful tools in developing a competitive information system is a profile of each competitor. Such a profile should delineate the business character of the competitor. One company constructed profiles of all competitors to focus on the following factors:

1. Background of key competitor personnel.
2. Characteristics of projects on which competitive proposals were made.
3. Characteristics of projects on which competitive proposals were not made.
4. Mix of competitor's in-house business.
5. Assessment of competitor's marketing strategy.
6. Assessment of relative value placed by competition on various performance measures, for example, product quality, service capability, etc.

From a compilation of basic public information and informed inferences about competitors emerged clear pictures that had not previously been perceived by the firm. For instance, one competitor clearly bid only on projects having a key common characteristic. Another was seen to be solidly in the control of managers with engineering backgrounds. The recent behavior of a third competitor was explained by the backgrounds of a number of nontechnical people who had recently moved into key executive positions. When these profiles were reported and discussed, some critical decisions were made concerning the company's future strategy. The key to the strategy was the company's ability to identify a place for itself in the market, one that provided it with a comparative advantage over the competition.

The profile concept can be instituted as a regular part of the information system. It should be linked to a clipping service and updated on a continuing basis. In more advanced applications, it can be supplemented with competitive image assessments made in parallel with the firm's own image assessment. Such information can form a data base when key questions or issues are being dealt with and a source of valuable information that can be summarized for use in the ongoing strategic planning process.

Chapter 11 deals with the details of competitive analysis and the development of a competitive information subsystem.

REGULATORY INFORMATION SUBSYSTEM. Every organization operates in an environment that imposes formal constraints on its activities. The most obvious such constraints are government regulations. Moreover, every organization also has individuals who are knowledgeable about the existing regulatory environment. However, their knowledge is often used only in an informal way and often after commitments have already been made in ignorance of the constraints.

The basic nature of strategic planning, which involves new and unfamiliar areas for an organization, normally mitigates against such regulatory information being readily available to those who are doing the planning. Managers may know the regulatory environment for the products and markets that they are used to dealing with, but they cannot be expected to be familiar with the regulations surrounding new areas. Thus, the strategic planning environment is fraught with the danger of expending planning and development resources in ignorance of crucial regulatory constraints. Such a situation cries out for a formalized data base with easy access by the many managers who participate in strategic planning.

The basic characteristic of a regulatory information subsystem is the same as that of any information retrieval system. The development of such a system requires that a taxonomy of the regulatory environment be developed. Then, key descriptors can be used by managers to access specific domains of the taxonomy. In this way, the regulations relevant to a particular product, industry, or political subdivision can be furnished to planners who have need for comprehensive regulatory information as it applies to a specific area for which planning is being accomplished.

Although there are clearly no general truths concerning the desirability and feasibility of such a subsystem, it is the experience of the authors that it plays a less important role in the minds of planning executives than do the other subsystems discussed here. Perhaps this is because it deals with boundaries rather than opportunities, and thus constrains action rather than promotes it. Or perhaps the particular design requirements of such a system, roughly analogous to that of developing a useful library indexing system, present a major cost deterrent. In any event, the authors have found that such subsystems, even though technically feasible, are generally considered only by those firms that already have been "burned" in the regulatory inferno. The current pervasiveness of such conflicts suggests that more attention may be paid to this area in the future.

CRITICAL INTELLIGENCE INFORMATION SUBSYSTEM. The term "intelligence" was used in the previous chapter in a fashion akin to that of military and political use of the term. Such a broad interpretation of the term makes it equally applicable to the subsystems dealing with competitors, potential customers, and customers. However, we have chosen to deal with the area of critical intelligence information separately, since what we define as such involves the determination of *specific facts or the answers to specific questions,* whereas these other subsystems have emphasized the continuous monitoring of a specific segment of the organization's environment. For instance, the answer to a question concerning a competitor's intentions to bid or not bid on a project is such a critical intelligence item, as is an assessment that a potential customer will soon be changing suppliers.

The salient aspects of such critical intelligence gathering are organization and systemization. It is not the purpose here to enumerate the myriad data sources and data collection requirements for a good business intelligence system, but rather to establish the desirability of having a formalized intelligence system, and the authority and responsibility patterns appropriate for effective intelligence activities. Chapter 11 discusses sources for intelligence activities in more detail.

The most important point in the critical intelligence subsystem, as in the potential customer and competitive subsystems, is to gather intelligence systematically, to have it evaluated, aggregated, and analyzed by trained people, and to ensure that it is distributed to those decision makers who can make use of it. If this can be done in a parsimonious fashion to ensure that the great amount of redundant and irrelevant information already flowing around in the organization is not merely made larger, the benefits can far outweigh the costs of such an operation.

In the development of a critical intelligence system, the most important element is the people who will develop and implement it. Moreover, the most important factor in determining its effectiveness is the recognition that everyone in an organization is involved both in the marketing function and in the process of intelligence gathering. The engineer who discusses specifications with the customer is both a marketer and an intelligence agent, as is the field marketing representative. Indeed, technical people can often have marketing impact of a far different and more significant variety than can the professional marketer or undercover agent. So, too, is top management involved both in marketing and in the collection of market intelligence. One of the most significant results of the image survey example described earlier was the recognition by the company that their top management, who had preached a customer-oriented marketing approach for years, were not themselves personally customer-oriented.

The ways in which nonprofessional marketers can be made aware of their marketing role and encouraged to perform as proficient marketers are diverse. Among those that the authors have successfully used are the conduct of joint technical .marketing seminars that begin with a discussion of image survey results and then go on to discuss each individual's role in remedying the problems that have been identified.

An effective approach to ensure that nonmarketers play their marketing intelligence roles is to specifically integrate them into the intelligence-gathering network. When engineers are to have customer contact, they must be made aware of the critical information that is needed and who in the customer's organization is likely to have it. Top management should be similarly briefed before their visits to customers and debriefed on return. In this way, a great deal of relevant information can be garnered and provided to those decision makers who are in need of it.

Of course, all of this presumes that an office in the organization has been set up for the collection and analysis of intelligence information. The analysis of intelligence involves a determination of the relevance, credibility, value, and appropriate dissemination of intelligence data. This central office can also perform the function of gathering together the key questions and identifying the voids in the knowledge necessary for effective strategic marketing planning. These questions can be asked in a routine fashion of field personnel and others who might be expected to have relevant information. Often, these people have the desired information in one form or another, but without a formalized intelligence system they have no way of getting it to the right people or of having it integrated with other information to form useful information aggregates.

This same intelligence organization, with its focus on analysis, eliminating redundancies, posing questions, and disseminating information to those who are in need of it, can also function as a part of the competitive and potential customer information subsystems. For example, data provided by clipping services require much the same analysis whether they relate to competitors or customers.

ENVIRONMENTAL SUBSYSTEM RELATIONSHIPS

In describing the various information subsystems that can make up an overall environmental information system for the support of strategic planning, this chapter relates information sources to various phases of the strategic marketing planning process. However, these relationships are not unique; there are clearly many other feasible interrelationships among the supporting information subsystems.

The taxonomy chosen in this chapter is one that the authors have found to be successful, whereas some other logical combinations have not worked well. For instance, the intelligence organization can play a role in the competitive and potential customer subsystems as well as in the critical intelligence subsystem. This suggests that the subsystems themselves might be combined. However, experience has shown that their differences in nature and function are more important than their commonalities. The competitive subsystem is designed to develop and maintain overall profiles of competitors. The critical intelligence subsystem is meant to develop answers to specific questions about competitors' activities and intentions. Even though the two are mutually supportive, they are quite different in their nature, their objective, and the subsystem functions necessary to sustain them. Thus, it is concluded that the two are best designed to be separate, but overlapping, subsystems.

The important area of integration of the various subsystems is in terms of *output* rather than function. The output of the various subsystems must be compatible and available in the aggregate for use in decision problem analysis if new and more sophisticated varieties of information systems are to lead to more effective strategic decision making. The design of the overall system must ensure this after the firm has determined which of the various modules are to be developed and the sequence of development. Of course, many firms will not find it economic to develop the entire system, so that this design phase must necessarily be idiosyncratic.

By developing such an integrated environmental information system, an organization can begin to routinely provide objective information to support strategic planning just as it provides objective data to support operational decision making. Since much of strategic planning is now based more on judgment and intuition than on reliable information, the quality of the decisions that determine the organization's future should be greatly enhanced.

Having suggested this outline of the potentially broad scope for environmentally generated information in supporting strategic planning, we shall, in the next chapter, go into greater detail with regard to one of these environmental subsystems—the competitive subsystem.

Summary

Management information systems may be developed to support strategic-planning activities, just as they may be used to support lower level management control and operational control activities. Of course, the nature of the planning

MIS may be different in that it will deal with less well-defined information from a broader variety of environmental sources. Indeed, the planning MIS may not be computerized and automated to the same degree as are lower level data processing systems. However, such a system is nonetheless important to planning.

Many of the information aspects discussed in prior chapters form a part of the overall planning MIS. For instance, strategic data bases, explicit assumptions, and forecasts represent planning information. So too, the output of planning models (corporate models) constitutes information that is useful for planning purposes.

However, an overall design for a planning MIS can be developed to specifically incorporate information on prospective customers, the organization's image as perceived by outsiders, regulatory happenings, and critical intelligence, all elements of information particularly useful in planning, which many organizations have no organized system for collecting, processing, and disseminating.

Chapter 10—Questions and Exercises

1. Describe a simple management situation with which you are familiar in which information could be used for strategic planning.
2. Distinguish between the formal, semiformal, and informal information systems in an organization.
3. What is the difference between data and information?
4. How is the management-by-exception principle related to the information that the manager should receive from an information system for strategic planning?
5. In what way might computer technology be harnessed to facilitate the operation of an information system for strategic planning? Do you think that it would be worth the cost?
6. How might an information system for operational matters in the organization be used for strategic planning?
7. What are some illustrative examples of important classes of strategic information? How can the interrelatedness of this information be demonstrated?
8. What are some examples of explicit assumptions that can qualify as strategic information? How might these assumptions be used in a manner similar to forecasts?
9. The authors state that environmental information is critical to effective strategic planning. Why is this so? Give some examples to verify your understanding of this statement.
10. Some management theorists have argued that strategic decisions are of such a unique and unstructured nature that it is not cost-effective to develop an information system to support them. How do you feel about this statement?
11. There are four basic questions that must be asked in any strategic planning process. How does an information system for strategic planning help the organization to find the answers to these questions?

12. What is an image assessment for an organization? What value does this image assessment have? What are some of the characteristics that might be evaluated in an image assessment?
13. "What is actually happening is often less important than what appears to be happening." Evaluate the significance of this statement in the context of an organization's image.
14. What is the value of a competitive information system? Is such an information system really necessary if your organization is a leader in its field?
15. What role do the strategic data bases of Chapter 5 play in the strategic planning information system?
16. What kind of system might one be able to develop to operate exclusively at interface 4 in Figure 10.1?
17. Describe a typical corporate information system in terms of the various system interfaces in Figure 10.1.
18. Why is a potential customer information system so important for strategic planning?

Chapter 10—Strategic Questions for the Manager

1. Do managers and planners understand the difference between strategic data and strategic information? Can I give illustrations of this difference?
2. Do techniques and processes exist whereby the strategic information in the organization can be interrelated and correlated?
3. What techniques are used to test the credibility of planning assumptions?
4. Do key managers and planners understand the difference between planning and forecasting?
5. Have the relative roles of computerized systems and noncomputerized systems for strategic information been determined?
6. Do key managers understand the difference between *predictive* and *optimization* models in strategic planning information?
7. Have provisions been made for the development of systematic and formal activities to provide decision-related information in support of strategic planning?
8. Has a focal point (in terms of authority and responsibility) been established for collecting and disseminating information for strategic decision making?
9. What means are currently in use to measure the organization's image with its customers? How might the current image be described?
10. What product and organizational characteristics are most important in establishing customer image?
11. How might image monitoring activities be integrated into existing organizational structures and management systems?
12. What information does the organization require on *potential* customers? What sources are available to obtain this information?
13. Would a formal clipping service prove beneficial to the organization?
14. Do the key decision makers in the organization have profiles of key competitors? What is the basis of this profile? hearsay? documented sources? other?

15. What executive has the responsibility for developing the regulatory information subsystem? Are periodic briefings held to acquaint key executives with changes in the regulatory information data base?
16. Has the individual who has been designated responsible for developing a market intelligence system acquainted himself with the many sources of published market data? What system has been designed to collect and disseminate this information?

References

Ackoff, R. L., "Management Misinformation Systems," *Management Science*, Dec. 1967, pp. 147–156.

Aguilar, F. J., *Scanning the Business Environment*, Macmillan, New York, 1976.

Baughman, J. P., Lodge, G. C. and Pifer, H. W., *Environmental Analysis for Management*, Richard D. Irwin, Homewood, Ill., 1974.

Daniel, D. R., "Management Information Crisis," *Harvard Business Review*, Vol. 39, Sept.–Oct. 1961.

De Carbonnel, F. E., and Dorrance, R. G., "Information Sources for Planning Decisions," *California Management Review*, Volume XV, Summer 1973, pp. 42–53.

Engster, C., "Corporate Planning in an Unstable Environment," *Futures*, Dec. 1971.

Fahey, L., and King, W. R., "Environmental Scanning in Corporate Planning," *Business Horizons*, Aug. 1977.

Grudnitski, G. M., "A Methodology for the Design of Decision-Maker Oriented Information Systems," Ph.D. Dissertation, University of Massachusetts, Amherst, Mass., 1975.

Kahn, H., and Weiner, A. J., *The Year 2000*, Macmillan, New York, 1967.

Kashyap, R. N., "Management Information Systems for Corporate Planning and Control," *Long Range Planning*, June 1972.

Kelley, W. T., "Marketing Intelligence for Top Management," *Journal of Marketing*, Oct. 1965.

King, W. R., "Intelligent Management Information Systems," *Business Horizons*, Vol. 16, Oct. 1973.

King, W. R., and Cleland, D. I., "Decision and Information System for Strategic Planning," *Business Horizons*, April 1973.

King, W. R., and Cleland, D. I., "Environmental Information Systems for Strategic Marketing Planning," *Journal of Marketing*, Oct. 1974.

King, W. R., and Cleland, D. I., "Information for More Effective Strategic Planning," *Long Range Planning*, Feb. 1977.

King, W. R., and Epstein, B., "Assessing the Value of Information," *Management Datamatics*, Sept. 1976.

Kotler, P., "A Design for the Firm's Marketing Nerve Center," *Business Horizons*, Fall 1966.

Kotler, P., "Marketing Intelligence Systems: A DEW Line for Marketing Men," *Business Management*, Jan. 1966.

Mason, R. O., Jr., "Basic Concepts for Designing Management Information Systems,'' AIS Research Paper #8, Graduate School of Business Administration, University of California, Oct. 1969.

McFarlan, F. W., ''Problems in Planning the Information System,'' *Harvard Business Review,* March–April 1971.

Montgomery, D. B., and Urban, G. L., ''Marketing Decision—Information Systems: An Emerging View,'' *Journal of Marketing Research,* May 1970.

Schewe, C. D., ''The Management Information System User: An Exploratory Behavioral Analysis,'' *Academy of Management Journal,* Dec. 1976.

Thomas, P. S., ''Environmental Analysis for Corporate Planning,'' *Business Horizons,* Oct. 1974, pp. 27–37.

STRATEGIC COMPETITIVE INFORMATION SYSTEMS[1]

The previous chapter described a broad framework for environmental information systems to support strategic planning. One of the most troublesome and ill-understood aspects of such an overall systems concept is dealing with the competitive sector of the organization's environment. Therefore, we seek in this chapter, through a more-detailed treatment of this subsystem, to demonstrate the feasibility and value of strategic information systems.

Some will think that in selecting the competitive information subsystem for detailed attention we are focusing exclusively on the strategic planning considerations of business firms. However, this is not the case at all. A wide range of organizations in our society are becoming aware of their need to study "the competition." Many recognize that they are competing against new forces and organizations that did not even exist when their original mission, objectives and strategy were originally determined. The U.S. Postal Services' concern with private delivery firms and the concern of various police departments with new roles being played by private security forces are illustrative of this growing awareness that public agencies like business firms, must be aware of those who can provide services to substitute for those now being provided under monopoly conditions.

Indeed, despite the fact that many public managers who are not involved in foreign affairs or foreign intelligence-gathering tend to respond to the suggestion that organizations should develop competitive intelligence systems by suggesting that such systems are appropriate only for business firms, the fact is that few business firms have adequate information about their competitors. In these times of post-Watergate morality, many firms may be tempted to ignore this information void, and many are likely to pay severe penalties for doing so.

Many business people who have not dealt with competitive information systems tend to disparage their utility or feasibility. Often some do so in

---

[1] Portions of this chapter are adapted from Cleland, D. I., and King, W. R. "Competitive Business Intelligence Systems," *Business Horizons,* Dec. 1975.

the belief that, although certain bits of information about competitors may be useful, there is little need for a system to collect and analyze it. Others feel that competitive intelligence would be useful, but it is impractical to obtain. Still others recognize the practicality of obtaining such intelligence, but doubt that it can be done legally and ethically.

The Need for Competitive Intelligence

"Intelligence" as the term is used in this chapter, refers to competitive and environmental data that has been evaluated to be useful in a specific situation, project, or class of situations, i.e., information. However, the term is not restricted to external data, since a great deal can be discovered about competition and the environment from internal organizational sources.

No person or organization can effectively operate in any competitive environment without a basic understanding of that environment or without up-to-date information on happenings in the environment. This point really needs no extensive logical justification. However, on a pragmatic level, one can simply point to the intelligence systems being developed by business firms. Witness, for example, the *Harvard Business Review* article[2] from the early 1960s which said:

> . . . commercial intelligence departments are appearing more and more on corporate organization charts . . .

The types of information about competitors that are generally considered to be "fair game" for collection, include a wide range of information on market pricing, discounts, terms, specifications, total market volume for a given product, historical trends, estimates of competitor's share, competitor's trends, evaluations of competitive product quality and performance, estimates of marketing policies and plans of each competitor, new competitive systems and/or trends, strengths, weaknesses, and probable strategies.[3]

The type of information required depends on the nature of the company, the competitive environment it faces, and many other relevant company and environmental characteristics. According to Greene[4]:

[2] Daniel, D. R., "Management Information Crisis," *Harvard Business Review,* Vol. 39, Sept.–Oct. 1961, pp. 111–121.

[3] The popular press has sometimes attempted to portray competitive business intelligence primarily as "espionage." For example, the book *The Secrets Business* by Stephen Barlay, Crowell, New York, 1973, reads like a Hollywood spy thriller. According to Barlay, "A multimillion-dollar industrial-espionage racket flourishes just beneath big business's respectable surface." Probably such activities exist to some extent. However, we believe that the greatest majority of business intelligence can be gleaned from overt ethical sources.

[4] Greene, R. M. (editor), *Business Intelligence and Espionage,* Richard D. Irwin, Homewood, Ill., 1966, p. 28.

The needs for intelligence differs according to the operation being run or planned. Companies may have long-range plans (strategic plans), tactical or short-range plans, and immediate operations, all of which require intelligence support.

Competitive Intelligence Concepts

In this chapter, we seek to address some of the common myths of competitive intelligence[5] by developing some basic competitive information system concepts, describing a model of competitive information systems that can be widely applicable and illustrating its use.

THE NATURE OF COMPETITIVE INTELLIGENCE

A "want list" of everything that an organization, such as a business firm, would like to know about a competitor would be almost endless. A representative list of what is required would serve to illustrate the usefulness of such intelligence. Although the details needed vary somewhat from company to company, there are basic elements required for most competitive analyses.

Marketing Information:
1. Pricing, discounts, terms, product specifications
2. Volume, history, trend and outlook for a given product
3. Market share and trend
4. Marketing policies and plans
5. Relations and image with customers
6. Size and deployment of sales force
7. Channels, policies, and methods of distribution
8. Advertising program

Production and Product Information:
1. Evaluation of quality and performance
2. Breadth of line
3. Processing and technology
4. Product cost
5. Production capacity
6. Location and size of production facilities and warehouses

---

[5] We shall use the term "intelligence" in this chapter in the way in which it is commonly used in the competitive environment, namely, to encompass all evaluated data concerning competition. In Chapter 10, we chose to distinguish between a competitive information subsystem and an intelligence subsystem to emphasize the need for both general background information and information concerning the competitor's ongoing activities.

7. Packaging
8. Delivery
9. Research and development capability

Organizational and Financial Information:
1. Identification of key decision makers
2. Philosophies of key decision makers
3. Financial condition and outlook
4. Expansion and acquisition programs
5. Major problems/opportunities
6. Research and development programs

A list such as this can be misleading since it may suggest to some that competitive intelligence is data rather than information. In fact, the meaning of intelligence is embodied in the basic elements of competitive behavior. Various illustrations of the use of business intelligence to be given later will serve to better define this distinction. However, it should be noted at this point that the issues of system feasibility and system utility rest on the *relevance* of the information that the system is designed to process, i.e., on the evaluation of competitive data as being relevant. If one specifies a wide variety of data in a basic system design, without regard for its relevance and known utility, the system may well prove to be infeasible, or at least, ineffective. On the other hand, systems that are designed to provide broad background information as well as specific information on well-defined areas can be both feasible and economic.

OBJECTIVES OF A STRATEGIC COMPETITIVE INFORMATION SYSTEM

The specification of some objectives for a competitive business intelligence subsystem serves to illuminate the operational concept of competitive intelligence. Such objectives might be as follows:

1. To assure the availability on a timely basis of credible and comprehensive information of the capabilities of, and the options open to, each key competitor.
2. To determine the manner in which key competitors' actions might affect current organizational interests.
3. To continuously monitor and provide credible and comprehensive information on situations and contingencies in the competitive environment and in the marketplace that might have an impact on the interests of the organization.
4. To achieve efficiency and eliminate unnecessary duplication of effort for the collection, analysis, and dissemination of competitive intelligence for the organization.

BASIC PREMISES FOR A STRATEGIC COMPETITIVE
INFORMATION SYSTEM

In working with companies on the development of strategic competitive information systems we have developed a number of basic premises to serve as guides for system development:

1. Competitive business intelligence is essential for ensuring success in competing in the market.
2. Markets today are changing so dramatically that informal means of maintaining competitive surveillance are inadequate.
3. Reliance on hit-or-miss methods for obtaining such information is ineffective in the long run. A total system in the true sense of the word is required for performing the intelligence function.
4. A business intelligence system can be highly personalized even though it is rigorously organized and operated.
5. Such a system should be action oriented. It should not simply produce reports of aggregated data. Rather it should also provide managers with exception-oriented information that indicates the *need to act* and suggests the preferred action.
6. Business intelligence can be gained from a variety of sources, many of which might superficially seem to be unprofitable.
7. A competitive intelligence system should include a security and counterintelligence capability. This capability should rest on the assumption that competitors have a similar system and that they may resort to illegal and/or unethical means to penetrate one's own system.
8. An intelligence system can be made most effective without resorting to unethical and/or illegal techniques of data collection.[6]

The use of unethical means of intelligence gathering can be counterproductive in the long run. If one pays an agent or bribes a competitor's agent to gain information, that person can undoubtedly be bought by the competitor, thus making the information potentially detrimental rather than beneficial. If one

---

[6] The predominantly public, semipublic basic nature of business intelligence, coupled with the fact that any good business intelligence system will operate with company personnel in visible positions in other organizations, determines that unethical or illegal methods using secret agents to collect competitive business information *is not likely to be necessary for attaining an effective level of intelligence*. A recent survey emphasizes the current ethical approach to intelligence gathering (see Wall, J. L., "What the Competition Is Doing: Your Need to Know," *Harvard Business Review,* Nov.–Dec. 1974. The data collected in this study ". . . contradict an expressed belief by the respondents that ethical standards have declined.", p. 22.) This supposition is supported in other literature of the field. For example "Guide to Gathering Market Intelligence," *Industrial Management* Vol. 47, March 1962, p. 84, says that ". . . the sources are so numerous . . . one need not stoop to any unethical practices. . . ."

then uses a counterintelligence system to preclude such erroneous data, the costs of data collection will rapidly escalate to the point of negating the benefit of the original system. This argument does not even take into account the risk of exposure and resultant loss of customer goodwill and possible fines or even imprisonment. It is our belief that illegal and unethical activities simply do not pay in the long run.

THE COMPETITIVE INTELLIGENCE CYCLE

Figure 11.1, portrays the overall intelligence cycle, which can form the basis for the strategic competitive information system, as a continuous process that is improved through feedback. The cycle starts off with the determination of the intelligence requirements and the organization of the resources for the collection of information. After the information is collected, it must be processed and analyzed; from this the desired intelligence is derived and then disseminated to the managers and organizational elements that have need for the intelligence. A continuous feedback process provides for the modification of the cycle wherever necessary to improve the total process. As new requirements are being levied on the intelligence collection agencies, information is being collected and continuously disseminated.

THE NEED FOR SYSTEMIZATION

To even attempt to address the broad diversity of business intelligence sources and uses without systemization would be utter folly. No individual or group could reasonably be expected to be aware, and much less, to have evaluated such a range of data. Therefore, any action taken without such a system is necessarily made without the full information that could contribute to that action.

Even subjective personally derived information needs to be systematized. The "slip of the lip" will stand a much greater chance of being caught and passed on to the key decision makers if the individual who hears it is aware of a need and of a system where it can be evaluated, put into its proper context, and highlighted as potentially useful intelligence.

To systematize the competitive intelligence process really means that questions such as those that follow be answered and the answers implemented.

What needs to be known?

Where can the data be obtained?

Who will gather the data?

How will the data be gathered?

Who will analyze and interpret the data?

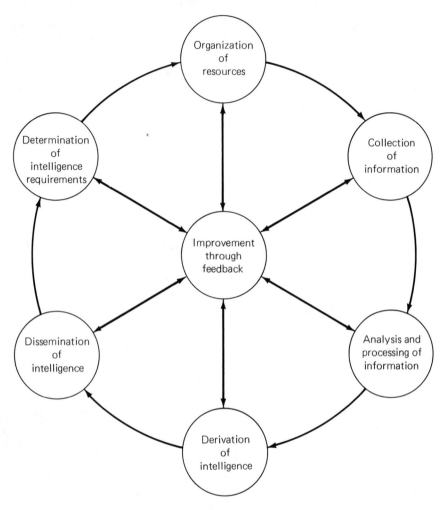

FIGURE 11.1   Competitive Intelligence System Cycle.

How will extracted information be stored most efficiently for equally efficient future retrieval?

How can extracted intelligence be disseminated to the proper parties at the right time for consideration?

How will the system be protected from "leakage" and sabotage?

Unless the intelligence problem is focused toward a single program or objective and can therefore be approached on a somewhat *ad hoc* basis, reasonable answers to these questions may dictate that a computer system be utilized for effective storage and retrieval operations. Dissemination and display over and above periodic briefings and responses to specific requests can be facilitated by assembling user interest profiles and feeding them into the computer. Then, as additions are made to the file, matchup with these profiles can automatically trigger intelligence outputs that might have been missed by the human data interpreter (evaluation function). This is a common approach taken by military intelligence units. This will permit a double check on the process and ensure rapid dissemination of vital information to the proper users. Such a system is shown in its broadest outline in Figure 11.2.

Even though a continuing formalized business intelligence system may require automation and computers, the *inputs* to the system can, and must, be highly personalized. The personalized nature of these inputs therefore requires that the system involve, in addition to automated processing equipment, *the right people at the right place to obtain information.*

Marketing people are only a small portion of the people part of such a system. Every executive of the company must be involved, as well as some personnel whose primary responsibility is defined to be intelligence gathering and processing. In some cases only high-level executives can penetrate competitors'' organizations, government agencies, and other organizations to gain useful information.

Therefore, although the intelligence-gathering skills of an individual can usually be improved, the primary emphasis should be on fitting individuals

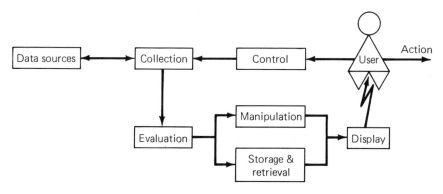

FIGURE 11.2   Competitive Intelligence Process.

into the system, having them recognize their intelligence responsibilities, and by providing them with easy data entry into the competitive business intelligence system.

A Strategic Competitive Information System Model

A basic model, or structure can be developed from the concepts presented thus far. This model has been tested in its various dimensions in a variety of real-world situations, but no one organization has adopted all of the model's elements. In this sense, it is a synthesis of ideas and elements found to be useful in a number of contexts, and on this basis, we believe that it is one that can be useful in a wide range of situations.

The model system may be thought of in terms of the three critical phases of the intelligence process: collecting, analyzing, and disseminating competitive intelligence information.

SYSTEM INPUT—THE COLLECTION OF INTELLIGENCE

Inputs to the competitive intelligence system may come from a wide variety of sources, both public and private. One thing that many people who are unfamiliar with intelligence often mistakenly presume is that most useful information comes from secret sources. They think of such things as the U.S.S.R.'s notable successes in obtaining U.S. atom bomb secrets after World War II and recent publication of the details of covert CIA operations as being typical of intelligence.

The truth is that *most intelligence activities* (even of the CIA and certainly of businesses) *operate primarily using public information.* Even in the military this is so, as exemplified by Admiral Ellis Zacharias' (Deputy Chief of Naval Intelligence during World War II) estimate that the U.S. Navy obtained 95% of its intelligence from public sources, 4% through semipublic sources, and only 1% through secret sources.[7]

Thus, the emphasis is on *organized search of publically available informa- tion sources.* Much of the basic information used by planners can come to them routinely from the vast outpourings of the business world in public media, business magazines, newspapers, government publications, scholarly or scientific treatises, and continuing informal feedback from the sales force.

However, although much can be obtained in this fashion, e.g., computerized search and organized search in a business library, the intelligence pro-

---

[7] Zacharias, E. M., *Secret Missions: The Story of an Intelligence Officer,* Putman, New York, 1946, pp. 117–118.

cess at the lowest level in the organization can be fruitful. A valuable intelligence collector may simply be a salesman who is assigned to join a plant tour at a competitor's facility and reports his findings to the sales office. A clerk who has been detailed to provide a clipping service from a newspaper located in a competitor's community may also be performing a vital intelligence function.

As noted in Chapter 10, the data collection takes the form of (a) the continuing collection of basic data for general encyclopedic intelligence or for maintaining a continuing awareness of the factors and forces in the competitive system and (b) the collection of specific items to fill critical information gaps in the intelligence base or to meet special requests for competitive information from a particular user-manager.

THE INTELLIGENCE COLLECTION PLAN

The collection phases of the overall intelligence cycle include the guidance, preparation, and transmittal of the collection plan (with goals and objectives) to those people and agencies responsible for the actual gathering of data.

In the guidance phase of the collection of information, the action is usually initiated by the intelligence office acting on their own initiative from a review of the organization's planning documents, or in response to a specific request from a ''consumer.'' The intelligence office receives guidance for their activities from their statement of organizational mission and from the specific guidance furnished in the various plans that exist in the organization. This office will also receive guidance and direction from the user-manager, his staff, and from higher, lateral, and subordinate organizational elements. The intelligence office should, of course, be kept informed of any changes in the planning of the organization, particularly if goals and objectives should be changed. Notice of new organizational direction or potential new direction is vital to the collection of adequate and relevant business intelligence.

The sources of potentially relevant information and the diversity of uses to which information may be put are so numerous that a plan for collection of information is essential to the success of such a system. *A competitive intelligence plan relates information needs to potential information sources* in such a way as to prescribe and delimit the information screening process.

Here, within the context of the collection plan, we provide an enumeration of the sources of competitive business intelligence and the process that the collectors might go through in gathering the necessary information. Despite the fact that the sources of potential competitive data are so numerous and varied that it would not be practical to attempt to list all the sources, a perusal of these sources will help to convince the reader that it is possible to obtain the competitive data needed to operate a business intelligence and still follow the highest standards of legal and ethical conduct.[8] *The following sources of information are offered as representative and can be augmented according to a particular company's needs:*

FIELD SALES FORCE. The salesman, because of his frequent contact with his customers and other salesmen, is one of the best information sources. However, a salesman is often subjected to half-truths and misleading information, particularly in the area of pricing. Intelligence gathered by salesmen should therefore be crosschecked and verified by data from other sources.

PURCHASING DEPARTMENT. Supplier salesmen frequently know a great deal about what is happening in an industry. Plant tours are often available to purchasing personnel. One may take advantage of this opportunity by briefing purchasing people on what to look for.

RESEARCH AND DEVELOPMENT ORGANIZATION. Research and development people keep up with the technical developments and breakthroughs in their various fields of interest. Their activity in technical associations and attention to technical papers and journals often give them considerable insight into competitor's product activities.

TREASURY DEPARTMENT. This information source can be valuable; if the competitor is also a customer, the treasury department will have knowledge of their payment habits and financial condition. Also, the treasury department can often arrange for an introduction to key people in the financial community who have in-depth knowledge of the competitor's finances.

KEY EXECUTIVES. Key executives are often in contact with peers in the industry. These contacts can give insight into what a competitor is doing.

BUSINESS PERIODICALS. Business periodicals are a must for careful scrutiny for articles dealing with a competitor's operation. The following periodicals are particularly valuable in this respect:

Wall Street Journal
Fortune

---

[8] The skeptical reader will react by saying that all of these sources are already known to him. Yet, in the authors' experience in developing such systems in industry, we have not yet found a fledgling effort that came close to utilizing the full range of valuable sources. In all of these instances, after a demonstration of the value of such sources was given, the analysts began making use of these known sources. Thus, our advice to the skeptic must take the form, "Try it. You'll like it!"

Business Week
Industrial Marketing
Printer's Ink
Harvard Business Review [9]
Business Horizons
Commerce & Business Daily
Dun's Review

BOOKS. Books dealing with a company can be very revealing. See for example, Greenwood, R. C., *Managerial Decentralization* Lexington Books, Boston, 1974, which provides a study of the General Electric Company management philosophy.

BUSINESS REFERENCE SERVICES. Financial information is the strong point of business reference services. However, do not overlook this as a source of additional intelligence on other matters as well. Some standard business reference services include:

Moody's Industrial Manual [10]
Barron's
Standard & Poor's Industrial Surveys
Funk & Scott Index of Corporations and Industries
The Value Line Investment Survey
Dun & Bradstreet Reports
Standard Corporation Descriptions (Standard & Poor's Corporation)
Thomas Register of American Manufacturers
Dun & Bradstreet Reports

BUSINESS LITERATURE INDICES. A careful perusal of company-oriented articles in the following indices can provide useful information about a competitor. For example, two articles referenced in the *Business Periodicals Index* provide

[9] For instance, a competitor should be interested in the article Goggin, W. C., "How the Multi-dimensional Structure Works at Dow Corning," *Harvard Business Review,* Jan.–Feb. 1973, pp. 54–65.

[10] In one example of a particular company, this manual provided several pages of detailed information along the following organization: Capital structure; history; business and products; sources of sales and earnings; principal plants and properties; management and organization; auditors; comparative consolidated income account; comparative consolidated balance sheet; financial and operating data (based on reports to Securities and Exchange Commission); long-term debt profile; and capital stock data.

valuable insight into the strategic-planning philosophy and approach of the General Electric Company.[11]

> The Reader's Guide to Periodical Literature
> The Business Periodicals Index
> The Wall Street Journal Index
> The New York Times Index
> Applied Science and Technology Index
> Business and Economic Index
> The London Times Index
> The Bulletin of the Public Affairs Information Service
> The Engineering Index
> The Agricultural Index

GOVERNMENT SOURCES. Government aerial maps are photographic maps that can help in determining the size of a competitor's facility. Securities and Exchange Commission Reports contain very detailed information on foreign investments as well as domestic data. Information is available at the local courthouse, e.g., if a competitor is embarking on an expansion program. Courthouse files may well reveal building permits, plans, etc. Also, Patent Department Reports, Federal Trade Commission Hearings, and Congressional Hearings are all sources for vital information.

PROFESSIONAL ASSOCIATIONS. Participation in professional associations can provide opportunity to talk unobtrusively with personnel of the competition.

LICENSE AGREEMENTS. Some competitors are also licensees. This may help in determining something about a competitor's volume and technology.

CUSTOMERS. Present and potential customers are usually interested in comparing a vendor's capabilities with those of competition. This information source is well worth developing.

SUPPLIERS. The supplier who sells to competition has a great deal of valuable information to offer. The cooperation of the purchasing department may effectively tap this source.

---

[11] See "GE's Jones Restructures His Top Team," Business Week, June 30, 1973, Springer, C. H., "Strategic Management in General Electric," Operations Research, Vol. 21, Nov.–Dec. 1973, and "Management: GE's Search for Synergy," New York Times, Apr. 16, 1978.

DISTRIBUTORS. This is an outstanding source of intelligence. Distributors are often familiar with a great many aspects of a competitor's businesses.

TRADE ASSOCIATIONS. Participation can yield valuable new information. The key is to gain useful intelligence without divulging very much about ones own operation.

LOCAL CHAMBER OF COMMERCE. This source can often give information on employment, the size of the competitor's facility, and the products being manufactured at a particular location.

LOCAL PRESS. Many times it is worthwhile to subscribe to the local newspaper of the community where a competitor is located. The smaller the community, the more information one might find on employment, organization, expansions, etc.

TRADE PRESS. A great deal of information is published here. It is almost mandatory to regularly review this material. Sources of information concerning trade associations may be found in such publications as:

Directory of National Associations of Businessmen
Encyclopedia of Associations
Standard Advertising Register

STOCKBROKERS. Stockbrokers, particularly those who have participated in the selling of a competitor's stock, often have made in-depth studies on a competitor's strengths and weaknesses.

ANNUAL REPORTS. Depending somewhat on a competitor's diversity of operation, the annual report will reveal profitability and financial health as well as the names of the officers and directors. Often, there will be information regarding expansion and acquisition programs.

PROSPECTUS. These will usually reveal the major stockholders along with financial and organizational details.

STOCKHOLDER MEETINGS. These can be very revealing or completely unrewarding. Owners of a share of stock are entitled to ask some very pointed questions and, under certain conditions, are entitled to request that responses be fully prepared in advance and distributed in writing to shareholders.

LOCAL BANKS. A competitor's principal bank is intimately familiar with his financial position.

INVESTMENT BANKERS. Investment bankers may be able to provide useful information. However, conflict of interest may present a problem.

Other miscellaneous sources include the following:

Technical journals (often, the first printed information about a new product or technology will be found here)

Competitor's house organ

Competitor's phone directory

Competitor's former employee

Published antitrust data

Gossip from customers

Trade show literature

Gossip by one competitor about another

Articles, papers presented at professional societies

Gossip from supplier salesmen about competitors

Information from dealers and distributors

Biographical listings (e.g., *Who's Who in America*)

ANALYSIS AND PROCESSING OF INFORMATION

Collected data are not information until analyzed and interpreted by the substantive experts. In cases of urgency, information can be passed to the decision makers without scrutiny by the substantive experts, but when time permits (and this means in the great majority of the cases), it is processed finished intelligence that is of greatest use by the decision maker.

The quality of the analysis and interpretation depends to a large degree on the credentials that the analyst holds. In the business organization, that means that the one having functional responsibility (production, marketing, finance, or research and development) is the best one to interpret a particular functional type of information. Determining the probable strategy of a competitor in the penetration of a new market area could be handled by a mix of people (set up as a task force) from several functional areas of the organization. The war gaming of a competitor's strategy would best be handled by setting up a 'microcompany'' within the organization to study the data that has intelligence value and then hypothesizing what the competitor's strategy might be.

In any case, there is the need for a centralized processing unit—in many cases of start up situations, perhaps only a single person. For instance, one company set up an individual who began by sending out a ''want list'' containing questions that needed to be answered concerning competitive actions on certain key company programs. This list was updated weekly. The field sales-man and others who received this list were urged to communicate anything that might be of significance about competitors to the intelligence office. Through this simple device, much was learned about competitive technical and market-ing strategy, particularly concerning a major government project on which the company was preparing a proposal.

In another instance, the development of up-to-date profiles on competitors led to an inference about a competitor's technical thrust. This was based on an analysis of the backgrounds of the people currently being promoted to positions of prominence in the competitor's organization. A knowledge of the common technical background of several key competitive people led to the inference that this technical thrust would come to dominate the competitor's strategy. The company designed a strategy to effectively combat this competitive thrust and succeeded in winning several key contracts.

ANALYZING THE CREDIBILITY AND RELIABILITY OF INFORMATION. Despite the legal, ethical, and public nature of the system being outlined, competitor infor-mation must always be analyzed in terms of the credibility and reliability of its source and its content. A simple evaluation system can be developed that expresses the viewpoints of the collector and others as to the source and con-tent. Many different guides have been developed to appraise the credibility of the information. One such guide drawn from a military intelligence context is indicated below.

Appraisal of Source	*Appraisal of Content*
A Completely reliable	A Confirmed by other means
B Usually reliable	B Probably true
C Fairly reliable	C Possibly true
D Not usually reliable	D Doubtful
E Unreliable	E Improbable
F Reliability cannot be judged	F Truth cannot be determined

The use of such a rating may be the only way for the analyst to judge the information when faced with confirming or contradictory information.

SYSTEM OUTPUT

Intelligence that has been evaluated can then be distributed to those persons and agencies entitled to receive it. If the nature of the intelligence relates to stra-tegic planning, then the people who prepare plans and are responsible for making strategic decisions should be the recipients of the finished intelligence. Certain information that is sensitive in nature may be distributed only to select individuals. Within the military establishment, the concept of "need to know" prevails. Regardless of an individual's organizational position, he should only receive the intelligence that is necessary for him to carry out his managerial duties. The same general idea can be applied in any organization.

Rules for dissemination should be developed to provide necessary safeguards, yet not deny the intelligence to those who need it. The Joint Congressional Committee on the World War II Pearl Harbor investigation condemned the overrestrictive circulation of intelligence derived from the decrypting of Japanese codes. The committee observed that "the fact that Japanese codes had been broken was regarded as of more importance than the information obtained from decoded traffic. The result of this rather specious premise was to leave large numbers of policy-making and enforcement officials in Washington completely oblivious of the most pertinent information concerning Japan." [12] Later evidence has shown that this protectiveness extended far beyond even those levels that were criticized in that investigation. [13]

A competitive business intelligence system should indicate to managers when action should be taken, and provide some indication of the best action to take. If the system simply provides volumes of reports on a continuing basis, action directives are left entirely to the manager; he must sift through the mire of data to evaluate its relevance and applicability. If the manager is to be relieved of this task, the business intelligence system should be exception-oriented; that is, in addition to providing a continuing flow of relevant information, it should provide red flag signals where action is required.

ADMINISTRATION OF THE COMPETITIVE BUSINESS INTELLIGENCE SYSTEM

The final consideration in designing a competitive business information system involves its administration, i.e., where should the system be placed in the organizational hierarchy and how should it be organized? This consideration is highly dependent upon the capability required, which in turn, will determine the operational plan.

If a successful marketing information system is in effect, the competitive intelligence group may be integrated into the organization within this system (most business firms position the group organizationally in this manner); however, this relatively low position in the hierarchy and specification to a func-

---

[12] U.S. Congress, *Joint Committee on Pearl Harbor Investigation,* U.S. Government Printing Office, Washington, D.C.

[13] See Winterbotham, F. W., *The Ultra Secret,* Harper and Row, New York, 1974, and Stevenson, W., *A Man called Intrepid,* Harcourt, Brace, Jovanovich, New York, 1976.

tional area (marketing) may be disadvantageous as the desirable flow of required information to other functional areas may be hampered.

As the competitive intelligence office should ideally be responsive to some degree to the requests of all functional areas, experience has shown that the most gainful output results if the office is autonomous and centralized for the product system area. An extreme diversity of product lines may necessitate decentralization of the intelligence group to some degree.

It is essential to the success of any program that in an office (perhaps just one individual) be assigned the responsibility for the coordination of the total competitive intelligence function, collecting, analyzing, and disseminating information. Once the overall authority and responsibility of the system office has been established, the following questions can provide valuable insight into how to start up operations.

WHAT INFORMATION IS NEEDED? It is necessary here to be quite specific. List the information that is essential to planning. Be specific as to competitors. Also, be realistic. One can never find out everything that one could possibly want to know.

HOW IS THE INFORMATION TO BE OBTAINED? Assess all the potential ethical sources of the specific information required.

WHICH PROMISES TO PROVIDE THE MOST RELEVANT INFORMATION? Be sure to involve other organizational functions in the search: purchasing, finance, engineering, manufacturing, and the controller's department may not be aware that they have a part to play in the evaluation of competition.

HOW WILL THE INFORMATION BE ORGANIZED? There are many ways to organize competitive information. Setting up a file for each important competitor has proven successful. Within this competitor file, sectionalize the information by major category such as Marketing, Product, Facilities, Organization and Finance, Strengths/Weaknesses, and Probable Strategies, etc. Consider the use of a computerized retrieval system.

HOW WILL THE INFORMATION BE ANALYZED AND TO WHOM WILL THE INTELLIGENCE BE DISSEMINATED?

WHAT POLICIES AND GUIDELINES SHOULD BE FOLLOWED? It is up to each user-manager to develop his own policies and guidelines for competitive intelligence use. However, each user-manager unit should be apprised of overall system policies, and during the start-up period each should be asked to submit policy guidelines (usually more restrictive) governing intelligence usage in their area.

ILLUSTRATIVE STRATEGY COMPETITIVE INFORMATION
SYSTEM POLICIES

The previously noted objectives and concepts for a strategic competitive information system will only be achieved within the context of a basic policy for system development and implementation. Here, we provide illustrative policies along with rationales for each.

RESPONSIBILITIES OF PARTICIPANTS. It is imperative that the roles and responsibilities of each participant be defined and made clear to all. This serves both to identify intelligence roles for many in the organization who may not previously have thought of themselves in such a context and to constrain the zeal of those who may become caught up in their intelligence role.

A broad and comprehensive system will require the participation of many elements of the organization. For example,

1. Finance division—Reviews statements on files with the state and federal securities offices. Provides continuing financial analysis of competitors.
2. Marketing division—Provides assessment of market forces affecting competitor behavior.
3. Industrial relations division—Interrogates job applicants who have competitive experience and maintain contact with employment agencies.
4. Manufacturing division—Maintains contact with equipment suppliers and with carriers (rail, truck and ship).
5. Purchasing division—Attends purchasing agent's meetings and maintains contact with raw material suppliers.
6. Engineering division—Costs out products and reviews engineering articles.
7. Research division—Searches patent applications and lab test products.
8. Corporate administration—Maintains contact with industry executives (avoiding price-cost discussions). Maintains contact with trade press and trade associations. Maintains contact with university officials and key consultants.

Thus total responsibility for intelligence collection should not be placed solely on the director of intelligence. The load must be shared by the entire enterprise with the obvious benefit of a comprehensive and penetrating collection system that is far superior to one operated by just a few individuals.

SECURITY IN A STRATEGIC COMPETITIVE INTELLIGENCE SYSTEM. An intelligence system must necessarily include sensitive information. Because one's own operation operates in an ethical fashion does not imply that competitors will do the same. Therefore, sensitive information must be protected. A valid approach to system security design would involve the assumption of the worst on the part of one's competitors. If they do not limit themselves to methods that we consider to be ethical, what impact will it have on the organization?

We believe that an intelligence system should have an associated security system patterned after that of the military. This should include limited counterintelligence and a classification system so that some information is available on a "need to know" basis, while some is open to all interested parties. This lends an aura of respectability to the entire operation and will also give it more importance so that a large enough budget can be justified to sustain the operations of data collection.

The following precautions should be considered in planning such an information security system:

1. Total responsibility for security vested in one individual.
2. Internal checks and balances.
3. Potential employees carefully screened.
4. Control system (document classification), periodic inventory, constant record of whereabouts, prompt return.
5. Soundproof area for discussion of highly proprietary information.
6. Files and desks kept locked.
7. Documents no longer useful burned or shredded under close supervision.
8. Identification cards for employees so that arriving and departing can be recorded.
9. Limiting employees' access to on-premises duplicating machines.
10. Confidential envelopes for internal transmission of confidential documents.
11. Strict security of model shops, research and development offices, engineering department labs.

Varieties of Strategic Competitive Information System

In the foregoing discussion, we have provided both the conceptual and practical bases for the development of a strategic competitive information system. We close this discussion by illustrating a number of varieties of such systems, i.e., strategic comeptitive intelligence systems can operate at various levels of sophistication.

INFORMATION RETRIEVAL SYSTEMS

The implicit level of the system descriptions previously given in this chapter are of the retrieval variety. In such a system, the potential user inquires into the system for a specific item of information. For instance, the user might ask for the "annual sales of XYZ Company for the past ten years."

Such systems are clearly useful, but they are limited in that they require the user to "know what he wants to know" in a very specific and precise fashion. This limitation serves to inhibit the potential value of the system, because the user-manager will not generally be knowledgeable about the structure and methods of operation of competitors. Thus, the user-manager's knowledge may be so limited that the most useful information cannot be readily identified.

For instance, suppose that a manager in a company that sells exclusively through regional sales offices inquires into a retrieval system concerning competitive sales by sales office, and suppose that the manager is unaware that the competitor sells both through sales offices and independent brokers. If the competitor's "sales office sales" information retrieved by the system is assumed to represent the total sales of the competitor, the retrieval system user will be misled. In this case, the misunderstanding would be caused by a lack of sufficient knowledge about the competitor's organization to properly pose his inquiry into the system.

Of course, good system documentation and the aid of user consultants can vitiate the impact of this system limitation, but it is a potentially serious one that should be considered in designing a strategic competitive information system.

STRATEGIC QUESTION-BASED SYSTEMS

An alternative to the pure retrieval system is a strategic question-based system. In such a system, rather than asking for specific items of information, the user merely poses a "strategic question" concerning competition and the system, through a series of information structure models, selects the information most relevant to the question.

For instance, a user might inquire about the capability of a particular competitor to introduce a new product in a particular product line by a specific date. With this strategic question as the input, the system is programmed to identify a wide range of competitive information dealing with the competitor's financial condition, research and development activity, marketing capability, etc., all addressed to permitting the manager to assess this strategic competitive capability without having to think about each of the myriad items of information to which it is related. As such, the manager is freed to concentrate on the assessment of the competitive capability rather than on identifying all of the relevant information.

Of course, such a system must be preprogammed as to the strategic questions which it will accept. We have not yet arrived at that computerized Nirvana of true man-machine communication at the operational level. Nonetheless, such a system can be expanded in scope as new strategic questions are identified in the strategic-planning process, thus making the strategic competitive information system into an integral supporting part of the overall strategic planning system.[14]

MODEL-ORIENTED INFORMATION SYSTEMS

The corporate model-oriented systems discussed in Chapter 8 may also incorporate a competitive element. Indeed, the schematic diagram of such a system (shown in Figure 8.5) shows a competitive module. Such systems are meant to provide the capability for asking what if questions, as opposed to strategic questions, concerning competitive capabilities. As such, strategic competitive information systems that incorporate a model capability represent a very sophisticated level of such systems, one that is not operationalized in the competitive area to the degree that it is in the other model module areas.[15]

Summary

Competitive information subsystems are treated in this chapter in detail to illustrate the practicability of developing MIS support for strategic planning. Competitive intelligence is one of the most important and least understood elements of planning information. There are many people who believe that competitive information is necessarily dealt with at a totally informal level.

In fact, competitive intelligence must be dealt with systematically if it is to have any chance of having impact, on a continuing basis, on strategic-planning decisions. A strategic competitive intelligence system should include an intelligence collection, a process for analyzing information, and a dissemination mechanism. All of these aspects must be developed to ensure the maximum value and credibility in the information and to enhance the likelihood that the information will be used by managers in their planning choices.

[14] See Rodriguez, J. I., and King, W. R., "Strategic Issue Competitive Information Systems, *Long Range Planning*, Dec. 1977.

[15] See King, W. R., Dutta, B. K., and Rodriguez, J. I., "Strategic Competitive Information Systems," *OMEGA*, Feb. 1978.

Chapter 11—Questions and Exercises

1. Some managers will profess that competitive information is useful but not worth the effort to gather on a systematic basis. How do you feel about this statement?
2. What kind of competitive information is considered to be fair game for collection?
3. Select an organization with which you are familiar. Develop a want list of competitive data that you might want to know about that organization.
4. What competitive information might be gleaned out of the article: "The Opposites: GE Grows While Westinghouse Shrinks," *Business Week*, January 31, 1977, p. 60?
5. What are some of the basic premises that might serve as guides for the development of a competitive business information system?
6. Can an effective competitive business intelligence system be developed without resorting to unethical and/or illegal techniques of data collection? Why, or why not?
7. What is the danger of using unethical means of collecting competitive information?
8. How can a business firm guard against a competitor's penetration of their organization?
9. Portray a competitive intelligence cycle. Relate this to the intelligence function of an organization with which you are familiar.
10. Which individuals in an organization should be involved in the collection of intelligence on the competitors? Who should manage the operation of the competitive business intelligence system?
11. Inputs to the competitive intelligence system may come from a wide variety of sources, both public and private. What are some of these sources?
12. What is the justification for the development of an intelligence collection plan? What is the composition of the plan?
13. Who should analyze the information that has been gathered on the competition to see if there is any intelligence involved?
14. How can the credibility and reliability of competitive information be determined?
15. Who should receive output from the competitive intelligence business system? How can access to this information be limited? What is meant by the idea of "need to know?"
16. Where should the competitive business information system be placed in the organizational hierarchy? How should the function be organized? What role might marketing play in the administration of the competitive business intelligence system?
17. What are some general guidelines for the protection of sensitive information in the organization? What should be the function of a counterintelligence officer in the organization?
18. What role should the legal counsel of the organization play in the operation of a competitive business intelligence system?
19. In practical terms, describe what is meant by the relevance of strategic information.
20. What is the importance of having an intelligence collection plan?

Chapter 11—Strategic Questions for the Manager

1. Who are the major competitors? What are their major strengths and weaknesses?
2. What are the probable strategies of the competitors? How do these strategies affect my competitive position?
3. What share of the market does the competitor hold? Is this share changing? What are the main products in the competitor's product line that threaten my market position?
4. What distinctive competence does the competitor bring to the industry? What counts for success in the industry? How do these factors compare to my own position?
5. What factors of the competitor's product provide an advantage? What roles do such factors as realiability, price, margins, technical quality, design, efficiency, maintainability, and service play?
6. How does the customer perceive the competitor's products? My products? Why do the customers buy a competitor's product?
7. What is the financial condition of the competitor? How do his financial ratios reflecting liquidity, profitability, and resource utilization compare with mine? What accounts for differentials in these ratios? How do differences in products, applications, geography, distribution channels, and customer groups affect these ratios?
8. With respect to the competitor's strategy: What went right? What went wrong? What can be learned from the competitor's successes and failures?
9. How do the competitor's facilities and equipment compare to mine in terms of efficiency, cost, capacity, age, tolerances, etc., resulting in productivity advantages or disadvantages?
10. How effective are the competitor's management systems? Does the competitor have an effective strategic planning system? How might the competitor's management philosophy be described?
11. What role does research and development play in the competitor's strategy? How does his research and development effectiveness compare with industry trends and with my research and development strategy? Does he innovate or imitate in his new product strategy?
12. What is the competency of the competitor's executive manpower? What image do his key managers have in the industry? Are any of his key managers dissatisfied? Why?
13. What image does the competitor have with his clientele? Are there any weaknesses with his clientele that can be turned to my advantage?
14. What are the five or six things that this competitor does best? How do these compare with my organization's competence?
15. Have I bought stock in my competitor's company so that I can be entitled to a shareholder's viewpoint? Have I utilized all ethical sources of information to learn about my competitors?

References

Barlay, S., *The Secrets Business,* Crowell, New York, 1973.

"Business Sharpens Its Spying Techniques," *Business Week,* August 4, 1975.

Greene, R. M. (editor), *Business Intelligence and Espionage,* Irwin, Homewood, Illinois, 1966.

"Guide to Gathering Market Intelligence," *Industrial Management,* Vol. 47, March 1962.

Hamilton, P., *Espionage and Subversion In an Industrial Society,* Hutchinson, London, 1967.

Houston, F. S., and Weiss, D. L., "Analysis of Competitive Market Behavior," *Journal of Marketing Research,* May 1974.

Robey, D., and Zeller, R. L., "Factors Affecting the Success and Failure of an Information System for Product Quality," *Interfaces,* Nov. 1977.

Schewe, C. D., and Wiek, J. L., "Innovative Strategies For Improving MIS Utilization," *Academy of Management Review,* Jan. 1977.

Springer, C. H., "Strategic Management in General Electric," *Operations Research,* Vol. 21, Nov.–Dec. 1973.

Thomas, P. S., "Gathering Competitive Information," *Chemical Engineering,* April 25, 1966.

Wall, J. L., "What the Competition Is Doing: Your Need to Know," *Harvard Business Review,* Nov.–Dec. 1974.

Wildt, A. R., "Multiterm Analysis of Competitive Decision Variables," *Journal of Marketing Research,* Feb. 1974.

Winterbotham, F. W., *Ultra Secret,* Harper and Row, New York, 1975.

Zacharias, E. M., Captain, USN, *Secret Missions, The Story of An Intelligence Officer,* Putnam, New York, 1946.

PART VI

The Planning–Organizational Subsystem

Chapter 12

THE ORGANIZATIONAL
STRATEGIC-PLANNING
CULTURE

Over a period of years, in the course of consulting experience with a variety of business organizations and public agencies in the development and implementation of long-range planning processes, the authors have drawn an empirically tested conclusion that *the success of long-range planning in an organization is less sensitive to the specifics of the planning techniques that are used than it is to the overall culture within which the planning is accomplished.*[1] Since most of the nonpontifical literature of planning focuses on planning techniques and specifications for planning processes, these conclusions suggest a critical void in planning methodology. This chapter focuses on the idea of an organizational culture and the importance of such a culture to the success of strategic planning.

The Organizational Culture

A usual concept of a *culture* deals with social and intellectual formation patterns within a group of people having some degree of common purpose, goals, language, customs, and traditions. The American Heritage dictionary[2] defines a culture as follows:

> The totality of socially transmitted behavior patterns, arts, beliefs, institutions, and all other products of human work and thought characteristic of a community or population.

In its broadest context, the idea of a culture, therefore, deals with the social and artistic expression manifest in a society or class.

---

[1] Portions of this chapter are adapted from Cleland, D. I., and King, W. R., "Developing a Planning Culture for More Effective Strategic Planning," *Long-Range Planning,* June 1974, and Cleland, D. I., and King, W. R., "Organizing for Long-Range Planning," *Business Horizons,* Aug. 1974.

[2] *American Heritage Dictionary of the English Language,* American Heritage and Houghton Mifflin Company, New York, 1969, p. 321.

In the organizational context, this idea can be applied by viewing a culture as *the integrated system of acquired behavioral patterns in the organization that are characteristic of the members of the organization and that influence the attitudes and the modus operandi of the organization.* Taken in this sense, culture is not a genetically predetermined condition. It is noninstinctive and is the result of social intercourse in the organization, transmitted and maintained primarily through a learning process.

Culture and society are not one. An organizational *society is made up of people:* superiors, subordinates, peers, associates. The *organizational culture is made up of the behavior of the people* within an organizational environment. Taken in this context then, a person may belong to a particular organizational society, but he may not belong to that culture.

An organization is therefore more than just people. It is a group of individuals united by organizational principles, policies, procedures, personal values, and authority and responsibility patterns. People within an organization have numerous contacts with their clientele; the majority of their activities are carried out in the organization in some group relationship. These relationships are not random, but are patterned and ordered according to learned norms of conduct and beliefs. Such relationships, ultimately expressed in some pattern of authority and responsibility, are distinctive, culturally defined, and limited.

Culture within an organization is acquired through behavior. Many of the basic behavioral patterns that make up a culture within an organization may be learned directly, as through the study of plans, policies, and procedures. This may be seen in the case of an executive who upon taking over a new position within the organization spends considerable time studying the policies and procedural documentation to determine the formal way of doing things. A study of such documentation exposes this executive to the formal authority and responsibility patterns within the organization.

Other values held within an organizational culture are not explicitly stated and are manifest only through the "informal organization" either because these values are taken for granted, or because people are so unused to reflecting about their beliefs that they are unable to state them. An executive, for example, may be so thoroughly imbued with a particular behavior pattern that he can only generalize about the principles that underlie such behavior. In such a cultural setting, an accepted way of behavior so permeates the organization that people who speak about the culture know only that a particular behavior is expected, and that another is not, without being able to express the underlying principle in so many words. This attitude is often demonstrated by an individual in an organizational setting who says, "Well, this is just the way we do things."

THE IMPORTANCE OF THE ORGANIZATIONAL CULTURE

The organizational culture importantly determines *what* the organization is able to effectively accomplish as well as *how* it will accomplish things. As Lee[3] observed in a more general context:

> The quality of a society will vary with the quality of its basic values . . . with their suitability to its needs and circumstances, and with the consistency and thoroughness with which they are worked out.

Specific illustrations of the significance of organizational culture are readily available. For instance, the cultural impact on executive attitudes toward decision-related questions can clearly affect the manner in which decisions are arrived at in the organization.

JAPANESE ORGANIZATIONAL CULTURE. In Japanese management, emphasis is initially placed on the *definition of the question,* the decision as to what is the real question or problem and whether it really needs to be addressed. In the western culture, emphasis is placed on solving of predefined problems that are already (implicitly) presumed to be worth solving.[4]

The Japanese process has been described further by Morgan:[5]

> During the process leading to the decision, the Japanese make no mention of what the answer might be. They do this to avoid forcing people to take sides. Once people take sides, a decision would be a victory for one side and a defeat for the other. So, the focus is on finding what the decision is really about, not what the decision should be. It results in a meeting of the minds that there is—or is not—a need to change behavior.
>
> The Japanese approach to a question takes time, which exasperates most Westerners. But when the question is defined and a consensus reached, action usually takes place with amazing speed—far more rapidly than in the West because everybody agrees on the action and no time is lost trying to "sell" any of the recalcitrant but powerful people who must be parties to the decision.

The Japanese technique of making decisions helps to facilitate a consideration of all the angles and alternatives, deferring the decision and commitment that the decision implies until all factors relative to the decision has been evaluated by those managers who will share in the responsibility for the execu-

---

[3] Lee, O., "Social Values and the Philosophy of Law," *Virginia Law Review,* Vol. 32, 1946, pp. 811–812; reprinted in Lee, O., *Freedom and Culture.*

[4] See Mitroff, I. I., and Featheringham, T. R., "On Systemic Problem Solving and the Error of the Third Kind," *Behavioral Science,* Vol. 19, Nov. 1974, and Ackoff, R. L., and Emery, F. E., *On Purposeful Systems,* Aldine-Atherton, Chicago, 1972.

[5] Morgan, J. S., *Managing Change,* McGraw-Hill, New York, 1972, pp. 94–95.

tion of the decision. Of course, an ancillary benefit is to strengthen the commitment of people to support the decision, once it has been made.

COMPLETED STAFF ACTION. The military concept of "Completed Staff Action"[6] means the evaluation of a problem and the presentation of a solution by a staff official in such a manner that all that remains on the part of the head of the organization (a line official or staff manager) is to indicate his approval or disapproval of the recommended action.[7] The lack of the ego involvement of the manager in such a decision process is obvious.

THE AMERICAN ORGANIZATIONAL CULTURE. In the context of recent happenings in American public and business administration, the impact of culture is clearly seen. For instance, according to Ways:[8]

> Management analysis of Watergate, then, must turn upon the question of why officials, whose ability ranged from average to very high, made so many mistakes. Much of the answer must lie in the ambience of the group, the cognitive and emotional patterns that permeated and shaped its organizational style. Such a collective atmosphere is not necessarily the exact sum of the attitudes, ideas, suppositions, desires, and values of the individuals who make up the group. Every organization has its own character, its own way of acting and reacting, and this quality powerfully colors what its members feel, think, say, and do within the organization.

The incredible series of events that surrounded the Watergate situation appear almost incomprehensible unless we try to understand the attitudes and emotional patterns of the principles employed at the White House and in the Committee to Re-elect the President. Again, to quote Ways[8]:

> . . . that ambience included a lot of fear, suspicion, and hostility . . . distress was in their minds . . . themselves as inhabitants of a beleaguered and distressed city, surrounded by enemies whose strength and malice they exaggerated. An intense will to win, coupled with the belief that the situation is desperate, can release a lot of energizing adrenalin. If it goes too far, such a state of mind can also trigger reckless misjudgments.

A parallel to the Watergate situation is found in the business community in the heavy electrical price-fixing conspiracy of the early 1960s. The business community was shocked and the question that was asked was this: How could

---

[6] There have been many versions of this concept. The reader is invited to go back to the original article for an unadulterated version. See "Completed Staff Action," *Army-Navy Journal*, Jan. 24, 1942.

[7] This view is also applied more broadly to U.S. corporate decision making by Galbraith in his conclusions concerning the impact of "technocrats" on top management decision-making. See Galbraith, J. K., *The New Industrial State*, Houghton-Mifflin, New York, 1967.

[8] Ways, M., "Watergate as a Case Study in Management," *Fortune*, Nov. 1973, pp. 110, 196.

intelligent, experienced, knowledgeable business executives in large sophisticated companies do anything so illegal and stupid? Ways observed:

> . . . much of the answer lay in the ambience of the conspirators. They felt overpressured—by their bosses, by rising costs, by government regulations they considered unfair.[8]

Many other examples could be described that point out the influence that the ambience, the culture, has on motivating the behavior of the members of an organization. The persecutions of the Jewish people during Nazi Germany's Third Reich is a case in point; again the question was asked: How could such a thing happen in modern times?

In the business context, there is no less influence of the organizational culture on the way organizations are managed. An analysis of the W. T. Grant Bankruptcy by *Fortune* magazine[9] is a case in point:

> New York headquarters had ordered the stores to begin selling furniture and large appliances. To bolster those sales, the company had entered the hazardous credit card business full steam ahead. (Store managers) . . . were ordered to push the credit card campaign above everything else . . . On New York's insistence, only cursory credit checks were conducted. *When one manager insisted on making thorough inquiries, New York threatened to fire him* . . . By last year Grant's credit-card receivables totaled $500 million, and half of that was deemed uncollectible.

In the W. T. Grant example, the evidence suggests that an "adversary" role was not culturally accepted. An "adversary" role would permit the questioning of objectives, goals, strategies, to ask the tough questions that have to be asked during the strategic choice process in an organization. Such an adversary role can help to provide an effective "checks and balances" to guard against poor strategic choice decisions that are unrealistic, optimistic, or that lack an adequate data base.

Another example of the lack of an adversary role is found in reviewing some of the difficulties of Playboy Enterprises, Inc.:[10]

> Decisions at Playboy often aren't based on normal business considerations. Hefner or another top guy will get excited about something and they'll plunge ahead without even taking out a pencil. *If you don't go along, you're put down as a negativist who can't be trusted.*

In one business situation, the authors were retained to do an analysis of a business organization's failure, a failure that cost the parent company in excess of $400 million. During the course of the investigation, in-depth interviews were conducted with key current and former managers. A top official was ques-

[9] "W. T. Grant's Last Days—As Seen from Store 1192," *Fortune*, April 1976, p. 110. Italics added.

[10] *The Wall Street Journal*, April 31, 1976, p. 1. Italics added.

tioned concerning the opportunity in the company for an adversary role during the period of time during which the seeds of disaster were being sown, in terms of unreasonable and unrealistic objectives, goals, and strategies. This executive replied: "Yes—we had adversaries—we didn't listen to them—we buried them and walked over their graves on to financial disaster!"

APPLICATION OF THE CULTURAL CONCEPT TO STRATEGIC PLANNING

The significance of the organizational culture to effective strategic planning may be directly inferred from a more general assessment of the impact of the ambience on all organizational activity. For instance, in Japan the culture directly influences organizational planning at all levels, from the family to the nation. This welding together of organizational and societal goals is the result of a practicing philosophy of planning. Even in small businesses, planning is carried out through weeks and even months of study and discussions at all management levels. According to Kano:[11]

> The process of plan formulation actually creates, through active participation, a concrete and detailed image of what is to be expected.

Kano's use of the idea of an "image of what is to be expected" emphasizes the future orientation of strategy planning. This concept of an "image of the future" is central to the thinking of the futurist Fred Polak.[12] Our reference to the term here is in terms of attempting to explain why some organizations appear to do a better job of strategic planning than do others. Our thesis can be summarized in several key words: "systems," "culture," and "future-orientation"; i.e., organizations with planning *systems* that reflect a *future-oriented* planning *culture* can do successful planning; those that do not are unlikely to be successful at planning.

The planning culture of an organization is a behavior pattern in which strategic planning is a way of life. Within such planning-oriented organizations, the total process of strategic planning is three dimensional: the *past periods* reflected in the tradition and mores of today; another world that deals in *current operational problems and opportunities;* and finally, *the world of tomorrow,* the design of goals, objectives, strategies, and future images that carry the organization to some future position.

In reality, these three dimensions flow together, suggesting that a culture for strategic planning is much more than its component parts. Such a culture includes, *and is motivated by,* the subsystems described in earlier chapters,

[11] Kano, H., "Managing for the Future in Japanese Industry," *The Future of the Corporation* (Herman Kahn, editor), Mason and Lipscomb Publishers, New York, 1974, p. 87.
[12] Polak, F., *The Image of the Future,* Elsevier, New York, 1973, see particularly p. 22.

e.g., a planning process, a decision subsystem, an information subsystem, a planning management subsystem, etc.

But, the strategic planning system is not sufficient to generate a planning culture. Such intangibles as the way in which behavior with regard to the future is accepted within the organization is as important as the intangible aspects of the culture such as the importance placed on planning by the organization's reward system.

Intangibles such as these may be difficult to accept by the traditional organization since "futuristic behavior" may be different from that which has traditionally been the norm in industrial and governmental organizations. As Polak says: [12]

> Thinking about the future requires faith and visionary powers mixed with philosophic detachment, a less emotional life, and creative fantasy.

Although "creative fantasy" has not been highly valued in traditional organizations, it is nonetheless being tolerated, even encouraged, in many organizations. According to James B. Webber, who directed a study of the role of futurists in business firms, as many as 20% of "Fortune 500" firms have people who "play the genie" in a practical sense, keeping firms abreast, so they don't get caught short. The role of one such genie perhaps describes the proliferating role of futurism. [13]

> Joseph L. Shapiro spends a good deal of his time in his sunny office in the planning department of Gillette Co. here contemplating what the changing role of women might bring about for the family in the decades ahead.
>
> He isn't exactly sure what that has to do with selling Gillette's razor blades and toiletries, if anything. No matter. As the company's resident crystal-ball gazer, he isn't paid to come up with the answer but rather to raise the questions.

The significance of such futuristic thinking can clearly only be great if the organization is imbued with an understanding of its importance, i.e., if a planning culture has been created. A guide to the creation of such a culture is given by Haggerty: [14]

> . . . we initiated the formal system to identify and state succinctly, yet completely, in writing, the strategies we would follow throughout our company for its growth and development. We also identified the tactics we would pursue in order to implement the strategies . . . there is little doubt that we have succeeded in diffusing throughout our management, both corporate and divisional, recognition of responsi-

[13] As quoted in Gallese, L. R., "The Soothsayers: More Companies Use 'Soothsayers' to Discern What Is Lying Ahead," *Wall Street Journal,* March 31, 1975, p. 1.

[14] Haggerty, P. E., "Strategies, Tactics, and Research," *Research Management,* Vol. IX, 1966, p. 154.

bility for initiating innovative programs, and an improved ability to conceive, describe and pursue such programs.

The key managers of an organization must also do everything possible to foster a legitimatized cultural ambience in which spontaneous adversary roles emerge whenever questionable goals, objectives, strategies, and such strategic choice opportunities (or problems) appear. Properly played adversary roles can be beneficial in a wide variety of situations such as:

1. Testing the credibility of planning assumptions.
2. Evaluating adequacy of data bases on which strategic choices are made.
3. Guarding against too active an influence of the key manager's values and prejudices on strategic choice.
4. Evaluating adequacy of the planning review process.
5. Relevance and realism of objectives, goals, strategies.
6. Serving as a watchdog for decisions whose strategic impact has not been sufficiently analyzed.
7. Testing the organizational culture for strategic planning effectiveness.

The Need for a Strategic Planning Culture

The development of a planning culture is not a straightforward task, since it requires that planning by made endemic to the value system of managers. In our experience, fully five to eight years may be required under optimum conditions. Yet, to ignore planning is to make oneself the victim of the planning of others, and to go through the motions of planning without inducing a planning culture is to simply make the same error in a more resource-consuming way.

There are a number of symptoms that can be found in modern organizations that serve to inhibit effective planning. The symptoms must be "treated" through the establishment of a planning culture if planning is to achieve its full potential. In the ensuing sections of this chapter, we discuss these symptoms as they are found in various organizations together with proven organizational approaches for alleviating them. Taken collectively, these organizational responses constitute the basis for an organizational planning culture.

DISCIPLINARY AND ORGANIZATIONAL PAROCHIALISM

An understandable tendency on the part of educated human beings to view the world from the standpoint of their particular experiential and educational background is one of the facts of organizational life that must be overcome if planning is to be effectively performed and implemented. Two varieties of such parochialism that abound in organizations as diverse as engineering-dominated technical firms and public school systems need be considered: disciplinary parochialism and organizational parochialism.

DISCIPLINARY PAROCHIALISM. The manager who is a victim of disciplinary parochialism thinks (even unknowingly) in a narrow, specialized function in which he was educated and in which he won his first kudos, despite the fact that he has left that function. Having won his credentials and a degree of success in a speciality such as engineering, he never totally recognizes the narrowness of his education and views that discipline as the most important one in the organization.[15] Such an individual is inclined to spend excess time supervising the engineering aspects of a strategy, since it is familiar and comfortable and to minimize his personal involvement in areas such as marketing, even though they may be of critical importance to success.

A good illustration of this sort of phenomenon is the aerospace firm whose top executive ranks were dominated by engineers. The firm considered itself to be the quality-leader in its field; yet, its record of obtaining contracts was poor. As the aerospace crunch of the early 1970s occurred, a formal study was conducted. The study revealed that the firm had seldom obtained a contract that was handled on a truly competitive basis. Moreover, when contrasted with its more successful competitors, it was apparent that its lack of success could be attributed to naive marketing. Such simple elements of modern aerospace marketing as frequent contact by high-level executives with customers, the allocation of salesmen (with a euphemistic title to embellish their image) to major customers, and the close control of these salesmen through briefings and debriefings were not recognized as deficiencies by the organization's executives. They had never recognized that they could not sit back and rely on the obvious quality of their products to sell themselves, because their concern was with the product and its technical performance rather than with the broader range of considerations that their job necessitated.

Of course, one way of avoiding this natural tendency toward parochialism is to surround the general manager with advisors chosen from various backgrounds. Since his success is reinforced by other specialists who have assisted him in moving up the ladder, the disciplinary parochialist often surrounds himself with those who are known and have been trusted within his field of speciality. Thus, even as he moves up the ladder into positions requiring a broader perspective, his view may not be broadened by his access to new advisors.

---

[15] This finding is substantiated by the information that managers specify as being most important to their decision making. See Ghymn, K. I., and King, W. R., "The Relative Importance of Marketing Information in Multi-National Management," *Proceedings of the American Marketing Association Educator's Conference*, August 1976.

ORGANIZATIONAL PAROCHIALISM. This variety of narrowness is similar to disciplinary parochialism; it describes the tendency of a manager to view his organization as the center of affairs and to focus attention on a coveted product line that has already been successful; another form of myopia. The pervasive tendency of some managers to spend product development funds in areas which are known and familiar, thus extending existing product lines, even in the face of overwhelming evidence of a changing market, is indicative of this sort of narrowness and reliance on the choice of comfortable alternatives.

The difficulties that can be created by organizational parochialism are made apparent by the fact that significant innovations have not necessarily been made in the organization, or even in the industry, in which they might logically be expected: [16]

> . . . it is almost axiomatic that major new technologies come from outside the industry they affect. There is the human and corporate dimension to the problem. The first jet engine, for instance, did not come out of the established aircraft industry, but out of the small, cluttered workshop of Sir Frank Whittle (the knighthood came later), who spent most of the 1930's trying in frustration to get government ministries and the British aircraft industry to develop it—a wall of opposition topped only by the war. Similarly, the first electronic computer came not from the business-machine industry, but from a wartime ballistics laboratory project; xerography came out of the home workshop of the late Chester F. Carlson, a sometime inventor and patent lawyer, not from the duplicating machine industry; the first synchronous communication satellite, Early Bird, came from Hughes Aircraft, not from anywhere in the communications industry.

People within an organization are often slow to accept new ideas, particularly when the ideas come from outsiders. Edison was not able to sell his patent to any of the electrical companies then in business. Alexander Graham Bell, failing to sell his telephone idea to the existing telegraph companies, had to found AT&T to promote his invention. Many other examples serve to remind us that good ideas that can affect the future of an organization can come from some remote person in the organization itself, from a competitor, or even from outside the "industry."

Indeed, there is evidence that many organizations tend to reject the results of their own research efforts. After making a study of a number of small electronic firms in the Boston, Massachusetts area that had been established in the 1950s and 1960s, Holloman concluded that many of them were started by frustrated engineers and scientists from large companies who failed to capitalize and make use of the ideas, forecasts, and research developed by their own employees. [17]

[16] Fortune, April 1972, p. 71.
[17] Morton, J. S., Managing Change, McGraw-Hill, New York, 1972.

The resolution of the problems of parochialism is not simple. The development of a planning culture is itself a partial answer, since a recognition and acceptance of the importance and pervasiveness of planning places pressures on the planning participants to produce plans that involve the consideration of wide ranges of alternatives. Thus, the desire for good planning in the planning culture sense is, in part, self-fulfilling.

Basic Tenets of a Strategic Planning Culture

Several organization-related tenets form the basis for the planning culture and the organization structure which is described in the next chapter. These tenets together with their consequent organizational structure and planning process, have been applied with success in a number of business and public organizations. Contemporary literature in behavioral science also supports these tenets.

MANAGERS ARE THE PLANNERS

The first tenet of the planning organizational approach to be presented is that *modern participative management is appropriate to the formalized strategic planning process of the organization* as well as to the planning aspects of the individual manager's job. Thus, the inference can be drawn from this basic assumption that *strategic planning is a job to be performed by managers, not for them.* However critical the role of the professional planning staff is to an effective strategic planning process, professional planners are not the doers of planning in this model; rather, they are the facilitators. In this respect Argenti cautions[18]:

> . . . The role of the corporate planner is to see that corporate planning is done, not to do the company's planning for it. He is there to see that a system is installed, that the obvious pitfalls (a forecast without an indication of its errors, for example) are avoided, that the full advantages of treating the company as a corporate whole and looking far enough ahead are reaped. He is not there to run the company nor to do its planning—only to see that it is done.

The distinction between the doers and facilitators of planning is borne out in the expression of the chief executive of Dow Corning[19]:

> Our corporate planning department develops the format and planning cycle that guides the activities of the businesses, functions, and areas.

[18] Argenti, J., *Corporate Planning,* A Practical Guide, Dow Jones-Irwin, Homewood, Ill., 1969, p. 227.
[19] Goggin, W. C., "How the Multidimensional Structure Works at Dow Corning," *Harvard Business Review,* Jan.–Feb. 1974.

The planning department does not do the planning. It simply develops, administers, and communicates the corporate ground rules. Each business, function, and area must do its own planning. The total effort is funneled into one- and five-year corporate plans that are reviewed and approved by the Corporate Business Board before they are presented to the board of directors for final approval.

THE PLANNING STAFF FACILITATES PLANNING

The organization of a corporate planning staff has to be done considering not only the future direction of the company, but the preservation of line official prerogatives within the company. An executive staff consisting of personnel who have been selected on the basis of their broad business backgrounds and their experience as successful line executives can strengthen the total corporate strategic planning process. Other personnel can be brought into the corporate strategic planning office because of their technical expertise and their experience in dealing with broad corporate problems.

The planning staff must play only a substantive facilitative role in providing forecasts, assumptions, alternative strategies, etc., to be considered by the manager-planners. If they try to play the planning cultural role of the chief executive, they may well be viewed as "technocrats with a cause." Then they, like the efficiency experts, operations researchers, and a host of others before them, will be relegated to the back room of the organization, and their cause will not play a significant role in determining the organization's destiny. The doers of strategic planning are managers, both top managers and lower-level line managers, thereby ensuring that the people who will be charged with implementing the plans are those who have generated the goals and developed and approved the plans. But, care must be taken to protect the prerogatives and viewpoints of both the *doers* and the *facilitators*. Although the line official should make the final selection of strategic alternatives available to him, the professional planners and other staff personnel that support the line managers should have full opportunity to present their viewpoints and recommendations to him *before the strategic decision is made.*

The dangers inherent in placing too much planning power in the hands of staff were illustrated in Gulf Oil. The Chief Executive, Jerry McAfee has noted that under a strong staff planning format intense competition quickly developed among the strategic operating units, with the heads of the units trying to make their results look good at each other's expense. One widespread result was inflated transfer payments among the Gulf units as each one vied to boost its own bottom line. This was remedied by going to a "managers are the planners" philosophy:[20]

---

[20] "Gulf Oil Goes Back to What It Knows Best," *Business Week,* Jan. 31, 1977, p. 78.

McAfee quickly turned the chairman's council into an advisory group, forcing responsibility back to the managers of the strategic units . . . the staff simply provides support services.

FULFILLING MANAGEMENT NEEDS

Another basic tenet of the planning organization approach is that there are unique needs inherent in the strategic planning processes and in the role of the line manager as an active participant in overall organizational planning. These needs cannot readily be met by the existing organization with its reliance on bureaucratic forms and procedures.

These needs range from substantive and objective to psychological and subjective. At the objective level, for instance, are informational needs. True organizational strategic planning requires that the planner-manager be provided with an understanding of information concerning the likely future environment in which the organization will operate. Such information for the overall organization is not normally supplied to the line manager. If it is, it is provided in a written summary that is an inadequate form for conveying real in-depth understanding and acceptance. Thus, in the traditional organization, even if the line manager is involved in overall organizational planning, he is not often supplied with adequate information to permit him to operate effectively and to have confidence in the credibility of strategic decisions.

The psychological constraints of the bureaucratic organization also serve to inhibit effective planning, thus creating a planning need for some "alternative organization." [21] For instance, the purview of a lower-level manager is necessarily restricted by his day-to-day activities as well as by his formal job description. When he becomes involved in higher level interorganizational decision-making, he is treading on the traditional ground of others who are higher in the organization. These "territorial imperatives" and their resulting impact on the people in the organization can be of great consequence to effective planning and to effective continued operation of the organization.

AUTHORITIES, ROLES, AND INFORMATION

Another tenet that forms the basis for the approach suggested here is that *organizational structure for strategic planning is largely prescribed by sets of two kinds:*

1. Definitions of the authorities, responsibilities, and roles of planning participants.

---

[21] We shall go further into the idea of an "alternative organization" in the next chapter.

2. Definitions of the information available to planning participants and the nature of the information flows among participants.

Thus, although the specification of the existing formal and informal organization is important to the determination of the kind of planning done, the nature of the process used, and the content of the plans formulated for any particular organization, it is assumed here that a planning organization, defined in terms of authorities, responsibilities, roles, and information, can be superimposed on the existing organization to effect better planning.

ACCOUNTABILITY AND PLANNING-RELATED INCENTIVES

In organizations that do not have a planning culture, the attitude that "long-range planning is not really important because we'll all be dead in the long run anyway" usually means that accountability for long-range results is poor. If the system of awards and punishments favors current performance at the expense of the long run, a powerful, antiplanning culture emerges to deter the executive from giving his attention to the long-range future of the organization.

If the manager has profit center responsibility, this short-run, tunnel vision is reinforced. This is illustrated by the division manager who, when asked to develop long-range strategy for his organization, came up with a strategy that essentially extended existing product lines. This manager had been successful and the prevailing incentive system provided for short-term profit performance. Indeed, there was little recognition, either in merit increases or promotion opportunity, for innovation in the development of long-range strategies. Thus, the success of a given product line reinforced a propensity to develop strategy along proven lines. The manager was doing just what could reasonably have been expected of him; yet the firm somehow naively believed that it could expect otherwise. Although planning should be participative and nonthreatening, once plans have been approved and accepted by the managers, they should be accountable for them. In this, as in perhaps no other way, can managers be forced to explicitly consider the short-term versus long-run trade-offs that are essential to good planning.

Of course, this principle has been accepted by many who have found it difficult to implement. The only effective way of doing so, within the context of an organizational environment in which personnel are constantly changing responsibilities, is to have the plans follow the individual, i.e., to trace the individual's planning performance back to previous jobs. The authors know of several firms who are trying to do this with varying degrees of success. If such a system can be developed, a reward structure that is, in part, based on planning performance can be implemented. When the organization does this, it reaps benefits that can go far beyond the reward-punishment syndrome, since the knowledge that "good planning pays" is itself a powerful element of a planning culture.

Another basic tenet of the planning culture is the need for a structured and carefully thought-out plan for the implementation of planning in the organization.

One of the most common reasons for the failure of planning to catch on in an organization is the commonly voiced assertion that the process is often more important than the product. Although it is true that the planning process can pay benefits for the organization in terms of the broader horizons, greater creativity, and better understanding of objectives on the part of planning participants, it is also true that a radically new planning process can disrupt an organization, threaten managers, and lead to ineffective planning.

The process of introducing a planning procedure into an organization is a subtle one of taking advantage of a preliminarily established planning culture and, in turn, of reinforcing that culture. Planning cannot be introduced into an organization not yet ready to accept it; and, conversely, successful planning reinforces itself.

Thus, the effective implementation of planning in an organization that has not previously done formalized planning requires that an *implementation strategy* be developed. An implementation strategy is a step-by-step procedure for taking advantage of the existing characteristics of the planning culture in such a way as to enhance the likelihood of planning being accepted and meaningfully used.

The basic nature of such a strategy is its sequential nature. An "all at once" introduction of a comprehensive planning process is almost inevitably doomed. A sequential process that has been successfully implemented by a technical products firm begins with a series of internal workshops that deal with the theory and state-of-the-art of long-range planning. These workshops focus on both the positive and negative aspects of planning in going into the advantages that can be gained as well as the practical failures with planning both within the firm itself and by other firms with which the consultant-seminar leaders are familiar.

The output of these seminars is a better appreciation of planning as well as some specific ideas as to the most fertile areas within the company for the initial implementation of planning. When the best area is selected, a planning activity can begin.

In one organization, the budgeting area was selected for major initial effort since it was well understood and because the seminars had revealed that the current system would be detrimental to innovative planning. In another organization, the new product area was selected for initial formalized planning because of its potential payoff.

In this way, the value of planning, so much talked about in the literature and by those executives who wish to make greater use of it in their organizations, can be demonstrated in concrete terms. As with the introduction of any major change in an organization, nothing succeeds like success, so that those who would oppose the *concept* of formalized planning, or ineffectively perform themselves in such a process are placed in the position of objecting to a proven approach. Usually, this approach attracts those who wish to join the coming thing, thus ensuring the success of planning.

Summary

Whatever may be the importance of a planning system to an organization, the culture within which that system operates is even more important. A planning culture can lead to effective strategic decisions even if the planning system in use is a rudimentary one. Conversely, an antiplanning culture can serve to make useless the most sophisticated planning system.

The idea of a planning culture is simple; it is an organizational ambiance that values and motivates good planning and the individual behavior associated with good planning. In such a culture, managers are rewarded for their planning performance and those who raise searching questions about the values of organizational objectives and strategies are answered and given encouragement rather than penalized.

A planning culture operationalizes the idea of a plan as a "future image," because it encourages speculation and creative thinking rather than discouraging it. That such a culture is needed is made apparent by those common organizational characteristics that serve to stifle creativity such as disciplinary and organizational parochialism.

The basic tenets of a planning culture are that managers are the planners, that the planning staff are facilitators, and that specific needs of managers must be addressed through planning. Authorities, roles, and information must be defined and prescribed with respect to planning as with the operational aspect of the organization. If these tenets are met, and if an accountability and reward structure is made a part of the system, the likelihood of effective planning can be enhanced.

Chapter 12—Questions and Exercises

1. How might a culture be defined? What are the elements of a society's culture?
2. Could the circumstances surrounding the resignation of Richard Nixon from the Presidency of the United States be described in terms of a cultural ambience? How would you describe this cultural ambience?
3. What role do the people of an organization play in determining the culture of that organization? Do the behavior, value systems, modus operandi, etc., of the chief executive of the organization do anything to condition the culture of the organization? Why, or why not?
4. Organization policies and procedures do not typically influence the culture of an organization. Defend or refute this statement.
5. Using the *Business Week* article: "The Opposites: GE Grows While Westinghouse Shrinks," January 31, 1977, portray a profile of the culture for strategic planning in these two corporations.
6. What is the relationship of the informal organization to the culture of that organization? Demonstrate by example that you understand this relationship.
7. Is there any relationship between the Japanese decision process and the Japanese culture? Why, or why not?
8. What cultural conditions are necessary in an organization to facilitate the effective operation of an adversary role? Would such an adversary role serve any purpose in the strategic-planning process in an organization?
9. Some organizations seem to do a better job of strategic planning than their competitors. What influence might the culture of an organization have on the motivation of the strategic-planning process?
10. What influence does a formal strategic-planning system have on the development of strategic thinking in an organization? Can you find some examples from the current business periodical literature (e.g., *Business Week, Fortune, The Wall Street Journal, Forbes*) illustrating this point?
11. The development of a strategic-planning culture takes a long time to develop, perhaps years. Why is this so?
12. What are some of the factors in an organization that tend to discourage the development of a cultural ambience for strategic planning?
13. What are several of the basic tenets that form the basis for the development of a strategic-planning culture in the organization?
14. What might a policy of participative management in an organization do toward developing a strategic-planning culture?
15. How might the actions of a staff planning adversely affect the development of a strategic-planning culture? How would you define the role that a staff planning office ought to have in the strategic-planning process?
16. Who would have accountability for strategic planning in the organization?
17. How does an implementation strategy for strategic planning in an organization help (or hinder) the development of a culture that encourages strategic planning?
18. Rewarding executives for the short-term financial performance of their organization may discourage the development of an effective strategic-planning system for their organization. Defend or refute this statement.

19. What is the relationship between a strategic-planning system and the culture for strategic planning in an organization?
20. The planning culture of an organization is a behavior pattern in which strategic planning is a way of life. What does this mean? Can you give a practical illustration of what this would mean in terms of the daily life of a manager?
21. What is disciplinary parochialism? What is organizational parochialism? What do they have to do with the way in which an organization may do its strategic planning?
22. Describe the role of the corporate staff planner in a strategic-planning culture.
23. What is meant by an "image of the future"? What role can such an image play in planning?

Chapter 12—Strategic Questions for the Manager

1. Can the strategic-planning culture of your organization be described?
2. Do the behavioral patterns of key managers in the organization tend to motivate or stifle planning? Why?
3. When was the last time you, as a key manager, discussed the implications of the organizational culture on the effectiveness with which strategic planning is carried out? Do you feel adequately prepared to have such a discussion?
4. Would a consensus type of decision process such as that employed in the Japanese culture be of any benefit to your organization? Why, or why not?
5. Do the decision techniques, policies, practices, etc., that are used in your organization help to strengthen the commitment of people to the decision?
6. What effect has the organizational culture had on past key decisions in the organization? Have these influences been favorable or unfavorable? Why?
7. Does an *adversary role* exist in the organization? How effective is this role?
8. How many "negativists" have been buried in your organization?
9. Is the organizational culture future-oriented as well as operationally oriented?
10. How much disciplinary or organizational parochialism is there in the organization? If such parochialism exists, how have strategic choices been influenced by it?
11. Have the organizational staff planners assumed any line manager prerogatives? In what respect?
12. Have the authorities and responsibilities of the planning participants been defined? Have the data bases to be used by planners and the flow of these data bases to the planning participants been established?
13. What can be done to the organizational reward system to help to motivate strategic planning?
14. What might the key managers do to develop and foster an adversary role in the organization?

References

Anthony, R. N., "The Trouble With Profit Maximization," *Harvard Business Review,* Vol. 38, Nov.–Dec. 1960, pp. 126–134.

Baker, C. R., "Behavioral Aspects of Corporate Planning," *Long Range Planning,* Aug. 1976.

Bennis, W. G. and Thomas, J. M., *The Management of Comparative Change and Conflict, Selected Readings,* Penguin, Baltimore, 1972.

Chambers, J. D., et. al., "Catalytic Agent For Effective Planning," *Harvard Business Review,* Jan.–Feb. 1971.

Cleland, D. I., and King, W. R., "Developing A Planning Culture For More Effective Strategic Planning," *Long Range Planning,* June 1974.

Currill, D. L., "Introducing Corporate Planning: A Case History," *Long Range Planning,* Vol. 10, No. 4, Aug. 1977.

Cyett, R., and March, R. G., *A Behavioral Theory of the Firm,* Prentice-Hall, Englewood Cliffs, N.J., p. 19.

Friedman, Y. and Segev, E., "Horizons for Strategic Planning," *Long Range Planning,* Vol. 9, No. 5, Oct. 1976.

Gluck, F. W., Foster, R. N. and Forbis, J. L., "Cure for Strategic Malnutrition," *Harvard Business Review,* Nov.–Dec. 1976.

Hammerton, J. C., "Management and Motivation," *California Management Review,* Vol. XIII, Winter 1970.

Irwin, P. H., and Langham, F. W., Jr., "The Change Seekers," *Harvard Business Review,* Jan.–Feb. 1966.

Kahalas, H., "Long Range Planning: An Open Systems View," *Long Range Planning,* Vol. 10, No. 5, Oct. 1977.

Kraar, L., "The Japanese Are Coming With Their Own Style of Management," *Fortune,* March 1975.

Kreitner, R., "People Are Systems, Too: Filling the Feedback Vacuum," *Business Horizons,* Dec. 1977.

Krober, A. L., and Kluckhohn, C. *Culture: A Critical Review of Concepts and Definitions,* Peabody Museum of American Archaeology and Ethnology, Harvard University, Vol. 47, 1952.

Lee, O., "Social Values and the Philosophy of Law," *Virginia Law Review,* Vol. 32, 1946.

Mansfield, E., *Industrial Research and Technological Innovation,* Norton, New York, 1968.

McGregor, D., *The Human Side of Enterprise,* McGraw-Hill Book Company, New York, 1960.

Mintzberg, H., "Planning On the Left Side and Managing On the Right," *Harvard Business Review,* July–Aug. 1976.

Morgan, J. S., *Managing Change,* McGraw-Hill, New York, 1972.

Morton, J. A., *Organizing For Innovation,* McGraw-Hill, New York, 1971.

Nurmi, R., "Developing a Climate for Planning," *Long Range Planning,* Vol. 9, No. 2, Apr. 1976.

"Patterns and Problems of Technological Innovation In American History," Report C-65344, Arthur D. Little, Cambridge, Massachusetts, 1963.

Ross, J. E., and Kami, M. J., *Corporate Management in Crisis: Why the Mighty Fall,* Prentice-Hall, Englewood Cliffs, N.J., 1973.

Schoen, D. R., "Managing Technological Innovation," *Harvard Business Review,* May–June 1969.

Sells, S. B., "Ecology and the Science of Psychology," *Multivariable Behavior Research,* April 1966.

Smith, R. A., *Corporations in Crisis,* Doubleday, Garden City, N.Y., 1963.

Ways, M., "Watergate As a Case Study in Management," *Fortune,* Nov. 1973.

Chapter 13

THE PLANNING
ORGANIZATION

The concept of a "planning organization" may be thought of by some in simple terms. To create such an organization, one simply hires professional planners, locates them in a staff position to the general manager, prints a new organization chart, and directs them to "plan strategically."

Of course, effective strategic planning is much more difficult to achieve than that, and the planning organization is much more important to good strategic planning than might be implied by the treatment of the planning organization as almost an afterthought at the end of many planning texts.

As indicated in the previous chapter, the planning organization is an integral part of the overall planning culture. Although many business firms attempt to operate as though planning were simply one of the many aspects of each manager's job, or as though only the top executives had responsibility for strategic planning, we have argued that this view is not likely to produce *effective* strategic planning.

Organizations

The idea of an organization is understood at some level by virtually everyone. However, few of us have stopped to think what it really means. It is a deceptively simple term. In common management usage, the term has come to mean an entity, a complex of people, cooperating in some common purpose. Inherent in meaning is the set of understandings established through the overall culture: policies, procedures, past behavior, goals, and objectives. Models of organization are usually thought of in terms of traditional organizational charts; more recently, the linear responsibility chart has been found useful in modeling authority and responsibility patterns within an organization's environment.[1]

In operational terms and within a strategic-planning context, it is useful to

[1] See Cleland, D. I., and King, W. R., *Systems Analysis and Project Management,* McGraw-Hill, New York, 1975, Chapter 12.

consider an organization as a dynamic goal-seeking system having the following:

1. An explicit or implicit objective toward which the participants are working.
2. A formal and/or an informal pattern of authority and responsibility among the participants.
3. A given quality and quantity of resources, both human and nonhuman.
4. A constant interaction between subsystems, as decisions are made, as strategies are designed for the implementation of decisions, and as decisions are themselves implemented.

With this simple operational definition of an organization as a basis, let us consider a modern form of organization that is useful to facilitate strategic planning.

The Multidimensional Organization

The variety of a planning organization that best implements the basic tenets discussed in Chapter 12 is one manifestation of the broader concept of the *multidimensional organization.* [2]

The multidimensional organization may be depicted as a *series of organization charts,* as shown in Figure 13.1. The leftmost chart depicts the legal *operating* organization as depicted on most organizational charts. It shows a chief executive who has authorities and responsibilities as defined by the organizational charter and by-laws, other line managers who report to him in the hierarchy, etc. As with all such organizations, the primary focus of this operating organization is the *control of existing operations.*

The middle chart in Figure 13.1 depicts the "strategic planning organization." *This organization is not made up of different people from those on the first chart; rather it represents the same people operating in new roles as dictated by the needs of the planning process.* It's focus is not on control of existing operations, but rather on the design and development of future organizational activities, its strategic plan or image of the future.

The planning organization is a continuous, parallel, ongoing organization that complements the basic operating organization. It operates with a different pattern of authorities and responsibilities than exist in the operating organization. This is so because it has different objectives than does the operating orga-

---

[2] Zand has referred to "collateral organizations" in a similar context. See Zand, D. C., "Collateral Organization: A New Change Strategy," *Journal of Applied Behavioral Science,* Vol. 10, 1974.

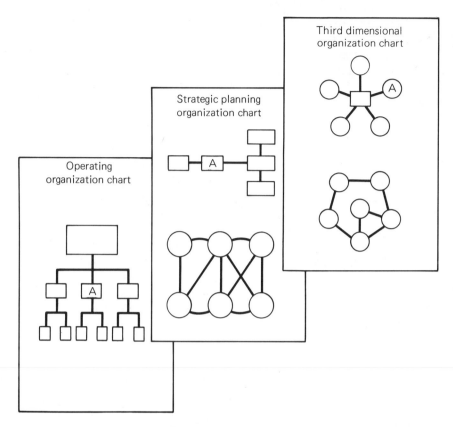

FIGURE 13.1   The Multidimensional Organization.

nization and because different people may have the knowledge and expertise necessary for leadership in such an environment.

The overall organization may also have other dimensions, as indicated by the rightmost chart in Figure 13.1. These other (undefined) organizations may be permanent and ongoing, as is the strategic-planning organization, or they may be temporary, e.g., a project team developed to solve a particular problem or to achieve a special goal and then disbanded.

A specific manager may play roles in various of these organizational elements. In the operating organization, he may have line responsibility for a department or function. In the strategic-planning organization, he may be a member of a board that reviews strategic proposals; in another organization he may be one member of a project team that is striving to develop and implement a major new management information system in the organization. The letter

"A" in Figure 13.1 depicts a manager playing such roles in each of the three organizational dimensions.

In each of these roles, he has varying relationships with other people. His boss in the operating organization may operate as his peer as a member of the planning review board; an individual from another department who ranks below him in the operating organization may be the project team manager in the third dimension of the organizational chart. In effect, the individual steps from chart to chart and plays different roles in performing one each chart.

Of course, to carry this to the extreme with many different dimensions to the organization would produce chaos. But it is certainly feasible to have a single ongoing planning organization superimposed on the operating organization in tandem with a temporary third dimension, to account for special activities that can be efficiently accomplished only outside of the operating organization.[3]

Moreover, although the explicit idea of the multidimensional organization is itself not well accepted, it is widely practiced. The idea of a matrix organization for example, involves the acceptance of a two-dimensional organizational concept. So too does the often-used idea of an individual who simultaneously wears many hats suggest the common acceptance of multidimensional organizational ideas, if not the formal concept itself.

The Need For a Strategic Planning Organization

The question of the need for a strategic planning direction in the multidimensinal organization, indeed, of the need for a multidimensional organizational concept at all, rests on some understanding of planning and modern organizations.

PEOPLE ARE PLANNERS

Strategic planning is inherently a people activity, a labor intensive aspect of the organization. Although many other activities (production and even management control with its emphasis on computers and reports) may be capital intensive, strategic planning is perhaps the most creative and ill-structured area of an organization's myriad activities.

One cannot expect people to operate cooperatively and creatively together, and to coordinate their acts and themselves into the strategic-planning system unless the norms and the climate of the organization encourage such behavior.

---

[3] See Cleland, D. I., and King, W. R., *Systems Analysis and Project Management,* McGraw-Hill, New York, 1975, for a discussion of this third dimension (the project dimension) or organizations.

Much has been written about how creative, specialized people should be organized and managed, not just in research and development but in any functional area of the business. No one really knows how to program such people to be creative, we do know if we try to direct such people in detail that creativity may be inhibited.

However, the organizational climate and the process that such people have to go through to plan can be provided. People can be motivated toward goals, objectives, and performance standards if they have the opportunity to contribute to such goals and objectives and understand them.

Unfortunately, it is difficult to provide this support for creativity within the confines of the existing operating organization. This is so because it necessarily and properly emphasizes *control and efficiency,* and creativity is not efficient in the usual sense.

THE NEED FOR CHANGE

The forces of change that beset modern organizations serve to remind us that doing strategic planning through a traditional organizational structure is inconsistent with the idea of change itself. Organizations do tend to perpetuate their existing structure and way of doing things; however, strategic planning is concerned with orderly change in organizations, change brought about through the *innovation* process in product, process, and market development. A simple, traditional organizational approach cannot provide the environment and motivation for creative people to innovate within a strategic-planning context. One must consider a variety of organizational designs and techniques for coping with the organizational complexity and interdependency.

THE DISTRIBUTION OF IDEAS IN AN ORGANIZATION

Coincident with the recognition of the inevitability of change has come the recognition that good ideas for the future are not the special prerogative of top managers or professional planners. The history of technological change is replete with examples of individuals with ideas who have caused profound change. James Watt is said to have developed the idea for he steam engine as the result of observing a boiling kettle in his boyhood days; Thomas Edison reportedly awaking from a nap with the idea for a filament that formed the basis for the electric light.

Ample evidence exists to demonstrate that if the planning process is to change organizations, a "stream of ideas" needs to be nurtured within the organization. In this regard, Schoen[4] has commented:

[4] Schoen, D. R., "Managing Technological Innovation," *Harvard Business Review,* May-June 1969, p. 160.

If there is any single point on which all who have written about the innovation process agree, it is the dependence of innovation on individuals committed to ideas.

THE NEED FOR "ORGANIZATION"

Despite the American mythology of the lonely genius and the importance of ideas in creating change, most important dsicoveries have not occurred in a vacuum. Morton[5] notes:

> Thus one vital aspect of technological change is context; it grows out of other discoveries, their communication, and economic developments which eventually come together to give birth to a needed change. They may come from a genius, *but not a lonely genius out of touch with the world around him.*

Thus, there would appear to be value in an organization to nurture the ideas of individuals. Clearly, since the implementing of most ideas in our complex society requires substantial resources, there is the need for organized activity to evaluate, test, and fulfill most ideas, however good they may inherently be.

Unfortunately, within complex organizations, particularly those that have not provided for an organizational process to encourage change, emerging ideas can be stifled by managers who desire (perhaps subconsciously) to resist change, an attitude that can be strengthened if the impending change would tend to threaten the position of the manager in the organization. This is, in part so, because the operating organization is most often structured in anticipation of serving an existing market. A total orientation to that market, which can be very effective for maximizing short-run performance, can tend to inhibit the process of change. In such a situation:[6]

> The policy, or system of values, of the organization may remain unexamined for long periods of time. If traditions and assumptions remain unquestioned, the policy of the company may come to be more of a liability than an asset. The reactions of the organization, like those of a person, will tend to become instinctive and habitual with a reduced ability to adjust to change.

Clearly, innovative ideas are the lifeblood of the organization's future and should constitute the basic building blocks of the planning system. If those ideas are truly new, they may easily be lost in the bureaucratic milieu. If, for instance, new products and markets that are not simply extensions of existing products and markets are to be developed, effective ways of generating ideas, evaluating those ideas, and developing them to fruition must be found.

[5] Morton, J. S., *Managing Change,* McGraw-Hill, New York, 1972, p. 53. Italics represent authors' emphasis.

[6] Suojanen, W. W., *The Dynamics of Management,* Holt, Rinehart, and Winston, New York, 1966, p. 134.

To give individuals with ideas a chance to have their ideas heard and evaluated, it is necessary to break out of the highly-structured operating organization. The complementary planning organization is the vehicle for doing this. However, if one merely creates a paper planning organization, it will not really operate differently from the operating organization. We shall therefore go into the structure and operating procedures of a planning organization that can make it a viable and independent entity.

Strategic-Planning Organizational Structures

The structure and operating procedures of planning organizations are not well developed, since many organizations have long treated planning as just one of the many jobs of each manager. However, great progress has been made in recent years toward developing new structures and procedures for implementing complementary planning organizations. These strategic-planning organizational structures generally reflect an underlying recognition that *the organizational structure that is best for operations may not as well be best for planning.*

THE STRATEGIC BUSINESS UNIT STRUCTURE

The question of the appropriate structure for performing strategic planning has been wrestled with by business firms for many years. A good description of the problem as well as the concept of a strategic business unit (SBU) is given by Springer: [7]

> In 1968, the General Electric Company was organized along decentralized lines with the usual corporate offices. Profit and loss responsibility was decentralized to department level; there were approximately 170 departments in existence. These departments were arrayed into some 50 divisions, and the divisions in turn were integrated into 10 groups in the typical hierarchical fashion. A subsequent reorganization of the company centered around the strategic planning done in the corporation. The existing department structure was retained for operational and control purposes; approximately 43 *Strategic Business Units* (SBU) were created for the primary purpose of planning for the company's future. A strategic business unit (SBU) was described as ". . . a business or collection of related businesses that has its own distinctive mission, competitors, markets, and so on, so that total business accountability, short and long range, can realistically be focused on one manager. This manager is responsible for the strategy of his SBU but his plan is fine-

---

[7] Springer, C. H., "Strategic Management in General Electric," *Operations Research,* Vol. 21, Nov.–Dec. 1973, p. 1177.

tuned, for resource allocation purposes, to the balanced interests of the company, as a whole.''

In more specific terms, the criteria for an SBU are described by Forsyth[8] as follows:

The component must have a unique mission independent of the business mission of any other component; It must have a clearly identified set of competitors;

It must be a full-fledged competitor in the external market;

It must be able to accomplish integrated strategic planning—in products, markets, facilities, and organization—relatively independent of other SBUs;

The component manager must be able to 'call the shots' within approved plans in areas of technology, manufacturing, marketing, and asset management which are crucial to the success of that business.

Thus, SBUs are those areas of the company that can be planned for as much as possible as if they were independent businesses. A strategic business unit can be a business department, a business division, or a business group; that is, it can be positioned at any point in the hierarchical structure. Examples of strategic business units within the General Electric Company are: (a) home entertainment, such as TV and audio; (b) transportation, such as locomotives, transit cars, diesel engines, and off-highway vehicles; and (c) aerospace.

Thus, in one sense the SBU organization is created for strategic-planning purposes, resulting in the superimposing of a different organizational structure on the existing organizational alignment. Although the hierarchical organizational structure of the company is maintained for management control purposes, a framework for innovation in the strategic sense is created, an organizational approach facilitating the bringing together under one line manager all of the factors relating to strategic purposes.

The apparent success of the SBU within the General Electric Company has been emulated by the Westinghouse Electric Corporation. Drawing on the General Electric SBU concept, the 110 Profit and Loss Divisions within Westinghouse have been integrated into 37 *Basic Business Units,* each headed by a general manager. The 120 divisions remain as profit centers, but strategic planning decisions on market growth and capital expansion are integrated in the Basic Business Unit level instead of at the division. The grouping of the divisions within Westinghouse by market area has been underway for several years; the final step in this integration has been to create the Basic Business Unit.[9]

[8] Forsyth, W. E., ''Strategic Planning in the '70s,'' *Financial Executive,* Oct. 1973, p. 98.

[9] For further information on this reorganization of Westinghouse along the Strategic Business Unit lines, see ''Westinghouse Opts for a GE Pattern,'' *Business Week,* February 3, 1975, pp. 18–19.

THE PROGRAMMATIC STRUCTURE

Another complementary structure within which strategic planning can be facilitated is the programmatic structure which has gained popularity as a result of the institution of Planning, Programming, and Budgeting Systems (PPBS) in many public organizations. The PPBS concept was introduced into the U.S. Federal Government in the late 1960s and has since been refined and adopted by many different levels of government (state, county, and city) and by various other public agencies. Despite the fact that PPBS has not been retained at its initial major level of importance in the strategic decision making of the federal government, it has had great impact there and is in use in many other governmental bodies.[10]

It is not our intention to go into detail concerning PPBS here, but rather to integrate the concept into our overall strategic planning model.[11]

The concept of a *program structure* has emerged into management theory as a way of helping organizations to design and carry out multiple strategies in a wide variety of different markets. Within business organizations, it is becoming increasingly common to find a program structure reflected in a program management unit with responsibility for developing planning and marketing strategies for a line of products, or for a unique group of the organization's customers. Indeed, the use of a program management unit may very well be considered to be a precursor of the strategic business unit. Corey and Star describe a program thusly[12]:

> ". . . is a total strategic plan for serving a particular market segment. It provides for product design, pricing channels of distribution, advertising, promotion, and field selling; for product supply and customer service. In the long run, it also includes the development of new products and services which the business is to supply to the market.

The program structure, of course, illustrates the point that an organizational structure should be reflective of the market opportunity. Corey and Star have determined in their research that organization design begins with the market and that successful businesses tend to be structured to carry out strategies in the markets they serve. As market opportunities change, strategies then change and organizational structure must change accordingly. Again, quoting Corey and Star:[12]

---

[10] For example, the city of Sunnyvale, California uses a "Resource Allocation Planning System" which has many of the elements of PPBS.

[11] The reader is encouraged to read Chapter 6 of Cleland, D. I. and King, W. R., *Systems Analysis and Project Management*, 1975, McGraw-Hill, New York, for a review of PPBS.

[12] Corey, E. and Star, S. H., *Organization Strategy–A Marketing Approach*,''' *Division of Research, Graduate School of Business Administration, Harvard University, Boston, 1971, p. 2.*

If a top corporate management is to pursue some set of long-term goals and is to allocate resources accordingly, it must, indeed, plan and appraise in terms of the individual businesses that make up the enterprise. It follows that the business structure should provide a suitable framework for planning and measuring.

Program structures thus appear to show promise for helping large corporations to deal with multiple strategies and widely ranging markets. Within these businesses, program management units organized along a group of customers are found. For example, Allegheny Ludlum Steel Corporation has product managers for stainless steel sheets, stainless steel castings, carbon steels, and silicon and electrical steels, among others. International Business Machines has program unit managers for such markets as airlines, utilities, distribution, and government.

THE MATRIX STRUCTURE

The program organizational concept is related to an organizational model for the identification, nurturing, and management of ideas in an organization that began in the U. S. aerospace industry where simple, formal theories of organization have been modified by *matrix forms*. In creating the matrix form, unified command and span-of-control concepts have been abandoned. Some of the success in the defense industry can be attributed in part to the early identification and management of ideas. To quote Merton J. Peck and Frederick M. Scherer[13]:

> The precipitating factor in the decision to begin serious development of a new weapons system is usually one or more technical or scientific ideas.

As these ideas emerge and show promise, a *project manager* (often called a team leader) can be put in charge of the idea; he becomes an entrepreneur, managing the idea across the organization by pulling together a team whose various members have the skills necessary to evaluate the emerging ideas and find answers to such questions as:

1. What is the nature of the future business opportunity: What function does it serve?
2. What and when is the need?
3. What is the marketability?
4. What is the competitive situation?
5. What is the organizational capability?
6. What investment is required'?

[13] Peck, M. J., and Scherer, F. M., "The Weapons Acquisition Process: An Economic Analysis, Boston, Division of Research, Graduate School of Business Administration, Harvard University, 1962, p. 326.

7. What is the influence of political, social, and economic considerations?
8. What specific strategy should be developed to satisfy a market need?

The results of the project team study is forwarded for final study by the body of executive-line officials responsible for selecting future alternative strategies. The composition and operation of these project teams, when coupled with the structural nature of the line organization, provide an adaptive and responsible approach for the development of strategy.

The use of horizontal project management techniques that cut across the vertical functionally oriented organization serves to create the ''matrix'' organization. Such an organization, as in Figure 13-2., shows a business firm in

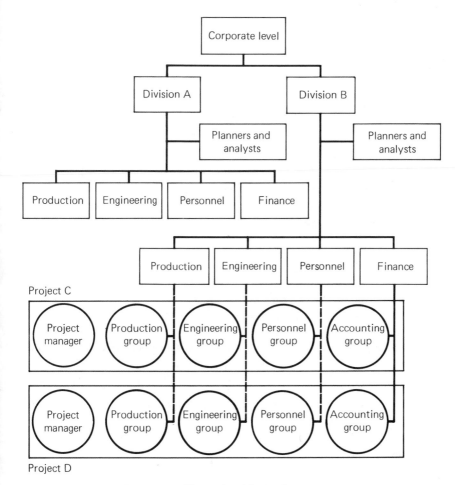

FIGURE 13.2 Illustrative Matrix Organization.

which Division A—an operating entity that produces a standardized product in high volume—is organized along traditional functional lines, whereas Division B has a matrix of vertical functions and horizontal projects, each of which draws on the services of the functional departments.[14]

The use of the matrix organizational structure is important both from the standpoint of its effectiveness and the message that it conveys to the rest of the organization: "Innovation is important in this organization—so important that an interdisciplinary-participative 'organization' has been created to manage innovation."

The varieties of matrix organizations that may be applied to achieving the organization's strategic objectives are virtually limitless. Although some who propose various approaches may proclaim that they are not matrix organizations at all, the two-dimensional organizational nature of most approaches suggests a striking commonality.

VENTURE TEAMS

Another adaptation of the two-dimensional organizational concept is directed toward the management of innovative ideas. As noted earlier, most organizations have determined that the operating organization serves to stifle new ideas and innovation in organizations.

The venture team approach is similar to that already discussed and is primarily included here for completeness. Figure 13.3 shows a company that has established a "New Ventures Division" that manages "projects" operated by "venture teams."[15] We shall further describe a possible operating procedure for such teams in a later section of this chapter.

A Comprehensive Strategic Planning Organization[16]

At Texas Instruments, two management modes with the company have been created: a *strategic* mode, and an *operating* mode. These modes can be viewed as an overlay or "matrix" organization, although the matrix organization is not used in its more familiar form. In the traditional matrix form, the matrix represents functions (or technologies) and projects; individuals in such organizations have dual reporting lines. At Texas Instruments, the matrix also creates dual

---

[14] For instance, see Sherwin, D. S., "Management *of* Objectives," *Harvard Business Review*, May–June, 1975, pp. 149–160.

[15] Adapted from Hill, R. M., and Hlavacek, J. D., "The Venture Team: A New Concept in Marketing Organization," *Journal of Marketing*, Vol. 36, July 1972, pp. 44–50.

[16] This section is based in large measure on Helms, E. W., "The OST System for Managing Innovation at Texas Instruments," presented, to the Armed Forces Management Association, April 7, 1971.

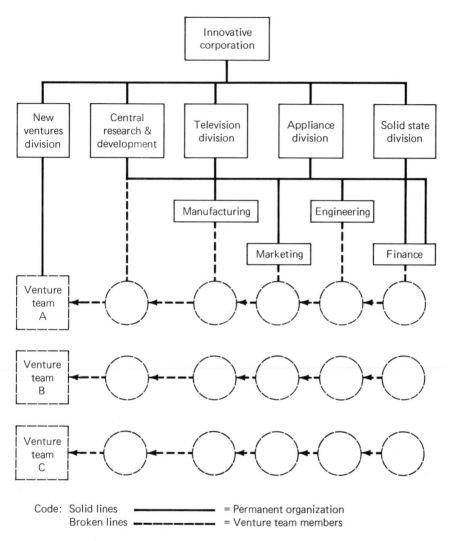

FIGURE 13.3 Innovative Matrix Organizational Structure.*

*Adapted from Hill, R. M. and J. D. Hlavacek, "The Venture Team: A New Concept in Marketing Organization," *Journal of Marketing*, Vol. 36, July 1972, pp. 44–50.

reporting relationships, but the distinction is between short range and long range, which provides for an explicit separation and visibility of what is going on for the present and what is being planned for the future. Figure 13.4 illustrates how this dual mode operates. The Corporate Objective establishes policies and specifies goals sought by the company. Goals are sought through various business objectives that operate within a business charter, and to understand opportunities and the selection of goals. Strategy concentrates on something new to reach the goals. Milestones and responsibilities come to play in the development of the strategy; it is here that the strategy manager considers alternative courses of action. Milestones help to measure progress and to help clear assignment of responsibility. A Tactical Action Program is a plan for going between two milestones in the strategy; it is an action plan with checkpoints every few weeks working toward a milestone that may be many months ahead. A Tactical Action Plan is a resource-allocation device and contains three elements: action plans with checkpoints, allocation of resources, and assignment of responsibilities.

Each objective, strategy, and tactic has a manager assigned so that accountability for progress at any level is clear. Such managers may be full-time in some cases, but normally they have operating responsibilities. They wear

FIGURE 13.4   Objectives-Strategy-Tactics Structure.*

*Helms, Eugene W., "The OST System for Managing Innovation at Texas Instruments," an Address to the Armed Forces Management Association, Washington, D.C., April 7, 1971.

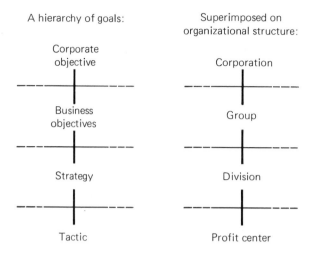

FIGURE 13.5   Hierarchy of Goals and Organizational Structure.*

*Helms, Eugene W., "The OST System for Managing Innovation at Texas Instruments," an Address to the Armed Forces Management Association, Washington, D.C., April 7, 1971.

two hats: An objective manager also may be a division manager; or a strategy manager also may be a profit center manager. What Texas Instruments has done is to take a hierarchy of goals and superimpose it on the traditional organization structure in which the corporation is divided into groups, divisions, and profit centers. Figure 13.5 portrays this model. Another way of portraying this is reflected in Figure 13.6 where an operating mode consisting of four groups (materials, components, equipment, and services) is complemented by eight business objectives: metallurgical materials, chemical materials, electronic functions, electrical controls, supply, government electronics, industrial electronics, and services. As the figure indicates, the objectives extend across group boundaries and are not restricted to traditional boundaries. *The business objective is TI's way of thinking about the future* business.[16]

The essence of the Texas Instrument approach is contained in Haggerty's comment: [17]

> Indeed, it is not too much of an over-simplification to state that our long-range planning system is fundamentally a system for managing innovation.

[17] Haggerty, P. E., "Strategies, Tactics, and Research," *Research Management,* Vol. IX, 1966, p. 146.

Operating modes

Corporate objectives	Materials group	Components group	Equipment group	Services group
Metallurgical materials				
Chemical materials				
Electronic functions				
Electrical controls				
Supply				
Government electronics				
Industrial electronics				
Services				

FIGURE 13.6 Matrix of Objectives and Operating Modes.*

*Helms, Eugene W., "The OST System for Managing Innovation at Texas Instruments," An address to the Armed Forces Management Association, Washington, D.C., April 7, 1971.

Using the Matrix Structure for Strategic Planning [18]

The basic question of organizational planning—"How (organizationally) can the planning be accomplished?"—goes beyond the question of organizational responsibility for strategic planning to the existence of a functioning organization that actually consumes resources (time and money) to produce the outputs that are called strategic plans. Of course, the project team approach is not a strategic-planning organization itself, even though the ideas that are being managed are related to strategic planning.

However, the same concept can be directly applied to the process of strategic planning through project teams that are responsible for the various aspects of strategic planning. For instance, project teams can be organized and held responsible for assisting in the development of alternative strategies in support of overall organizational opportunities, that is, an interdisciplinary, interorganizational project team is pulled together to study a broad market opportunity or charged with developing a statement of goals for the organization.

The interdisciplinary, interorganizational character of these teams is critical since it ensures that various points of view and experiential bases will be brought to bear. In this way, both disciplinary and organizational parochialism [19] are reduced.

[18] See Cleland, D. I., King, W. R., *Systems Analysis and Project Management*, McGraw-Hill, New York, 1975, for detailed discussions of the matrix organizational concept and applications.

[19] As discussed in Chapter 13.

The matrix planning organization has many advantages over the traditional way in which planning is done. Among the advantages are these:

1. Personal involvement through participation is enhanced; an individual feeling of belonging is strengthened.
2. A checks and balances through consensus decision making is provided.
3. An organization is created to facilitate innovation, thus complementing the organization designed for efficiency, control, and discipline.
4. The chief executive has another organization he can draw upon to assist him in developing long-range strategies.
5. The effect of organizational and disciplinary parochialism is reduced.

Of course, if project techniques are to be used by an organization to assist in the development of long-range strategies, then the people who will be serving on the project teams (or will be supervising project team efforts) need to be familiarized with project management techniques and concepts. This training is essential simply because bureaucratic organizational structures are still very much a way of life in our society, even though the bureaucratic form of organization is ''out of joint with contemporary realities.''[20]

We have already alluded, in previous chapters, to the use of project team structures to accomplish the development of specific planning informational inputs. Here, we shall summarize some of these to give operational significance to the concept of a parallel strategic-planning organization.

PROJECT TEAM DEVELOPMENT OF STRATEGIC DATA BASES

In Chapter 5, we introduced the idea of using various strategic data bases as vehicles for initiating the strategic-planning process. Strategic data bases were defined in Chapter 6 as concise statements of the *most significant* strategic items related to various clientele or environments that affect the organization's strategic choices. As such, they are the mechanisms through which the current situation and future opportunities are assessed. The strategic data bases reflect the influence of various forces (the environment, competitors, top management, the business in which the organization operates, as well as the organization itself) on the strategic options that are available.

The project team approach to the development of strategic data bases involves the charging of project teams, which are made up of managers representing various of the parochial interests within the organization, with gathering and evaluating the data in each of a number of areas and *choosing* through the

---

[20] Bennis, Warren G., ''The Coming Death of Bureaucracy,'' *THINK*, International Business Machines Corporation, 1966.

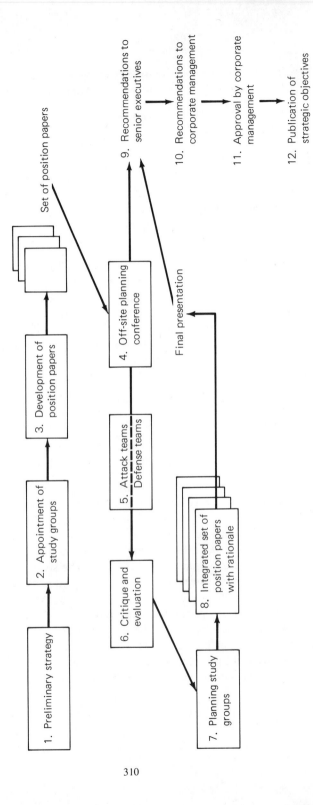

FIGURE 13.7 A Task Force New Business Opportunity Planning Process.

consensual process that guides most project team decision making—those that are the most important to the development of the organization's strategy.

Thus, the strategic data bases represent information rather than data in the sense that large quantities of data have been evaluated and condensed to a form that can feasibly be used in the strategic-planning process. There is with the SDB approach, a greater likelihood that some of the information that is so universally regarded as being important to strategic planning will actually become an integral part of the strategic-planning process.

Chapter 5 gives illustrations of strategic data bases of a number of varieties. The task force approach to their development represents *one* possible dimension of a collateral organization for strategic planning.

TASK FORCE DEVELOPMENT OF CLAIMANT-BASED OBJECTIVES

The claimant model and analysis described in Chapter 7 represents another opportunity for the significant employment of interdisciplinary project teams in strategic planning. This is so because such an analysis, to be truly meaningful as an input to the development of objectives, must be negotiated and evaluated in much the same sense as must the strategic data bases.

Thus, only some mechanism such as a project team, which is charged with developing significant and concise informational inputs, can have any hope of resolving the inevitable conflicting viewpoints that will be reflected by the various subunits of the organization. Attempts undertaken in other fashions, such as through staff analysis, are often doomed to failure since they will probably not be accepted by some of the organizational participants or departments.

TASK FORCE DEVELOPMENT OF NEW BUSINESS OPPORTUNITIES

One business firm that has adopted the strategic planning organization approach did so in a process involving a number of phases. Annual cycles that involved successively more sophisticated complementary organizations were used as vehicles for developing the planning organization to its fullest potential.

The first cycle devoted primary attention to the identification and evaluation of new product-market opportunities. Subsequent cycles have continued this focus while complementing it with other foci, such as the evaluation of existing company businesses that are potential candidates for divestment and the development of strategic organizational and management development plans. Figure 13.7 shows the process used by the firm in establishing and utilizing the task force studies of new business opportunities. The major elements of Figure 13.7 are explained in the following sections.

PRELIMINARY STRATEGY. To initiate the process, a planning guide was prepared to guide the study groups (task forces). This guide contained a preliminary statement of the firm's objectives, the general areas of opportunity that are foreseen by the corporate planning staff and anticipated environmental changes over the period for which planning is to be done.

STUDY GROUPS. The firm established thirteen task forces, each charged with investigating an area of opportunity for new business. Each group was to begin with a specified set of federal executive agencies and work from the documented plans of those agencies to identify areas of opportunity. Emphasis was to be placed on nongovernmental areas that would be enhanced, or developed as a result of current and future activities of the various federal agencies.

POSITION PAPERS. Each study group was asked to develop a position paper for each area of opportunity that they wished to recommend. The specification of the content of these opportunity areas is shown in Table 13.1. A perusal of that table identifies the activities that each study group was required to perform.

PLANNING CONFERENCE. Once the study groups have developed a set of position papers supporting their choices, an off-site planning conference was conducted to further refine the output of the study groups efforts. Such a conference provided an opportunity for officials at various levels to input their judgments into the opportunities being defined.

ATTACK/DEFENSE EXERCISE. An attack team can be charged with responsibility for reviewing, analyzing, and critiquing the preliminary reports of each study group. This review was brought into focus through a face-to-face exchange between the study group (defense) and the attack team. In such a dialectic approach, emphasis is placed on sharpening each study group's analysis through the critical and aggressive review of a comparable group of managers.

CORPORATE REVIEW. After the task forces have had an opportunity to revise their recommendations based on the conference results and the attack/defense exercise, their position papers were forwarded to corporate level for review and consolidation as indicated in the planning process diagram in Figures 4.1 and 4.2.

TASK FORCES IN PLANNING REVIEW

Task forces may also be used to aid in the planning review function. For instance, in one company the chief executive appointed a task force made up of managers from other business areas to review each planning unit's strategic plan and to make recommendations to a senior corporate committee. Not all of

TABLE 13.1 / Summary Form. Evaluation of Business Opportunity Areas

I. *Description of Business and Function It Serves*
Keep it brief. Be sure to identify in terms of product, service, software, leasing, franchise, etc.

II. *Establish the Need*
   1. Timing
   When should activity begin? Indicate milestones. Assess each milestone on the basis of present best estimates, also indicate range of dates that could occur. What options are available to management based upon the range of dates?
   2. Growth
      a. Show value of *specific* market by year as a curve. Indicate risk or uncertainty by showing maximum and minimum growth that could *reasonably* happen. (Could business be replaced, superseded, never materialize?)
      b. Table enumerating *facts* and *assumptions* with respect to timing and growth. Consider market, economy, technologic development, politics, and public policy. Assess the risk of the assumption changing.

III. *Market*
Who is the customer(s)? How is the marketing done now? Is it the only way? Why? Is there an international market? Should it be included now or later? Why?

IV. *Competitive Situation*
Who are the present competitors? What are their strengths and weaknesses? Comparisons on the basis of research and development capability, engineering, marketing, contracting base, manufacturing capability, and image with customer, i.e., price, service, reliability, maintainability.

V. *Capability Analysis*
Chart of capability required versus capability available. Short recommendation of way to meet the capability requirements where there is a company lack. Estimate cost and time required. Highlight strengths and weaknesses!

VI. *Investment*
Dollars invested/dollar sales, industry experience in time and amount invested before there is income. Front end load? Typical return on investment. Demand analysis; i.e., what is history of ups and downs in the particular business area? Range of swings, length of cycles, etc.

VII. *Political, Social, and Economic Considerations*
Relate to company and its image. Image of the business.

VIII. *Strategy*
Based upon the picture developed in the steps above, what actions and strategies are recommended?

Note: With respect to everything listed, in your report question whether it is fact or assumption and then with respect to each assumption evaluate the risk; i.e., what limits can be placed about the assumption? What alternatives are available based upon the swings that could occur to the assumption.

the planning unit strategic plans were reviewed by a task force. The following selection criteria were used to determine which units would be reviewed:

1. The planning unit was having significant performance difficulties thus casting serious doubt as to the suitability of the existing strategy.
2. The planning unit had overestimated its performance potential given historical performance and strategies.
3. The previous year's strategic plan was not sufficiently complete to permit a good analysis for the business potential.
4. The planning unit's strategic plan had not undergone formal review by the senior corporate committee in the past planning period.
5. Significant events in the environment or in the competition dictated a review of the strategic direction of the planning unit.

Organizational Roles for the Strategic-Planning Organizations

There are a variety of adaptations of the basic planning organization structure that can prove equally effective. For instance, a council of top executives has been used as a "murder board," which critiques and evaluates the results of the planning teams. An assistant who acts as an alter ego and planning facilitator for the chief executive can also be useful. As Steiner[21] has said:

> There is no single method or formula, or standard way to start and conduct a formal corporate planning system. What is done is a function of such factors as managerial style, size of organization, whether the firm is centralized or decentralized, managerial authority extended to decentralized managers, types of problems the company faces, managerial knowledge, types of products, and other comparable factors. So each system is fitted to each company.

However, there are a number of critical roles, and corresponding patterns of authority and responsibility, that are crucial to the success of a planning organization. These roles reflect the basic premises of the "planning culture" discussed in Chapter 12. Here, we make them more specific in light of the organizational structure that is developed in this chapter.

Many companies and other organizations have experimented with giving a central planning department the responsibility to develop organizational strategies but with no carry-through responsibility to see that the strategies are

---

[21] Steiner, G. A., *Comprehensive Managerial Planning in Contemporary Management, Issues and Viewpoints* (Joseph W. McGuire, editor), Prentice-Hall, Englewood Cliffs, N.J., 1974, p. 343.

implemented. This type of approach can cause resentment on the part of line managers who see such planning as an interference with their prerogatives. In other approaches, a line manager is assigned an individual within the central planning department that is responsive to the particular line manager as well as within the context of the overall company strategies. In this design, the planning activities still tend to be apart from the line manager responsible for executing plans.

Organizations will put the planning function in the hands of the senior executives hoping to avoid the problem of separating the actual planning from the execution of plans, since the senior executives, acting as a body (e.g., the board of directors), have to approve the strategies and allocate the resources for the implementation of plans. A major disadvantage of this approach is that the chief executives are often too far removed from the actual operation of the company and cannot know about some of the local problems that affect the operation of the company. In addition, the complexity of planning in large organizations serving different markets requires the amassing and study of extensive data bases and is beyond the time or capability of a few executives. Means have to be found to delegate the process of strategic planning and at the same time provide for the protection of the managerial prerogatives of all executives concerned.

The relative roles of planners and managers should create a symbiotic relationship where planners and managers live together in mutually supportive roles. The following descriptions of the roles of various people and organizational elements are developed to achieve that sort of relationship.

THE LINE MANAGER'S ROLE IN PLANNING

In consonance with the basic premise of the line organization, the line manager should be responsible for and actively involved in the strategic-planning process. The manager who is responsible for the current operational efficacy of the organization must also be a member of the planning organization; he must explicitly participate and devote his energy and attention to it. Moreover, a corollary to the basic premise about participation serves to further integrate subordinate line managers into planning; in essence, *those who must implement planning should be charged with doing it.*

The strategy for the role of the line manager is to charge those who have generated, developed, and nurtured ideas during the planning process with the responsibility for carrying them out after they become an accepted part of the strategic plan. With this simple policy, a variety of knowledge and commitment is secured for the plan which no quantity of formal orders or no volume of exhortation could achieve.

THE TOP MANAGER'S ROLE IN PLANNING

The first role of the manager of the planning organization is the establishment of that concept as reality. If there is any new idea that must come from the top, it is the creation of a radically new and innovative way of planning. Such an organization should provide for checks and balances and provide a maximum opportunity for participation on the part of those executives who will ultimately be responsible for implementing the decision. In addition, the long-range-planning organization should provide an opportunity for widespread participation by technical people at all levels.

In creating this organization, the chief executive must provide the necessary incentives whereby people are rewarded for contributing to the development of future strategy. He should also demonstrate, by his personal involvement, that the continuous development of future strategy is of vital concern in the organization.

Of course, the development of a long-range sense of direction and purpose for an organization is usually touted as the primary challenge to chief executives. Although the problems of controlling current operations is a key responsibility of chief executives, the forces of change in our society clearly challenge the provident executive to devote more time to his role as an organizational strategist.

But the chief executive clearly cannot be a planner in the sense of doing the planning. Obviously, he has limited time. He simply cannot either do or direct the myriad of studies necessary to build forecasts, test assumptions, and conduct cost-effectiveness studies; an organization must be created to do this for him. His responsibility is developing future organizational strategy centers around the final evaluation and selection of strategic alternatives and the design of a master plan of implementation for those alternatives.

More importantly however, the chief executive can provide an environment in which the development of long-range strategy is a way of life. This requires that he create an organization where there is a continuing assessment of future environmental trends and a more-or-less continuous effort to develop a range of strategic alternatives for evaluation by the senior executives. If such an environment has been created, the chief executive makes the final choice of strategic alternatives for the organization to pursue.

The chief executive, therefore, functions as a "linking pin" among various project teams, planning teams, suborganizations, and executives in this sort of planning organization. He also serves as a balancing force that ensures the emergence and development of ideas to form the organization's future.

THE ROLE OF THE STAFF PLANNER

The staff planner has four basic functions with regard to the planning process. First, he plays a role in the initiation of the process. This role is shared with other staff specialists, who provide informational input to planning, and it is also shared with top management. Second, the staff planner is the facilitator of the planning process. He schedules all aspects of the process and makes sure that they are carried out. The third major staff planning function is that of review and evaluation. Staff planners review the various plans prepared by line managers, evaluate them for a consistency with each other and with the assumptions and guidelines that have been laid down, and synthesize them into a plan, which is then passed on to other staff specialists, e.g., financial analysts, and finally to top management for a review. Top management can then approve the plans or send them back through the cycle to be redone. The fourth function of the staff planner is consultation. He must be available for consultation with task force members during the planning process so that they have access to such items as interpretations of assumptions and forecasts, clarification of planning guidelines, and preliminary evaluation of the feasibility of plans.

The latter aspect of this consultative role is of primary importance. Although the staff planner performs a review and evaluation function, it is clearly inefficient for the process to become so formal that plans are developed and then rejected on the basis of criteria that could be communicated between staff planner and managerial planner early enough in the planning process to avoid wasted planning effort.

This concept of a staff planner's role in a central planning staff assumes that planning has been decentralized to the line managers that will be responsible for implementing the plans; the planning activity is tightly coordinated, monitored, and evaluated by a headquarters central planning staff, thus centralizing policy and strategic functions. Other staff activities (such as those in support of the current operations), are separated from strategic planning so that operational problems do not drive out longer range planning activities.

The executive who heads up the central planning staff should be an individual of stature; preferably an executive who has successfully demonstrated his ability to manage effectively a line organization, and to produce viable strategic plans in that line capacity. An illustration of the importance placed on strategic planning by the General Electric Company can serve to illustrate this point. Within the General Electric Company in 1973, the head of the Corporate Strategic Planning Office was an executive, Rubin Gutoff, who was formerly chief executive for the Components and Materials Group, one of the ten operating groups within the company. According to R. H. Jones, chairman of the board, and chief executive officer of General Electric, Gutoff ". . . was outstanding in laying out strategic plans and profitably implementing them" during his position as chief executive officer for the Components and Materials Group.[22] Thus, in selecting a successful line manager to head the planning staff, General Electric signaled the importance of planning and ensured that a realistic management-oriented viewpoint would guide the planning activity.

The central planning staff exists to oversee the total organizational planning function—*to see that the planning is done but not to do the planning.* Such a staff can examine the total planning and provide the organizational mechanisms and facilitating services required to support planning throughout the entire organization. The composition of the planning staff should include a balance of both line and staff officials—managers and analysts who are detailed for 2–3 year periods to function as planners. This rotation would provide managerial input to planning analysis as well as an educational experience for managers.

Summary

Planning may be most effectively accomplished in the context of a multidimensional organization, in which the operating organization and the planning organization operate in parallel to complement one another. This relieves the operating-planning conflict, which commonly inhibits planning effectiveness.

The multidimensional organization is needed because planning is so labor intensive that it needs to be organized. Moreover, if change and innovation are to be fostered, the operating organization will generally serve as an inhibiting factor. This means that some way of breaking out of the confines of the operating organization must be found. The multidimensional organization, which incorporates parallel, or collateral, organizations for operations and planning, is one way of accomplishing this.

Multidimensional organizational concepts have been implemented under various nomenclatures. The strategic business unit planning concept of General Electric, governmental program structures, the matrix structure, venture team organizations, and the objective-strategy-tactic system of Texas Instruments are illustrative of the various approaches that have been taken.

A matrix structure may itself be used in planning in a variety of ways. Task forces or project teams may be used to develop strategic data bases, to perform claimant analyses, to establish objectives, to review new business opportunities or to review the plans of individual business units.

The roles and duties of the various actors in the planning system (the chief executive, planners, and line managers) must be spelled out clearly if the mul-

---

[22] For more information on the restructuring of the General Electric Company to emphasize strategic planning, see the article "GE's Jones Restructures His Top Team," *Business Week,* June 30, 1973.

tidimensional system is to work effectively. Once this has been done, the various participants can complement one another and the operating and planning organizations can, as well, play complementary roles in the overall organization.

Chapter 13—Questions and Exercises

1. The planning organization should be an integral part of the overall organizational planning culture. What is meant by this statement?
2. An organization may be defined in operational terms as a dynamic, goal-seeking, purposeful system. What are the characteristics of such a system?
3. The planning organization is a continuous, parallel, ongoing organization that complements the basic operating organization. Explain this.
4. A line manager in an operating organization may have different authority and responsibility patterns than he has in the role that he plays in the strategic-planning organization. Describe this situation in practical terms such as who works for whom, who can give orders to whom, and how decisions are arrived at in the two contexts.
5. Strategic planning is inherently a people activity. Why is this so?
6. An operating organization can be characterized as emphasizing control and efficiency. Contrast these operating organization objectives with those of a strategic planning organization.
7. Why do ideas in an organization form the basis for developing a strategic direction for the organization?
8. Emerging ideas in an organization can be stifled by managers who desire (perhaps subconsciously) to resist change. Give an example of how this can happen.
9. Why is the organization structure that is best for efficient day-to-day operation not the best organizational approach for strategic planning?
10. What are the criteria for a Strategic Business Unit (SBU) as used by the General Electric Company?
11. What other varieties of parallel organizations might be useful in addition to the operating and planning organizations?
12. What is the concept of a program structure? What value does this concept have in strategic planning?
13. The authors encourage the use of a matrix organizational structure in facilitating the strategic planning process. What is the value of such a matrix organizational structure in strategic planning?
14. Compare the similarities and differences between the strategic planning organizations of the General Electric Company and Texas Instruments, Inc.
15. What are some of the advantages of the matrix planning organization over the traditional way in which planning is accomplished? What relevance do these advantages have in facilitating a strategic-planning culture?
16. The way in which the relevant roles of managers is defined in an organization has an influence on the efficacy of the planning process. Summarize the typical roles of

the following people in an organizational planning context: (a) the line manager's role; (b) the top manager's role.

17. What are the four basic functions that the staff planner should deal with in the strategic planning process?
18. How might a task force in strategic planning be used to enhance the effectiveness of an adversary role in the organization?
19. An old adage in management theory holds that the existing organizational structure should complement the market strategy of the organization. Explain what is meant by this statement.
20. Strategic planning is too important to an organization to be left to the chief executive. Why is this so?
21. What criteria might prove to be useful in determining how many parallel organizations an organization might usefully create?
22. How does our knowledge of the distribution of ideas in an organization conflict with the basic underlying assumptions of bureaucracy?

Chapter 13—Strategic Questions for the Manager

1. Does the present organizational structure help to encourage and facilitate strategic planning? Why, or why not?
2. What has been the history or idea identification and development within the organization? Is there any evidence to suggest that these ideas emerged randomly in the organization? Or did the ideas only come from key managers?
3. Does the current ambience in the organization tend to encourage individuals to come forth with ideas for improvement of the organization's effectiveness?
4. What have organizational managers done to encourage (or stifle) the emergence of ideas within the organization?
5. What opportunities exist in the organization for the creation of a strategic-business-unit type of planning organization?
6. Are line executives responsible for seeing that strategic planning is accomplished in the organization?
7. Does the existing organization reflect the market opportunity?
8. Has the use of project teams to study and evaluate market/product opportunities ever been tried? Would the current organizational ambience permit the use of such teams?
9. What checks and balances are used in the organization to test the credibility and attainability of goals and objectives?
10. Have performance standards been developed to evaluate strategic opportunities in the organization?
11. Have tentative strategic purposes been set forth by the chief executive to use as a point of departure in strategic planning?
12. What are the methods and techniques used to determine organizational strengths and weaknesses?
13. What is the stratelic planning role of the line manager in the organization?
14. What is the strategic planning role of the staff?

References

Anshen, M., "The Management of Ideas," *Harvard Business Review,* July–Aug. 1969.

Anshen, M., "Organization Structure and the New Decision-Making Technology," in *Management: Organization and Planning,* Donald M. Bowman and Francis M. Fillerup, editors, McGraw-Hill, New York, 1963, Chapter 2.

Bennis, W. G., *Changing Organizations,* McGraw-Hill, New York, 1966.

Bennis, W. G., "The Coming Death of Bureaucracy," *Think,* International Business Machines Corporation, New York, 1966.

Cleland, D. I., and King, W. R. "Organizing For Long-Range Planning," *Business Horizons,* Aug. 1974.

Dale, E., and Urwick, L. F., *Staff in Organizations,* McGraw-Hill, New York, 1960.

Forsyth, W. E., "Strategic Planning in the Seventies," *Financial Executive,* Oct. 1973.

"GE's Jones Restructures His Top Team," *Business Week,* June 30, 1973.

George, W. W., "Task Teams for Rapid Growth," *Harvard Business Review,* Mar.–Apr. 1977.

Goggin, W. C., "How the Multidimensional Structure Works at Dow Corning," *Harvard Business Review,* Jan.–Feb. 1974.

Greiner, L. E., "Evolution and Revolution as Organizations Grow," *Harvard Business Review,* July–Aug. 1972.

Hall, W. K., "*SBUs*: Hot New Topic in the Management of Diversification," *Business Horizons,* Feb. 1978.

Harvard Business Review, "Participation Management at Work. An Interview with John F. Donnelly," Jan.–Feb. 1977.

Higgins, J. C., and Finn, R., "The Organization and Practice of Corporate Planning in the U.K.," *Long Range Planning,* Vol. 10, No. 4, Aug. 1977.

Kraushar, P. M., "Organization for Corporate Development," *Long Range Planning,* Vol. 9, No. 3, June 1976.

Mace, M. L., "The President and Corporate Planning," *Harvard Business Review,* Jan.–Feb. 1965.

Mee, J. F., "Speculation About Human Organization in the 21st Century," *Business Horizons,* Feb. 1971.

Mason, R. O., "A Dialectical Approach to Strategic Planning," *Management Science,* Apr. 1969.

Miller, D., "Common Syndromes of Business Failure," *Business Horizons,* Dec. 1977.

Morton, J. A., *Organizing For Innovation,* McGraw-Hill, New York, 1971.

Nott, P. C., "The Merits of Using Experts or Consumers as Members of Planning Groups: A Field Experiment in Health Planning," *Academy of Management Journal,* Sept. 1976.

Reichman, W., and Levy, M., "Psychological Constraints on Effective Planning, *Management Review,* Oct. 1975.

Ross, D. J., "For LRP-Rotating Planners and Doers," *Harvard Business Review,* Jan.–Feb. 1962.

Schoen, D. R., "Managing Technological Innovation," *Harvard Business Review,* May–June 1969.

Steiner, G. A., "Rise of the Corporate Planner," *Harvard Business Review,* Sept.–Oct. 1970.

Vancil, R. F., "So You're Going to Have a Planning Department," *Harvard Business Review,* May–June 1967.

"Westinghouse Opts for a GE Pattern," *Business Week,* Feb. 3, 1975.

Vancil, R. F., "Strategy Formulation in Complex Organizations," *Sloan Management Review,* Winter 1976.

Wrapp, H. E., "Organization for Long Range Planning," *Harvard Business Review,* Jan.–Feb. 1957.

Zand, D. C., "Collateral Organization: A New Change Strategy," *Journal of Applied Behavioral Science,* Vol. 10, 1974.

PART VII

The Planning–Management Subsystem

Chapter 14

IMPLEMENTING
STRATEGIC PLANNING
IN ORGANIZATIONS

In many organizations, the greatest difficulties in instituting change, be it change involving new ways of doing things, new ways of making choices, or new products and services, do not lie in the design and development of the changes themselves. Rather, the greatest obstructions to positive change lie in the processes that are used to implement them.

In many of the preceeding chapters, we have focused on the nature of a modern effective strategic-planning system per se. Now, we focus explicitly on the issues involved in getting such a system operationalized in the organization.

Of course, the several phases involved in the design, development, and implementation of a strategic-planning system cannot be separate and distinct. If they are made to be seperate, the system is quite likely to fail.

Although this point has not become a basic tenet of the field of strategic planning, it is becoming quite well understood in other areas of systems design. For instance, the authors have written in the context of a systems design MIS methodology:[1]

> . . . the methodology involves participation on the part of the managers who will use the MIS. It emphasizes this manager participation to such a great degree as to require the acceptance of a *broader definition of optimality* than that usually adopted by MIS designers. Of course, many approaches to MIS design involve management participation in specifying information needs and in reviewing the system development effort. However, this approach involves user participation in basic systems design decisions which are usually thought of as "technical" in nature. Thus, the methodology can produce systems which cannot be thought of as optimum in the technical sense.
>
> In this regard, the approach is addressed to a broader variety of optimality which considers *both* technical cost-benefit considerations *and* the manager's perception of the potential utility of the system in enhancing his decision-making effectiveness. The essence of this broader view of optimality is the belief that a tech-

[1] King, W. R., and Cleland, D. I., "The Design of Management Information Systems: An Information Analysis Approach," *Management Science,* Vol. 22, Nov. 1975, p. 287.

nically-optimum system which goes unused is inferior to a system which is technically inferior, but perceived to be useful by the organization's managers.

This methodological approach is as applicable to strategic-planning systems as it is to other organizational management processes and systems.

In prior chapters, we have implicitly applied this principle to the design and development of the overall strategic-planning system as well as to each of its subsystems. For instance, our focus on *participation*, in strategic choice, in developing informational inputs, and in the planning process in general, has implementation as one of its primary motivations.

In this chapter, we therefore seek to focus these ideas more directly on the issue of implementation and to develop an operational approach to a strategic-planning system that will enhance its likelihood of being implemented in the organization and accepted and used by those organizational participants for whom it is intended.

The Need for a Planning Implementation Strategy

Implementation of planning is important because the objective of a strategic-planning system is organizational change. Organizational change has not, in the past, been viewed as necessary or even desirable. However as Drucker noted[2]:

> The ruling assumption of an innovative strategy is that whatever exists is aging.

A strategic-planning system is one significant way that an organization can enhance its ability to cope with change. *However, an innovative strategic-planning system itself represents change* to the organization's participants. Moreover, it is usually introduced as a part of a *change strategy* developed by a top manager or the organization's top management group.[3]

The need for such innovative systems in organizations is described by Morton[4]:

> Innovation means renewal. It means the improvement of the old and the development of new capabilities of people and their organizations. Innovation is not the anarchistic destruction of the old—rather, it is the adaptive change and improvement of existing systems.

[2] Drucker, P. F., *Management: Tasks Responsibilities and Practices,* Harper and Row, New York, 1973, p. 791.

[3] Kudla has found that the introduction of formalized strategic planning in an organization can often be associated with changes in top management in the organization. See Kudla, R. J., "A Study of Corporate Planning in Fourteen Large Corporations," *Long Range Planning,* in press.

[4] Morton, J. A., *Organizing for Innovation,* McGraw-Hill, New York, 1971, p. 1.

To effectively introduce such systems change requires a strategy, just as a strategy is required to proactively induce change in the organization's products and materials. We can be sure that change will occur, but we cannot be assured that it will be desirable change. Therefore, a strategy for change is necessary if positive and desirable change is to be facilitated.

The nature of a strategy for implementing strategic planning is a *change strategy*. Such a strategy has two interrelated varieties of components in the strategic-planning context, a *systems design strategy* and an *implementation strategy*. We shall discuss the implementation strategy first and then relate it to the design strategy in terms of many of the ideas that have already been developed.

A Strategic Planning Implementation Strategy

The successful implementation of an innovative strategic-planning system presumes that the responsible executive has a commitment to succeed and that by words and actions the executive uses strategic planning as the common denominator for managing the organization. Among the important things to consider in developing an implementation strategy are timing, attitude, change, gaining the support of top level management team, and the delegation of operational matters.

TIMING THE INTRODUCTION OF STRATEGIC PLANNING

The variety of comprehensive strategic-planning system with which this book deals will represent a radical change for many organizations. Thus, a gradual approach to implementing strategic planning is suggested. In view of the substantial investment required in time and personal commitment, it is advisable to proceed slowly. Until an organization understands its peculiar needs for a planning staff, its information requirements, and a suitable planning process, it would be unwise to fully implement a comprehensive planning activity. Indeed, the development of knowledgeable people at both the central headquarters and the operating levels would have to be initiated to ensure an effective planning system, and such personnel development simply takes time.

The implementation strategy should be a phased one, a process of slowly introducing strategic planning in a few organizational elements, and then gradually expanding to the rest of the organization. The strategy for implementing a planning process should be carried out in such a manner that it builds on the strengths of the organization and simultaneously makes it clear that a new importance is to be given to planning in the organization.

ATTITUDE CHANGE

The achievement of a positive *attitude change* about planning should be a primary initial goal of the implementation process. To assist in developing such change, planning workshops can be conducted using consultants as well as organizational executives who have been successful in strategic planning for their own purpose. More specialized workshops on other aspects of planning such as modeling and forecasting should be held using practical examples of successful modeling that has been done in similar organizational environments.

Initially, these workshops should focus on the need for planning, the essentials of a planning process, the values of planning, and on soliciting ideas about the specifics of how a planning system might be designed. Subsequently, they can become devices for promulgating the overall planning systems design and for educating managers as to how to effectively participate and *to use the system to get their personal ideas across.*

The planning workshops can serve to emphasize the need and value of planning, as well as asking for ideas and participation in the design of specific aspects of the planning process. The subject matter to be dealt with in the planning workshops might include:

1. An analysis of "where we are today"—our current organizational problems and opportunities.
2. An assessment of the factors critical to succeed (and failure) in our industry; a preliminary evaluation of the competition.
3. A dialogue on the basic conceptual design of the organization, or in other words, what business the organization is currently in, and what future business it should be in.
4. A description of planning process, the steps and techniques that may be followed in designing and operating strategic planning systems.
5. Identification of the information that is needed to plan adequately—sources, availability, retrival methods, etc.
6. After the planning process has been in operation for some time, a discussion of the effectiveness of such planning. What went right? What went wrong? How might the planning effectiveness be improved?

Many attempts at implementing strategic planning fail simply because the approach has been piecemeal; too often little forethought had been devoted to determine what was involved and to develop a strategic approach.

GAINING TOP MANAGEMENT SUPPORT

Assuming that the chief executive has made a basic strategic decision to initiate a planning process, an important step is to gain the support and enthusiasm of the top management team. Initially, the chief executive can hold private, personal discussions with key managers about strategic planning. This begins a familiarization with planning and helps the chief executive to perceive the fears, hopes, and prejudices that these managers have about strategic planning. The chief executive will also get to know them a little better as individuals and be in a better position to assess their predilections toward improving strategic effectiveness. An effective way to do this is to gain their early participation in the decision to launch a strategic planning system. This can be facilitated through an informal, off-site workshop to discuss the need for, and the timeliness of, strategic planning. Discussing several topics such as the following can serve to help create a need for strategic planning:

1. A few success stories on strategic planning taken from articles in management literature.
2. How things might be done differently in the organization if strategic planning were being carried.
3. How strategic planning might be carried out in the organization.
4. How strategic planning could be motivated in the organization.

The chief executive who plans to introduce a planning system must spend some time getting educated and committed to accept the value of the process. When fully conversant with the aspects of planning, the chief executive must delegate enough of his other work to provide sufficient time for planning matters. Top management is a demanding job, with the responsibility of satisfying his organizations's clientele; when the chief executive is deeply involved in the theory and practice of planning, his enthusiasm will catch on with the other executives. In this respect, Hussey[5] cautions:

> The success or failure of corporate planning greatly depends on the attitude of the chief executive—whether he believes in it, understands and actively participates in the process, and provides the strong leadership necessary to really benefit from corporate planning. Or, if the chief executive introduces planning merely because it's the fashionable thing to do, does not believe nor understand it, and thus loses interest in the process, it's bound to fail. For successful corporate planning, the chief executive must be almost as expert at it as his planner—and know when to become involved at "key points" without getting bogged down in detail to the detriment of the other duties of his position.

For successful planning, the operating managers as well as the chief executive must be committed to develop a strategic awareness in their management of the organization. The role played by the chief planner is important as well as the image he portrays in the organization. There is no simple and easy

[5] Paraphrased from David Hussey, *Corporate Planning: Theory and Practice*, Pergamon Press, New York, 1974, pp. 302–303.

way to do this; it has to be done within the context of their operating responsibilities. Defining an organizational purpose as an outgrowth of a strategic-
planning process is a time-consuming and continuous process. The executive
must regard such work as a key requirement of his or her position, to be done
along with operational activities. This means that operational matters must be
managed more effectively and where possible some of the executive's work
must be delegated.

DELEGATING OPERATIONAL MATTERS

A good place to start thinking about a strategic-planning system is to review the
adequacy of delegation of authority in the organization. An executive who
wants to start working on attitude change for strategic planning should examine
his or her work to see which part can be delegated to peers and subordinates.
This process of delegation normally involves (a) the assignment of certain tasks
to other people, (b) delegating authority to accomplish these tasks, and (c) establishing the charge of responsibility for doing the tasks.

An effective delegation of authority and exaction of responsibility by the
executive helps to free time for the introspective thinking about the organization's future that is so important to strategic planning. Also, the example set by
the executive of the effective delegation of operational matters will serve to encourage the managers to do likewise, and free more time for their role in strategic planning.

A PLANNING-NEEDS STRATEGY

One company that was about to introduce strategic planning developed and
expressed their strategy in terms that reflected their planning needs. This
strategy serves to illustrate the concept of a strategy for implementing strategic
planning.

Planning Needs

1. A strong statement, reaffirming the president's commitment to the strategic planning process, and indicating his direct involvement in the
   process.
2. Redefinition of a broad statement of strategies and goals, focusing on
   such issues as growth strategy and areas of primary endeavor, to reflect
   recent changes in the environment.
3. A statement defining the strategic planning unit and how it will operate.
4. A procedure for assessing the relationship between plans of individual
   Strategic Planning Units and overall corporate goals and a process for
   allocating corporate resources accordingly.

5. Initiation of a program to train planners and to develop greater planning sensitivities in present and potential managers.

6. The development of alternative strategies for each Strategic Planning Unit.

7. An iterative procedure for finalizing plans including a mechanism to provide a corporate overview of the implications of the entire planning effort for the corporation.

8. A strengthened and continuous evaluative process.

9. Establishment of the capability to develop corporate positions on key environmental factors that affect plans (e.g., the state of the economy) and a method to disseminate this information to all organizational units involved in planning.

This statement of planning needs was developed in a series of workshops held by the corporation's key managers. During these workshops it became obvious that the corporation was seriously ineffective in its current planning; the development of these planning needs served to motivate the diverse managers to work together to seek overall improvement in their planning capability.

A Strategic-Planning Systems Design Strategy

The basic "optimality criterion" for systems design, which was referred to in the introduction to this chapter, must be applied to every phase of the design of a strategic-planning system.

To effectively design any variety of management system, such as an MIS or strategic-planning systems, which will have a high likelihood of achieving positive organizational change, requires manager-designer mutual understanding.[6] This understanding must be developed to overcome such poor systems design results as have been reported. For instance, a McKinsey and Co.[7] report reveals that:

> . . . many otherwise effective top managements are in trouble with their computer efforts because they have abdicted control to staff specialists.

And Diebold[8] reports in the MIS area that ". . . technicians, not management, are setting goals for the computers."

---

[6] Churchman and Schainblatt discuss this concept as a basis for systems design in Churchman, C. W., and Schainblatt, A. H., "The Researcher and the Manager: A Dialectic of Implementation," *Management Science,* Vol. II, Feb. 1965, pp. B69–B87.

[7] McKinsey and Co., "Unlocking the Computer's Profit Potential," *Computers and Automation,* April 1969.

[8] Diebold, J., "Bad Decisions on Computer Use," *Harvard Business Review,* Jan.–Feb. 1969.

Activity	#1 City council	#2 Mayor	#3 Comptroller com / budget director	#4 Police commissioner	#5 Deputy commissioner	#6 Inspector	#7 Captain	#8 Uniformed patrolman	#9 Police administrator	#10 Other city departments	#11 Board and agencies	#12 Federal government
Analysis of routine complaints				A	C_4	S	E	C_7		7^i	7^i	
Observation of field practices				A	S	E	C_6					
Crime analysis				A	S	E	C_6			6^i	6^i	
Court decision analysis				A	E	C				5^i	5^i	
Analysis of social problems				A	S	E	C_6			6^i	6^i	6^i
Analysis of new legislation				A	S	E	C_6			6^i	6^i	6^i
Issue clarification & definition				A	S	E	C_6			6^i		6^i
Selection of alternatives				A	E	C_5						
Obtaining relevant facts				A	S	E	C_6	C_6		6^i	6^i	
Analysis of facts				A	E	C_5						
Review	A	A		E						$4^{i,o}$	$4^{i,o}$	
Formulation			A	E	C	S	E					
Articulation		A	A	A	C_4	S	E			6°	6°	
Training for implementation					E	E						
Execution and control	A	A		A	S	E	C_6			6°	6°	

FIGURE 14.1 LRC System Model.

Of course, the achievement of manager-analyst cooperation in systems design, whether it be information systems design or planning systems design, requires that a design process be developed that explicitly considers this need.

IMPLEMENTATION-ORIENTED DESIGN STRATEGY

The strategic-planning systems design approach most appropriate in this context is one that focuses on incorporating the system users into the design process.[9] Such an approach permits the development of systems that are, in part, designed by the people who best understand the job that the systems are to do, the user managers; it also permits the development of systems that incorporate many of the information indicators and practices that managers commonly develop and use outside of the domain of formalized management systems. Such a methodology is based on the concept that the system should be designed by those who best know the business and who will be users of the systems. It is addressed to a broad variety of optimality that encompasses both technical cost-benefit concerns and the user's perception of the usefulness of the system. Thus, the design process involves not only managerial input and review but also managerial decision making in the systems *design* process.

AN IMPLEMENTATION-ORIENTED DESIGN PROCESS[10]

The systems design process suggested here has been developed by the authors and applied in a number of organizations. The design process serves to operationalize the overall implementation strategy. This design process initially involves the definition, by the analyst in close cooperation with the organization's managers, of "user sets" and "decision areas." The user sets are defined so as to permit the system design to be oriented toward a reasonable number of user groups, each of which is treated as a homogeneous entity. The decision areas are delineated to represent the major decision categories of the organization using the same informal process. Each of these areas is then specifically defined in terms of the subdecisions and tasks which constitute the important elements of the decision area.

These user sets and decision subtasks are then consolidated in terms of a general-level system model such as that shown in Figure 14.1. The decision area represented in that figure is that of "establishing policies concerning the environment." Such a model, which is based on the concept of a linear respon-

[9] See King, W. R., and Cleland, D. I., "Manager-Analyst Teamwork in MIS Design," *Business Horizons,* April 1971, for a description of the basis for such an approach.

[10] Portions of this section are adapted with permission from the authors' paper. King, W. R., and Cleland, D. I., "The Design of MIS: An Information Analysis Approach," *Management Science,* Nov. 1975.

sibility chart (LRC),[11] shows system characteristics in terms of (a) authority and responsibility relationships, (b) initiation characteristics, and (c) information input-output characteristics among the various user sets as well as interacting environmental organizations.

Figure 14.1 represents a single decision area of the organization with the constituent subdecisions and tasks listed on the left and user sets and relevant environmental organizations listed across the top. The codes used in the figure to describe these characteristics for internal user sets are I, initiation; E, execution; A, approval; C, consultation; S, supervision. Numbers subscripts on these role descriptors serve to identify the specific relationship.

For instance, the figure shows on the first row that the analysis of routine complaints (E) is handled at the police captain level under the supervision of an inspector (S) with the police commissioner having approval authority (A). In performing this function, the captain has the consultation of uniformed patrolmen (C_7, where the subscript 7 indicates with whom the consultation takes place). Another consultation takes place when the Deputy Commissioner consults with the Commissioner (C_4) at the approval stage.

Various informational linkages with interfacing environmental organizations are also depicted in the figure—e.g., both "city departments" and "boards and agencies" provide input (i) to the police captain level (7) in the analysis of routine complaints.

The strategic planning systems design process involves the construction of *three different models* of the LRC variety. The three models are respectively: (a) a *descriptive* model describing existing system characteristics; (b) a *normative* model defining the ideal system[12]; (c) a *consensus* model integrating elements of both (a) and (b) and provides the basis for detailed systems design. The descriptive model is developed by analysts on the basis of observation and discussion with operatives in the system, much as in the traditional systems design mode. So too is the normative model developed in quite traditional fashion by analysts using criteria of technical optimality. However, the different and crucial aspect of this design process is the consensus model. This model is developed using the descriptive ("how we do it") and normative ("how we *should* do it") models as the basis for organizational discussion and design decision making. One format that has been successfully used is that of a participative executive development program, in which the descriptive and normative models were explained in detail to managers in lecture/discussion sessions and manager/analyst workshops were used to develop the consensus

---

[11] See Cleland, D. I., and King, W. R., *Systems Analysis and Project Management,* McGraw-Hill, New York, Chapter 12.

[12] See Ackoff, R. L., *A Concept of Corporate Planning,* John Wiley, New York, 1970, for a discussion of "idealized system design."

model (the one that is the best blend of theory and practical limitations to theory).

The considerations that go into the development of a consensus model are many and varied. "We can't do it the way the books say we should because of some unique feature of our organization," is a frequently heard comment in the consensus-seeking process. Sometimes, such comments are entirely valid. The recognition of this validity and its incorporation into the consensus model serves to make the systems design more useful, since the system is being designed in terms of this practical consideration, which otherwise might have provided a basis for rejecting a more nearly optimal design. This design process also serves to make the managers feel that they have, in fact, designed their own systems—a not insignificant element in gaining their acceptance of it.

This variety of process directly implements the systems design optimality criterion since it incorporates practical implementation content into every aspect of the consensus model that is used as the final system design. So long as the managers who participate in the development of the consensus model are not allowed to simply have their own way by being required to justify any deviations from the normative model, such a process has the potential of producing a general design that is both a significant improvement over the existing system and is feasible, usuable, and useful.

A Plan for Implementing Planning

Once both a strategic-planning system design strategy and an implementation strategy have been developed and design processes that are based on them have been defined, a plan for the implementation of planning can be formally developed. Just as it is important to have an organizational plan, the documented output of a planning process, so too is it important to develop a formal plan for implementation, for this is the only way that will ensure that the desired activities are actually carried out.

Figure 14.2 shows one important element of such a plan as developed by one business firm. This plan defines a wide variety of activities that must be performed over a three-year period in order to introduce planning. This firm also developed a network plan for depicting the activities and events of a planning effort. Figure 14.3 shows such a plan. Such techniques are useful as both planning and control tools; the participants in a strategic planning effort will gain a better understanding of the processes of planning if they participate in designing a network description of the strategy for the development of strategy.

Another firm that had adopted the project team planning organizational philosophy developed a nine-phase plan for implementing planning:

Planning organization	Year 1	Year 2	Year 3
Planning executive at decentralized level	X		
Acquire new skills			
(a) modeling management	X		
(b) planning analyst	X		
(c) planning services	X		
(d) information systems design	X		
Task force planning-extend to other areas	X———————————————→		
Introduce adversary role in review process		X—————————→	
Assign managers as staff planners	X		
Formal reorganization of planning effects			X
Major project review committee design	X		
Planning process			
Preliminary design	X—X		
Testing-workshops	X————X		
Documentation and workshops		X————X	
Design planning review process	X—X		
Implement review process	X————————————————→		
Attitude change			
Reward system			
(a) Preliminary design	X————X		
(b) Workshop testing		X—X	
(c) Implementation			X
Modeling workshops		X—X	
Decision philosophy			
Business simulation modeling	X————————————————→		
PIMS-established planning standards	X————————X		
Technological forecasting			X
Risk Analysis			X
Delphi			X
Information systems			
Develop organizational data banks	X————————————————→		
Integrate into planning system	X———————————————→		
Develop competitive business intelligence systems	X————————————————→		
Integrate into planning system	X———————————————→		
Forecasting			
(a) economic	X————————————————→		
(b) social	X———————————————→		
(c) legal	X————————————————→		
(d) political		X————————→	
(e) technological	X————————————————→		

FIGURE 14.2 Portion of Plan for Implementary Planning.

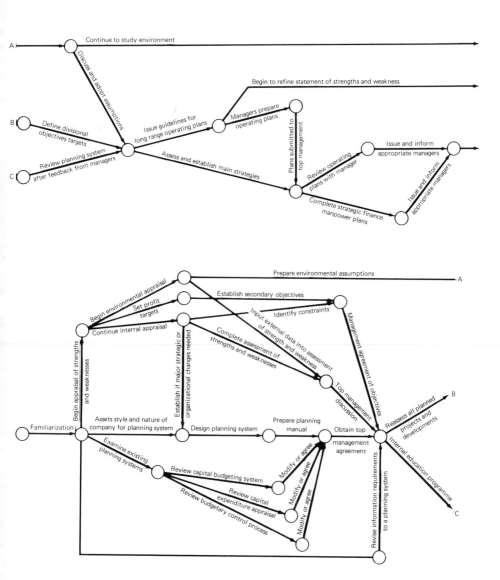

FIGURE 14.3 Network of main events on introduction of corporate long-range planning.

Phase 1. A philosophical orientation of the project team personnel in the concept of *project management and strategic planning.*

Phase 2. The establishment of a set of standards by which to evaluate strategic opportunities.

Phase 3. The postulation of *tentative* strategic purposes for the organization.

Phase 4. The development of data bases reflecting expected models of future environments.

Phase 5. An assessment of competitive strengths, weaknesses, and strategies.

Phase 6. An assessment of internal organizational strengths and weaknesses.

Phase 7. An evaluation of strategic objectives, goals, and tactics.

Phase 8. The proposal of tentative implementation strategies.

Phase 9. Building the staff planning organization.

Each of these phases was connected through a feedback process; the phases were repeated as necessary to develop credible data bases and to bring about meaningful strategic evaluation. Each of these phases is briefly described in the following sections as they were accomplished by this firm.

PHILOSOPHICAL ORIENTATION

A philosophical orientation in project management and the process of strategic planning was believed essential for the project team effort. This orientation included a dialogue in the philosophies and techniques of project management, particularly the organization implications of using project teams, and how authority and responsibility patterns would vary as organizational lines were crossed in the planning process. The orientation phase helped to establish a common language for the project team in dealing with the executives of the organization and provided the climate for the project team to function. Key executives of the organization were present during the orientation period. Their presence not only facilitated the communication process but served to highlight the importance that strategic planning would play in the organization.

ESTABLISHING STRATEGIC-PLANNING STANDARDS

Strategic-planning standards are necessary to facilitate the evaluation of potential market and product strategies and serve to give the project team members an assessment of how well they are doing. The significance of these standards can best be illustrated by citing the primary criteria used to evaluate market opportunity:

Significant (measurable) marketing potential.

Acceptable organizational financial performance.
1. A sales growth to a size of organizational involvement.
2. Income after taxes/sales of 5% in 5 years.
3. Return on equity of not less than 20%.
4. A discounted cash flow return on investment of not less than 15%.
5. An annual sales and profitability growth of 10%.

Acceptable risk versus payoff.

Acceptable level of competition.

An acceptable implementation strategy.

The standards will, of course, depend on the organization's sense of purpose. The above standards are only illustrative.

POSTULATION OF TENTATIVE STRATEGIC PURPOSE

As a point of departure, the chief executive put forth a statement of the business he believed the organization to be currently in and a tentative statement of future business purpose. Project teams made recommendations for the validation, amendment, redirection, etc., of this tentative business purpose as they carried out their analysis work.

DEVELOPMENT OF DATA BASES

A major undertaking of the project teams was to develop data bases for the building of environmental models of the future. Data bases, which include intelligence about future periods as well as the assumptions surrounding this intelligence, were developed in the following areas:

Social changes
Economic factors
Technological progress
Legislative actions
Political expectations
Market potential

These forces were related to the organization's industry to assist in developing an assessment of the anticipated market from both the supply and demand point of view.

ASSESSMENT OF COMPETITION

Simulataneous with the building of the future environmental models, an assessment of the competition was carried out. This assessment contained a review of
the competitors' strengths and weaknesses, financial performance, market strategies, pricing policies, product development practices, and such related material. Insofar as possible, the competitors were studied along parallel lines with
the organization itself. This was not always possible since adequate data on the
competitor were frequently inadequate or lacking. Brainstorming, assumption
construction, war gaming, simulation, etc., were used to augment the inadequate data on competition.

ASSESSMENT OF INTERNAL STRENGTHS AND WEAKNESSES

Too often organizations will do a good analysis of market, environment, and
competitive forces yet fail to look critically at their own organization and its
ability to compete. A task force is especially suited to do such analysis since
the task force tends to subsume parochial organizational loyalties that often
tend to limit one's self-analysis.

A critical part of the self-analysis in this case was the matter of executive
skills and the expected capability of the future strategies to be adequately
implemented within existing executive skills. For example, the project team
concluded that:

> Existing executive and technology administration skills are inadequate to cope with
> the new market that the company intends to enter. Consequently, major effort
> should be put forth to acquire these resources.

The task force report noted further:

> A realistic entry strategy for the market could only be developed if certain competi-
> tor personnel could be persuaded to join our company.

Assessing internal strengths/weaknesses was a challenging and difficult job.
The use of task forces to perform the analysis brought an element of objectivity
to the process that might not otherwise have been obtainable.

EVALUATION OF STRATEGIC OBJECTIVES AND GOALS

It was at this time that the chief executive and his staff began to intensity their
efforts. The data bases had been garnered, the competition analyzed, and the
organization's strengths and weaknesses assessed. The chief executive began
his process of evaluating strategic alternatives. The task force's role at this time
was to recycle data, perform specific analysis, and act as a ''murder board'' for

evaluating emerging strategic alternatives. At the same time the task force began to develop preliminary implementation strategy.

PROPOSAL OF TENTATIVE IMPLEMENTATION STRATEGIES

The project team's work provided an opportunity to propose tentative implementation plans, particularly to test the probability and reality of proposed goals and objectives. This required the project team to address the techniques and skills of administration in the allocation of resources.

The project team played an important adversary role; they asked the questions that managers who sought to protect their parochial interests avoided. For example, a division manager's strategic plan highlighted a simple product line extension for this organization even though the long-term market and competitive data indicated he was in a losing game. The data pooled together by the project team clearly indicated a pessimistic outlook for the product line. This data base was forwarded through the matrix organization on to the chief executive who quickly grasped the need for development of alternative product lines. Had the chief executive depended on this division manager's recommendations without the counsel of the project team, the company might have pursued an irrelevant strategy at an enormous cost.

BUILDING THE STAFF PLANNING ORGANIZATION

Simultaneous with this nine-phase participative effort, the chief executive went about the task of developing a planning staff support organization to interface with, support, and alleviate the burdens placed on line managers during the implementation process. The hope was that the staff planning organization could, during annual cycles after the initial implementation cycle, perform some of the data gathering and analysis tasks that had been performed by task forces in the implementation cycle. This approach was not intended to replace the task force effort, but rather to complement it and to enhance its potential for effectively and efficiently using managerial resources in planning.

The elements of the following subsections represent paraphrasings of materials describing the sort of staff planning organization that was envisioned.

HEADQUARTERS-LEVEL PLANNING ORGANIZATION. The Headquarters-Level Planning Staff should be made up of both analysts and managers who are detailed for one to three year periods to operate as planners. This provides managerial input to planning analysis as well as an educational experience for managers. Specialists that represent the decentralized organizational entities on the planning staff should be responsible for liaison with the planning staff in the decentralized units. These specialists should also represent the decentralized entity's interests in planning activities at the centralized headquarters. Final review of decentralized plans can be conducted by a project team that draws membership from all functional units in planning, decentralized specialists responsible line officials, and the chief planning executive in the organization.

A major element of the central headquarters planning staff should be a management science modeling-oriented group with responsibilities for building decision models and eventually integrating them into a central organizational model. A decision philosophy must be instituted in parallel with a new planning system. This philosophy should recognize that major planning decisions will always be made by managers, but that significant valuable inputs to those decisions can be obtained through management science simulation modeling and other sophisticated techniques. To this end, business simulation models should be further developed at the planning unit level with the expectation that they will be integrated into higher levels over a longer period.

Other sophisticated approaches to planning analysis should be evaluated by the planning group and developed as needed. Of special significance in this set of techniques is technological forecasting, Delphi techniques, and risk analysis using subjective probabilities. Figure 14.4 protrays a staff planning organization and Table 14.1 describes the functional elements in this organization.

THE SENIOR PLANNING EXECUTIVE. Both central headquarters and the decentralized unit planning executives should be people of stature. The senior planning executive of the organization should have outstanding credentials and be recognized as a person of stature in the organization. He should have had in-depth functional experience and tenure as a line or general manager. He must have demonstrated his ability to manage a profit center successfully and have unassailable credentials in both the theory and practice of strategic planning.

The chief planner should have enough seniority to function as a peer with the top operating executives of the organization. If the organization operates through a senior executive management committee, the chief planner should be a member of that group. The image he portrays is crucial to the success of strategic planning. If the chief planner is someone who is waiting out retirement, this fact will not go unrecognized by the other people connected with planning, and their efforts will tend to reflect this image. As the alter ego of the top executive, the chief planner not only must have a first class track record, but also be able to develop rapport with many line and staff people.

People in the organization identified as emerging crown princes should have an early assignment in strategic planning. If this is done, highly motivated young people will view this as a fast way up the organizational ladder; creative talent will tend to gravitate to the strategic-planning activities in the organization and reinforce the planning culture that exists.

TABLE 14.1 / Description of Functions of Planning Organizational Elements on Figure 14.4

1. *Planning Services*	performs planning systems design, development and monitoring
	consulting group for decentralized units
	monitors planning related activities such as promotions, incentives
2. *Financial Analysis*	performs financial analyses of plans submitted by decentralized units
3. *Planning Analysis*	performs nonfinancial analysis of plans submitted by decentralized units
4. *Forecasting*	provides economic, social, political, technological, etc., forecasts for guidance of planning process
5. *Management Science*	performs simulation modeling and evaluates advanced modeling tools for use in planning
6. *Planning Information*	designs, develops, and administers planning data bases and a competitive information system
7. *Decentralized Specialists*	provide liaison with Decentralized Unit Planning Executives and participate in planning review task forces
8. *Planning Review Task Forces*	perform final overall evaluations of plans submitted by decentralized units after individual reviews by planning functional elements (includes reps. from 1–7 plus decentralized planning reps)
9. *Major Project Review Committee*	deals with evaluation of major project proposals. This review committee consists of major line managers who are competing for limited funds as well as representatives of planning staff. Planning staff analysts should make an adversary-like presentation the best case *against* the proposal after a presentation has been made for it. This will give line managers the chance to hear both sides before a decision is made without putting them in the position of direct adversaries.

Contingency Planning for Implementation

The manager who wishes to introduce planning may well find that the time is not right to do so. If the current problems of the organization are so vexing and time consuming that strategic planning cannot be carried out (and this can happen to organizations that are grappling with bad times) then the executive should, as a minimum, try to do the following:

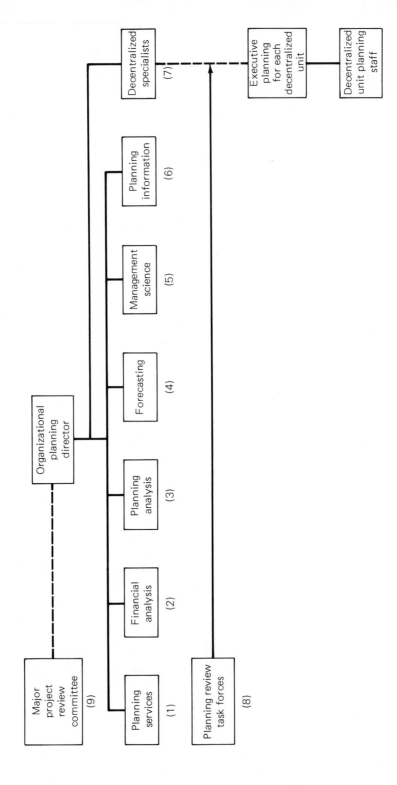

FIGURE 14.4 Proposed planning Organization.

1. Approach each major decision in the organization with the query, "How might this decision affect the organization's future?"
2. Set a future date for launching strategic planning.
3. Develop a set of lessons learned from the current problems that can be related to strategic-planning failures.
4. Assemble a bibliography on strategic planning and circulate pertinent material to key line and staff executives.
5. Hold some workshops on the subject of strategic planning as a prelude to developing a formal system.

The foregoing actions will help to keep the idea of strategic planning alive in the minds of key personnel and should help to strengthen the need for the process. Some of the concepts and techniques of strategic planning are bound to rub off! In times of organizational disaster this may be about all of the strategic planning that an organization can afford. But it is well to keep the idea active in the minds of the executives who will eventually become actively involved in planning.

Summary

The introduction of a planning system into an organization is a significant change with which the organizational participants must cope. Just as planning leads to changes in products, job assignments, etc. so a new way of planning represents a significant change. The effective introduction of this change (the planning system) requires that an implementation strategy be consciously developed. Such a strategy considers the timing of the introduction of various elements of a new planning system, the ways in which the support of top management may be gained and used to good effect, the allocation of time to the process of implementing the planning system, and the explication of the need for and benefits of the planning system.

If implementation considerations have been incorporated into the systems design strategy, the implementation of the planning system should be relatively easy. If this has not been done, the planning system may represent such a threat to managers that it will be ignored or even sabotaged.

A plan for implementing planning should therefore be developed at the earliest possible moment in the process of introducing a planning system into an organization. Such a plan can guide the design process as well as the implementation of the planning system. It serves to ensure that the same principles are used to guide the development of the planning system as the system will itself impose on the development of organizational strategy.

Chapter 14—Questions and Exercises

1. The greatest obstruction to change in organizations may lie in the planning process. What is the reason for this?
2. An innovative strategic-planning system itself represents change to the organization. Such change may be threatening to individuals in the organization. How can this threat factor be reduced?
3. What are the two interrelated components in a change strategy?
4. What is meant by using strategic planning as the common denominator for managing an organization?
5. The authors suggest a gradual approach to implementing strategic planning in organizations. Why do you suppose they have taken this position? What might happen if the strategy were not gradual?
6. How can a chief executive motivate strategic planning on the part of his subordinate managers?
7. If a university wished to launch a strategic-planning effort through a series of planning workshops, what might be appropriate subjects for these workshops? What administrator at the university might be the logical one to assume the chairmanship for the operation of these workshops? Should students participate in these workshops?
8. If a church organization decided to initiate a strategic-planning approach in their organization through a series of workshops, what might be the appropriate people in the community to participate in such workshops? Would it be worthwhile to spend some time in these workshops to discuss "what business the church is in?" Isn't the mission of a church organization obvious to all? If so, won't the discussion of it lead to boredom?
9. There are many reasons why strategic planning fails in organizations; conversely, there are many reasons why strategic planning succeeds. Develop a set of statements describing why you believe strategic planning succeeds or fails. What are the lessons to be learned from such a list?
10. The chief executive's attitude toward strategic opportunities in the organization is reflected in the attitudes of his subordinate managers. Why is this so?
11. What is meant by the statement: " . . . operating managers as well as the chief executive must be committed to developing a strategic awareness in their management of an organization?"
12. Why should the adequacy of delegation of authority in an organization be an important first step in setting up a strategic-planning system?
13. What are planning needs?
14. The strategic-planning systems design approach that is most appropriate in initiating a planning system focuses on incorporating the system users into the design process. Who are these users?
15. The strategic-planning systems design process involves the construction of three different models of a Linear Responsibility Chart variety. Identify and explain these three models.
16. What is a plan for implementing planning? What should be the major elements of such a plan?

17. In one large U.S. corporation, the current problems of that corporation simply preclude any real effort being given to strategic planning by the chief executives. What might such executives do to keep the idea of strategic planning alive in the organization until the time is more appropriate?

18. Addressing the question of Where are we today? is a useful point of departure for initiating a strategic planning system in an organization. Why is this so?

19. What role can an outside consultant play in helping an organization initiate a strategic-planning system? What part of planning should such a consultant attempt to do?

20. What is the value in developing a network plan for the introduction of corporate strategic planning? Demonstrate this value using the example of Figure 14.3.

21. Develop a linear responsibility chart for your family. Show how various family members play roles in the various activities that the family routinely performs.

Chapter 14—Strategic Questions for the Manager

1. What provisions exist for implementing strategic planning in the organization? Is there a strategy for the development of strategy?

2. Are there effective organizational policies and procedures that emphasize the opportunity for participation in the development of organizational strategies?

3. Do the key managers and planners recognize that an existing strategy may in fact be obsolete?

4. How would the key managers and planners in the organization assess the climate for innovation?

5. Do the key executives exhibit a commitment to succeed in strategic planning? Do these executives demonstrate by their words and actions that strategic planning is important to the organization?

6. Does the implementation strategy for strategic planning provide for a process of slowly introducing change? Are provisions provided for gradually expanding the change element to the rest of the organization?

7. Has the question of attitude changed relating to strategic planning been addressed? Has thought been given to using outside consultants to conduct planning workshops designed to motivate a need for strategic planning within the organization?

8. Have the essentials of the planning process, the expected outcome of planning and the process for soliciting ideas about strategic decision, been considered in the organization?

9. How has the question of where we are today been addressed in terms of current organizational problems and opportunities?

10. Have discussions been held in the organization concerning the effectiveness of current planning? Have such questions as what went right? what went wrong? how might the planning effectiveness be improved? been addressed?

11. Has the chief executive of the organization ever held private personal discussions with his key managers about strategic planning?

12. What things might have been done differently in the organization if a successful strategic-planning system were in operation?

13. Have the maximum of operational matters been delegated in the organization in order to provide more time for key managers to think about the organization's future?
14. Are major decisions in the organization addressed with the query "How might this organization's future be affected by this decision?"

References

Arthur D. Little Co., "Patterns and Problems of Technological Innovation in American History," Report C-65344, Cambridge, Mass., 1963.

Currill, D. L. "Introducing Corporate Planning: A Case History," *Long Range Planning,* Vol. 10, No. 4, Aug. 1977.

Galbraith, J. K., *The New Industrial State,* Houghton-Mifflin, Boston, 1967.

Gilmore, F. F., and Brandenburg, R. G., "Anatomy of Corporate Planning," *Harvard Business Review,* Nov.–Dec. 1962.

Hunt, M. M., "Bell Labs' 230 Long-Range Planners," *Fortune,* Vol. 49, May 1954, pp. 120–123 and 129–136.

Kirby, W. E., "Where Long-Range Planning Goes Wrong," *Management Review,* May 1962, pp. 11–12.

Kraar, L., "The Japanese Are Coming With Their Own Style of Management," *Fortune,* March 1975.

Kudla, R. J., "Elements of Effective Corporate Planning," *Long Range Planning,* Vol. 9, No. 4, Aug. 1976.

Linneman, R. E., and Kennell, J. D., "Shirt-Sleeve Approach to Long-Range Plans," *Harvard Business Review,* Mar.–Apr. 1977.

Mackenzie, R. A., "The Management Process in 3D," *Harvard Business Review,* 1969.

Payne, B., "Steps in LRP," *Harvard Business Review,* March-April 1957.

Pennington, M. W., "Why Has Planning Failed?," *Long Range Planning,* March 1972.

Schultz, R. L., and Sleving, D. P. (eds), *Implementing Operations Research Management Science,* American Elsevier Co., New York, 1975.

Steiner, G. A., "How to Improve Your Long-Range Planning," presented at the 16th Institute Conference on Corporate Planning, Chicago, Illinois, March 8, 1974.

Taylor, R. W., "Psychological Aspects of Planning," *Long Range Planning,* Vol. 9, No. 2, April 1976.

Chapter 15

PLANNING
EVALUATION
AND CONTROL

The planning management subsystem consists of all of those activities and processes necessary for the management of planning. Some of these activities have been treated in Chapter 14 in the context of implementing planning. These implementation concerns recognize that, as with any other choice, a decision to plan more effectively does not mean that more effective planning will ensue. The decision to have the organization do better planning cannot merely be made and ordered into being; it must be implemented, monitored and controlled if it is to have the desired effect.

Planning must be managed in much the same way as any other organizational activity, for unless those activities and processes that are generally thought of as comprising good management are applied to it, the planning activity will inevitably lose its direction and focus. This is true at the onset of formalized planning, when the good intentions of top managers and planners must be translated into reality. It is also true for an established planning process, which must be re-evaluated and changed to adapt to changing organizational and environmental conditions.

Thus, all of the activities and processes that constitute the field of management can be applied to the strategic-planning activities of the organization. Since both the systems design and implementation aspects of good planning management have been addressed in the previous chapter, it remains for us here to deal with the follow up aspects of good management (evaluation and control) as they apply to the strategic-planning system.

The Need for Planning Evaluation and Control

The concept of planning evaluation and control implies that both the *process* and *results* of strategic planning must be evaluated periodically to ask such questions as: What went right? What went wrong? How might our strategic planning processes be improved? A planning system that does not have a strategy for review and improvement of the efficacy of strategic-planning efforts in the organization is unlikely to achieve its fullest potential.

This chapter details some of the ways planning processes and results can be measured and evaluated. We stress the importance for planners accepting the need for a philosophy of control to be applied to strategic planning in much the same way that control techniques are applied to the operating activities of the organization. Thus, strategic-planning evaluation and control becomes a part of the overall management-control function in the organization.

The need for this special variety of control is created by the obvious, but sometimes overlooked, fact that planning is not inherently good. The planning era of the past two decades seems to have led to a degree of ''faith'' in planning per se which may not be justified. Poor planning may be worse than no planning at all merely because no planning really means an absence of *organized* planning activities. In a no planning environment, planning is done in a decentralized and often uncoordinated way which may sometimes be superior to organized planning that is done badly.

Thus, if planning is to be effective and constitute a positive force for organizational change, it must be good planning. Yet, it is difficult to distinguish between good planning and poor planning on a prima facie basis. The outputs from planning processes that vary greatly in quality may look very much alike when the plan is produced. It is only upon careful perusal and after time has elapsed that the quality can definitively be assessed.

Such careful perusal and tracking of planning as is required will simply not occur unless a formal process is developed for doing it. Many organizations have made the error of thinking that this is not so and found that the relief that comes from knowing that the annual planning cycle is completed is not conducive to careful evaluation and control of planning and of the plans that the planning process produces. Such organizations blunder from one planning cycle to the next with little attention to building on the outdated plans or to improving those elements of the process that did not prove to be effective. In doing so, they repeat the mistakes of history and eventually conclude that the planning process is itself not valuable. Periods of high planning activity followed by periods of low planning activity in many organizations attest to the pervasiveness of this phenomenon.

Indeed, the simple process of reviewing last year's plans before beginning a new planning cycle can be very enlightening and can lead to improvements in planning. One planning executive told the authors that, upon assuming his planning position, he had sought copies of the plans developed over the past ten years. These were very difficult to obtain, but the persistent executive even went to the length of seeking out executives who had left the company to find if they possessed copies. When he finally obtained all of the plans, he summarized their significance with a chart such as that shown in Figure 15.1.

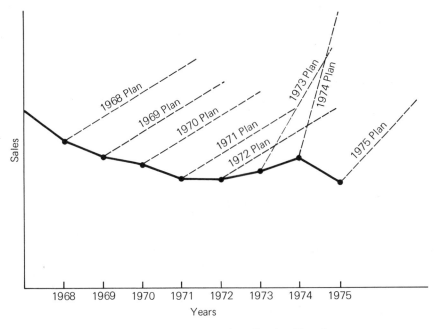

FIGURE 15.1 Illustration of Ineffective Planning.

The plans which are succinctly described in dotted lines in Figure 15.1 show a continuing optimism that is not borne out by the actual performance shown in the solid line. Each year's plans foresee either a turnaround or an acceleration in sales growth, which is never realized. From 1968 through 1971, the anticipated turnaround did not occur. In 1972, its occurrence signalled even greater planning optimism that continued until an unforeseen downturn in 1975, at which point the sort of planning that always foresees a coming turnaround appears to begin anew.

Perhaps there is no better way to demonstrate the need for continuous planning evaluation and control than to see a graph such as Figure 15.1 and to realize that such planning takes place each year in many business firms and public agencies.

Planning Control Systems

To control is to constrain activities in consonance with plans that have been established. In this case, the activities to be controlled are the activities and outputs of the planning process itself.

Since the planning process is complex, this suggests the need for a planning evaluation and control system. The description of a *control system* calls to mind our earlier definition of a system as a collection of interrelated and interdependent parts or subsystems collectively seeking an objective or goal. In any control system, there are necessary elements—an objective, inputs, outputs, etc. These elements are outlined below for a strategic-planning evaluation and control system.

1. An *Objective*—a strategy for the development of strategy which establishes the purpose of and the results desired from the strategic-planning system of the organization.
2. *Inputs*—internal audit, environmental and competitive information that predicts what the world is expected to look like in the future for the organization.
3. *Outputs*—information reflecting the missions, objectives, strategies, programs, and resource allocations that have been selected.
4. A *Sequence*—indicating the precedence of actions for converting inputs into outputs, which is the planning process itself.
5. *Resources*—the current state of commitment of organizational resources supporting the development of strategies.
6. *Feedback Loops*—information to evaluate existing strategies and the efficacy of the planning system and to institute corrective action as needed.
7. *Standards*—against which the process and its output may be compared.
8. An *Environmental Setting*—a facilitative organizational structure to permit the development and critical evaluation of existing strategies and of the planning system.

All of these essential elements of a strategic planning evaluation and control system have been treated in previous chapters except one: the *standards* against which the planning process is to be compared.

Planning Standards

Planning standards may be both process and output oriented, i.e., they may be standards against which the planning *process* is to be compared or standards against which the planning output (the plan) is to be compared.

STANDARDS FOR THE PLAN

One company developed the checklist shown in Table 15.1 as a basis for guiding the evaluation of the comprehensiveness and worth of its planning. Note

TABLE 15.1 Guidelines for the Evolution of Planning

Strategy for Development of Strategy

Assignment of authority and responsibility for developing organizational strategy
Reward system for effective planning
Facilitative organizational structure and process for strategic planning
Organizational climate which stimulates innovation and creativity
Strategic planning milestone charts
Specific planned inputs and outputs required at each stage of process standards for planning documentation

Analysis of Present Position

Current problems, successes, failures
Current market performance
Production, financial, research and development strengths and weaknesses
Personnel capabilities
Customer image
Adequacy of organizational structure

Analysis of Past Performance

Financial performance trends
Marketing strengths and weaknesses
Major successes and failures
Production and logistics effectiveness

Competitive Audit

Strengths and weaknesses of most threatening competitors
Probable strategies and tactics
Technological, financial, production, market capabilities
Effectiveness of leadership
Performance differentials between competitors and own company

Environmental Factors

Analysis and projection of key political, economic, legal, social and technological systems
Adequate, timely, and relevant quantitative and qualitative data bases
Trends and rate of change factors
What counts for success in the industry?

Objectives and Goals

Compatibility with organizational strengths and weaknesses
Compatibility with environmental forces
Problems with current objectives and goals
Measurability and support ability of goals and objectives
Probability of attainment

Evaluation of Alternatives

Adequacy of data bases and evaluation procedures
Invention, design, and evaluation of new alternatives
Asking of most ridiculous, searching, compelling questions
Which alternatives offer the best competitive advantage?

TABLE 15.1 (continued)

Contingency Strategies

Identification of key contingency events
Modification of objectives, goals, and strategies to meet contingencies
Confidence levels in forecasts, assumptions, and strategies
Uncertainty levels in key environmental and competitive events
"What if everything went wrong" analysis?

Implementation Strategies

Adequacy of organizational structure and management processes
Established landmarks and milestones to measure strategic credibility
Performance standards
Allocation of resources, authority, and responsibility
Suitable organizational culture

Feedback Mechanisms

Reporting of deviations from performance standards
Budget variance
Strategic policy review
Mechanisms for strategic review
Resource allocation review

---

that most of the items in the table are output oriented rather than process orien-ted. This checklist was not intended to be all-inclusive; rather it was meant to be used as a guideline for delineating some of the primary factors that have to be evaluated in evaluating a strategic plan.

STANDARDS FOR THE PLANNING SYSTEM

The planning system may itself be evaluated in terms of a set of standards. These standards are the criteria on which the planning system design was to be based. The issue of the standards to be applied to a planning system is therefore a simple one: "To what degree does the system do what it was intended to do?" "Does the system entail those elements and features that were established for it?"

In terms of the planning system outlined in this book, the criteria, or basic premises, were stated in the Preface as follows:

1. Professional planners can facilitate a planning process, but they cannot themselves do the organization's planning.
2. Planning activities should be performed by the managers who will ul-timately be responsible for the implementation of the plans.
3. Creative strategic planning is inherently a group activity, since it must involve many different subunits of the organization and many different varieties of expertise.

4. A "planning organization" must be created to deal with the conception and development of strategic plans. This organization provides the climate and mechanisms through which individuals at various levels are provided a greater opportunity to participate in determining the organization's future.

5. Strategic planning involves much more than numerical extrapolations of trends; it involves as well the selection of missions, objectives, and strategic alternatives.

6. Managers must be motivated to spend time on strategic planning through a formalized system and organization approach that also permits their contribution to the planning process to be assessed.

7. The planning process must provide for the development of relevant data bases, qualitative as well as quantitative, that facilitate the development of environmental forecasts and the evaluation of strategic alternatives.

8. An evaluation of future environmental trends, competitive threats, and internal organizational strengths and weaknesses is essential to the strategic planning process.

9. Evolving ideas within the organization provide the point of departure to develop future products and markets.

10. The chief executive's responsibility for developing future organizational strategy centers around the development of a "strategic culture" in the organization, the final evaluation and selection of strategic alternatives, and the design of a master plan of implementation for those alternatives.

Both the plan and the planning system may be evaluated in terms of the standards of Table 15.1 and the preceding list *as soon as the system and plan have been developed and exist in final form.* Of course, the final evaluation of both the plan and the system can be made only after a period of time has elapsed over which the process has been used and the strategic choices reflected in the plan have been put into effect.

Evaluating the Planning System

The primary measure through which a planning process can be evaluated is the *quality* of the choices reflected in the plan, not merely the nature of its content. Thus, the quality of these strategic choices is the only valid measure of the worth of a planning system. However, a checklist such as that of Table 15.1 reflects a first approximation to a measure of a planning system's worth. This is so because the quality of the choices reflected in a plan are difficult to assess except after a long time period has elapsed, a characteristic that is inherent in the nature of strategic choice. Moreover, despite the fact that some simple performance measure may be reflected in a plan, such as the sales measure applied in Figure 16.1, many of the bases for evaluating the quality of a plan are qualitative in nature.

Two basic questions represent a valid starting point for evaluating the quality of a planning system:

1. What actions are reflected in the plan that probably would not otherwise have been taken?
2. What actions that might otherwise have been taken have been foregone as a result of the planning process?

Despite the generality of these two questions, it is usually possible for the top managers of an organization to make an explicit listing in response to each. This is especially easy in the case of a newly introduced planning system. If such answers are developed as soon as the plan is finalized, it can provide a basis for the continuing planning evaluation and control process. If answers to these questions are not made explicit, it will subsequently be much more difficult to ferret out those things that were a direct result of planning and those that would have taken place with or without planning.

Once lists have been made in response to each of these basic questions, it will usually be possible to identify specific actions with specific phases or elements of the planning process. For instance, if a task force planning effort identified a new product opportunity, the relationship of that product to that planning element should be noted. Alternately, if a strategic data base identified strategic business factors that eventually led to a decision not to follow a specific line of research and development, this should also be noted.

After a period of time has elapsed, it will be possible to begin evaluating the quality of the choices and relating these evaluations to phases or elements of the planning system. For instance, a new product that is successful lends credibility to the task force process that produced the idea. Similarly, a foregone product idea introduced successfully by a competitor detracts from the worth attributed to those planning elements that suggested that the opportunity be foregone.

Through this process, over time, a planning system may be thoroughly evaluated in terms of both the quality of the strategic choices that it produced and the relationship of those choices to the various elements of the process.

The Control Aspect of Planning

The control of the plan and the strategic choices it reflects is directed toward either maintaining the direction established in the plan or determining that a mid-course correction must be made. It is the fear of following an obsolete strategy that haunts most managers. The challenge that faces the strategic manager is simple to pose but difficult to meet: How to test periodically the validity and credibility of selected strategies? How to establish *strategic checkpoints?*

One might post a simple solution to this challenge: provide a *continuous* planning process within the organization. One can argue for the need for such a continuous planning process, but such a continuous process is probably more theoretical than real. Most managers, and in particular *general managers,* simply have too much to do in serving their diverse clientele to significantly engage in formalized planning on a continuous basis.

STRATEGIC CHECKPOINTS

The establishment and review of strategic checkpoints should be done at an organizational echelon immediately above the echelon that has developed the strategy. The principal function of such a review is to determine if competitive, environmental, and internal organizational forces have developed to justify continuing a particular course of action, or alternatively, to redirect the strategy. This review should examine the strategic alternates and the present organizational direction by:

1. Checking the credibility of alternatives, objectives, goals and supporting strategies by probing into the underlying assumptions and data bases.
2. Creating, where necessary, other alternative strategies and objectives for further consideration.
3. Reviewing the effect on the employment of organizational resources, in relation to the planned resource allocation scheme.

Strategic checkpoints are benchmarks that may be used to evaluate progress toward the fulfillment of a given strategy. These benchmarks establish thresholds of organizational performance which, if met, establish the validity of a given strategy. Examples of such benchmarks might include:

Percentage share gain in existing market.

Degree of penetration of a new market.

Specific financial goals within a stipulated time period.

Degree of customer acceptance.

Emergence of certain environmental conditions, e.g., passage of National Health legislation.

Advancement of state-of-the-art leading to anticipated technological breakthrough.

Meeting or exceeding competitor actions.

Development of executive talent.

Percentage of reduction of known risk.

Corporate exposure and vulnerability.

The strategic checkpoints along the pathway of a strategy must be designed to become an inherent part of the planning system. A review of the checkpoints for each strategy should be accomplished within the context of periodic overall strategy reviews. The people that accomplish the review should be given a clear mandate to function in an adversary capacity, to call the shots as they are, and not as they should be or as someone wants them. An executive may be blinded to the realities of the situation because of his pride of plan authorship. Often such an executive is unable to see the realities of the situation and cannot evaluate objectively progress toward an objective or goal. The determination of strategic checkpoints for review can help to determine if a strategy is emerging as contemplated, and the necessary corrective action can be taken.

THE REVIEW PROCESS

The continuing review of strategic plans starts with the development of a strategy for the development of strategy. Although this may appear as a play on words, what is meant is that the review process has to be planned as an outgrowth of the documentation and processes that guide planning in the organization. We offer a few criteria for this review process:

1. The process must be disciplined with specific inputs and outputs required for each step of the review.
2. The review must be systematized with specific activities scheduled according to a schedule that provides feedback on an exception basis to the executives who control organizational resources.
3. The review should be done on some cyclical basis which provides all organizational levels a chance to conduct their planning and participate in reviews in an orderly fashion.
4. Standards for the documentation of plans and data bases should be included so that uniformity in the quality and quantity of the written material can be ensured.
5. The review should provide for the integration of internal, competitive, and environmental data affecting the organization and its strategies.

6. Whenever possible task forces, peer groups and similar organizational mechanisms should be provided for the review to facilitate a checks and balances approach. This safeguards against organizational and disciplinary parochialism in the organization.

The review itself should start with each strategic checkpoint and proceed *generally* along lines similar to the strategic planning process model portrayed in Chapter 4. The data bases supporting each of these steps should be available for analysis. The critical assumptions should be evaluated, first in terms of the degree of confidence in the assumption, and second in terms of the degree of influence the organization has over the assumption. An assumption concerning a competitor's actions is obviously less controllable than an assumption concerning the application of internal resources to a strategy, for instance. If the data base and the assumptions surrounding the data base are risky, then they should become candidates for an even more thorough examination.

CONTINGENCY PLANNING—TRIGGER POINTS

If the organization has performed its planning to incorporate the contingency planning approach, it has identified strategic trigger points. These trigger points are similar to the strategic checkpoints noted earlier, except that they identify specific levels of some indicators that are to automatically trigger action, or at least review. For instance, a trigger point might involve the rate of growth of GNP, e.g., "if the rate of growth of GNP falls in a quarter below the prior year's level, our strategy should be reviewed (changed)." Such a trigger point would indicate that the current plan is intrinsically tied to a forecasted greater growth rate in GNP. It also indicates that a prior strategic choice has been made that the plan should be discarded and a contingency plan or strategy should be adopted in its place should the forecasted GNP not transpire.

In theory, a specific contingency plan should be available that would be automatically adopted once a trigger point is reached. In practice, while contingency plans must be available, they are rarely adopted on such a routine basis. Usually, the occurrence of a trigger point means that a previously-prepared contingency plan is dusted off and reviewed for possible implementation.

REASSESSING STRATEGY

Once a series of strategic checkpoints are reviewed or trigger points have been identified as having occurred, it may be necessary to reassess and alter the organization's strategy on other strategic choice elements. Such strategy revisions should be undertaken only after the same level of analysis has been applied as was initially used in the selection of the strategy. If this direction is followed, it will prevent the panicky and premature altering of a sound strategy that may momentarily appear to be ineffective.

The key questions should be, "Why is the strategy not working?," and, "Why do we believe that a proposed revised strategy will work any better?" If these questions cannot be definitely answered, it is probably wise to postpone a strategy change. This philosophy will avoid the implicit choice of an all-too-common strategy: "Don't just stand there, do something!"

Moreover, this approach avoids the alteration of strategies before they have had an opportunity to take effect and have impact. Almost no strategy had immediate discernible impact and some good strategies may require time before they can produce impact even in the desired direction. Few managers expect a new product to break-even in its first month, yet some behave as though other complex strategies should not require the same break in period. Such premature strategy change can lead to no strategy at all, because since a strategy is a general direction, frequently changing strategies provide no coherent direction.

However, if the resons for the failure of a strategy can be isolated and the reasons that a revised strategy is expected to be successful can be delineated convincingly, a strategy choice should be made. For instance, Bridewater et al,[1] illustrates a strategy change based on changing assumptions and forecasts. This change, shown in Table 15.2, incorporates an original strategy that was presented in Chapter 7 as well as a revised strategy along with the assumptions on which each is based. In the after case, changing assumptions about consumer behavior and changing forecasts concerning growth have led to significant strategy revisions.

The Psychological Aspect of Control

This view of contingency planning as a guiding theme that controls planning, rather than as a system to which one slavishly adheres, is consistent with the philosophy of control. Just as a plan should not be considered as cast in concrete, so too a control mechanism should not be applied without regard to the current judgments of the strategic manager.

Thus, people perform control; not machines, computers, or procedures. People must institute corrective action to redirect organizational resources toward the objectives and goals. Drucker[2] notes:

> . . . One has to realize that even the most powerful 'instrument board' complete with computers, operations research, and simulation, is secondary to the invisible,

---

[1] Bridgewater, B. A., Jr., Clifford, D. K., and Hardy, T., "The Competition Game Has Changed," *Business Horizons,* October 1975.

[2] Drucker, P. F., *Management: Tasks, Responsibilities, Practices,* Harper and Row, New York, 1973, p. 505.

TABLE 15.2* Before and After Strategies and Their Assumption Bases

THE "GIVENS"	STRATEGIC IMPLICATIONS

BEFORE

Consumer will put premium on convenience, range of choice, and diversity

Volume gains possible through new products

→ Emphasize value-added products

→ Enrich mix via new forms, sizes, varieties, products, private label lines

→ Emphasize marketing and distribution

→ Open more and bigger stores

Spending on nonfood items will rise sharply

→ Stimulate volume through promotion

→ Broaden mix with nonfood lines

→ Diversify into other consumer goods and services

AFTER

Consumers are increasingly price-conscious—putting premium on value, nutrition

→ Focus development on nutrition, on building value into products

→ Prune, take out marginal, uneconomical forms, sizes, varieties

Potential growth in absolute volume is limited → Emphasize cost control, resource utilization, productivity

Consumers have less to spend on non food items

→ Promote more selectively

→ Focus on core business

→ Get out of unsuccessful nonfood ventures

*Adapted from Bridgewater, B. A., Jr., Clifford, D. K., and Hardy, T., "The Competition Game Has Changed," *Business Horizons*, October 1975.

qualitative control of any human organization, its systems of rewards and punishments, of values and taboos.

In managing (controlling) the strategic planning process, the chief executive must depend on the quality and motivation of his managers. Further delegation of planning control by these managers requires confidence in their abilities and motivation to seek objectivity and rigor in the strategic planning process.

TOP EXECUTIVE ATTITUDES

Control is inherently a process operating through people in the organization. People evaluate strategic planning-related information through a feedback process and initiate corrective action to get things back on track. Management control, according to Anthony, "is essentially applied social psychology." [3] An important aspect of control, albeit subtle in its operation, is the attitude that the chief executives of the organization profess and demonstrate about the value of strategic planning in the organization. The chief executive and other key executives charged with the responsibility for developing and executing strategic plans must be deeply committed to strategic planning. This means more than just a verbal commitment, it means committing top talent's time and energies to developing strategic plans and using these plans as a basis for decision making. Such a commitment of top management also means designing and operating a disciplined process for evaluating the soundness of the plans and the planning process itself, actively participating in counseling junior managers in the values and techniques of strategic planning, and setting up a reward system that recognizes the strategic as well as the operational contributions that executives have made to the organization.

A chief executive can do much to instill a strategic sense of responsibility in the organization by the example that he sets through frequently asking questions such as the following whenever important matters come before him: What will be the strategic impact of this decision? Have we addressed the relationship this decision has to our long-term objectives and goals? Does this decision commit our organization to a particular direction in the future whose total impact has not been fully measured? Such a constant querying of subordinates in strategic terms motivates them to have the answers prepared when the next issue arises. Thus, the middle managers are motivated to think strategically.

Indeed, the chief executive's actions may speak louder than all the pronouncements he can make about the value of strategic planning. For example, if the chief executive is willing to sacrifice longer term aspects of the strategic plan to short-term operational achievements such as short-term profitability, then his behavior will be emulated by subordinate managers. Such managers quickly perceive how their performance is to be evaluated, whether by short-term results or by a combination of current effectiveness and ability to develop a strategic direction for the organization. Remember that:

> . . . The president who keeps his organization involved continuously in appraising its performance against its goals, appraising its goals against the company's concept of its place in its industry and in society, and debating openly and often the continued validity of its strategy will find corporate attention to strategic questions gradually proving effective in letting the organization know what it is, what its activities are about, where it is going, and why its existence and growth are worth the best contributions of its members. [4]

[3] Anthony, R. N., Dearden, J., and Vancil, R. F., *Management Control Systems: Text, Cases and Readings,* Richard D. Irwin, Homewood, Ill., 1972, p. 8.

[4] Christensen, C. R., Andrews, K. R., and Bower, J. L., *Business Policy, Text and Cases,* Richard D. Irwin, Homewood, Ill., 1973, p. 867.

If the chief executive participates directly in the planning reviews and is able to demonstrate that he has thoroughly examined each subunit's strategic plan, the subordinate managers will be motivated to do likewise.

AN EXAMPLE OF STRATEGIC AWARENESS. In a very large company known to the authors, the chief executive does just this and more. This chief executive believes (and demonstrates by his actions) that the name of the game is strategy through strategic planning. Here are some of the things that he does to make this pronouncement credible:

1. He reads each strategic plan that his 1st and 2nd tier operational managers have put together.
2. He participates directly in the review of these plans along with his operational managers and staff people.
3. When strategic issues are at stake he confronts these issues by bringing together relevant people in a problem-solving environment, without regard to organizational level but rather based on the individual's ability to contribute to the strategic question.
4. He holds regular workshops on strategic planning dealing with the theory and practice of planning and addressing such questions as: What went right? What went wrong? How can we improve on a strategic planning process?
5. He insists that each major decision or policy that is addressed by top management be related in *specific terms* to the strategic planning of the corporation.
6. He provides an executives' incentive system which rewards line (and certain key staff people) for short-term profitability *and* strategic planning results.
7. He provides for decentralization of planning with tight guidelines for the planning process, a stringent review, but considerable latitude for the details of planning format.

It is easy to recognize the importance that strategic planning has in this company, for the chief executive's leadership in planning is evident in both his words and actions.

Rewards and Punishments for Planning Effectiveness

One of the ways in which a desire for the good management of some activity is often translated into practice is through the institution of a system of rewards and punishments. Most enterprises have formal or informal systems to reward and punish managers for performance. In business firms, these systems are often reflected through formalized incentive or bonus schemes that directly tie monetary rewards to the organization's performance.

This may be accomplished on an overall basis, as with a profit sharing system through which individuals are rewarded in proportion to the profits that accrue to the corporation as a whole. The system also may operate on a profit center scheme, in which individual units are designated as profit centers and their managers are rewarded in proportion to the profit center's performance which they presumably directly control to a large degree.

THE FUTURE VERSUS THE PRESENT

Whatever may be the reward system concept, rewards are usually tied more directly to *current performance* than to *planning performance*. This is so primarily because it is so difficult to assess the quality of an individual's performance in planning relative to the degree of difficulty that exists in assessing current performance. The bottom line may fairly well reflect the present, but it may inadequately reflect the future potential created by current strategic decisions.

There are many managers who have used the bias of reward systems toward the present as a basis for personal advancement that is detrimental to the organization's future. A goal of maximizing current profit will inevitably lead to shortchanging the future in terms of current investments from which the primary return will be in the future. If this is done, it can lead to good current performance, but it will invariably lead to long-run difficulties.

Steiner[5] has put it well in saying:

> No manager will spend time on long-range planning if top management does not review his plans and give him some sort of feedback, and if his personal financial well being is based strictly on the bottom line of his annual profit and loss statement.

Reward systems that permit the trading off of the long run for performance in the short run will inevitably catch up with someone. In some cases, however, the individual who is responsible will have moved on to other responsibilities. When the difficulties that result from past failures to invest in the future come to light, such an individual will usually disclaim responsibility, and it is difficult in such circumstances to prove that he is responsible.

Thus, a good reward system should provide planning payoffs for the creation of future potential performance as well as for current performance. Moreover, a good system will provide a basis for tracking the performance of an

---

[5] Steiner, G. A., "How to Improve Your Long-Range Planning," presented at the Sixteenth Institute Conference on Corporate Planning and the Annual Seminar of the Chicago Chapter of the Planning Executive Institute, March 8, 1974, Chicago, Ill.

individual through various jobs so that a record of planning performance is created on which reward decision may be based.

TOP EXECUTIVE'S ROLE IN PLANNING REWARDS

Of course, rewards and punishments for planning performance can probably never be entirely objective as can (presumably) those for current performance. As Drucker[6] has noted:

> . . . There is a fundamental, incurable, basic limitation to controls in a social institution. This lies in the fact that a social institution is both a true entity and a fiction. As an entity it has purposes of its own, a performance of its own, results of its own—and survival and death of its own . . . But a special institution is comprised of persons, each with his own purpose, his own ambitions, his own ideas, his own needs. No matter how authoritarian the institution, it has to satisfy the ambitions and needs of its members, and do so in their capacity as individuals but through *institutional* rewards and punishments, incentives, and deterrents. The expression of this may be quantifiable—such as a raise in salary. But the system itself is not quantitative in character and cannot be quantified.

Because of the inherent qualitative and subjective nature of the system to which Drucker notes, top executives must take much of the responsibility for identifying and rewarding good planning performance. They can do this by taking note, both explicitly and implicitly, of such performance and by promoting those people whose performance has been consistently good. Moreover, they can make it known that such promotions are based, in part, on superior strategic planning performance.

Eventually, it will be necessary to introduce headquarters level control on promotions and incentives to ensure that strategic-planning performance is considered in evaluating executive performance. It should be made clear to general managers that an executive evaluation system will review all proposed promotions and rewards to assess the contributions the individual has made to strategic planning in his organization. In addition, the executive's commitment to planning will, in turn, be evaluated partly on the basis of his use of planning as a criterion for the advancement of his own people. Rewarding executives for strategic planning assumes that a high degree of participation in strategic planning does exist and that planning is being carried out by those executives responsible for implementing the plans. In such circumstances, executives can be encouraged to design strategic planning objectives and goals against which performance can be measured and rewarded. The dialogue that a superior carries out in reviewing this subordinate's strategic planning can help to establish

[6] Drucker, P. F., *Management: Tasks, Responsibilities, Practices*, Harper and Row, New York, p. 504.

TABLE 15.3 Simplified
Profit Center
Profit/Loss Statement

Net Sales Billed	000
Direct Product Costs	000
Gross Product Margin	000
Operating Expense	000
Operating Profit	000
Strategic Expense	000
Organization Profit	000

performance standards to measure efficacy in planning. Simply put, if strategic planning really counts in the organization, then it must be rewarded.

A SIMPLE OPERATING-STRATEGIC DICHOTOMY

However difficult it may be to quantify all of the measures on which planning rewards and punishments are to be based, it is essential that an attempt be made to do so. For instance, Texas Instruments bases current performance on operating profit rather than the overall profit of a profit center. This distinction separates out strategic expense as shown in Table 15.3 to create a measure of operating profit on which current rewards can be based.

Although this simple idea does not resolve the difficulty in determining appropriate rewards for planning performance, it does serve to distinguish between current performance and future performance on an explicit basis. This reflects the basic philosophy expounded by Helms[7] that:

> According to some fundamental law of nature . . . there is a powerful tendency for all resources to gravitate toward a short-term orientation. The inevitable problems and crises occur, and where do you find the resources to handle them? They always come from the strategic programs, because, . . . they are the ones which are postponable. The end result of this process is that, in the absence of restraining forces, after a period of time, all resources are absorbed in short-term activities. This is what happens to the organization which stays so busy that it can never think about the future. It is well down the road toward "playing out its string."

If managers are rewarded for current performance in terms of their operating profit rather than organizational profit, a basis is created for "separating out" strategic performance. One simple view of this might be that high levels of strategic expense represents a commitment to the future. However, of

[7]Helms, E. W., "The OST System for Manager Innovation at Texas Instruments," presented to Armed Forces Management Association, Washington, D.C., April 7, 1971.

course, strategic allocations must be effectively deployed and employed for an assessment of "good planning" to directly follow. This means that an analysis of the efficacy of strategic investments must be carried out as well. However, the separation of the long-run from the short-run is the basic thing that must be accomplished before rewards based on planning performance can be effectively instituted.

Summary

Planning management refers to the process that is used to manage planning activities. This includes the implementation of planning, as treated in Chapter 14 and the evaluation and control of the ongoing planning system.

One of the real problems with sophisticated planning systems is that, although they often produce good plans, the mechanisms for continuous monitoring and evaluation are not as sophisticated as are those for producing the plans. This means that well-founded plans may sometimes go astray because they are not quickly adapted to changing conditions. On the other hand, a lack of evaluation and control mechanisms may lead to ad hoc decisions, made in response to environmental changes, which are inconsistent with the plan. In either case, the worth of planning is significantly reduced.

Because plans are complex, there is a need for a formal control system for planning. Such a system entails planning standards and mechanisms for matching results with the standards. This process of matching obviously cannot take place continuously. Strategic checkpoints should be defined at which planning results are reviewed and evaluated in terms that will permit the reassessment of strategy.

The broader psychologic aspects of control should also be considered in the design of a planning control system. Since people are the ultimate control mechanisms, they must be motivated to continuously assess performance with respect to the plan, to suggest changes in the plan when environmental changes appear to warrant such action, to act within the scope of the plan, and to report deviations from the plan for assessment at higher levels. If such motivation is coupled with a reward system that truly recognizes the contribution of individuals to planning and to the planning control function, sophisticated planning has a chance of significantly improving organizational effectiveness.

Chapter 15—Questions and Exercises

1. What are the components of the planning management subsystem?
2. A decision to plan more effectively in an organization does not mean that more effective planning will ensue. Why is this so?

3. All of the activities and processes that constitute the field of management can be applied to the strategic-planning activities of the organization. Explain what is meant by this statement. Demonstrate by example that such a statement has validity.

4. What is the classical control cycle in management theory? How can this control cycle be applied to strategic planning?

5. Where should one start in setting up a planning evaluation and control system?

6. The strategic-planning cycle that many companies follow in doing strategic planning can work against effective strategic planning. Why?

7. Define the concept of control. Relate that definition to the strategic-planning process.

8. Develop a planning control system in model form. Relate the elements of this control system to a strategic-planning system.

9. What are planning standards? What are some examples? What role do these planning standards play in the planning process?

10. What is the primary measure through which a planning process can be evaluated? What are the two basic questions that can represent a valid starting point for evaluating the quality of a planning system?

11. To test periodically the validity and credibility of selected strategies a series of strategic checkpoints have to be established. What is a strategic checkpoint? Who should be responsible for establishing such checkpoints?

12. What value can an adversary role play in the testing of strategic checkpoints?

13. What are some criteria for designing a review process for strategic planning? Who should participate in such a review? Who should have the responsibility for seeing that such a review is carried out?

14. What is the relationship between contingency planning and strategic checkpoints? What is an example of a contingency plan?

15. The bottom line may fairly well reflect the present, but it may inadequately reflect the future potential of the organization. What is meant by this statement?

16. If a manager's reward system emphasizes the short-term performance of his organization, he will not be motivated to do strategic planning. Why?

17. The continuing review of strategic plans starts with the development of a strategy for the development of strategy. What does this mean?

18. What is the value in using task forces, peer groups, and similar organizational mechanisms in the strategic planning review?

19. What are some of the key questions to be asked in reassessing an organization's strategy?

Chapter 15—Strategic Questions for the Manager

1. Do key managers and planners accept the principle that the salient activities and processes of management can be applied to the strategic activities of the organization?

2. Have the concepts of control, evaluating and guiding progress to objectives and goals, been integrated into the strategic planning system?

3. Have the successes and failures of previous years' strategic plans been evaluated to determine the credibility and accuracy of these historical plans?
4. What strategic planning standards have been developed in the organization? Are these standards both *process* and *output* oriented?
5. Has any consideration been given to developing a strategic checklist as a basis for guiding the evaluation and efficacy of strategic planning within the organization?
6. Are strategic planning activities being performed by those managers who are ultimately responsible for the implementation of the plans?
7. Has a planning organization been created to deal with the conception and development of strategic planning? Does this planning organization provide the mechanism and the climate for assessing future opportunities and problems?
8. Are relevant data bases, qualitative and quantitative, developed to facilitate the planning process?
9. What motivational techniques exist to encourage key managers to spend adequate time on strategic planning?
10. How is the quality of strategic choices determined in the organization? Who maintains quality control over this process?
11. Has the organization ever followed an obsolete strategy? Why was this obsolete strategy followed? What safeguards exist currently to avoid an obsolete strategy?
12. What strategic checkpoints have been designed for evaluating strategic direction within the organization?
13. Are the strategic checkpoints truly benchmarks which can be used to evaluate progress towards the fulfillment of a given strategy?
14. Are the people to review strategic checkpoints given a mandate to function legitimately and candidly in an adversary capacity?
15. Do managers really believe that they will be directly and explicitly rewarded for doing good planning?

References

Anthony, R. N., Dearden, J., and Vancil, R. F., *Management Control Systems: Text, Cases and Readings,* Richard D. Irwin, Inc., Homewood, Ill., 1972.

Bales, C. F. "Strategic Control: The President's Paradox," *Business Horizons,* Aug. 1977.

Bower, J. L., Managing the Research Allocation Process: A Study of Corporate Planning and Investment, Harvard Business School, Boston, 1970.

Christopher, W. F., "Achievement Reporting: Controlling Performance Against Objectives," *Long Range Planning,* Vol. 10, No. 5, Oct. 1977.

Helms, E. W., "The OST System for Managing Innovation at Texas Instruments," presented to the Armed Forces Management Association, Washington, D.C., April 7, 1971.

Kreitner, R., "People are Systems Too: Filling the Feedback Vacuum," *Business Horizons,* Dec. 1977.

Pekar, P. P., Jr., and Burack, E. H., "Management Control of Strategies Plans Through Adaptive Techniques," *Academy of Management Journal,* March 1976.

Pennington, M. W., "Why Has Planning Failed?," *Long Range Planning,* March 1972.

Suojanen, W. W., *The Dynamics of Management,* Holt, Rinehart, and Winston, New York, 1966.

Taylor, B., "Managing the Process of Corporate Development," *Long Range Planning,* Vol. 9, No. 3, June 1976.

Tilles, S., "How to Evaluate Corporate Strategy," *Harvard Business Review,* Vol. 41, July–Aug. 1963.

Vancil, R. F., "The Accuracy of Long Range Planning," *Harvard Business Review,* Sept.–Oct. 1970.

INDEX